NEW YORK BY GASLIGHT

BARTHOLDI'S STATUE—LIBERTY ENLIGHTENING THE WORLD.

NEW YORK BY GASLIGHT

CLASSIC 1882 EDITION ·

A Work Descriptive of The

GREAT AMERICAN METROPOLIS

ITS HIGH AND LOW LIFE; ITS SPLENDORS AND MISERIES;
ITS VIRTUES AND VICES; ITS GORGEOUS PALACES
AND DARK HOMES OF POVERTY AND CRIME;
ITS PUBLIC MEN, POLITICIANS, ADVENTURERS;
ITS CHARITIES, FRAUDS, MYSTERIES, ETC., ETC.

By James D. McCabe, Jr.

WITH A NEW FOREWORD BY GERARD R. WOLFE, PH.D.
PROFESSOR OF CONTINUING EDUCATION, NEW YORK UNIVERSITY AND
MEMBER OF THE NATIONAL TRUST FOR HISTORIC PRESERVATION
AND THE SOCIETY OF ARCHITECTURAL HISTORIANS

ILLUSTRATED WITH FINE ENGRAVINGS

GREENWICH HOUSE
Distributed by Crown Publishers, Inc.
New York

A NOTE TO THE READER:
The author of this book has used some racial and ethnic refer-
ences that may be offensive to modern readers. Readers should
be aware, however, that these do not reflect the attitudes of the
publisher of this edition and that they merely reflect the language, and its usage, of the late nineteenth century.

Copyright © 1984 by Arlington House, Inc.
All rights reserved.

This 1984 edition is published by Greenwich House,
a division of Arlington House, Inc.,
distributed by Crown Publishers, Inc.,
One Park Avenue, New York, New York 10016

Originally published as *New York by Sunlight and Gaslight*

Manufactured in the United States of America

Library of Congress Cataloging in Publication Data

McCabe, James Dabney, 1842-1883.
  New York by gaslight.

  Reprint. Originally published: New York by sunlight and
gaslight. Philadelphia, PA : Hubbard Brothers, 1882.
  1. New York (N.Y.)—Description.   2. New York (N.Y.)
—Social life and customs.   I. Title.
F128.47.M46   1984   974.7'1   84-4001

ISBN: 0-517-43153X

h g f e d c b a

CONTENTS

FOREWORD   25

PREFACE   29

CHAPTER I

THE GREAT METROPOLIS

GENERAL DESCRIPTION OF NEW YORK CITY—LOCATION—NATURAL ADVANTAGES—COMMERCIAL ADVANTAGES—THE STREETS—BUILDINGS—CLIMATE—HEALTHFULNESS—MORTALITY—RAPID GROWTH OF THE CITY—LOFTY BUILDINGS—DESCRIPTION OF THE MOST NOTED AND THE HIGHEST STRUCTURES IN THE CITY—REASONS FOR BUILDING SO HIGH—LAND CHEAP UP STAIRS.   33

CHAPTER II

THE PEOPLE OF NEW YORK.

POPULATION OF NEW YORK IN 1870—THE STATE CENSUS OF 1875—WHAT CHANGES IT SHOWED—POPULATION IN 1880—POPULATION AFFECTED BY THE IMPROVEMENTS IN THE LOWER PART OF THE CITY—THE MOST DENSELY SETTLED PART OF NEW YORK—THE FLOATING POPULATION—STRANGERS IN NEW YORK—FOREIGN DISTRICTS—COSMOPOLITAN CHARACTER OF THE PEOPLE—CHARACTERISTICS OF NEW YORKERS—LACK OF PUBLIC SPIRIT—INDIFFERENCE TO POLITICAL AFFAIRS—THE RESULT—THE RACE FOR WEALTH—HOW BUSINESS IS DONE IN NEW YORK—WEARING OUT BODY AND SOUL—A PHILOSOPHICAL MERCHANT—A NEW COMER'S IMPRESSIONS—LIVING TOO FAST—NO CHANCE FOR LAGGARDS—HOW SUCCESS IS WON—MERIT THE TEST—NEW YORK FROM A MORAL POINT OF VIEW—ITS CHARITIES AND BENEVOLENCE—TOLERATION OF OPINIONS AND BELIEFS—MENTAL CULTURE OF THE PEOPLE—WHAT IT COSTS TO LIVE IN NEW YORK—THE RICH AND THE MIDDLE CLASSES—NEW YORK AS A PLACE OF RESIDENCE—ATTACHMENT OF THE PEOPLE TO THE CITY.   51

CHAPTER III

THE GROWTH OF NEW YORK.

RAPID GROWTH OF NEW YORK DURING THE PAST THIRTY-FIVE YEARS—THE FLUSH TIMES AFTER THE WAR—EFFECTS OF THE PANIC OF 1873—A MOMENTARY CHECK—RETURN OF PROSPERITY—PROSPECTS FOR THE FUTURE—INCREASE IN BUILDING OPERATIONS—HOW REAL ESTATE APPRECIATES IN VALUE—THE SECRET OF THE GREAT INCREASE OF WEALTH IN NEW YORK—FUTURE CENTRES OF POPULATION—WHAT NEW YORK WILL BE FIFTY YEARS HENCE—A GRAND DESTINY.   65

CHAPTER IV

THE HARBOR OF NEW YORK

NATURAL ADVANTAGES OF THE HARBOR—THE OUTER AND INNER BAYS—EXCURSIONS—A TRIP DOWN THE HARBOR—SCENES ALONG THE ROUTE—THE SHIPPING—THROUGH THE INNER BAY—GOVERNOR'S ISLAND—BEDLOE'S AND ELLIS' ISLANDS—BARTHOLDI'S STATUE—LIBERTY ENLIGHTENING THE WORLD—THE KILL VAN KULL—STATEN ISLAND—THE NARROWS—THE FORTIFICATIONS—THE OUTER BAY—QUARANTINE—CONEY ISLAND—SCENES IN THE LOWER BAY—SANDY HOOK—OUT TO SEA—BACK TO NEW YORK.   88

13

CHAPTER V
SANDY HOOK

DESCRIPTION OF "THE HOOK"—A NOTED LANDMARK—A SANDY WASTE—THE COVE—THE BEACH —THE LIGHT-SHIPS—THE LIFE SAVING STATION—SANDY HOOK LIGHTHOUSE—ITS HISTORY —THE KEEPER'S HOUSE—WRECKS—IN THE LIGHT-TOWER—A GRAND VIEW—OCEAN CEME-TERY—THE FORTIFICATIONS—TESTING THE HEAVY GUNS—THE NORTH LIGHT—THE SYRENS —THE TELEGRAPH STATION. 104

CHAPTER VI
THE NEVERSINK HIGHLANDS

SITUATION OF THE HIGHLANDS—THE SHREWSBURY RIVER—RED BANK—ORIGIN OF THE NAME OF THE HIGHLANDS—AS SEEN FROM THE SEA—THE LIGHT TOWERS— A MAGNIFICENT LIGHT —VIEW FROM THE TOWER—THE PICTURES IN THE LENSES—A GLIMPSE OF FAIRY LAND. 113

CHAPTER VII
MUNICIPAL GOVERNMENT

ORGANIZATION OF THE CITY GOVERNMENT—THE MAYOR AND BOARD OF ALDERMEN—THE COM-MISSIONERS—DESCRIPTION OF THE VARIOUS MUNICIPAL DEPARTMENTS—POWERS OF OFFI-CIALS—THE COURTS—POLICE JUSTICES—THE MEN BY WHOM NEW YORK IS GOVERNED—RESPON-SIBILITY OF THE BETTER CLASSES—FROM THE GROG SHOP TO CIVIL POWER—WHO THE LEAD-ERS ARE—THE "BOSS"—THE RING—HOW BOSS TWEED MAINTAINED HIS POWER—SPASMODIC EFFORTS AT REFORM—MULHOOLYISM IN NEW YORK—AN INSIDE VIEW OF MUNICIPAL POLITICS —THE SLAVE OF THE RING—LOOKING OUT FOR THE "BOYS"—THE INTERESTS OF THE CITY NEGLECTED—THE POPULAR WILL DEFIED BY THE RING. 118

CHAPTER VIII
BROADWAY

EARLY HISTORY OF BROADWAY—UNDER THE DUTCH AND ENGLISH RULE—PRIMITIVE NAME OF THE STREET—IT COMMENCES TO GROW—THE GREAT FIRE OF 1776—THE BROADWAY OF TO-DAY—APPEARANCE OF THE STREET—A STROLL ON BROADWAY—THE LOWER STREET—TRINITY CHURCH—THE INSURANCE COMPANIES—THE TELEGRAPH WIRES—MAGNIFICENT BUILDINGS—SCENE FROM THE POST-OFFICE—A BROADWAY JAM—LOWER BROADWAY BY NIGHT—CHARACTERISTICS OF THE VARIOUS PORTIONS OF THE STREET—VIEW FROM CANAL STREET—THE HOTELS—AMONG THE PUBLISHERS—"STEWART'S"—GRACE CHURCH—BROADWAY AT UNION SQUARE—THE NARROWEST PART—MADISON SQUARE—A GRAND SIGHT—UPPER BROADWAY—A STREET OF MARBLE—THE GREAT HOTELS—THE CENTRAL PARK REACHED—STREET CARS AND OMNIBUSES—THE NIGHT LIFE OF BROADWAY—SCENES ON THE STREET—THE STREET WALKERS—THE ELECTRIC LIGHT—THE MIDNIGHT HOUR—BUSINESS ON BROADWAY. 134

CHAPTER IX
THE BROADWAY STAGES

POPULARITY OF THIS MODE OF CONVEYANCE—A CHEAP PLEASURE—DESCRIPTION OF THE VARI-OUS LINES—THE STAGES AS REGARDS COMFORT—THE OUTSIDE SEATS—"KNOCKING DOWN IN BY-GONE DAYS"—THE PATENT CASH BOX SYSTEM—THE "SPOTTERS"—A NIGHT RIDE WITH JEHU—THE "BOSS" ON THE WATCH—MYSTERIOUS SIGNALS—SKILL OF THE STAGE DRIVERS—A STAGE DRIVER PHOTOGRAPHED—SUFFERINGS OF THE DRIVERS—UPS AND DOWNS OF THE CRAFT—THE MUTUAL BENEFIT ASSOCIATION. 157

CONTENTS

CHAPTER X
THE FIFTH AVENUE

FIFTH AVENUE THE CENTRE OF FASHION AND WEALTH—DESCRIPTION OF THE STREET—A
GRAND PANORAMA—LOWER FIFTH AVENUE—ENCROACHMENTS OF BUSINESS—FOURTEENTH
STREET—THE "SWALLOW-TAIL" DEMOCRACY—AMONG THE PIANO MAKERS—CHICKERING
HALL—CHURCHES—CLUBS AND ART GALLERIES—TWENTY-THIRD STREET—DELMONICO'S—
THE ASTOR RESIDENCES—STEWART'S MARBLE PALACE—A REGION OF BROWN STONE—UPPER
FIFTH AVENUE—THE HOTELS—THE CATHEDRAL—THE VANDERBILT MANSIONS—ALONG
THE CENTRAL PARK—THE LENOX LIBRARY—THE FIFTH AVENUE MANSIONS—HOMES OF
WEALTH AND LUXURY—HOW THEY ARE FITTED UP—FIFTH AVENUE ON NEW YEAR'S NIGHT—
LIFE IN FIFTH AVENUE—THE WHIRL OF DISSIPATION—WHAT IT COSTS—THE STRUGGLE FOR
SHOW—THE "NEWLY RICH"—DARK SIDE OF FIFTH AVENUE LIFE—THE SKELETONS—FIFTH
AVENUE HUSBANDS AND WIVES—THE CHILDREN—"ALL IS NOT GOLD THAT GLITTERS." 165

CHAPTER XI
THE ELEVATED RAILROADS

INCONVENIENCES OF OLD-STYLE TRAVEL—PLANS FOR RAPID TRANSIT—THE FIRST ELEVATED
RAILROAD—THE PRESENT SYSTEM—THE METROPOLITAN AND NEW YORK ELEVATED ROADS—
THE MANHATTAN COMPANY—DESCRIPTION OF THE ROADS—HOW THEY ARE BUILT—MODE OF
OPERATIONS—STATIONS—EMPLOYEES—RAPID TRAINS—ADVANTAGES OF THE SYSTEM—ITS
DRAWBACKS—IMMENSE TRAFFIC—RESULTS OF THE ELEVATED SYSTEM—RAPID GROWTH OF
THE UPPER PART OF THE CITY—A RIDE ON THE ELEVATED RAILROADS—THE NIGHT TRAINS
—FROM THE BATTERY TO HARLEM BY NIGHT. 178

CHAPTER XII
SOCIETY

THE VARIOUS CLASSES OF SOCIETY—THE BEST OF ALL—THE "OLD KNICKERBOCKERS"—A HEAVY
SET OF SWELLS—RICHES AND CULTURE COMBINED—THE NEWLY RICH—THE CONTROLLING
ELEMENT—HOW SHODDY GETS INTO SOCIETY—THE POWER OF MONEY—FASHIONABLE SNOB-
BERY—FROM THE TENEMENT HOUSE TO THE FIFTH AVENUE MANSION—MANIA FOR COATS
OF ARMS—HOW BOSS TWEED WAS VICTIMIZED—SUDDEN APPEARANCES AND DISAPPEAR-
ANCES IN SOCIETY—"RICHES HAVE WINGS"—A FAILURE AND A TRIUMPH—WHAT IT COSTS—
MONEY THE ONE THING NEEDFUL—EXTRAVAGANCE OF NEW YORK SOCIETY—LOVE OF DRESS
—A FASHIONABLE LADY'S WARDROBE—FOLLIES OF THE MEN—PASSION FOR THE LEG BUSI-
NESS—FASHIONABLE ENTERTAINMENTS—THE END OF EXTRAVAGANT CAREERS—THE SKELE-
TONS SOMETIMES COME OUT OF THEIR CLOSETS—FASHIONABLE BALLS AND PARTIES—HOW
THEY ARE GIVEN—INVITATIONS—BALL ROOM SCENES—THE SUPPERS—A SWELL CONVERSATION
—FASHIONABLE THIEVES—AN ARISTOCRATIC SNEAK THIEF—HOW A BROKER KEPT HIS PLACE
IN SOCIETY—A DETECTIVE'S EXPERIENCE IN FASHIONABLE LIFE—THE PRETTY WIDOW AND
THE LACES—FASHIONABLE RECEPTIONS—WEDDINGS IN HIGH LIFE—ARRANGED ON A PECU-
NIARY BASIS—MONEY THE ATTRACTION—HOW HEARTS ARE BOUGHT AND SOLD—THE WED-
DING FESTIVITIES—GUARDING THE BRIDAL PRESENTS—WHAT IT ALL COSTS—FASHIONABLE
DEATH—ONLY THE RICH CAN AFFORD TO DIE IN NEW YORK—COST OF A FASHIONABLE
FUNERAL—INTERESTING DETAILS. 195

CHAPTER XIII
THE STREET RAILWAYS

THE PRESENT STREET-RAILWAY SYSTEM—IMMENSE BUSINESS DONE BY THE SURFACE ROADS—
EXPENSES AND RECEIPTS—HOW THE ELEVATED ROADS HAVE AFFECTED THE HORSE RAIL-
WAYS—DISCOMFORTS OF THE STREET CARS—THE CONDUCTORS AND DRIVERS—STORY OF A
CONDUCTOR'S LOT—HARD WORK AND POOR PAY—KNOCKING DOWN—HOW IT IS DONE—BEAT-
ING THE BELL-PUNCH. 238

CHAPTER XIV
SIXTH AVENUE

RAPID ADVANCE OF SIXTH AVENUE IN PROSPERITY—DESCRIPTION OF THE STREET—THE LOWER PORTION—THE TENEMENT HOUSES—FRENCH FLATS—THE ELEVATED RAILROAD AND ITS STATIONS—A BUSY SCENE—SIXTH-AVENUE STORES—"MACEY'S"—THE JEFFERSON MARKET POLICE COURT—BOOTH'S THEATRE—THE MASONIC TEMPLE—"THE TABERNACLE"—SIXTH AVENUE BY NIGHT—A CHANGE OF SCENE—THE STREET-WALKERS—BRAZEN VICE—THE FRENCH WOMEN—SNARING A VICTIM—SHAMEFUL SCENES ON THE AVENUE—THE STREET A TERROR TO DECENT PEOPLE—THE ROUGHS—SIXTH-AVENUE OYSTER HOUSES AND BEER SALOONS—SCENE IN A FLASH SALOON—A YOUTHFUL CRIMINAL—THE DETECTIVE'S PRIZE—SIXTH AVENUE AFTER MIDNIGHT—A DRUNKEN SINGER—"IN THE SWEET BYE-AND-BYE"—NO EFFORT MADE TO CHECK THE EVIL. 250

CHAPTER XV
COACHING DAY

MEMORIES OF BYGONE DAYS—STAGE COACHING IN FORMER YEARS—REVIVAL OF COACHING IN NEW YORK—COLONEL KANE'S ENTERPRISE—THE "TALLY HO"—A HANDSOME SUCCESS—SOCIETY ADOPTS COACHING AS THE "CORRECT THING"—THE COACHING CLUB ORGANIZED—COACHING DAY—THE ANNUAL PARADE—A BRILLIANT SIGHT. 258

CHAPTER XVI
THE STREETS OF NEW YORK

MADISON AVENUE—MILES OF BROWN STONE—PARK AVENUE—LEXINGTON AVENUE—THIRTY-FOURTH AND FIFTY-SEVENTH STREETS—MAGNIFICENT RESIDENCES—THIRD AVENUE THE GREAT HIGHWAY OF THE EAST SIDE—EIGHTH AVENUE THE SMALL TRADERS' PARADISE—THE SATURDAY NIGHT MARKET—TWENTY-THIRD AND FOURTEENTH STREETS—DISAPPEARANCE OF LANDMARKS—CHANGES IN THE CHARACTER OF THE STREETS—A GLANCE AT TWENTY-THIRD STREET TO-DAY—"THE BEGGARS' PARADISE"—STREET CHARACTERS—A YOUNG IMPOSTOR—KICKED FROM A HORSE CAR INTO A HOME—BLEECKER STREET—LIFE IN BOHEMIA—A STREET WHERE NO QUESTIONS ARE ASKED—GRAND STREET—CHATHAM STREET—THE CHILDREN OF ISRAEL AND THEIR WAYS—FULTON STREET—NASSAU STREET—A CROWDED NEIGHBORHOOD—PECULIARITIES OF THE STREET—PINE STREET—AMONG THE MONEYED MEN—WEST AND SOUTH STREETS—ALONG THE WATER SIDE—BUSY SCENES. 265

CHAPTER XVII
DIVORCES WITHOUT PUBLICITY

QUEER ADVERTISEMENTS—THE "DIVORCE RING"—ITS FIELD OF OPERATIONS—THE DIVORCE LAWYER—WHO HE IS—HEADQUARTERS OF THE MEMBERS OF THE RING—SCENE IN A LAWYER'S OFFICE—A RICH CLIENT—"OFF WITH THE OLD LOVE AND ON WITH THE NEW"—A CHARACTERISTIC CASE—"THE EASIEST THING IN THE WORLD TO GET A DIVORCE"—WESTERN DIVORCES—HOW A MERCHANT MADE A MISTRESS OF HIS WIFE—WHO ARE THE CLIENTS—COST OF A DIVORCE—HOW IT IS MANAGED—THE REFEREE SYSTEM—SPOTTING A HUSBAND—MANUFACTURING EVIDENCE—THE "OLD MAN" ENTRAPPED—PROFESSIONAL WITNESSES—THE DIVORCE LAWYER'S SYSTEM OF DRUMMING UP BUSINESS—DIRTY WORK FOR TEN PER CENT.—SERVING A SUMMONS—A MOCKERY OF JUSTICE—POWER OF THE RING—THE COURTS AND BAR AFRAID TO BREAK IT UP. 281

CHAPTER XVIII
CHRISTMAS IN NEW YORK

PREPARATIONS FOR CHRISTMAS—HOLIDAY APPEARANCE OF THE CITY—STREET SCENES—BUSINESS BOOMING—SCENES IN THE CITY BY NIGHT—A NOVEL SIGHT ON THE ELEVATED RAILROAD TRAINS—BUSY TIMES IN THE MARKETS—THE TURKEYS—TRINITY CHIMES—MIDNIGHT SERVICES—CHRISTMAS DAY—HOW IT IS OBSERVED IN NEW YORK—CHRISTMAS WITH THE POOR. 290

CHAPTER XIX

PUBLIC BUILDINGS

THE CITY HALL—THE GOVERNOR'S ROOM—THE COUNTY COURT HOUSE—REMINISCENCES OF THE "TWEED RING"—THE HALL OF RECORDS—THE UNITED STATES SUB-TREASURY—THE GREAT VAULTS—HOW UNCLE SAM'S MONEY IS GUARDED—THE ASSAY OFFICE—THE CUSTOM HOUSE—A NOBLE EDIFICE—THE BUSINESS OF THE PORT OF NEW YORK—DUTIES OF OFFICIALS—THE BARGE OFFICE—PASSING THROUGH THE CUSTOM HOUSE—CUSTOM HOUSE BROKERS—TAMMANY HALL—THE TAMMANY SOCIETY—POLITICAL ORGANIZATION—"BOSS KELLY"—THE COOPER UNION—WORK OF THE INSTITUTION—THE BIBLE HOUSE—A GREAT WORK DONE—THE NATIONAL ACADEMY OF DESIGN—HOW THE SCHOOLS ARE CONDUCTED—ANNUAL EXHIBITIONS—THE YOUNG MEN'S CHRISTIAN ASSOCIATION BUILDING—THE LECTURE ROOM—A REFUGE FOR YOUNG MEN—THE GRAND CENTRAL RAILROAD DEPOT—INTERNAL ARRANGEMENTS—THE CAR HOUSE—THE FOURTH AVENUE TUNNELS. 296

CHAPTER XX

NEW YEAR'S CALLS

NEW YORK'S GREAT FESTAL DAY—PREPARATIONS FOR NEW YEAR'S DAY—THE HAIR-DRESSERS' ROUNDS—RECEPTION CARDS—HOW THEY ARE ISSUED—JOINT RECEPTIONS—THE CARD-BASKET AND ITS MEANING—LADIES' TOILETS—A CHANCE FOR REFORM—THE FIRST CALLERS—THE VETERANS—ADVANTAGES OF A LIST—SCENES TOWARD NIGHTFALL—TOO MUCH PUNCH—MRS. B.'S RECEPTION—A SWEET FINALE—NEW YEAR IN THE KITCHEN—HOW THE SALOONS CELEBRATE THE DAY—REFRESHMENTS AND PUNCH FOR ALL—NEW YORK WITH A HEADACHE—LADIES' DAY. 320

CHAPTER XXI

AMONG THE BULLS AND BEARS OF WALL STREET

DESCRIPTION OF WALL STREET—VALUE OF REAL ESTATE—ENORMOUS RENTS—ORIGIN OF THE NAME OF THE STREET—NOTABLE BUILDINGS—TRANSACTIONS OF THE STREET—THE SCENE AT NOON—THE STOCK EXCHANGE—THE LONG ROOM—OUTSIDE DEALERS—THE REGULAR BOARD—HOW BUSINESS IS CONDUCTED IN THE EXCHANGE—THE VICE-PRESIDENT—RULES OF THE EXCHANGE—GOOD FAITH EXACTED OF ITS MEMBERS—THE GOVERNMENT BOARD—CHARACTERISTIC SCENES—THE VAULTS AND THEIR TREASURES—THE TELEGRAPH INSTRUMENTS—THE "TICKERS"—LIFE OF A STOCK BROKER—SPORTS OF THE EXCHANGE—THE CLEARING HOUSE AND ITS OPERATIONS—CURBSTONE BROKERS—RECKLESS TRANSACTIONS—STOCK SPECULATIONS—BUYING AND SELLING ON COMMISSION—UNCERTAINTIES OF THE STREET—HOW FORTUNES ARE MADE AND LOST ON WALL STREET—STOCK GAMBLING—WHO ARE THE SPECULATORS—A DARING BROKER—"BLACK FRIDAY"—HOW AN OPERATOR WAS RUINED—STOCK SWINDLERS—SHARPERS IN WALL STREET—THE COMBINATION SYSTEM—A BAREFACED SWINDLE—ACTION OF THE GENERAL GOVERNMENT—HOW BOGUS OPERATORS FLEECE UNSUSPECTING CUSTOMERS—AN INSIDE VIEW OF THE COMBINATION SYSTEM—ENORMOUS PROFITS—THE SWINDLE EXPOSED—A WARNING TO WOULD-BE SPECULATORS. 330

CHAPTER XXII

ALONG THE WHARVES

WRETCHED CHARACTER OF THE WHARVES—PLAN FOR A NEW SYSTEM—THE NORTH RIVER FRONT—THE RAILROAD PIERS—THE FERRY HOUSES—THE FOREIGN STEAMSHIPS—THE FLOATING PALACES OF THE HUDSON AND LONG ISLAND SOUND—THE BETHEL—THE BOAT STORES—THE GRAIN ELEVATORS—THE EAST RIVER FRONT—SAILING VESSELS—THE SHIP YARDS—THE DRY DOCKS—THE CANAL BOATS—SCENES ON BOARD—THE FRUIT TRADE—THE FISH MARKET—SCENES ALONG THE WHARVES—ACCIDENTS—THE RESCUE STATIONS—THE VOLUNTEER LIFE-SAVING CORPS—"NAN, THE LIFE SAVER." 360

CHAPTER XXIII

POLICE

ORIGIN OF THE NEW YORK POLICE FORCE—THE OLD TIME POLICEMEN—"OLD HAYES"—INCREASE OF CRIME—GEORGE W. MATSELL—THE FIRST REGULAR POLICE FORCE—OPPOSITION TO IT—THE METROPOLITAN POLICE FORCE ORGANIZED—THE MUNICIPAL POLICE—POLICE HEADQUARTERS—THE COMMISSIONERS—SUPERINTENDENT WALLING—THE SUBORDINATE OFFICERS—THE PATROLMEN—QUALIFICATIONS OF A POLICEMAN—THE BROADWAY SQUAD—DUTIES OF THE FORCE—OMNIPRESENCE OF THE POLICE—POWER OVER THE ROUGHS—DANGERS OF A POLICEMAN'S LIFE—DARING EXPLOITS OF CAPTAINS WILLIAMS AND ALLAIRE—FIGHTING A MOB—FEAR OF THE "LOCUSTS"—UNIFORM OF THE FORCE—HOW THE CITY IS PATROLLED—HOURS OF DUTY—A SINGULAR POLICEMAN—HOW PETE JOINED THE FORCE—HIS SERVICES—ARRESTS—THE STATION HOUSES—INTERNAL ARRANGEMENTS—THE "BUMMERS' ROOMS"—HOW VAGRANTS ARE LODGED—THE SERGEANT IN CHARGE—A NIGHT IN A POLICE STATION—A FEMALE TRAMP—"DRUNK AND DISORDERLY"—A CASE OF DISTRESS—A FRUITLESS ERRAND—A NEW WAY TO GET HOME AT NIGHT—SEARCH FOR A MISSING HUSBAND—A POLITICAL ROW—YOUNG BLOODS ON A LARK—COSTLY FUN—A WOULD-BE-SUICIDE—BROUGHT BACK FROM THE GRAVE—A JOLLY TRAMP—A GHASTLY SPECTACLE—MASKERS IN A STATION HOUSE—THE MOUNTED POLICE—A SENSIBLE HORSE—THE HARBOR POLICE—A HARD LIFE—PROVISION FOR DISABLED POLICEMEN AND THEIR FAMILIES. 368

CHAPTER XXIV

FERRIES

NEW YORK'S ONLY MEANS OF COMMUNICATION WITH THE MAIN LAND—NUMBER OF FERRIES—THE FERRY BOATS—CROSSING IN A FOG—ANNOYANCES OF FERRY TRAVEL—THE FERRY HOUSES—A MOONLIGHT RIDE ON A FERRY BOAT—A SUICIDE—ACCIDENTS. . . . 404

CHAPTER XXV

THE PRISONS OF NEW YORK

THE TOMBS—DESCRIPTION OF THE BUILDING—THE INTERIOR—THE "BRIDGE OF SIGHS"—PLACE OF EXECUTION—THE MALE PRISON—THE CELLS—THE WOMEN'S PRISON—THE "BUMMERS' HALL"—THE WARDEN'S OFFICE—THE "SWELL CELLS"—THE BOYS' PRISON—RELIGIOUS SERVICES—GOVERNMENT OF THE TOMBS—WARDEN FINN—THE MATRON—A PRISON OF DETENTION—NOTED ESCAPES FROM THE TOMBS—"BLACK MARIA"—THE POLICE COURT—HOW PRISONERS ARE DISPOSED OF—THE COURT OF SPECIAL SESSIONS—THE "TOMBS SHYSTERS"—LUDLOW STREET JAIL—THE SHERIFF'S PRISON—IMPRISONMENT FOR DEBT—CAPTIVE MILITIAMEN—FEDERAL PRISONERS—EXTORTIONS PRACTICED UPON PRISONERS—HOW THE DEPUTY SHERIFFS BLEED THEIR VICTIMS. 409

CHAPTER XXVI

PUBLIC SQUARES

THE BATTERY PARK—ITS HISTORY—THE BATTERY IN OLD TIMES—ITS PRESENT CONDITION—A DELIGHTFUL BREATHING PLACE—THE BARGE OFFICE—THE BOWLING GREEN—THE CITY HALL PARK—TOMPKINS SQUARE—SQUANDERING THE PUBLIC FUNDS—A FINE PARK RUINED—WASHINGTON SQUARE—UNION SQUARE AND ITS SURROUNDINGS—THE "SLAVE MARKET"—STUYVESANT SQUARE—MADISON SQUARE—A DELIGHTFUL PLEASURE-GROUND—MAGNIFICENT SURROUNDINGS—GRAMMERCY PARK—RESERVOIR SQUARE—MOUNT MORRIS SQUARE—MORNINGSIDE PARK—RIVERSIDE PARK. 422

CHAPTER XXVII
THE PAWNBROKERS AND THEIR WAYS

THE SIGN OF THE THREE BALLS—LAWS RESPECTING PAWNBROKERS—HOW LICENSES ARE ISSUED—DISREGARD OF THE LAW BY THE PAWNBROKERS—SOURCES OF PROFIT—EXCESSIVE INTEREST—STORAGE CHARGES—SALES OF UNREDEEMED GOODS—WHO ARE THE PAWNBROKERS—THE JEWS—A DISHONEST CLASS—SUCKING THE LIFE-BLOOD OF THE POOR—HOW CUSTOMERS ARE SWINDLED—CHARACTERISTIC SCENE IN A PAWN SHOP—THE JEWS' ONE PER CENT.—AN INSIDE VIEW OF THE BUSINESS—DRUMMING UP CUSTOM. 432

CHAPTER XXVIII
THE CENTRAL PARK

PLANS FOR A GRAND PARK—CHOICE OF A SITE—THE PARK COMMISSION ORGANIZED—DIFFICUL-TIES IN THE WAY—THE WORK BEGUN—THE RESULT—THE CENTRAL PARK OF TO-DAY—COST OF THE PARK—THE UPPER AND LOWER PARKS—THE ENTRANCES—THE POND—THE OLD ARSENAL—THE MENAGERIE—THE METEOROLOGICAL OBSERVATORY—THE BALL GROUND—THE DAIRY—AMUSEMENTS FOR CHILDREN—THE GREEN—THE SHEEPFOLD—THE SEVENTH REGIMENT STATUE—STATUE OF WEBSTER—THE MARBLE ARCH—THE MALL—STATUES ON THE MALL—THE PLAZA—THE VINE-COVERED WALK—THE ARCADE—THE TERRACE—THE ESPLAN-ADE—THE BETHESDA FOUNTAIN—THE LAKE—BOATING—SKATING SCENES—THE CONSERVA-TORY WATER—THE RAMBLE—THE CAVE—THE BELVEDERE—THE CROTON RESERVOIRS—THE UPPER PARK—HARLEM BEER—THE OLD POWDER HOUSE—THE METROPOLITAN MUSEUM OF ART—THE DI CESNOLA COLLECTION—THE OBELISK—A VENERABLE RELIC OF THE ANCIENT WORLD—THE AMERICAN MUSEUM OF NATURAL HISTORY—THE TRANSVERSE ROADS— A TRI-UMPH OF ENGINEERING—THE PARK COMMISSION—THE POLICE REGULATIONS—PARK TRAFFIC. 440

CHAPTER XXIX
TRINITY CHURCH

"OLD TRINITY"—THE THREE CHURCHES—DESCRIPTION OF TRINITY CHURCH—THE INTERIOR—THE ALTAR AND REREDOS—THE WINDOWS—THE SERVICES—FINE MUSIC—DAILY SIGHTS IN TRINITY—THE SPIRE—THE CHIMES—VIEW FROM THE SPIRE—THE CHURCHYARD—NOTED TOMBS—TRINITY PARISH—THE CHAPELS—WEALTH OF THE PARISH—ITS NOBLE WORK. 469

CHAPTER XXX
THE LOST SISTERHOOD

PREVALENCE OF PROSTITUTION IN NEW YORK—POLICE STATISTICS—FIRST-CLASS HOUSES—THE PROPRIETRESS—THE INMATES—THE ARISTOCRACY OF SHAME—THE VISITORS—VISITS OF MARRIED MEN—AVERAGE LIFE OF A FASHIONABLE PROSTITUTE—THE NEXT STEP—THE SECOND-CLASS HOUSES—TERRORS OF THESE PLACES—THE GREENE STREET BAGNIOS—GOING DOWN INTO THE DEPTHS—THE NEXT STEP—THE WATER STREET HELLS—AVERAGE LIFE OF A PROSTITUTE—"THE WAGES OF SIN IS DEATH"—HOW YOUNG GIRLS ARE TEMPTED INTO SIN—EFFORTS TO SAVE AN ERRING DAUGHTER—THE STREET WALK-ERS—THE PANEL HOUSES—HOW MEN ARE ROBBED AND MURDERED IN THESE HOUSES—THE CONCERT SALOONS—THE WAITER GIRLS—THE DANCE HALLS—THE "BUCKINGHAM"—THE "CREMORNE"—BUCKINGHAM BALLS—ASSIGNATION HOUSES—PERSONALS—THE MID-NIGHT MISSION—REFORMATORY ESTABLISHMENTS—ABORTIONISTS—THE WICKEDEST WOMAN IN NEW YORK. 474

CHAPTER XXXI

JAY GOULD

EARLY LIFE OF THE GREAT FINANCIER—PERSONAL APPEARANCE—KNOWLEDGE OF LAW—
ENTERS THE ERIE ROAD—BLACK FRIDAY—HOW GOULD CAME OUT OF IT—A SHREWD
GAME IN "ERIE"—HIS WEALTH—ATTACKED IN WALL STREET—HIS METHOD OF OPER-
ATING. 496

CHAPTER XXXII

THE NATIONAL GUARD

THE FIRST DIVISION—ITS ORGANIZATION—HOW ARMED—APPROPRIATIONS BY THE CITY—
PRIVATE EXPENSES—THE COMMANDER-IN-CHIEF—EFFICIENCY OF THE TROOPS—PAST
SERVICES OF THE FORCE—OVERAWING THE MOB—PUTTING DOWN RIOTS—A REINFORCE-
MENT TO THE POLICE—DISCIPLINE—THE ARMORIES—THE SEVENTH REGIMENT ARMORY—
PARADES. 499

CHAPTER XXXIII

WILLIAM H. VANDERBILT

THE RICHEST MAN IN NEW YORK—EARLY LIFE—BECOMES A FARMER—ENTERS THE RAILROAD
WORLD—BECOMES VICE-PRESIDENT OF THE NEW YORK CENTRAL SYSTEM—SUCCEEDS THE
OLD COMMODORE—THE VANDERBILT PALACES—LOVE OF FAST HORSES. . . 503

CHAPTER XXXIV

CRIME IN NEW YORK

PROFESSIONAL CRIMINALS—THEIR NUMBERS—THE THIEVES—SUPERINTENDENT WALLING'S DE-
SCRIPTION OF THEM—THE THIEF LANGUAGE—GRADES OF THIEVES—BURGLARS—BANK ROB-
BERS—SNEAK THIEVES—CONFIDENCE MEN—HOW THEY OPERATE—THE PICKPOCKETS—
WHERE THEY COME FROM—THE ROGUES' GALLERY—THE RIVER THIEVES—DARING CRIMES
—THE FENCES—HOW STOLEN GOODS ARE DISPOSED OF—TRICKS OF THE FENCES—THE
ROUGHS—BLACKMAILERS—HOW THEY FLEECE THEIR VICTIMS. 506

CHAPTER XXXV

CREEDMOOR

THE NATIONAL RIFLE ASSOCIATION OF AMERICA—THE CREEDMOOR RANGE—THE GROUNDS
—THE TARGETS—SHOOTING MATCHES—NATIONAL GUARD PRACTICE—AMATEUR MARKS-
MEN. 527

CHAPTER XXXVI

BAR-ROOMS

ARRESTS FOR DRUNKENNESS AND DISORDER—NUMBER OF LICENSED BAR-ROOMS—THE DRINK-
ING CAPACITY OF WALL STREET—AMOUNT OF BEER DRANK—THE LARGEST BAR IN THE
WORLD—AN ENORMOUS BUSINESS IN RUM—HIGH RENTS ASKED FOR BAR-ROOMS—THE ALL-
NIGHT HOUSES—THE BUCKET-SHOPS—GREAT AMOUNT OF DRUNKENNESS—WOMEN AS
DRINKERS—WHERE THEY GET THEIR LIQUOR. 530

CHAPTER XXXVII

HENRY BERGH

THE FRIEND OF THE BRUTE CREATION—ESTABLISHMENT OF THE "SOCIETY FOR THE PRE-VENTION OF CRUELTY TO ANIMALS"—WORK OF MR. BERGH—HOW HE BECAME A TERROR TO TWO-LEGGED BRUTES—A NOBLE RECORD. 534

CHAPTER XXXVIII

THE EAST RIVER BRIDGE

TRAVEL AND TRAFFIC BETWEEN NEW YORK AND BROOKLYN—THE FERRIES—PLANS FOR A BRIDGE—THE WORK BEGUN—THE GREAT BRIDGE—THE TOWERS—THE BRIDGE PROPER —THE CENTRAL SPAN—THE CABLES—THE ANCHORAGES—THE APPROACHES—PLANS FOR TRAVEL ACROSS THE BRIDGE. 537

CHAPTER XXXIX

GAMBLERS AND THEIR WAYS

LAWS AGAINST GAMBLING—NUMBER OF GAMBLERS IN THE CITY—THE FARO BANKS—FIRST-CLASS ESTABLISHMENTS—SPLENDID VICE—THE BROADWAY HELLS—THE SKIN GAME—DANGERS OF SUCH PLACES—THE DAY HOUSES—POOL-SELLING—TRICKS OF POOL-SELLERS —LOTTERIES—HOW THEY ARE CONDUCTED—POLICY DEALING—AN INSIDE VIEW OF THE GAME. 542

CHAPTER XL

THE HUDSON RIVER TUNNEL

A DARING UNDERTAKING—THE WORK BEGUN—ACCIDENTS—DESCRIPTION OF THE TUNNELS—THE PROPOSED DEPOT IN NEW YORK—PROSPECTS OF THE SCHEME. . . . 553

CHAPTER XLI

FASHIONABLE SHOPPING

FASHIONABLE STORES—HANDSOME GOODS—THE FIXED-PRICE SYSTEM—DETECTIVES ON THE WATCH—"STEWART'S"—ENORMOUS TRANSACTIONS THERE. 556

CHAPTER XLII

TENEMENT HOUSES

DENSITY OF POPULATION IN NEW YORK—NUMBER OF TENEMENT HOUSES AND INHABITANTS —CAUSES OF LIVING IN TENEMENT HOUSES—HIGH RENTS—HOMES OF THE WORKING CLASS—HOPES FOR THE FUTURE—VARIETIES OF TENEMENT HOUSES—A SPECIMEN—CLOSE PACKING—RENTS OF APARTMENTS—EVILS OF THE SYSTEM. 559

CHAPTER XLIII

JERRY McAULEY'S MISSION

WATER STREET—THE MISSION—ITS SUCCESS—JERRY M'AULEY—THE REFORMED THIEF—MRS. M'AULEY—THE PRAYER-MEETINGS—THE AUDIENCE—JERRY M'AULEY'S METHODS—A SCENE AT A PRAYER-MEETING—A WONDERFUL WORK. 563

CHAPTER XLIV

METROPOLITAN AMUSEMENTS

THE PRINCIPAL THEATRES—METROPOLITAN AUDIENCES—EXPENSES OF A FIRST-CLASS THEATRE
—SALARIES OF ACTORS—PRODUCTION OF NEW PLAYS—LONG RUNS—"BOOTH'S" THEATRE
A MODEL ESTABLISHMENT—THE GRAND OPERA HOUSE—"WALLACK'S"—"THE UNION
SQUARE"—"DALY'S"—THE ACADEMY OF MUSIC—VARIETY THEATRES—THE GRAND
DUKE'S THEATRE—NEGRO MINSTRELS—CONCERTS—LECTURES. 571

CHAPTER XLV

LIFE UNDER THE SHADOW.

POVERTY IN NEW YORK—THE DESERVING POOR—SAD SCENES—"RAGPICKERS' ROW"—HOW
THE RAGPICKERS LIVE—AN ITALIAN COLONY—SOUR BEER—DRUNKENNESS IN "RAGPICK-
ERS' ROW"—BOTTLE ALLEY—A RELIC OF THE FIVE POINTS—A WRETCHED QUARTER—
THE DWELLINGS OF POVERTY—THE CELLARS—LIFE BELOW GROUND—BAXTER STREET—
THE CHINESE QUARTER—A HOSPITAL FOR CATS. 581

CHAPTER XLVI

THE METROPOLITAN PRESS

THE DAILY NEWSPAPERS—HOW THE LEADING JOURNALS ARE CONDUCTED—THE VARIOUS DE-
PARTMENTS—PRINTING-HOUSE SQUARE—EDITORS' SALARIES—THE "NEW YORK HERALD"
—THE HERALD OFFICE—JAMES GORDON BENNETT—CIRCULATION OF "THE HERALD"—
THE TRIBUNE "THE TALL TOWER"—WHITELAW REID—PROFITS OF "THE TRIBUNE"—
"THE TIMES," THE LEADING REPUBLICAN JOURNAL—"THE SUN," A LIVELY PAPER—
CHARLES A. DANA—PROFITS OF "THE SUN"—THE EVENING PAPERS—WEEKLIES—MAGA-
ZINES. 592

CHAPTER XLVII

THE FIRE DEPARTMENT

THE METROPOLITAN FIRE DEPARTMENT—FIREMAN'S HALL—THE BOARD OF FIRE COMMIS-
SIONERS—DIVISIONS OF THE DEPARTMENT—THE FORCE—UNIFORM—THE ENGINE-HOUSES
—INTERNAL ARRANGEMENTS—THE ENGINES—THE HORSES—HOW THEY ARE TRAINED—
THE SIGNAL TOWERS—THE ALARM BOXES—FIRE DISTRICTS—THE FORCE ON DUTY—SCENES
AT A FIRE—THE INSURANCE PATROL AND ITS DUTIES—THE "FIRE DEPARTMENT RELIEF
FUND"—LIFE OF A NEW YORK FIREMAN—HEROIC DEEDS. 602

CHAPTER XLVIII

HARRY HILL'S

THE BEST KNOWN DANCE-HOUSE IN NEW YORK—THE HALL—THE AUDIENCE—THE FEMALE
VISITORS—THE PERFORMANCES—DANCING—HARRY HILL—THE MIDNIGHT HOUR—HARRY
HILL ON DUTY. 612

CHAPTER XLIX

JOHN KELLY.

"BOSS KELLY"—BIRTH AND EARLY LIFE—EDUCATION—BEGINS LIFE AS A STONE-CUTTER—
ENTERS POLITICAL LIFE—BECOMES AN ALDERMAN—ELECTED TO CONGRESS—HIS CAREER
IN THE HOUSE OF REPRESENTATIVES—IS ELECTED SHERIFF—LOSS OF HIS FAMILY—

ASSISTS IN OVERTHROWING THE TWEED RING—LEADER OF TAMMANY HALL—APPOINTED COMPTROLLER—REMOVAL FROM OFFICE—PERSONAL CHARACTERISTICS. . . 616

CHAPTER L

RELIGION IN NEW YORK

NUMBER OF CHURCHES IN NEW YORK—VALUE OF CHURCH PROPERTY—THE DUTCH REFORMED CHURCH—THE EPISCOPALIANS—GRACE CHURCH—ST. THOMAS'S—"THE LITTLE CHURCH AROUND THE CORNER"—THE LUTHERANS—THE PRESBYTERIANS—THE FIFTH AVENUE CHURCH—THE BAPTISTS—THE METHODISTS—ST. PAUL'S CHURCH—THE CONGREGATIONAL- ISTS—THE QUAKERS—THE UNITARIANS—THE ROMAN CATHOLIC CHURCH—ST. STEPHEN'S— ST. PATRICK'S CATHEDRAL—THE JEWS—THE TEMPLE EMANU-EL—LOWER NEW YORK DES- TITUTE OF CHURCHES—FASHIONABLE RELIGION—STRANGERS IN CHURCH—THE MUSIC— PROFESSIONAL SINGERS—A TENOR'S SENSATION—THE FIFTH AVENUE PROMENADE—PEW RENTS—CHURCH DEBTS—RECKLESS EXTRAVAGANCE. 620

CHAPTER LI

ALONG THE BOWERY

ORIGIN OF THE NAME OF THE STREET—NOTABLE BUILDINGS—CHEAP RETAIL SHOPS—BEER SALOONS—CONCERT HALLS—THE JEWS—THE BOWERY BECOMING GERMANIZED—THE BOW- ERY IN BY-GONE DAYS—THE "BOWERY BOY"—THE "BOWERY GIRL"—A GORGEOUS CREA- TURE—SUNDAY IN THE BOWERY—NIGHT SCENES IN THE BOWERY—THE STREET-WALKERS —THE GERMAN BEER GARDENS—THE SHOOTING-GALLERIES—THE THEATRES. . 639

CHAPTER LII

NEW YORK HOTELS

GREAT NUMBER OF HOTELS IN NEW YORK—FIRST-CLASS HOTELS—THE AMERICAN AND EURO- PEAN PLANS—THE ASTOR HOUSE—THE ST. NICHOLAS—THE METROPOLITAN—THE GRAND CENTRAL—THE NEW YORK—THE FIFTH AVENUE—THE WINDSOR—OTHER HOTELS—INTE- RIOR ARRANGEMENTS—NIGHT SCENES—COST OF FURNISHING A HOTEL—DEAD BEATS— HOW THE DETECTIVES WATCH SUSPICIOUS CHARACTERS. 645

CHAPTER LIII

THE TRAMPS

NEW YORK THE PARADISE OF TRAMPS—WHO THEY ARE—THEIR MODE OF LIFE—WORTHLESS CHARACTERS—SLEEPING IN THE PARK—THE TRAMPS' ABLUTIONS—THE TRAMPS' LODGING- HOUSE—UNFORTUNATE WANDERERS. 652

CHAPTER LIV

THE POST-OFFICE

THE MODEL POST-OFFICE OF THE UNION—THE BUILDING—THE POST-OFFICE PROPER—THE BOX AND STAMP DEPARTMENT—INTERNAL ARRANGEMENTS OF THE POST-OFFICE—BUSI- NESS OF THE OFFICE—HOW THE WORK IS CONDUCTED. 656

CHAPTER LV

CASTLE GARDEN

THE BUILDING—THE OLD FORT—EARLY HISTORY OF CASTLE GARDEN—BECOMES AN EMIGRANT DEPOT—ARRIVALS OF FOREIGN STEAMERS—LANDING THE EMIGRANTS—AVERAGE WEALTH OF THE NEW-COMERS—PASSING THE SURGEON—REGISTERING EMIGRANTS—INTERNAL ARRANGEMENTS OF CASTLE GARDEN. 660

CHAPTER LVI

THE MARKETS OF NEW YORK

THE MARKET-HOUSES—UNSIGHTLY STRUCTURES—THE MANHATTAN MARKET—SCENES IN THE MARKETS—NEW YORK'S SOURCE OF SUPPLY—THE MORNING HOURS—SATURDAY-NIGHT MARKETS—THE OYSTER-SALOONS—FULTON MARKET—THE "CORNER GROCERIES." 663

CHAPTER LVII

THE CROTON WATER-WORKS

THE SOURCE OF NEW YORK'S WATER SUPPLY—CROTON LAKE—THE CROTON AQUEDUCT—A WONDERFUL WORK—THE HIGH BRIDGE—THE "HIGH SERVICE" SYSTEM—THE CENTRAL PARK RESERVOIRS—HOW THE WATER IS SUPPLIED TO THE CITY—ENORMOUS WASTE. . 667

FOREWORD

Sit back and let *New York by Gaslight* re-create the sights and sounds of the year 1882. Here is the city exactly as James W. McCabe, Jr., observed it more than one hundred years ago—dynamic, tumultuous, glittering, and corrupt...and growing at a dizzying pace. In just twenty-five years, New York had doubled in area and population and boasted over one and one-half million inhabitants. Then, the city consisted only of the island of Manhattan, a few small surrounding islands (Governor's, Ellis, Bedloe's, Blackwell's) and a tiny chunk of southern Westchester County that is now part of the Bronx; consolidation with the other boroughs was still sixteen years in the offing. And across the East River, arch-rival Brooklyn, then the third largest city in the country, was rumored to be entertaining ambitions of annexing Manhattan soon after the Great East River Bridge opened the following May.

The city was suffering from mismanagement and the ill effects of years of Tweed Ring frauds. Public services, with a few exceptions, were "the most inefficient and the most shamefully neglected of any city in the land"; while the nation at large was still in shock over the assassination of President Garfield, the year before.

New York was then in the throes of the "Elegant Eighties," which were elegant for only a precious few. The enormous gap between the poor and wealthy classes was ever widening, with the cost of living making it impossible for the city to number a strong middle class. And to the minions of the poor were added thousands of daily newcomers, as crowded immigrant ships disgorged their human cargo upon our shores. Life in the city, charming and delightful as it could be for the élite in their mansions and town houses, was for the most drudgery and despair for the working classes huddled in their tenements; and rents were so high that many people of moderate means were forced to reside outside the city and commute.

Yet, for the privileged as well as the benighted, New York did offer excitement, pleasures, inspiration, and opportunity. The great metropolis was reveling in the Age of Invention and was enjoying a love affair with the new machine technology. The telephone, invented only six years before, could be found in every major business establishment; the era of electricity was creating new marvels daily; and construction was going on everywhere,

25

elevating the city skyline in every direction. Broadway and Fifth Avenue, between 14th and 34th streets, were ablaze in dazzling arc-light illumination, and within a few short months, Thomas Edison would throw the switches on his dynamos and flood an entire square mile below Wall Street with incandescent light for the first time.

To acquaint his readers with the city, author James D. McCabe escorted them—and now escorts us—on a host of adventurous tours to view, at first hand, its wonders as well as its seamy side. No superficial observer, he delved into all he saw in great detail, supplying a wealth of historical, technical, and sociological information, as well as a good measure of advice and admonition. For the first sightseeing trip McCabe took a ride on the recently completed Second Avenue Elevated, in comfortable open-platform wooden coaches drawn by a diminutive steam locomotive, two stories above the street (the els were not electrified until 1899). At the northern terminus in Harlem, then a quiet village, he boarded an excursion steamer for a ride down the East River to the Battery, and then another el train up the west side of Manhattan on the Ninth Avenue Line, with a return ride on the Sixth Avenue El. The fare was five cents, except during rush hours when it was a dime. McCabe pointed out that rush hours were five to seven A.M. and five to seven P.M., Monday through Saturday, which gives some idea of the length of the work week.

Other itineraries that the reader of today can enjoy only vicariously were on the Fifth and Madison Avenue stages, or horse-drawn omnibuses. These forerunners of today's buses were described in the minutest detail, from their traditional lack of comfort, and the rivalry between omnibuses to grab passengers, to the tricks used by drivers to defraud the company. McCabe also treated readers to a ride on one of the city's ubiquitous horse railroads. Among the minutiae of daily life that might otherwise have been lost to posterity, he described how passengers would often try to pass the unpopular twenty-cent coin as a quarter; and how in return, the conductor, in making change, was not averse to passing a silver three-cent piece as a half-dime.

New Yorkers' pace of living has not changed much since 1882. The author pointed in astonishment to the "torrents of pedestrians, each in his race for wealth, forming steady streams of human beings, hurrying as if his life depended on his speed, taking no notice of his fellows, pushing and jostling . . . each with a weary, jaded, anxious look upon his face."

McCabe's enthusiam for the city, was however, boundless ("New York combines the solidity of London with the beauty of Paris, over which hangs a sky bluer and clearer than that of Italy"), and he marveled at how the city was growing upward as well as northward. He conducted his readers along each major thoroughfare, describing every point of interest enroute. On Fifth Avenue, he lamented the passing of "the precincts of the wealthy," as the avenue gave way to "fancy shops, jewelers, hotels, and boarding houses ... its exclusiveness vanished forever... with nearby Murray Hill soon to pass into shabby gentility." Riding up Madison Avenue, he decried the construction of the "continuous and interminable series of brown-stone boxes" that filled each block as far north as 72nd Street.

Another deligtful excursion possible only by armchair today was the trip by side-wheel steamer from lower Manhattan down the bay to Sandy Hook, a voyage that some still living today may still recall with nostalgia. And neither did the vast number of ferries that connected Manhattan with Long Island (fare 3¢) and New Jersey (2¢) escape McCabes' interest.

A shopping tour of "Ladies' Mile" covered the grand emporiums of the gaslight era—A.T. Stewart, Tiffany's, Lord & Taylor, and Arnold Constable—all situated along Broadway, between 9th and 23rd streets.

A visit to the New York Stock Exchange will entertain readers with descriptions of the frenetic action on the floor of the exchange and the disciplining of Board members for infractions such as smoking cigars, standing on chairs or tables, throwing paper darts or balls, or smashing a hat over the eyes of a fellow member.

Among the many aspects of city life examined here is high society. Not only did McCabe scrutinize the various levels of high society but he also described it all so vividly that a reader might feel he or she accompanied him on carriage rides to society balls and soirées in opulent Fifth Avenue mansions, to wonder at the extravagant and ostentatious lifestyles of the super-rich, newly rich, and would-be rich.

McCabe didn't shrink, on the other hand, from portraying the dark side of the metropolis. "New York is the wickedest city, with the gaudiest and vilest haunts of sin, where the devil's work is done upon a large scale," declared McCabe, as he prowled crowded tenement houses, gambling dens, "first-class" houses of ill repute, venial oyster saloons, and into a local police precinct where he encountered the nightly parade of sneak thieves, tramps, river pirates, ladies of the evening, homeless urchins, and the professional vagrants who slept regularly at the station-houses.

The evidence of the author's detailed knowledge of and insight into the character of New York City, would lead any reader to expect he was a native, or at least a lifelong resident of Manhattan. But James Dabney McCabe, Jr., was not; he was, in fact, born in Richmond, Virginia, in 1842 and spent half his life in the South. The son of a clergyman (which may explain his reverential description of the tall spire of Trinity Church "which points solemnly heavenward, as if to lift the soul above the vulgar worship of Mammon in the city below...telling that wealth is not all, folly is not all, pleasure is not all, business is not all, but that there is something purer, nobler, waiting high above the golden cross which the sunlight bathes so lovingly"), he joined the Confederate Army in 1861, wrote war poems and plays in praise of the Rebel cause, contributed to and edited the *Magnolia Weekly,* a Southern literary magazine, and in his lifetime produced several hundred short stories, essays, poems, and translations. McCabe also authored a number of histories and guidebooks, including *The Life and Campaigns of General Robert E. Lee, Paris by Gaslight, Pathways of the Holy Land,* and a history of the Turko-Russian War.

He visited New York in 1867 and soon thereafter produced his first book on the city, *The Secrets of the Great City,* "a work descriptive of the virtues, vices, mysteries, miseries, and crimes of New York City." In 1872 he produced *Lights and Shadows of New York Life, or The Sights and Sensations of the Great City.* The present *New York by Gaslight* was his last work—a splendid tribute to the city he came to adore. Alas, he did not live to enjoy the fruits of his labors, for he died on January 27, 1883, soon after the book was published. There is an unusual postscript to the story: In Chapter XXXVIII, he described in generous detail the gala opening ceremony of the Brooklyn Bridge, which took place on May 24, 1883—four months *after* his death! Not a clairvoyant, but an assiduous researcher, McCabe had uncovered the plans for the opening months in advance, and accurately described the event as if it had just occurred!

New York   GERARD R. WOLFE
February 1984

PREFACE

What Paris is to the Frenchman, or London to the Briton, New York is to the American. It is not only the Great Metropolis of the New World, but it is the chief attraction upon this continent, the great centre to which our people resort for business and pleasure, and as such, is a source of never-failing interest.

This being the case, it is natural that every American should desire to visit New York, to see the city for himself, behold its beauties, its wonderful sights, and participate in the pleasures which are to be enjoyed only in the Metropolis. Thousands avail themselves of this privilege every year; but the great mass of our people know our chief city only by the descriptions of their friends, and the brief accounts of its sights and scenes which occur from time to time in the newspapers of the day. Even those who visit the city bring away but a superficial knowledge of it, as to *know* New York requires years of constant study and investigation. Strangers see only the surface; they cannot penetrate into its inner life, and examine the countless influences at work every day in shaping the destiny of the beautiful city. Few, even of the residents of the Metropolis, have either the time or the means for such investigations. Few have a correct idea of the terrible romance and hard reality of the daily lives of a vast portion of the dwellers in New York, or of the splendor and luxury of the wealthier classes.

One of the chief characteristics of New York is the rapidity with which changes occur in it. Those who were familiar with the city in the past will find it new to them now. The march of progress and improvement presses on with giant strides, and the city of to-day is widely separated from the city of a few years ago. Only one who has devoted himself to watching its onward career, either in prosperity and magnificence or in misery and crime, can form any idea of the magnitude and character of the wonderful changes of the past ten years.

The volume now offered to the reader aims to be a faithful and graphic picture of the *New York of to-day*, and to give, in life-like

29

colors, views of its magnificent streets and buildings, its busy, bustling crowds, its rushing elevated trains, its countless sights, its romance, its mystery, its nobler and better efforts in the cause of humanity, its dark crimes, and terrible tragedies. In short, the work endeavors to hold up to the reader a faithful mirror, in which shall pass all the varied scenes that transpire in New York, by sunlight and by gaslight. To those who have seen the great city, the work is offered as a means of recalling some of the pleasantest experiences of their lives; while to the still larger class who have never enjoyed this pleasure, it is hoped that it will be the medium of their acquiring an intimate acquaintance with New York in the quiet of their own homes, and without the expense or fatigue of a journey.

This volume is not a work of fiction, but a narrative of well authenticated, though often startling facts. The darker sides of New York life are shown in their true colors, and without any effort to tone them down. Foul blots are to be found upon the life of the great city. Sin, vice, crime and shame are terrible realities there, and they have been presented here as they actually exist.

Throughout the work, the aim of the author has been to warn those who wish to see for themselves the darker side of city life, of the dangers attending such undertakings. A man who seeks the haunts of vice and crime in New York takes his life in his hand, exposes himself to dangers of the most real kind, and deserves all the harm that may come to him in his quest of knowledge. Enough is told in this volume to satisfy legitimate curiosity, and to convince the reader that the only path of safety in New York is to avoid all places of doubtful repute. The city is bright and beautiful enough to occupy all one's time with its wonderful sights and innocent pleasures. To venture under the shadow, is to court danger in all its forms. No matter how "wise in his own conceit" a stranger may be, he is but a child in the hands of the disreputable classes of the great city.

In the preparation of this work the author has drawn freely upon his own experience, the result of a long and intimate acquaintance with all the various phases of New York life. He ventures to hope that those who are familiar with the subject will recognize the truthfulness of the statements made, and that the book may prove a source of pleasure and profit to all who may honor it with a perusal.

November 1st, 1882.   J. D. M'C.

NEW YORK BY GASLIGHT

CHAPTER I

THE GREAT METROPOLIS

GENERAL DESCRIPTION OF NEW YORK CITY—LOCATION—NATURAL ADVANTAGES—COMMERCIAL ADVANTAGES—THE STREETS—BUILDINGS—CLIMATE—HEALTHFULNESS—MORTALITY—RAPID GROWTH OF THE CITY—LOFTY BUILDINGS—DESCRIPTION OF THE MOST NOTED AND THE HIGHEST STRUCTURES IN THE CITY—REASONS FOR BUILDING SO HIGH—LAND CHEAP UP STAIRS.

New York, the commercial metropolis of America, is also the largest city of the Western Hemisphere. It lies at the mouth of the Hudson River, and occupies the whole of Manhattan Island, Randall's, Wards, and Blackwell's Islands, in the East River, Bedloe's, Ellis's and Governor's Islands in the Bay, and a portion of the main land of West Chester County, north of Manhattan Island, and separated from it by the Harlem River and Spuyten Duyvel Creek. Its extreme length northward from the Battery is sixteen miles; its greatest width, from the Hudson to the mouth of the Bronx River, is four and a half miles; thus giving it an area of forty-one and a half square miles, or twenty-six thousand five hundred acres. Of these, twelve thousand one hundred acres are on the main land. The city proper—the true

33

New York—stands on Manhattan Island, which is thirteen and a half miles in length, and varies in breadth from a few hundred yards to two and a half miles. It has an area of nearly twenty-two square miles, or about fourteen thousand square acres. The island is irregular in formation, having somewhat the shape of a fan. It is very narrow at *The Battery*, its southern end, and widens rapidly as it proceeds northward. Its extreme length on the western or Hudson River side is thirteen and a half miles, while on the East River side it is nine miles long. It attains its greatest breadth at Fourteenth and Eighty-seventh streets, where it is about two and a half miles wide. At *The Battery* the land is but a few inches above the surface of the water, but from that point it rises steadily until it reaches its northern limit, at Washington Heights, a range of bold and beautiful cliffs, 130 feet above the Hudson. The lower part of the island is sandy; the upper part very rocky. Several bridges over the Harlem River and Spuyten Duyvel Creek afford connection with the main land, and numerous lines of ferry boats maintain constant intercourse on the Long Island and New Jersey shores. The city is compactly built along the western side, from the Battery to Fifty-ninth street, the lower end of the Central Park. From that point to Manhattanville, One Hundred and Twenty-fifth street, the buildings are straggling, and above Manhattanville the west side is very rural, abounding in country seats, market gardens and miniature farms. The east side is built up compactly almost the whole way, there being only about two miles of space that does not merit this description.

Situated between two broad, deep rivers, and within sixteen miles of the sea, upon which it looks out from the safety of its well-sheltered harbor, Manhattan Island was designed by nature as the seat of a great commercial metropolis. Its waters are deep enough for the largest vessels, and in its commodious harbor the fleets of the world could ride at ease. It commands all the chief routes of communication with the great West and South, and steam and electricity have enabled it to reach the various quarters of the globe as easily and as quickly as any of its old world rivals.

New York is a magnificently built city. The lower portion is a dense mass of houses, with narrow and often crooked streets. This is the business quarter, and is not so thickly populated as the middle districts. Above Canal street the streets assume a more regular formation. They are broad and straight, crossing each other at right angles, and are laid off at regular intervals. In the lower portion of the city all the streets are designated by names. Above Houston street, the cross streets, or those extending from river to river, are designated by numbers. The avenues start from about Third street, and extend to the northern end of the island. The city is substantially, as well as handsomely built. It contains few frame houses, the prevailing materials being marble, stone, iron and brick. Marble, iron, and the lighter colored stones are used principally in the construction of business edifices, but the residences are chiefly of brick and brown stone. Land being very high in price, the buildings are generally lofty, often reaching an altitude of seven and eight, and sometimes ten and twelve stories. The business edifices have generally two cellars below the pavement, with vaults extending out under the street. These are dry, are well lighted and ventilated, and are used for the storage of goods. As a rule, the business houses of the city are handsome and elegant. Every convenience is provided for the prompt and proper despatch of the business of the establishment. Time is everything in New York, and nothing is neglected that can possibly aid in saving it. Within these magnificent edifices is gathered the wealth of the world. Compared with the treasures they contain, the fabled wealth of Tyre of old sinks into insignificance. The private residences of the city are among the handsomest in the world, and, as a rule, are furnished with elegance and taste. The city has all the substantial appearance of London, and a large part of the brightness and beauty of Paris. It is a worthy rival to either, and is in many respects their superior.

New York is highly favored as regards its climate. Its proximity to the sea mitigates the cold of the winters, and the cool ocean breezes temper the fierce heats of the summer In the latter season the lower part of the city may be stifling, but above Thirty-fourth street, and in all the upper quarters, the breeze is constant and refreshing. If New York were not a great city it would unquestionably be the principal watering place of the continent. Snow rarely lies in its streets, and the people consider themselves in high good fortune when the winter is sufficiently cold to hold the snow long enough to give them a few days of sleighing.

I have said that New York combines the solidity of London with the beauty of Paris. Over it hangs a sky bluer and clearer than that of Italy. Days will pass without a cloud to mar the calm blue depths above, and against this exquisite background the spires and domes of the city stand out as clear and sharply defined as if cut on a cameo.

Possessing such a climate, drained by such broad, deep rivers, New York cannot be other than healthy. The death rate compares favorably with that of other cities. It is largest during the summer months. At this period children swell the list of deaths to a high figure. The great infantile mortality occurs in the tenement districts. The largest number of deaths occur from diarrhœal disease. The *New York Tribune*, some time since, thus summed up the most interesting facts in relation to this subject, as gained from a report of the Board of Health —

"The great infantile mortality occurs mainly in the tenement districts. The largest number of cases of death from diarrhœal disease have been reported from the Nineteenth Ward. The Thirteenth, Fourteenth, Sixteenth, Twenty-first, Twenty-second, and Twenty-fourth Wards follow closely. The other Wards have been comparatively free from deaths of this sort. The greatest number of cases of diarrhœal disease have been found in tenements containing from eight to ten families, but the location has had considerable influence upon the death rate. Very few if any cases of death from this cause have been reported from houses containing only one family. A prominent physician said recently that poverty and neglect are the true causes of the large mortality among children under five years of age. The hard times and the scarcity of work compel the mothers to search for work, to labor from morning until night in order to obtain the means of bare subsistence. The infant, at the most critical time of its life, is left to the uncertain care of one of the other children, and is sure to be neglected. It is scantily fed, and what food it gets is of such a bad quality that instead of nourishing it only irritates the alimentary canal. The hot weather attacks, with its debilitating influences, the poorly fed, weakened constitution of the neglected child, and it is hurried into its grave.

"There is a large part of this city—that covering the central division of the island, between Third and Eighth, avenues—which is considered by physicians to be as healthy as any part of this country. This quarter is well-drained, and there are very few tenements within its boundaries. The mortality in this district has always been very small. There have been very few cases of diphtheria or smallpox reported within its limits, and hardly any deaths from diarrhœal diseases. On the east side of the city tenements are thickly planted, some of them being crowded with more than fifty families. Here the deaths from diarrhœal diseases reach an appalling number. The infants three months old die in hosts, and those from nine to twelve months of age, together with those who are passing through the period of dentition, perish in large numbers. On the west side of the city, also, there are many large and badly constructed tenements, where the mortality has always been very great in hot weather.

"Physicians who attend the sick in the tenements give pitiful statements of poverty and want that prevail so largely. One physician said that he had a case where

the infant each day was fed upon only one tablespoon-
ful of condensed milk dissolved in a quart of water.
It lived upon this daily supply for six months, growing
thinner daily, and then died.   The mothers, he added,
are not able to supply their offspring with natural food,
in which case the infant is fed upon condensed milk,
for they are so poorly fed themselves that they can give
little nourishment to their children.   In either case,
what should be nourishment is only an irritant, and the
child dies of some one of the many forms of diarrhœal
disease.   In the tenement districts it is easy to point
out the infants that are rapidly passing into their graves
from the want of proper nourishment.   Their faces
look pinched and drawn.   Besides the want of proper
nourishment, neglect of cleanliness and want of suitable clothing add to the other causes that are hurrying
so many to death."

New York grows rapidly.   In spite of the trying
times that have afflicted the whole country since the
panic of 1873, the city has grown steadily, and has
improved in a marked degree.   One of the most notable features of this growth is the *upward* tendency of
the new structures.   Land is so dear that property
owners endeavor to build as lofty edifices as their
means will permit, in order to offset the lack of ground
and space.   An old resident of the city writes as follows concerning this feature of New York architecture:

"The manner in which New York city has grown
upward, or rather skyward, during the past ten and
fifteen years, has heretofore attracted the attention of
visitors to the American metropolis.   It is just now a
subject of considerable discussion among architects

and builders, who are busily engaged in drawing plans
for numerous new buildings to be erected within the
city precincts during the coming twelve months, now
that labor and material are cheaper than they have
been for several years.   This growth of New York in
altitude is particularly noticeable in the lower part of
the city, from the Battery to Canal street, where high
buildings, averaging ninety to one hundred feet, have
taken the place of small structures and of those not
higher than forty-five to fifty feet.   Some eight years
ago, as one looked from the ferry-boats of either the
North or East River, or from the bay, the then new
Herald Building, on Broadway, towered many feet
above the mass of adjoining structures.   Now it is in-
distinguishable from either point named, the neighboring buildings entirely overshadowing it.

"This growth of New York thus illustrated in height
is attributed by the architects to the high price at which
each foot of real estate is held all over the island, and
notably in the lower section of the city; but it has also
been greatly facilitated by the use of elevators, which
enable some of the most prominent firms to occupy
offices on the fourth and fifth floors, and even higher
floors, where only a few years ago they would not entertain the idea of asking their customers to call upon
them above the second story.   This "mania" for high
buildings, which the architects as yet regard only in its
infancy, is, however, not original with New York; the
new part of the city of Edinburgh, in Scotland, being
full of buildings ten and eleven stories high.   There,
however, the stories do not average over nine feet,
while high basements and sub-cellars, like those of New

York, are unknown. Old architects state that they can hardly conceive the wonderful changes, wrought mainly by their own hands, on taking a retrospect of the city of their youth, and they stand amazed at the giant structures rising all over the city to take the place of buildings which less than twenty years ago were considered ornaments of New York. Forty years ago, when Griffith Thomas arrived in New York, he says he found only two architects here, Messrs. Dacon and Davis. To-day there are about five hundred architects in this city; and the practice, then quite general, of a builder's making his own plans and designs is entirely abandoned. Thirty years ago Mr. Renwick, then only twenty-three years old, built Grace Church, at Tenth street and Broadway, as the building, forty feet high, formerly occupied by that congregation at Rector street and Broadway had to be changed into offices; it was in 1846 that Dr. Wainwright and Dr. Taylor preached their last sermons in the old church, which was soon changed to an eighty-feet building. In the immediate vicinity of the old Grace Church used to stand Bunker's Hotel, a well-known landmark of the time. It was surrounded by buildings all three stories high; to-day not a vestige remains of any of these small buildings, and the lower part of Broadway is filled with structures ranging from six to seven stories. One of the highest residences of New York, on Broadway, at the time named was the house occupied by John F. Delaplaine. It was forty-five feet high, and considerably overshadowed the adjoining two-story residence. The ground is to-day occupied by what is known as the Exchange Building, at Nos. 78 and 80 Broadway, which is filled with offices, and is not less than eighty-five feet high. The Franklin House—which was considered a rather high building, being sixty feet in height—at Dey street, and Broadway, has had to make room for the building of the Western Union Telegraph Company, which is one hundred and sixty feet in height to the roof (the tower being two hundred and thirty feet above the sidewalk). On the other side of Broadway, the Park Bank Building, ninety-five feet high, has now for several years overlapped *The Herald* office, and these two again have been recently overtopped by the nine-story building of *The Evening Post.*

"On the side streets, the same principle of building upward appears to have guided the various improvements, even the old Tontine Building, at Wall and Water streets, having been raised fifteen feet higher than it was formerly, when the old coffee-house attracted the attention and the cash of old New Yorkers. The staid old Bank of New York, at William and Wall streets, where Commodore Vanderbilt could always be found at certain hours of the day, during his latter years, is now a six-story building, where before only two stories were considered ample accommodation for all those transacting business within its walls. The Drexel Building, at Broad and Wall streets, with its high basement and seven stories, looms up gigantically on the spot where only a few years ago stood an unpretending three-story building—which, however, was sold for the highest price ever paid for real estate in New York—while the Stock Exchange, right across Broad street, is fully eighty-five feet high, and has taken the place of a number of brick stores thirty feet less in height. The beautiful white

EVENING POST BUILDING.

marble building at Nos. 50 and 52 Wall street, is now eighty feet high, while it measured only sixty a few years back; while the Union Bank, at Pine and William streets, has had its height increased twenty feet. The Metropolitan Bank, on the corner of Pine street, is a

ODD-FELLOWS' HALL.

building eighty feet high, and stands upon a lot previously occupied by a house of fifty feet.

"The corner of Leonard street and Broadway used to be marked by the old Athenæum, with its peculiar pillars and low ceilings. Messrs. Appleton had their place of business there for some time, and removed to make room for the stately building now owned and occupied by the New York Life Insurance Company. This building, erected by Thomas and finished in 1868, has four stories in front and eight in the back, and part of it stands on very high ground. The Knickerbocker Life Insurance Company's building on the corner of

NEW YORK LIFE INSURANCE COMPANY'S BUILDING.

Park Place is ninety-five feet high, and has taken the place of some four-story brick houses, where the Mechanics' Library Association, in times past, kept its books and held its meetings.

"But not only are there high buildings occupied by public institutions, insurance companies, banks, and newspaper offices; throughout the lower part of the city there are many buildings six and seven, often eight stories high, used as warehouses, especially by dry goods firms. In Walker street, between Cortlandt alley and Elm street, are several six and seven-story buildings on the ground where once stood the St. Matthew's (German Lutheran) Church. The stores at Nos. 555 and 557 Broadway, ninety feet high, have taken the place of several very diminutive establishments, and the upholsterers' warehouse of Sloane and Solomon are also ninety feet high, instead of the three-story buildings of fifteen years ago. Baxter's high building of six stories and mansard roof, at Canal and Mulberry streets, has taken the place of numerous small shanties, which looked anything but attractive before East Canal street was made the street it is to-day. On the spot where Samuel Ward, "the King of the Lobby," was born, in the two-story and attic building erected by his father, John Ward, is now the establishment of Brooks Brothers, fully ninety-five feet high.

"The corner of Fourteenth street and Union Square, where once stood the residence of the late Judge Roosevelt's brother, fifty feet in height, is now occupied by the Domestic Building, which is one hundred and twelve feet high. A few doors west, the new building of the Wheeler and Wilson Manufacturing Company, one hundred feet high, has taken the place of the Old Maison Dorée, which was a low building not over forty-five feet in height. Tiffany's store, at Fifteenth street and Union Square, with its roof ninety feet from the sidewalk, fills the place formerly occupied by the Rev. Dr. Cheever's Church—the Church of the Puritans—the roof of which was only thirty-five feet from the

DOMESTIC SEWING MACHINE BUILDING.

ground. Across the Square, on the corner of East Fourteenth street, the German Savings Bank building of ninety feet, with its mansard and high basement, has replaced the old Belvidere Hotel, while a block further up, on the corner of East Fifteenth street, the Union Square Hotel, remodeled, has had forty feet added to its height. The building owned by the Singer Sewing Machine Company, at East Sixteenth street and Union Square, is nearly one hundred feet high, while looking beyond the Square, the eye takes in at once the prominent store of Arnold, Constable & Co., filling the entire block between Eighteenth and Nineteenth streets, on the ground where only a very few years ago stood nothing but two-story shanties.

TRIBUNE BUILDING.

"Further up town the Stevens Apartment House, at Twenty-seventh street and Fifth avenue, attracts attention by its extraordinary height, one hundred and ten feet, where before stood only three and four-story houses, and on the corner of Forty-seventh street a number of three-story houses have made room for Brewster's high factory, of eighty feet. It is doubtful if any new buildings up town will surpass in height the new Roman Catholic Cathedral, which is one hundred and forty-five feet to the top of the roof.

"In order to show the upward progress made in the growth of New York during the past ten years, buildings like the Fifth Avenue Hotel, Grand Opera House,

STAATS-ZEITUNG BUILDING.

Claflin's Warehouses, and others, have been omitted from this enumeration. These were erected at intervals, and not in such rapid succession, as, for instance, the Equitable Life Building with its one hundred and sixty-four feet of height, 'The Tribune Building' of one hundred and seventy-one feet, 'The Evening Post,' with its nine stories, 'The Staats-Zeitung,' with its one hundred feet, and the building of the Delaware and Hudson Canal Company, in Cortlandt street. All these, taken in connection with those mentioned above, have fully doubled the capacity of New York for accommodating all those who desire to transact business within its borders, while at the same time not an inch more ground has been taken for that purpose than was the case before this increase in altitude set in. On the contrary, it is believed that, owing to the widening of streets, like South Fifth avenue and New Church street, as well as New Chambers street and the New Bowery, there is actually to-day less ground occupied by buildings, small and large, down town, than fifteen years ago. And yet there is considerably more room for all purposes of business."

CHAPTER II

THE PEOPLE OF NEW YORK

POPULATION OF NEW YORK IN 1870—THE STATE CENSUS OF 1875—WHAT CHANGES IT SHOWED—POPU-
LATION IN 1880—POPULATION AFFECTED BY THE IMPROVEMENTS IN THE LOWER PART OF THE
CITY—THE MOST DENSELY SETTLED PART OF NEW YORK—THE FLOATING POPULATION—
STRANGERS IN NEW YORK—FOREIGN DISTRICTS—COSMOPOLITAN CHARACTER OF THE PEOPLE
—CHARACTERISTICS OF NEW YORKERS—LACK OF PUBLIC SPIRIT—INDIFFERENCE TO POLITI-
CAL AFFAIRS—THE RESULT—THE RACE FOR WEALTH—HOW BUSINESS IS DONE IN NEW YORK—
WEARING OUT BODY AND SOUL—A PHILOSOPHICAL MERCHANT—A NEW COMER'S IMPRESSIONS
—LIVING TOO FAST—NO CHANCE FOR LAGGARDS—HOW SUCCESS IS WON—MERIT THE TEST—
NEW YORK FROM A MORAL POINT OF VIEW—ITS CHARITIES AND BENEVOLENCE—TOLERATION
OF OPINIONS AND BELIEFS—MENTAL CULTURE OF THE PEOPLE—WHAT IT COSTS TO LIVE IN
NEW YORK—THE RICH AND THE MIDDLE CLASSES—NEW YORK AS A PLACE OF RESIDENCE—
ATTACHMENT OF THE PEOPLE TO THE CITY.

According to the Ninth Census of the United States,
the population of New York in 1870 was 973,106 souls.
This return was not satisfactory to the citizens of the
Metropolis, who claimed that it greatly under-estimated
the actual number of residents. In the summer of 1875
a census of the city was taken, by order of the Legislature of the State. This enumeration showed the
population in that year to be 1,064,272, an increase of
91,166 inhabitants since 1870. In 1880, the Tenth Census of the United States gave the population as 1,209,-
561.

The census of 1875 was deeply interesting, imperfect as it was conceded to be. It showed many changes
in various portions of the city, recording a gain for
some sections and a decrease for others. The falling
off was mainly in the lower wards, where business
houses predominate. In the strictly commercial quarters dwellings are very rare, and the population is made
up almost entirely of janitors and their families, who

occupy the upper floors of business houses and public buildings. The population of the Sixth Ward was shown to be 1100 less in 1875 than in 1870. In 1880 it had regained about 150 of its loss. This is one of the most wretched and wicked sections of the city; "the Five Points" is its centre. For some years it has been improving in character, though "the Five Points" and Baxter street are bad enough yet. During the past ten or twelve years many of its old haunts have been broken up, numerous factories and business establishments have been erected on their sites, and Worth street has been widened and opened from Broadway to the Bowery, making a clear, wide path through what was once an eyesore to the city and a chosen haunt of vice and crime. In 1875 the greatest increase was in the wards adjoining the Central Park, in which the gain was over fifty thousand, and in 1880 the increase was proportionally larger. This is accounted for by the steady up-town movement of the population, which will no doubt be greatly accelerated by the elevated railroads, which now bring all parts of the city within easy and rapid reach of each other. The largest increase of all, in 1875, was in the Nineteenth Ward, which lies east of the Sixth avenue, and between Fortieth and Eightieth streets. In 1870 the population of this ward was 86,090, in 1875 it was 125,196, showing an increase of 39,106 in five years. In 1880 it had reached the enormous figure of 158,108 inhabitants, thus gaining 32,912 people since 1875, or 72,018 in ten years.

The most densely populated portion of New York is the region embraced in the Seventh, Tenth, and Thirteenth wards, which lie upon either side of East

Broadway and Grand street, in the extreme lower part
of the city, and cover a comparatively small area. In
1870 these wards contained 119,603 inhabitants, and a
further increase seemed impossible, so densely were
they packed. Yet in 1875 the population numbered
124,093, and in 1880 it was 135,456. It is believed
that some of the blocks within this section are more
densely populated than those of any European city.
Yet in ten years the increase of the district was
15,843.

The census of 1875, as has been said, did not fairly
represent the population of the city at that time. It
was taken in the summer, when large numbers of people were absent, and it was asserted that many of the
persons entrusted with making enumerations were
incompetent to their task. The census of 1880 was
taken with more care, and more faithfully represents
the actual number of inhabitants.

In a fair estimate of the people of New York, one
must add to the number of actual residents, the strangers temporarily residing in the metropolis, and the immense number of persons who enter and leave the city
every day in the year. It is estimated that there are more
than seventy thousand strangers from distant parts of
the country temporarily sojourning in New York at all
periods of the year. Thousands of persons doing business in the City, and residing in the suburbs, are not
counted in the population. They come from Brooklyn
and Long Island, from Staten Island, from the mainland of New York, from New Jersey, and even from
Connecticut. They crowd the trains and the ferry
boats, and pour into the city in the morning and leave

it in the afternoon, with clock-like regularity. To these also must be added the persons of both sexes and all ages, who come into the city to do a day's shopping, or to attend the matinees of the theatres and other places of amusement, or to visit friends. It is estimated that at high noon, on any fair day during the season, the Island of New York contains at least two millions of people.

In 1880 the native population was 727,743, and the foreign 478,834.

The annual number of births in New York is about 40,000. The number of deaths in 1880 was 31,937.

The foreign classes generally congregate in distinct quarters of the city, which they seem to regard as their own, as they constitute the majority of the dwellers in these sections, and give to them their leading characteristics. In certain portions, whole blocks may be found in which English is rarely heard, the dwellers using the tongues of their native countries in their intercourse with each other, and having little communication with their neighbors.

The people of New York represent every nationality upon the globe, and thus give to the city the cosmopolitan character which is one of its most prominent features. But no city on the continent is so thoroughly American as this. The native population is the ruling element, and makes the great city what it is, whether for good or for evil. The children and grandchildren of foreigners soon lose their old world ideas and habits, and the third generation sees them as genuine and devoted Americans as any on the Island.

The besetting sin of the people of New York is their

lack of public spirit. The race for wealth, the very struggle for existence, is so eager and intense here, that the people think little of public affairs, and leave their city government, with all its vast interests, in the hands of a few professional politicians. They pay dearly for this neglect of such important interests. They are taxed and plundered by rings and tricksters, and are forced to bear burdens and submit to losses which could be avoided by a more patriotic and sensible treatment of their affairs. Business men here regard the time spent in casting their votes at the polls, or in arranging a political canvass so that good men only shall be secured for public officers, as so much time lost. They say they cannot afford to take it from their business. The result is they are put to greater loss by unnecessary and unjust taxes.

The race for wealth is a very exciting one in the great city. The interests at stake are so vast, the competition so constant and close, that men are compelled to be on the watch all the time, and to work with rapidity and almost without rest. Business hours are from nine until five. In the larger establishments but little is done after four o'clock, except at certain seasons. During these seven or eight hours the work of twenty-four is done. Every nerve, every muscle, every power and faculty of body and mind, is taxed to the utmost to discharge the duty of the day. Go into any of the large establishments of the city during business hours, and you will be amazed at the ceaseless rush and push of clerks and customers. It is one unending drive. Everything must be finished up to the closing hour, so that the morrow may be begun with a series of new and clear transactions. Merchants from other cities coming into these establishments to make purchases, find themselves caught in this whirl of work, and are carried along and made to decide questions and make purchases with a rapidity utterly unknown to them in their own homes.

Two merchants from a Western city met one night, not long since, in the sitting-room of the St. Nicholas Hotel.

"How do you get on with your purchases?" asked one of the other.

"I am through buying," was the reply.

"Going home to-morrow, then, I suppose?"

"No; I shall not do so for several days yet. The truth is I am tired, and I want to rest. I used to go back home as soon as I had finished my business here, and when I got there I invariably found myself too tired to do anything for several days. I couldn't understand it. It was the same thing year after year, and I set to work to think it out. I know now that it is the effect of the hard work I do here in a few days. I come here, stay a week, and during that time do an amount of work, both physical and mental, greater than I would undergo in a month at home. Now, instead of going home as soon as I am done, I stay here and rest; go out to the Central Park, and loaf for a whole afternoon; take a ride on the steamer up the East River; go down to Coney Island, or down the Bay, and amuse myself in every way I can. Then I go home bright and fresh, and able to take hold of my work there properly."

The clerks in the large houses of the city have a

weary, jaded look, always. The heads of the houses have the same expression intensified. They are always tired. They crowd too much work into a day. The result is that New York can show comparatively few old merchants or clerks. They cannot always stand the strain upon them, and die off by hundreds, at a time of life when they ought to be looking forward to a hearty old age.

A gentleman once said to the writer of these pages: "I came to New York at the close of our civil war, to seek employment. I came up the Bay from Monmouth County, New Jersey, full of hope and confidence. The sail up the broad blue water gave new life to this feeling. I knew I was competent, and I was resolved to succeed. I landed at Pier Number One, near the Battery, and taking up my valise started up town. I turned into Broadway at the Bowling Green, and as I did so, found myself in a steady stream of human beings, each hurrying by as if his life depended upon his speed, taking no notice of his fellows, pushing and jostling them, and each with a weary, jaded, anxious look upon his face. As I gazed at this mighty torrent I was dismayed. I got as far as Trinity Churchyard, and then I put my valise upon the pavement, and leaning against the railing, watched the people as they passed me by. They came by hundreds, thousands, all with that eager, restless gait that I now know so well, all with the weary, anxious, care-worn expression I have mentioned, as if trying to reach some distant goal within a given time. They seemed to say to me, 'We would gladly stop if we could, and rest by the way; but we must go on, on, and know no rest.' I asked myself, 'What chance have I here? Can I keep up with this eager, restless throng, or will they pass me, and leave me behind?' Well," he added, with a smile, "I have managed to keep up with them, but I tell you it's a hard strain. We are all living too fast; we are working too hard. Instead of taking a leisurely stroll to our business in the morning, we rush down town at a furious pace. We grind, grind at our treadmills all day, and grind too hard. We bolt our meals in a fourth of the time we should give to them; we rush back home at night as furiously as we left it in the morning, and our evenings are spent in an effort to keep up the excitement of the day. We are living too fast, too hard. We break down long before we should. This haste, this furious pace at which we are going, at business, at pleasure, at everything, is the great curse of New York life."

Now my friend's opinion is shared by hundreds, thousands of the most sensible men of the city, but they are powerless to save themselves from the curse they know to be upon them. Should they attempt to go more slowly, to live more reasonably, they would be left behind in the race for wealth; they would fail in their hopes and plans. So they must join the crowd, and rush on and on, seeking the glittering prize of wealth and fame, well knowing all the time that, in all probability, when they have grasped it tired nature will give way and leave them incapable of enjoying it, if indeed they do not die before attaining their end.

The common opinion that New York is the paradise of humbugs and tricksters is untrue. These people do abound here, beyond, a doubt; but they are short-lived. They flourish to-day and are gone to-morrow.

They take no root, and have no hold upon any genuine interest; they attain no permanent success. It is only genuine merit that succeeds in the great city. Men are here subjected to a test that soon takes the conceit out of them. They are taken for just what they are worth, and no more, and he must show himself a man indeed who would take his place among the princes of trade, or among the leaders of thought and opinion. He may bring with him from his distant home the brightest of reputations, but here he will have to begin at the very bottom of the ladder and mount upward again. It is slow work, so slow that it tries every quality of true manhood to its utmost. The daily life of the dwellers in the great city makes them keen, shrewd judges of human nature, and they are proficients in the art of studying character.

It is said that New York is the wickedest city in the country. It is the largest, and vice thrives in crowded communities. How great this wickedness is we may see in the subsequent portions of this work. Yet, if it is the wickedest city, it is also the best on the Continent. If it contains thousands of the worst men and women in our land, it contains also thousands of the brightest and best of Christians. In point of morality, it will compare favorably with any city in the world. It is unhappily true that the devil's work is done here upon a large scale; but so is the work of God, upon an even greater scale. If the city contains the gaudiest, the most alluring, and the vilest haunts of sin, it also boasts the noblest and grandest institutions of religion, of charity, and virtue. Being the great centre of wealth and culture, New York is also the centre of everything that is good and beautiful in life.

In its charities, New York is, as in other respects, the leading city of the Continent. It maintains its own charitable and benevolent institutions with a liberality, and upon a scale of magnificence and comfort, unequaled in other parts of the country. It spends millions to relieve suffering and disease within its own limits, and at the same time lends an open ear and a ready hand to the cry of distress from other quarters. There is no portion of the globe to which the charity of New York does not extend; and when it gives, it gives liberally. When the yellow fever laid its heavy hand upon the Southern States during the summer of 1878, it was to New York that the sufferers first turned for aid; and the Metropolis responded nobly. In the course of a few months assistance in money and supplies was sent to the amount of several hundred thousand dollars. During the recent war between Russia and Turkey, New York, with characteristic liberality, sent generous assistance to the sick and wounded of both armies. When Chicago was burned, the people of New York literally showered relief upon the afflicted citizens of the western Metropolis. It is enough for the great city to hear the cry of distress, no matter from what quarter; its action is prompt and generous. The city authorities annually expend one million of dollars in public charities, while the various religious denominations and charitable associations expend annually about five millions more. No record can be had of private charities—but they are large. This is the charity that begins at home. Of the aid sent to suffer-

THE GRAND CENTRAL DEPOT, NEW YORK.

ing persons and communities in other parts of the country no proper estimate can be made; the sum is princely, and we may be sure is recorded above.

I have spoken of the energy of the people in matters of business. They are in all respects the most enterprising in the Union. While others are timid and hesitating, they are bold and self-reliant. They take risks in business from which others shrink, and carry their ventures forward with a resolution and vigor that cannot fail of success. It is this that has made the city the metropolis of America. Its people take a large, liberal view of matters. There is nothing narrow or provincial in their way of dealing with questions. They are cosmopolitan in all things.

This liberality extends to matters of opinion. Men rarely trouble themselves to inquire into a neighbor's views of religion or politics, or to hold him to account for them. One may think as he pleases here, and so long as he observes the ordinary rules of decent living he will retain his place in society. Christian, Jew, Turk, Heathen, all mingle together in pleasant social intercourse, careless of each other's opinions, and taking each other for just what the individual man is worth. And so it is in politics. The most decided political antagonists may be in private life intimate friends. New York cares nothing for individual opinions. It welcomes every man, and uses him as best it can.

Indeed, this indifference is carried to such an excess that men often live by each other, as next-door neighbors, for years, without interchanging salutations or holding any neighborly intercourse at all. It may be said that this prevents gossip and adds to the privacy of one's domestic affairs; but at-the same time it breeds an amount of coldness between people and prevents the pleasantness of neighborly intercourse, which is not in all respects desirable.

In mental culture the people of New York compare favorably with those of any American city. The conditions of success in the various pursuits of life require and develop the highest order of intelligence. Every faculty of the human being is sharpened in the struggle for mere existence. In addition to this, the surroundings of the people contribute daily and almost imperceptibly to their culture. The magnificent streets, the imposing buildings, the rare and beautiful displays in the shops of the city, all go to cultivate the taste and impart knowledge to the people who behold them. The libraries are extensive and well patronized; the theatrical displays and other amusements are upon the most elaborate and imposing scale; and the schools and educational institutions are among the most excellent in the world. Those who have leisure for study, of course, have great advantages here, but the great mass of the people who have not leisure find means of improvement in the sights which greet them in their daily walks along the street.

All sorts of people come to New York. You may watch the throng on a fair afternoon, in any of the principal streets of the city, and you will see pass before you representatives of every land and clime, of all professions, trades and callings.

The great cost of living in New York makes it impossible for the city to number a strong middle class among its people. The very rich can afford the expense, since it brings them pleasures and compensations they can obtain nowhere else in America for their outlay. The very poor and the laboring class huddle in the tenement houses, and put up with discomfort at a cost which would enable them to do far better in the other cities of the country. What a workingman pays for his two or three rooms in a New York tenement house would give him a separate house and a comfortable home in almost any other American city.

Persons of moderate means doing business in New York who desire the comforts of a home for their families are, as a rule, obliged to reside out of the city. They come into New York in the morning, and leave it in the evening. It is a severe tax upon their strength, but it enables them to enjoy the business advantages of the metropolis, and at the same time to provide for their families homes of comfort and taste at a cost within their means, which they could not do as residents of the city.

This leaves New York but a comparatively small representation of the class which is the mainstay of modern communities. The pauper population is large, the number of those who live by manual labor is larger, and against these are set the rich men of the city. The class which should be strongest, and which should stand as the harmonizers of the extremes we have mentioned, is conspicuous by its absence.

Persons who do business in the city and reside in the suburbs are subjected to many inconveniences, especially during the winter season. A heavy snow or a dangerous storm may keep them from their business when their presence is imperatively demanded, or may prevent them from reaching home at night.

As a place of residence, to those who have the money to justify it, New York is by far the most delightful home in the country. Its cosmopolitan and metropolitan character, its glorious climate, and its thousand and one attractions, added to the solid comfort one may enjoy here, make it the most attractive of our great cities. It possesses a peculiar charm, which all who have dwelt within its borders feel and own. As a rule, the people would rather be uncomfortable here than comfortable elsewhere. They leave it with regret, and return to it with delight whenever able to do so.

CHAPTER III

THE GROWTH OF NEW YORK

RAPID GROWTH OF NEW YORK DURING THE PAST THIRTY-FIVE YEARS—THE FLUSH TIMES AFTER
THE WAR—EFFECTS OF THE PANIC OF 1873—A MOMENTARY CHECK—RETURN OF PROS-
PERITY—PROSPECTS FOR THE FUTURE—INCREASE IN BUILDING OPERATIONS—HOW REAL
ESTATE APPRECIATES IN VALUE—THE SECRET OF THE GREAT INCREASE OF WEALTH IN NEW
YORK—FUTURE CENTRES OF POPULATION—WHAT NEW YORK WILL BE FIFTY YEARS HENCE—
A GRAND DESTINY.

We have already given the population of the metropolis according to the last three censuses, but before
passing on, it will be interesting to glance at the growth
of the city for the last thirty-five years. The United
States Census is taken every ten years, and shows a
marked change in every decade; but the State Census,
which is taken every five years, enables us to obtain
a view of the movement of the city's population at
shorter intervals. From it we learn that, notwithstanding the phenomenal growth of New York, there
was a period, covering the duration of our civil war,
when the metropolis, instead of increasing, actually de-
clined in population. The returns since the year 1845,
record the population as follows:

In 1845, ...	371,223
In 1850, ...	515,547
In 1855, ...	629,810
In 1860, ...	813,669
In 1865, ...	726,386
In 1870, ...	942,292
In 1875, ...	1,064,272
In 1880, ...	1,209,561

The close of the civil war marked the opening of a new era of prosperity, which New York shared with the rest of the country. The panic of 1873 began another period of depression, which had its effect in keeping down the city's growth. The hard times drove numbers of laboring people and those in humble circumstances to the West and other portions of the country, to seek the rewards which the stagnation of business in the great commercial centre denied them. During the past two years the onward march of prosperity has been resumed, and the census of 1880 shows a growth of 267,269 inhabitants over the population of 1870, and of 145,289 over that of 1875. It is confidently expected that the next five years will show a still greater improvement, and should the next decade be favorable to the general prosperity of the country, there can be little doubt that in 1890 New York will contain nearly, if not quite, two millions of inhabitants. With wise foresight, the city is preparing to accommodate this vast number of human beings which will soon crowd its limits. What changes will take place in the next ten years no one can with certainty predict, but it is safe to assert that 1890 will see a city far more splendid, far more enterprising, and in every way more worthy of the proud title of " Metropolis," than that to which we now invite the reader's attention.

Not long since, a gentleman who had carefully studied the progress of New York, and who, as a statistician of great and acknowledged experience, is entitled to speak with authority, said : " Basing my calculations on tables corrected by external and internal influences which are clearly apparent to any one giving attention to the subject, I anticipate an increase in our population in New York, during the next five years, of fully three hundred and fifty thousand. First of all, the bad state of trade in Great Britain, and the wretched poverty existing among the tillers of the soil, must greatly swell the tide of immigration. Moreover, we are of late getting a better class of immigrants. That is because skilled artisans, attracted by the glowing accounts of the better wages and more liberal treatment prevailing here, sent to them by fellow workmen who have already made their home in the United States, are now coming out here in force, and will emigrate in even larger numbers as the good news is disseminated among them. These men, unlike the unskilled laborers, who must needs travel on to less populated States, where alone their labor is in demand, will readily find a market for their skilled labor in New York, and here, consequently, they will make their home. Rapid transit, too, now so fully developed, will not only keep the present population resident in their own city, but will, I think, draw thousands of men resident in Brooklyn, Jersey, Long Island and Connecticut towns and elsewhere, whose places of business are in New York, back within the city limits."

The increase of the population necessarily brings an increase in the means of accommodating it, and of providing for its various requirements. Consequently, New York is rapidly growing in the number of its business edifices, its dwellings, churches, theatres, and public buildings. In spite of the hard times and general depression which have marked the past ten years building operations have been carried on upon a gigantic scale. According to the returns furnished by the city authorities, the number of buildings erected from 1872 to 1879, was as follows:

In 1872	. . . . . .	1,728
In 1873	. . . . . .	1,311
In 1874	. . . . . .	1,388
In 1875	. . . . . .	1,406
In 1876	. . . . . .	1,379
In 1877	. . . . . .	1,432
In 1878	. . . . . .	1,672
In 1879	. . . . . .	2,065

In all, a total of 12,381 buildings erected in eight years.

"The first thing that strikes the eye on perusing these figures," says the gentleman we have quoted, "is the large increase in the number of buildings that went up in 1879, as compared with previous years, during which the increase of population and number of buildings erected were about proportionate. Hence the activity in building is clearly traceable to the general improvement of trade and freer circulation of money that has recently taken place." On this subject, the gentleman whose remarks are quoted above spoke as follows :— "The erection of buildings in New York during the past eight years has been carried on upon an enormous scale. Mere figures give to the reader but a poor idea of the vast nature of these operations. From a careful calculation I have made, I find that were it possible to mass in one whole all the buildings erected in New York since 1872, they would cover an area equal in extent to the ground lying between 110th and 140th streets, from Fifth to Ninth avenue inclusive, and from 60th street to 110th, between Eighth and Ninth avenues. It is, in short, perfectly safe to say that 11,000 full lots have been built upon during the period indicated—considering that the Seventh regiment armory alone covers thirty-two lots, and many other enormous buildings have also gone up. This increase of building is, I think, likely to go on indefinitely, and real estate, in sympathy, will, I believe, rise greatly in value. It may be advanced against the views I take upon this head that no matter how great an activity may prevail in building operations, there is so much vacant land on hand that real estate will not greatly advance in price. A very cogent argument in my favor will be found in a growing disposition on the part of large capitalists to buy up large pieces of land as an investment, after the manner adopted by Robert Lennox, whose farm at the five-mile stone has proved such a veritable El Dorado to the two generations succeeding him.

"The following extracts from the will of Robert Lennox have, at this time, such a peculiar significance, in the face of the renewed demand for real estate for building operations, as to be worth reproducing. Section 9 of the will, bearing date of May 23d, 1829, June 23d, 1832, and October 4th, 1839, read as follows:—

" ' I give, devise and bequeath to my son, my only son, James Lennox, my farm at the five-mile stone, purchased in part from the Corporation of the city of New York and containing about thirty acres, with all improvements, stock of horses, cattle and farming utensils, for and during the term of his life, and after his death to his heirs forever.

My motive for so leaving this property, is a firm per-
suasion that it may, at no distant date, be the site of a
village, and as it cost me much more than its present
worth, from circumstances known to my family, I like
to cherish the belief it may be realized to them. At all
events, I want the experiment made, by keeping the
property from being sold.'

"Under the second date on the will—namely, June
23d, 1832—the foregoing bequest is thus modified:—

"'Whereas, in my said will I have left my farm, situ-
ate in the Twelfth (formerly Ninth) ward of the city of
New York, near the five-mile stone, to my son, James
Lennox, for and during the term of his natural life, and
after his death to his heirs, forever; now I do hereby
give and devise the said farm to my said son, James
Lennox, and to his heirs, forever. At the same time,
I wish him to understand that my opinion respecting
the property is not changed, and though I withdraw
all legal restrictions to his making sale of the whole or
part of the same, yet I enforce on him my advice not to
do so.'

"A wise man in his generation was Robert Lennox.
The farm at the five-mile stone originally cost the tes-
tator somewhere in the neighborhood of $40,000.
Early in 1864, Mr. James Lennox, the fortunate legatee
under the will quoted from, of the now historic farm,
conveyed to his nephew, Robert Lennox Kennedy,
the whole block between 72d and 73d streets, Madi-
ison and Fifth avenues—a block 204 feet 4 inches
in width on Fifth and Madison avenues and 420 feet
in length on each street named. The consideration
paid for this slice out of the golden farm was

$250,000. To Clarence S. Brown, on December 11th, 1866, Mr. Kennedy, for $240,000, disposed of twenty lots on this block, comprising the whole front on 72d street, between Fifth and Madison avenues, and the plot 120 feet 2 inches by 100 feet, on the southwest corner of 73d street and Madison avenue. But four years had elapsed when Clarence Brown disposed of these identical lots to John Crosby Brown for $430,000.

" Not to enter into further detail," said the gentleman who had furnished these particulars, " I may first add, that in 1875 the farm at the five-mile stone was valued at $9,000,000, without a building upon it. To-day I judge that the lot on the corner of 72d street and Fifth avenue, 27 feet by 100, would fetch in the open market in the neighborhood of $100,000, being more than twice as much as the shrewd old Scotchman paid for the whole thirty acres. At the present time the whole estate is probably worth $12,000,000. Many brokers have concurred in the correctness of these views. Hall J. How said to me, only yesterday, 'Why, Amos Clark, of Boston, owns the lot on 72d street and Fifth avenue, and he would not sell it for $100,000.'

"The late John D. Phillips was hardly so wise as the owner of 'the farm at the five-mile stone.' On the 2d of June, 1851, he purchased of Peter McLaughlin the lot on the southeast corner of 84th street and Fifth avenue for $540. Tempted by the rapid rise in the value of the property, Mr. Phillips sold this lot to Stephen Roberts on the 18th day of August, 1853, for $1900. On Thursday last this identical property was purchased by George Kemp for $40,000. I wonder if it ever occurs to capitalists that, in the long run, more

money can be made out of things of substance than
things of paper—certificates representing the Manhattan shares, for example? If it does not, let them in
quire of those foolish Senators who rushed in where
angels never tread—to wit, the Board of Brokers. In
real estate operations, loaded dice cannot well be employed, and midnight decrees doubling its value are
things unheard of; and it might be well for our million-
aires to remember that the Legislature, forced on by
public sentiment, manifests a disposition to lessen the
burdens that have hitherto fallen upon real estate, by
forcing the corporations to bear their fair share of the
expense of government. I would observe, *en passant*,
that the corporations of Pennsylvania pay almost the
whole amount of the State taxes. Says the Attorney-
General of that State: 'The greater portion of the
revenues of Pennsylvania are derived from the taxes
levied on corporations.'

"All my observations lead me to the conclusion that
building operations will be carried on still more extensively during the next few years.

"I am strongly impressed with the belief that the
west side of the city will be the locality wherein the
greatest activity in building will manifest itself. The
fashionable locality bounded by 60th and 90th streets,
and Madison and Fourth and Fifth avenues, is now
pretty well built up, and within a couple of years
or so will, I imagine, be completely covered. Again,
the recent enormous rise in prices of lots in the fashionable eastern districts will cause builders to at
least ponder over Horace Greeley's advice as to
going West. That portion of the city will, I think,

prove the home of the well-to-do class of the future. I understand that the series of large buildings recently erected by Mr. Edward Clark, of sewing machine fame, on the north side of 73d street, between Ninth and Tenth avenues, are already all rented on good terms. Mr. Clark is a large owner of lots in this particular locality. These and other projected and already begun building operations on the west side will encourage other extensive property holders and capitalists to invest largely in similar enterprises. The natural advantages of the western side, comprising the peerless riverside drive, with its panoramic views of the Hudson, the Palisades, Jersey, and its glimpses of the sea, and its health-giving breezes from the mountains, the Boulevards, Manhattan Square and the Morningside Park, combine to render this western portion of our city a highly desirable place of residence. By reason of bill No. 206, that has recently passed the Senate, Morningside Park—hitherto a park only on paper—will speedily be transformed into 'a thing of beauty and a joy forever.' It is to be at once graded, and the approaches appropriately arranged; and better still, the bill provides that $150,000 shall at once be spent by the Department in its cultivation and adornment. By the 1st of May, too, the squatters—whose rudely constructed huts in various stages of dilapidation and decay are at present notable disfigurements of the district—will disappear, as the property owners have recently combined with the view of effecting this desirable reformation. The superior equipments, too, of the western elevated road, the better class of passengers using the cars, and the convenient situation and frequent recurrence of the stations, are all important factors in enhancing the growing popularity of the western district as a residential suburb.

"Riding over the western elevated road, as the eye rests upon the little groups of houses and cottages, clinging, tendril-like, around the stations of the elevated road, anywhere above, say, 125th street, one is forcibly reminded of the words of Victor Hugo. Writing of the populating effects of railroads on the suburbs of Paris, in 'Les Miserables,' he says: 'Whenever a station is built on the skirts of a city, it is the death of a suburb and the birth of a town.' Those who had the courage to invest their money in real estate in the worst of time (about eighteen months ago), have been enabled in many instances to dispose of their purchases at prices almost approaching, and in some instances actually exceeding, the prices prevailing in 1872–73, and have reason to exclaim with Macbeth:—

> " 'Things at the worst will cease, or else climb upward
> To where they were before.' "

About a year ago, the New York *Herald*, in a carefully-prepared paper, thus predicted the future of New York:—

"The growth and development of this city are without a parallel and without a precedent. Its future has been often prophesied, but not always understood. When we undertake to trace the causes that have led to its commercial supremacy, and those that are now operating to increase its prosperity, we are met by singular and fortuitous circumstances, which it was impossible to foresee, and not easy to comprehend. One thing is, however, certain, that the anticipations of the most sanguine have always been more than realized, while the prognostications of the doubtful have only been remembered for their fallacy.

"The progressive growth of the city has been often capricious, so far as locality is concerned, but the important factor of topography has always asserted itself, in spite of all efforts to ignore it in the interests of individual projects. Going back to the early settlement and Dutch supremacy, we find both commerce and social life progressing along the east side of the city, on the line of what is now Pearl street, where the Dutch burgher sat on his 'stoop,' with his long pipe, and held social commune with his neighbor over the way. The early occupation of that section was due to the fact that from the east side of the city, on account of the prevailing winds, sailing vessels may always be got under way more readily than from the west side, where it is often impossible for a vessel to leave her berth without the aid of a tug. When the English occupation took place, the Dutch had already monopolized the east side of the city, as far up as the 'Bowerie,' or Bowery, including the Stuyvesant meadows— Peter Stuyvesant himself owning a large tract, where is now the Stuyvesant Park. The natural social and business antagonism between the Dutch and English necessitated the selection of a new locality on the part of the latter, and Broadway became the choice, where were erected the English churches—Trinity and St. Paul—and here the English merchants built their residences and their stores. The Dutch churches were in Fulton and Nassau streets, and as the religious element, especially in small communities, is always an important factor in social life, we find two distinct centres of civic progress developing themselves, and maintained with great energy and determination for many years. The topographical advantages were, however, in favor of the English, and the building up of New York along the line of Broadway, the 'backbone' of the island, was the result. But time and prosperity causing a rapid increase of population, the city assumed a cosmopolitan character, local religious or social influences ceased to have the same force that they formerly exerted, and new influences arose to determine the direction and character of the city's growth. Yet no one anticipated then, or for years afterward, what the city might become. There are many persons still living who can remember Canal street as out of town, where they went for a day's shooting in its swampy surroundings, or to fish from the bridge that spanned the sluggish stream on Broadway; and there are at present residents of Fourteenth street who were once regarded with amazement by their friends, for establishing their homes in such a remote locality. Yet the city has continued to grow, the centre of active trade shifting from place to place as the city extended itself. This has been especially the case with the dry goods trade, which at one time centred itself in Pearl street, in the old homes of the Dutch, shifting thence to lower Broadway, afterward occupying the streets running from that thoroughfare on the west side, most of which were widened from forty to sixty feet to make accommodations for this rapidly-increasing trade, and were lined with fine marble buildings, soon, however, to be abandoned for Church street, middle Broadway, and the streets connecting them, where it now rests for a season.　Other lines of trade have apparently followed in the wake, and occupied the localities deserted by the jobbing trade, leaving no vacancies, but filling up, as it were, the interstices as fast as they were made; but from the very force of numbers and the great bulk of this business, the dry-goods traders have always led the way.　On the other hand, in the development of the area appropriated for the purposes of residences, the governing elements have been of an entirely different character.　Any one who will take the pains to examine, from one decade to another, the progressive northward extension of the building limits, will observe a remarkable fluctuation, similar to the irregular and spasmodic lines that indicate on a diagram the rise and fall of gold during the inflation period.　At one time, this line runs forward along the course of Second avenue, leaving all others behind. Again, the extension is transferred to Seventh avenue, which in 1844 was far ahead of all others.　At another period it advanced with great rapidity on the line of Third avenue, which has distanced all competitors and prolonged itself to Harlem.　With the better class of residences, Fifth avenue rushed onward, leaving Madison avenue behind, in quite an insignificant position; but again Madison avenue takes up the race, and has now outstripped Fifth avenue.

" These apparently capricious fluctuations are due to such obvious causes that, instead of being singular, they are directly the reverse, since, with the circumstances that brought about these results, it would have been remarkable had they been otherwise. Take, for instance, Second avenue. An extensive tract in this locality belonged to the heirs of the Stuyvesant estate, many of whom had sufficient means to erect expensive structures for their own residences, and encouraged others to do the same in their vicinity. The consequence was, that for a time many first-class improvements were made in the neighborhood of Stuyvesant Square, and along that region of the avenue alluded to. But the disposition to erect fine buildings in that section soon passed away, and it has never gone beyond an oasis of respectability in a desert of mediocrity. Again, St. Mark's place was selected by an enterprising citizen as an exclusive faubourg, but it proved a mere halting place of fashion. Bond street was another effort, where enough gentlemen of taste and means established themselves to render the entire street an exclusive precinct for a decade or more, but its glory has long since faded.

"Some thirty years ago the movement in Fifth avenue was initiated, and it has held its own, with a growth above and decay below, from that time to the present day. This fine avenue has now become thoroughly invaded, from Washington square almost to the Central Park, with fancy shops, jewelers, hotels and boarding houses, and its exclusiveness has vanished forever. 'Murray Hill,' the line of which it crosses, was for a considerable time regarded as the synonym of fashion, but in time it will be more strictly synonymous with shabby gentility. Fifth avenue northward is limited to the east side of the Park, and has a 'jumping off' place at 102d street, into the Harlem flats, which checks its career of availability. Madison avenue has to some extent usurped the place of Fifth avenue, due in a large measure to the convenience afforded originally by the extension of the Fourth avenue surface road into that avenue. The Third avenue road, which in its incipient stages had been a losing concern (the stock of which at one time sold for three cents on the dollar), began at last, through the mere element of convenience, to cause the building up of the desert of vacant lots through which it was originally projected, and at the time of the construction of the elevated line along its route, was paying its stockholders every year a hundred cents on the dollar of its original cost, and twenty cents per annum on its enormously watered capital. Of course this involved the transportation of very great masses of people, amounting to many millions annually, accompanied by much crowding and discomfort. This immense volume of travel is now being absorbed by the East Side Elevated Railroad.

"Lennox Hill, on the line of Fifth and Madison avenues, from the very nature of its elevated position, affords very attractive building sites, which the large and opulent class of our Hebrew fellow citizens have not been slow to appreciate. In this vicinity they have, with a generous and noble liberality, erected the superb Mount Sinai Hospital, for the care and comfort of the sick of their own people, and many of the handsomest private residences in this fine locality have been erected by them.

"In fact, as this favored territory is really limited by the sudden descent into Harlem Flats at 100th street, it is very doubtful whether it will be sufficient even to accommodate all of that faith who are likely to erect here their 'lares and penates.' The inquiry naturally presents itself, where, then, shall the growth of the city thus limited and circumscribed in the channels it has pursued for three decades, be now directed?

"The answer to this question is to be found in the irresistible logic of facts that we propose now to present. In the glance we have taken at the great capitals of Europe, over some of which not only centuries, but tens of centuries have rolled since their foundation, and on which successive monarchs have sought, in lavish expenditure, to stamp the glory of their brief reigns, by splendid architectural adornments, by parks and promenades, avenues and squares, by grand monuments of brass and marble, triumphal arches and gorgeous palaces—unlike what the New World has yet dreamed of and may never possess—in this glance we see what an important element the broad shaded avenues and fine parks have been in their development. We have recognized that, regardless of all other considerations, these avenues and drives have been the fixed centres of attraction, the final resting place of fashion and elegance, along which and around which cluster the homes of the æsthetic and the opulent, where the citizen who entertains a just civic pride has sought to embellish with his own wealth and taste the choice spots where natural topography, aided by well-ordered public improvements, invite him to a salubrious and permanent home.

"The conclusion is inevitable, therefore, that the section of the city that has been held in reserve until the time when the progress of wealth and refinement shall have attained that period of its development when our citizens can appreciate and are ready to take advantage of the situation, is the section that is to be the most favored and the most sought after. At an expense unparalleled except in the lavish periods of imperial opulence, the great West End plateau, extending from the Central Park to the North River, has been laid out and ornamented with a series of magnificent avenues not excelled by any other city in the world. Moreover, this entire region combines in its general aspect all that is magnificent in the leading capitals of Europe. In our Central Park we have the fine Prater of Vienna; in our grand boulevard the rival of the finest avenues of the gay capital of France; in our Riverside avenue the equivalent of the Chiaja of Naples and the Corso of Rome; while the beautiful "Unter den Linden" of Berlin, and the finest portions of the West End of London, are reproduced again and again. Let us look more closely at the topography of this section, and see whether it will bear out the impressions that are given in regard to it, by a study of its plan.

"Originally, the highest portions of the 'backbone' of the island were rough and unsightly, rocky eminences alternated with intervening valleys. By a process of uniform grading these have been transformed into a generally level plateau, from seventy-five to a hundred feet above the river. On the east, the Central Park, with all its luxuriant beauty, stretches out its long line of trees and shrubs. On the west, the stately Hudson bathes the foot of the green slope in which it terminates, while from the splendid avenue on the crest above, this beautiful sheet of water, with its teeming life of sail and steamer, is viewed for more than three

miles of drive and promenade.   On the south the busy
city stretches out from below the Park, and on the
north the Boulevard extends its length away into the
picturesque and inviting region of Fort Washington,
with the Morningside Park on the east to break the
view of Harlem Plains, while Long Island Sound and
its beautiful islands are seen in the distance.

"In the details of draining, sewering and water supply, the highest skill of the city engineers has been
here employed, and these important public necessities
have been provided in anticipation, with scrupulous
regard to thoroughly studied general plans.   The ignorance and carelessness of the past have been replaced
by intelligence and conscientious work, and the errors
elsewhere committed have here been avoided, these
errors furnishing both a lesson and a guide to perfection.
The drainage of this region flows principally towards the
west side, in some portions of which there has accumulated a great deal of contaminated soil, which may
never be purified.   The underground drains in that
region, which were constructed at a late day, to remove
the water from the soil, after much of the grading had
been done, are found, in some instances, to run sewage
matter of the most offensive description.   Whether this
escapes from imperfect sewers, or from the polluted
condition of the soil, cannot readily be ascertained; but
such is the case.   That side must necessarily partake
of the disadvantages arising from the great pressure
of travel incident to the crowded population that
already monopolizes the larger portion of the territory,
to be increased in the near future by all that is to ac-
cumulate on Harlem Plains.   It is believed that the

density of the future population of the east side will exceed anything now conceived of. With the improvement of the Harlem River, soon to be accomplished, a cordon of business and second-class dwellings will be drawn closely around that side, which can by no possibility invade the West End plateau. The business capacity of the Harlem River is yet to be developed. More of a river than the Thames at London; twice as much as the Seine at Paris, and compared with which the Spree, which runs through Berlin, is a mere open sewer, it has yet been almost ignored in discussing the immediate future of New York. We are soon to realize the fact that this fine river is the proper terminus of the Erie Canal. When the contemplated improvements of this river are completed, a commercial channel will be opened that will render unnecessary the transportation of the canal freight the entire length of the island and around the Battery, to interfere with the shipping and the ferries. It will, instead of making this long detour, be discharged into warehouses and elevators on the Harlem River and at Port Morris, whence the foreign shipping can receive it. The grain and lumber trade of the city will centre here, and a large amount of business now crowded into the lower end of the island will be transacted at this point. The facilities offered by the rapid transit railways have made all this not only possible, but certain.

"Overlooking the whole of this vast and accumulating traffic and commerce, but separated from it forever by topographical lines as clearly defined and obstructive as the bastions that surround the fashionable residences of the Viennese, the West End plateau will undoubtedly always be held intact for the development of a higher order of domestic architecture than it has been the good fortune of New York heretofore to possess. We have become so accustomed to being victimized and led by speculative builders, that the average citizen has come to believe that any attempt of his own to form a conception of the house that he would desire to live in, or any expectation of finding such a house if he indulged himself in such ideas, would be perfectly absurd. It is time for us to ask ourselves if such a state of things is absolutely necessary, if we are to go on and be shelved away in a continuous and interminable series of brown-stone boxes, the dimensions of which are growing less year by year, until they may finally become but little larger than the vaults into which our mortal remains are to be thrust away out of sight forever. A stroll into the upper sections of the east side, where house manufacturing is going on by the mile, is enough to alarm a thoughtful person as to the possible future of New York in this respect. The sanitary feature of this condition of things is a most serious one, as it is almost impossible to secure in such constructions those appliances for ventilation and house drainage that are absolutely necessary to health. The curse of the tenement-house has been almost irrevocably stamped upon the poorer class, and the curse of the speculative builder is rapidly stamping itself upon the more prosperous. The truth is that, as a people, we have almost lost the idea of what a real house is. The few attempts at architectural display have been principally made on 'corner lots.' This unfortunate fancy for corners began with the extension of building on the Fifth avenue. We say unfortunate, because out of it has come that style of corner-lot architecture that has dominated for so many years, at the expense of symmetry and completeness, and has almost given a permanent stamp to domestic architecture in the city. These corner lots have been eagerly sought after by those who could afford to buy them, and few persons, no matter what their wealth or æsthetic culture, have thought of constructing anything more than what appears to be three-quarters of a house. With marked exceptions, no one has seemed to consider it worth while to erect a really complete house, although possessed of ample land for the purpose. The otherwise tasteful residence of Mr. R. L. Stewart, at the corner of 20th street and Fifth avenue, is an example of this defect to a marked degree. So also are the handsome mansions of the Astors, at 33d and 34th streets, on the same avenue, where the connecting fence between the houses on each corner seems labeled, 'This space to be filled in solid.' This jug-handle style of architecture has become so universal that we have grown accustomed to it, and the incongruity does not strike us as it does all intelligent visitors from other cities.

" The plans of improvement at the West End that have now been completed afford the opportunity for that change in style of house construction that has so long been a desideratum with us. There are a number of cities in the United States that are far in advance of New York in this respect, where the residences of the leading citizens are marked by æsthetic surroundings, and an individuality that are not seen here. The territory at the West End is so admirably divided up by the broad boulevard through the centre, the open space of Central Park on the east and the Riverside Park on the west—that the interminable vistas of brown stone that characterize the rest of the city are impossible, while unexampled facilities are supplied for the erection of elegant homes that will do credit to their owners and will be ornaments to the city. Instead of expending from $30,000 to $50,000 for a corner lot on Fifth avenue, from four to six lots can here be now purchased for that sum, and the indications are that men of foresight and good judgment are availing themselves of the chances that are thus offered. Steam transit has accomplished in a year what a decade would have failed to do without it. The admirable service on the elevated roads has shown with what comfort and facility a home in this vicinity can be reached, and as these roads will be running through the West End this spring, a decided movement has already begun, and building operations on an extensive scale have been commenced, the most marked of which is that at 72d street and Eighth avenue, where there is to be erected an edifice that will be equal to anything of the kind in this or any other city. Some fine private residences will also be erected this spring on the unrivaled Riverside avenue. This splendid avenue is to be fully completed and opened during the coming season. Visitors to the City and the Central Park, in 1890, will probably find the entire region westward to the river built up in a manner consistent with the surrounding public improvements.

"If there appears to be the least exaggeration in this

statement let us reflect for a moment on the striking
fact that, with the exceptions of the immediate vicinity
of the General Post Office and that of Madison
Square, 23d street, there is no spot in the city where
a larger number of people can be concentrated, in the
shortest space of time, with the readiest means of locomotion, than 'The Circle' at the Eighth avenue and
59th street entrance of the Central Park; and yet, in
ignorance of this fact, this point is probably regarded
by nine-tenths of our citizens as comparatively isolated.
The elevated railways, which in this immediate vicinity
come together, and meet eight lines of surface railways,
have accomplished this result. While the triangle between St. Paul's and the Post Office will be for many
years to come what it now is, the most active focus of
the business portion of the city, 'The Circle' has been
made, by the facilities for locomotion afforded at that
point, the chief centre of social life. Here will be
erected in a shorter period of time than most people
imagine the great Palace Hotel, combining the elegance
of the Windsor with the comfort of the Fifth Avenue
and the convenience of the Astor. In close proximity
will be the Conservatory of Music, which will be the
permanent home of both English and Italian opera, with
adjoining accommodations that can afford ample space
for social entertainments, both in winter and summer,
on a scale that the increasing size of the city demands.
The other leading places of amusement will also congregate in the vicinity, on account of the facility with
which they can be reached from all other parts of the
city."

CHAPTER IV

THE HARBOR OF NEW YORK

NATURAL ADVANTAGES OF THE HARBOR—THE OUTER AND INNER BAYS—EXCURSIONS—A TRIP
DOWN THE HARBOR—SCENES ALONG THE ROUTE—THE SHIPPING—THROUGH THE INNER BAY
—GOVERNOR'S ISLAND—BEDLOE'S AND ELLIS' ISLANDS—BARTHOLDI'S STATUE—LIBERTY
ENLIGHTENING THE WORLD—THE KILL VAN KULL—STATEN ISLAND—THE NARROWS—THE
FORTIFICATIONS—THE OUTER BAY—QUARANTINE—CONEY ISLAND—SCENES IN THE LOWER
BAY—SANDY HOOK—OUT TO SEA—BACK TO NEW YORK.

The Harbor of New York is one of the most beautiful sheets of water in the world. It consists of an Inner and an Outer Bay, connected by the strait known as "The Narrows." Between them lie Staten and Long Islands, two natural barriers which render the Inner Bay one of the safest of snug harbors. The Outer Bay, though less sheltered than the Inner, affords safe and commodious anchorage for the fleets of the world.

In the summer and early fall steamers make daily trips from the city to the ocean and back, and carry thousands of passengers bent on enjoying the sea breeze and the glorious scenery of the harbor. We invite the reader to take passage with us on one of these.

We start from one of the up-town piers on the North River side, and make several landings between our point of departure and the Battery, at each of which we add largely to our cargo of human freight. The steamer glides swiftly along the city front, by the hundreds of vessels lying at the piers and anchored in the stream. Here, moored to their piers, each of which is covered by an enormous wooden shed, are the great European steamships. You may tell them by the color of and the marks upon their smoke stacks. Two or three are anchored in the river, having just come in from the ocean voyage, and are still dingy and dirty with the smoke and grime of travel. Further down are the steamers plying between New York and American ports, the floating palaces of the Hudson and Long Island Sound, and numbers of river craft. The huge ferry boats, black with passengers, cross and recross our track, and it requires not a little skill on the part of our steersman to keep safely out of their way. Tugs are puffing by us with heavily laden vessels, or vessels in ballast, guiding them skillfully along their course. The flags of all the countries of the world are floating out from ship and shore, and the river presents a gay and animated scene. On the opposite side is Jersey City, the most conspicuous objects of the shore line being the great ferry houses which mark the depots of the various railway lines leading south and west from New York. In the not distant future the tunnel now in construction under the Hudson will connect New Jersey with New York, and the railways will enter the city by means of it.

The last landing has been made, and our steamer now turns her head toward the Inner Bay. Just off the Battery we pass a fine frigate and a monitor, flying the national flag, and near them notice several foreign men of war riding at their anchors. From the steamer's deck the lower end of the city and the spires and towers that rise from it make a pleasing picture, while across the East River is Brooklyn, its heights crowned with stately mansions, and between the two cities swings the great bridge that is to connect them.

PAVONIA DOCKS, JERSEY CITY.

On our left is Governor's Island, with the half round fort of Castle William, and the more formidable works of Fort Columbus beyond it.   The American flag is flying from a tall staff about the centre of the island, and the troops of the garrison can be seen engaged at their manœuvres on the parade ground.   Across the harbor, near the Jersey shore, is Ellis's Island, on which is situated Fort Gibson, armed with twenty heavy guns. To the south of it is a larger island, known as Bedloe's, on which stands Fort Wood, which mounts eighty guns. This island is well out in the bay, and commands an unobstructed view through the Narrows, out to sea. Upon this island is to stand Bartholdi's great statue of "Liberty Enlightening the World."   This remarkable work is the gift of numbers of French citizens, to New York, and is gigantic in size, being intended as a light-house as well as an ornament to the harbor.   A writer in *Scribner's Magazine* for June, 1877, thus describes the statue and the site chosen for it: "One can see that Bedloe's Island is a very central point in the complex of rivers and islands forming what is really the city of New York—Manhattan Island is only one and the chief portion of our city.   Hoboken, Jersey City, Staten Island, Bay Ridge, and Brooklyn are already parts of it ; in the future they will always tend to be bound more closely around New York proper.   Bedloe's Island is therefore a nearly central point in the Upper Bay, about which lie those detached portions of the future, if not of the present city, and its small size will only add to the effect of any gigantic statue erected on it.   The fort will be an advanced part or terrace to the pedestal of the figure, which will rise high above any other object in the immediate neighborhood.

"Allowing twenty feet for the height of the island above the water, the pedestal is to be one hundred and ten feet high, and the statue, to the flame of the torch, one hundred and forty-five. This makes the torch at least two hundred and seventy-five feet above the level of the Bay. It will equal in height the column of the Place Vendome, at Paris, and will be larger than the Collossus at Rhodes, so much celebrated by antiquity. Like that statue, it will have to be cast in pieces of manageable size, and built up, much after the manner of an armored frigate. The construction will be a curious piece of engineering skill. At night it is proposed that a halo of jets of light shall radiate from the temples of the enormous goddess, and perhaps the flame of the torch may be fashioned in crystal, in order that it may catch the light of the sun by day, and at night form a glowing object illuminated by electricity.

"In respect to the pose of the statue, that has been calculated with care. A Liberty would have to be draped, even if a draped statue were not advisable, in a climate as cold as ours, where nude figures suggest extreme discomfort. But M. Bartholdi has also used his drapery to give a tower-like and therefore solid look to the lofty woman, without forgetting the necessity for variety in the upward lines.   *   *   *   *

"She will stand so as to suggest that the strongest hurricane could never budge her from the pedestal she has chosen. Her gesture is meant to call the attention of the most distant person, and, moreover, to let him know unmistakably what the figure

BIRD'S-EYE VIEW OF NEW YORK.

means. For in this statue M. Bartholdi has applied his science to fine effect in getting the figure outlined against the sky, while the energetic attitude has not interfered with a certain dignified repose which inheres in the resting position, and which may be owing to the weight of the body being thrown on the left leg, as well as to the grave folds of ample drapery. Even if a stranger approaching from the Narrows should not know at once what she is holding up for him to see, the energy of her action will awaken his curiosity, and the dignity of it will make him await a nearer approach with confidence. When he can make out the tablets of the law which jut out from her left side as they rest on her bent arm, and the flaming torch which she holds high up above her head, while her eyes are fixed on the horizon, he will be dull indeed if he does not understand what she wishes to tell."

This grand statue will be the most notable ornament of the harbor, and one of the most prominent attractions of the city. A model of the arm with the uplifted torch is now standing in Madison Square, where it has been much admired. It was originally exhibited at the Centennial Exhibition at Philadelphia, and was removed to New York after the close of the World's Fair. The statue will be of bronze, and, it is hoped, will be completed and erected within a year or two.

Looking back up the harbor, we see the broad Hudson stretching away to the northward, with the high bluffs of New Jersey on the west, and the stately spires of New York on the east. Between Governor's Island and the city, the East River, crowded with shipping, and full of moving steamers, stretches away until its shores seem to meet. Brooklyn unrolls itself like a vast panorama as our steamer speeds by it, and the shores of Long Island spread away beyond it. On our right is now a little white lighthouse, situated on a shoal, marking the entrance to the Kill Van Kull, or Staten Island Sound, a placid sheet of water separating Staten Island from the Jersey shore. It is full of small craft, and looks very inviting as we sail by it. The bold heights of Staten Island rise up on our right, lined from shore to summit with picturesque villages and villas, all embowered in bright green foliage. Pretty villas are also seen on the distant shores of Long Island, and we can see the steamers darting swiftly towards the landing at Bay Ridge, where the passengers will take the cars for Coney Island.

The shores of Staten and Long Island now draw nearer together, the former rising to a bold headland, the summit of which is over one hundred feet from the water. The strip of water between the islands is about a mile in width, and is known as the Narrows. It connects the Outer and Inner Bays, and is strongly fortified. The principal defences of the city are at this point, and the shores on either hand bristle with guns. On the Long Island shore is Fort Hamilton, a large casemated work, built in the old-fashioned style. It was begun in 1824, and was finished in 1832. It cost $550,000, and mounts eighty heavy guns. Since the Civil War, extensive additions have been made to it in the shape of outer batteries, mortar batteries, etc. The fort is a pretty place, and is visited by thousands every year from New York and Brooklyn. It is one of the principal military stations on the Atlantic coast, and its officers are noted for their hospitality. It looks very peaceful as it lies back amid its grass-covered parapets, and the rows of guns which project from it seem innocent enough in this soft summer light.

At the very entrance to the Narrows, and on a shoal a few hundred yards distant from Fort Hamilton, stands Fort Lafayette. It was begun in 1812, and occupies the best of all positions for the defence of New York Harbor. During the Civil War it was used as a prison for political offenders. In December, 1868, it was injured by fire to such an extent as to make it practically worthless, unless repaired at a very considerable outlay; and as it was adapted to guns of small calibre only, it was not thought worth while to restore it, but to replace it by a construction which should meet the demands of modern armaments. The defence of New York Harbor requires a new work on this shoal which will admit of the mounting of eighty one-hundred-ton guns. It will require several years to construct such a work as is needed, and it is expected that it will be begun without delay. The old fort cost $350,000, and was armed with seventy-three guns.

The Staten Island shore bristles with guns, from the water line to the summit of the bluff. These works are eight in number, and are admirably constructed and strongly armed. They are known as Forts Wadsworth and Tompkins (the latter of which will probably be called Fort Richmond), the Glacis Gun Battery, north of Fort Tompkins, the Glacis Mortar Battery, south of Fort Tompkins, Battery Hudson, South Mortar Battery, North Cliff Battery, and South Cliff Battery.

Fort Wadsworth was commenced in 1847, and constitutes a part of the second line of defence of the
southern water approach to New York. It is an
enclosed work, built of granite, containing three tiers
of guns in casemates and one *en barbette*, the lower tier
being only a few feet above the water level. The
work, in connection with those adjacent to it on either
side of Fort Tompkins and the two adjacent glacis batteries on the hill in rear, is designed to throw a heavy
concentrated fire on vessels approaching or attempting
to pass through the Narrows, crossing its fire with that
of Fort Hamilton and batteries on the opposite side
of the channel.

Fort Tompkins occupies the site of an old work, and
was commenced in 1858. The main work, with the glacis
gun battery on its left and the glacis mortar battery on
its right, crowns the hill in rear of Fort Wadsworth
and the earthen batteries known as North Cliff Battery, South Cliff Battery, Battery Hudson, and the
South Mortar Battery. It is an inclosed pentagonal
work, having on its four land faces two tiers of case-
mate quarters, a deep dry ditch and a heavy battery to
resist a land attack, and on its channel front seventeen
large casemates for storage and other purposes. It
mounts its channel-bearing guns *en barbette*. It is
intended to supply quarters for the garrison and act as
a keep or citadel for all the defensive works occupying
this position. This work will be able to throw a heavy
fire from a commanding position upon vessels attempting to pass through the Narrows. The four land faces
were, for all defensive purposes, finished in 1865. In
December, 1869, a plan giving such increased depth

to the casemates that heavy rifled guns could be mounted over them *en barbette*, was adopted and carried into execution.

Battery Hudson was commenced in 1841, and was finished in 1843. Together with the North and South Cliff Batteries, it occupies the slope of the hill between Fort Tompkins and the water. These works are able to bring a powerful direct fire upon the channel leading up to and through the Narrows.

The South Mortar Battery was commenced in 1872, and is situated south of Fort Tompkins, and directly in the rear of Battery Hudson extension. It is designed to throw a heavy vertical fire upon vessels approaching the Narrows from the Lower Bay.

These powerful works are as yet unfinished, but when completed and properly armed, will render the passage of an enemy's fleet through The Narrows a doubtful, if not an impossible, undertaking. They are so peaceful now in repose that we cannot obtain anything like an accurate idea of their formidable character. On the Fourth of July, and on other national holidays, during the firing of the noonday salute, they present a grand sight. From both sides of the Narrows tongues of fire dart forth from the heavy guns, and the waters of the bay tremble under the prolonged roar of artillery.

Our steamer passes through the Narrows, and now darts out into the broad Lower Bay. The Staten Island Hills sweep away in a graceful curve to the southwest, and under them lies Raritan Bay, a small arm of New York Bay, through which the Raritan River empties into the sea.

Out in the Bay, a mile or so below the Narrows, are Dix and Hoffman Islands, occupied by the State of New York as a Quarantine Station. This is *the Lower Quarantine.* One hears so much of Quarantine that it may be interesting to look a little more closely at this famous place.

"Quarantine is divided into two sections, generally known as 'upper' and 'lower' Quarantine. From October to April the boarding is done at the upper station, the grounds of which lie between Fort Wadsworth and Clifton Landing, on Staten Island, a little over a half mile from either point. It is here that the health officers reside, viz: Dr. Vanderpoel, the senior officer, and his deputies, Drs. J. McCartney and Thompson. During the other months of the year vessels coming from the West Indies, South America, the west coast of Africa, and from infected ports, are visited at the lower station, which is situated at West Bank, about two miles below Fort Wadsworth, and the same distance from shore. The boarding station is the old hulk Illinois, formerly belonging to the Government, and transferred to the use of the State for an indefinite period. She can also be used as a hospital, having all the appurtenances on board for such a purpose. Near it are the two quarantine islands, known as Dix and Hoffman Islands. The former is used for the reception of cholera and yellow fever patients, except when both diseases prevail at the same time, when those sick with one disease are quartered on one island and the remainder on the other, as the law prescribes that persons sick with different diseases are not to be put in the same hospital. Smallpox patients are sent to Blackwell's Island, and those with Typhus or ship fever are sent to Ward's Island. On the arrival of infected vessels, all well persons are given their freedom as soon as practicable, after having their clothing thoroughly fumigated. Before being admitted to the hospital the clothing of the sick is removed and thrown into a solution of carbolic acid, and the persons thoroughly fumigated. The only diseases against which quarantine applies are yellow fever, cholera, typhus, or ship fever, smallpox, and any disease of a contagious or pestilential nature. Vessels from foreign ports, and from domestic ports south of Cape Henlopen, and vessels upon which any persons shall have been sick during the voyage, are subject to visitation by the health officer, but are not detained beyond the time requisite for proper examination, unless an infectious disease shall have occurred during the voyage. Persons recently exposed to smallpox, with insufficient evidence of effective vaccination, are vaccinated as soon as practicable, and detained until the operation has taken effect. Vessels arriving from any place where disease subject to quarantine existed at the time of their departure, or which have had cases of such disease on board during the voyage, are quarantined at least thirty days after their arrival, provided this occurs between the first of April and first of November. If a vessel be found in a condition which the health officer should deem dangerous to the public health, the vessel and cargo are detained until the case is duly considered by him. Vessels in an unhealthy state, whether there has been sickness on board or not, are not passed by the doctor until they have been cleansed and ventilated.

If in the judgment of the health officer the vessel requires it, he may order a complete purification, and remand it to quarantine anchorage until disinfection is perfected. A vessel has the right, before breaking out her cargo, in preference to being quarantined, of putting to sea; but before exercising this right the health officer is required to satisfy himself that the sick in such cases will be taken care of for the voyage, and to take care of those who prefer to remain.

"During the past summer a vigilant inspection has been made of all vessels arriving from Savannah as well as other ports where yellow fever was prevalent. Every vessel has been fumigated with chlorine gas, special attention being giving to European vessels carrying a large number of steerage passengers. Many complaints have been made on account of the charges for fumigation, which range from $10 to $25 for each vessel. At first glance these may seem exorbitant, but it is not the material alone which costs, but the work is attended with much danger, and hence large wages are paid. It requires at least three persons, besides the doctor, to fumigate a vessel. The schedule of prices was not made by the Health Board, but by a board constituted for that purpose, of which the Mayors of New York and Brooklyn were members. It is stated that a new board, to establish a new schedule, is to be appointed.

"The two deputy health officers divide their duties by taking alternate days of duty, twenty-four hours each time. Though they are not obliged to visit vessels after sunset, as a matter of accommodation to sailing vessels in tow, which are under extra expense, they

frequently make visits until midnight. They also board
coasting vessels after sunset, when it is almost certain
that they have had no sickness which would subject
them to quarantine, but all vessels with a large number of passengers must lie at anchor until sunrise before
being boarded, so that they may undergo careful inspection.   Between the first of November and the first of
April, vessels from domestic ports are permitted to go
to the city without being boarded by the health officer,
the quarantine regulations for them being declared
"off" during that interval.   It frequently happens that
at sunrise a fleet of a dozen or fifteen vessels may have
anchored off Quarantine Station during the night, and
the doctor is several hours in making his tour.   As the
first round of visitations is made before breakfast, it
sometimes delays the taking of that meal until late in
the day; in fact, regular hours are an impossibility to
those attached to the station.   Usually vessels are
boarded from the quarantine tug Governor Fenton, but
it happened a short time since, during the first part of
a storm, that the tug broke her shaft, and a small boat
was used.   The doctor appeared at sunrise fully
equipped in his storm-clothes, and started on his tour.
A large fleet had collected, and through a driving rain
and choppy sea, for four hours, he went from one vessel
to another in pursuit of his investigations, and his labors
were not ended until after eleven o'clock.   During the
gale, though very few vessels arrived, the duties of the
health officer were arduous.   Running alongside a great
ocean steamer with a "Jacob's ladder" over the side,
the doctor would wait his chances for the sea to lift the
boat, and then grasping the "man-ropes," scramble up

the side of the ship and make the necessary investigation of the vessel and persons on board. The present board has been in office since 1871, while some of the deputies have seen longer service."

To the northward, or on our left, are the immense hotels and other structures of Coney Island, all plainly visible, and seemingly alive with people. As we steam on, now turning our course to the eastward, Rockaway and Rockaway Beach come in sight, and on their white and distant shores we see the monster hotel and the other caravansaries which make this place a formidable rival to Coney Island as a breathing place for the Metropolis.

The Bay grows wider, and the swell increases as we speed to the Eastward. On the south we now see plainly the bold headlands of the Neversink Highlands, and in a short while Sandy Hook, with its tall lighthouses and dark, frowning fort, are directly off our starboard quarter. Over the whole scene the clear sun sends a flood of brilliancy; the air is cool and bracing, and the water smooth. The boat dances gaily over the waves, and at length we pass the bar and are at sea. The Light-ship nods dreamily to us far out on the blue waters, as if inviting a visit from us ; but we do not go so far to sea. A short distance beyond the bar the steamer puts about, and turning its head to the westward, starts on its return to the city. We enjoy a delightful sail up the Bay, and as the sun is sinking behind the distant Jersey hills, we pass through the Narrows, and speeding over the gold-tinged waters of the Inner Bay, are soon landed at the pier from which we started on our voyage of delight.

CHAPTER V

SANDY HOOK

DESCRIPTION OF "THE HOOK"—A NOTED LANDMARK—A SANDY WASTE—THE COVE—THE BEACH
—THE LIGHT-SHIPS—THE LIFE SAVING STATION—SANDY HOOK LIGHTHOUSE—ITS HISTORY
—THE KEEPER'S HOUSE—WRECKS—IN THE LIGHT-TOWER—A GRAND VIEW—OCEAN CEME-
TERY—THE FORTIFICATIONS—TESTING THE HEAVY GUNS—THE NORTH LIGHT—THE SYRENS
—THE TELEGRAPH STATION.

Nineteen miles seaward from New York, on the western side of the Bay, is a narrow strip of white sand, projecting northward into the bright waters. Seen from a steamer's deck on a clear day it gleams like a streak of polished silver; but when the skies are dull and gray, or overhung with clouds, it lies leaden and dead in the half light.   This is Sandy Hook, a long, low, sandy peninsular of drift formation, the continuation of a sand reef skirting the New Jersey coast.   It projects northward five miles into the Lower Bay of New York, and forms the eastern breakwater of Sandy Hook Bay.   In width it varies from fifty yards at the Neck, near Highlands Bridge, where jetties of brushwood form but a frail protection against easterly storms, to a full mile at the point where the main light is located.

Many an eye has watched this strip of sand sadly as some outgoing steamer turned its head to the sea and began its long way across the Atlantic; and many a heart has beat more quickly as it came plainly into view, the homeward voyage over, for beyond it lie the bright waters and the smiling shores of home.

A pleasant and profitable afternoon may be spent in a visit to this interesting spot. Taking the Long Branch steamer, we are carried swiftly down the Inner Bay, through the Narrows, and out upon the broad bosom of the Lower Bay, which is finally left to the eastward, and our steamer passing into the calmer waters of Sandy Hook Bay, or, as it is more commonly called, "the Cove," lands us at the wharf of the New Jersey Southern Railway. Once on shore, we see a waste of sand all around us, covered thickly in parts with cedars and a scrub undergrowth, with clear patches of shining white here and there, and at intervals are a number of buildings which are used for various purposes. Leaving the railroad, we take our way over the sands towards the point of the Hook, and soon reach the bright and shining beach. At our feet the breakers roll in lazily with a monotonous plash as they waste themselves on the shore. Far away stretches the blue Atlantic, calm and fair to look upon now, but terrible at times. When the fierce gales of winter sweep down upon the coast, the surf comes rolling in "mountain high," and dashes upon the beach with a wild, angry roar, never to be forgotten by those who have listened to it. About a mile and a half to the eastward is the Scotland Light-ship, rocking lazily upon the placid sea, and six miles further east the Sandy Hook Light-ship is seen rising and falling with the long, regular heave of the ocean. The latter ship marks the point from which all vessels bound for New York shape their course for the Lower Bay, and from which the European steamers begin to reckon their voyages to the Old World. It is painted red, and carries two fixed

red lights elevated forty-five feet above the surface of
the water. At night they glare out upon the waves
like two great sleepless eyes, welcoming the seaman
home, and telling him of the dangers that lie in his
path. When the mists settle down over sea and shore,
you can hear the hoarse voice of its great fog horn
moaning across the deep, warning the watchful mari-
ner that the shore and the breakers are near. Now,
in the bright calm day, it sways idly with the waves,
and looks lonely and forlorn. Far down toward the
horizon is the long black trail of the smoke of one of the
outward bound steamers, and in every direction the
sunlight flashes back from the white sails of various
kinds of craft, leaving and making for the Bay.

Close at hand is a low, red building, used as a life-
saving station. It is provided with all the appliances
necessary to the humane work to which it is devoted,
and is in charge of a keeper and a competent force.
From April 15th to September 15th a careful watch is
kept along the beach, and two patrols nightly pace the
sands on the lookout for vessels in distress. For some
years, however, they have had but little opportunity to
show their skill. Few vessels now come ashore at
Sandy Hook. Long Branch, Squan, and Barnegat,
lower down the Jersey coast, have been the scenes of
almost all the recent wrecks. Yet the Hook has had
its share of disasters, as the light-keeper will tell you,
if you are fortunate enough to draw him into conversation.

Before us, and not far back from the point of the
Hook, is the main light-tower, and pressing on, we are
soon at the foot of it. This spot has been the site of

one of the principal lighthouses on our coast from a very early period of our history. In 1679–80, Governor Andrews, of New York, urged upon Governor Carteret, of East Jersey, the necessity of establishing a light, or "sea marks for shipping upon Sandy Point," as the Hook was then called. Nothing came of this suggestion, and for eighty years the shore remained in darkness. The necessity for a light grew more apparent every day, however; and in 1761 the merchants of New York began to take steps toward establishing one. The money was raised by two lotteries, which were authorized for the purpose by the Assembly of New York, and in May, 1762, the merchants of New York purchased a tract of four acres at the point of the Hook, from Robert and Isaiah Hartshorne, the owners of the peninsula, for the sum of £750, or about $3750 in United States money. By this purchase New York acquired the northern part of the peninsula. It remained the property of that State until it was ceded by it to the General Government, which, some years later, purchased from the Hartshorne family all the remainder of the peninsula as far south as Young's creek. The first lighthouse was completed, and the lamps were lit, in 1764. It was built of stone, and "measured from the surface of the ground to the top of the lighthouse 106 feet." The claim of the Province of New York to the original four acres was confirmed by the British Government, and an act of George the Third, dated May 22d, 1762, provided that actions for trespasses on Sandy Hook should be tried by the courts of New York. To defray the cost of maintaining the light, New York levied a duty of three pence per ton on all vessels entering the port. During the first year after the lamps were lit, this duty realized the handsome sum of £487, 6s., 9d., from which it will be seen that the commerce of New York had grown to very respectable proportions. In March, 1776, the British fleet being daily expected in the Bay, the Provincial Congress caused the lights to be removed. It seems, however, that the walls were not destroyed, and at a later period of the war of the Revolution the building was occupied and fortified by the British.

The present lighthouse is identical with that of 1764, as far as the walls are concerned. Various improvements have been made in the edifice, such as lining the interior with brick, and replacing the old wooden stairs with a more substantial structure of iron. The lens is of French construction, and is ninety feet from the ground, and the lamps are of the most improved style. Near the foot of the tower is the cottage of the keeper, with its pleasant shade trees and pretty garden, and close at hand is the barn, with its cow sheds, built of wreck wood, that has been cast ashore by the merciless waves. Many a stout vessel has contributed its share to the construction of these humble sheds, and each plank and post, each rafter and beam, has its story of manly daring, high hopes, storm and wreck, despair and death, all swallowed up by the dark waters that beat upon the sands. Nightly, for nineteen long years, has Keeper Patterson climbed the long iron stairs, trimmed his lamps, and sent their bright rays far over the waves, and many an interesting story can he relate of the wrecks that have strewn the beach during this long period. Since he first lit these lamps, more than fifty wrecks have occurred within sight of Sandy Hook light. "Here almost every object offers a suggestion of storm and disaster. That arm-chair on the piazza drifted ashore from the brig *Swett*, which foundered off the east shore during the winter of 1868. Here is a remnant from the English ship *Clyde*, and that one from the brig *Prosper*, which, during a terrific gale, drove on the bar near the west beacon. Here is a figure-head that once danced over the waves, defiant of storms, now warped and weather-stained; and on the side of the barn, just below the dove cot, is a stern-board, bearing the name *Trojan*, close to which nestle the cooing doves. One side of the hencoop is enclosed by a panel from a French brig, elaborately carved with sprays of foliage, which, when it was disentangled in fragments from the seawrack upon the beach, was gorgeous with gilding, but which, with the exception of a bright speck here and there, is now bare and brown."

From the lantern the eye rests upon a glorious sight. On one side is the ocean, stretching away to the horizon, with vessels of all classes dotting its surface; and on the other the lower bay, studded with ships, and drawing in to the Narrows, beyond which rise the shipping of the inner bay and the distant spires of New York. Near the end of the Hook is the unfinished fort, which guards the anchorage within Sandy Hook Bay, where safe at anchor ride numbers of craft of all descriptions. Far across the bay is Long Island, and you can make out with a glass the great hotels at Rockaway; while nearer to New York Coney Island looms up, with its iron tower, its famous pier, and the

huge hostelries that form so marked a feature of New
York summer life.   Across Sandy Hook Bay are the
picturesque Highlands of Neversink, with their trim
lighthouses, and the white hotels nestling at their feet;
and beyond this the bold heights of Staten Island close
in the view to the westward.   Down the coast Long
Branch is dimly seen, and along the shore a railway
train is speeding swiftly towards the Hook.   Overhead
the fish-hawks wheel and scream,watching for whatever
prey chance may bring within reach of their skillful
swoop.

Not far distant from the lighthouse is " Ocean Cemetery," a small enclosure, dark with cedars.   Here,
under the humble crosses and headboards, sleep the
unknown sailors whom the sea, merciful in its cruelty,
cast ashore from storm and wreck, for kindly hands to
bless with Christian burial.   The sand grass and
brambles grow thickly over the lowly, lonely graves,
and the winds shriek and the surf roars by them
through winter's cold and summer's heat; yet they
sleep well, the men that lie below; and from time to
time new tenants come to the little graveyard, craving
the rest that wind and wave denied them in life.

Leaving the eastern beach and the sea, we cross the
peninsula to the west beach, the fort and the point of
the Hook, guided by the thunder tones of heavy ordnance, which grow louder as we press onward.

Before reaching the fort we come to the Barracks,
two long lines of two-story houses separated by a
sandy street a hundred feet wide, in the midst of which
are the pump and the school-house.   In the latter, a
school is taught, the attendants being the children

of the dwellers upon the Hook. The Barracks were built in 1856–57, and were designed for the accommodation of the men engaged in the work of building the fort. This force amounted to five hundred men at one period of the late Civil War, when the work was pushed forward with great energy. They are now occupied by the government employees connected with the ordnance department and the lighthouse, life-saving and signal services, and by the Western Union Telegraph operators. These, with their families, number about fifty souls, and constitute more than one-half of the population of the Hook. Immediately to the east of the Barracks are the old and new quarters for officials, the latter a handsome brick building.

Beyond the Barracks lies the fort, an unfinished structure, upon which the work has been suspended for many years. The works occupy a commanding position, and from them one can obtain a fine view of the ocean and the Bay. The fort, which is at present nameless, will probaby be called "Fort Clinton." It ranks next to Fortress Monroe, and will be the second in size in the United States, covering with its outworks eighteen or twenty acres. It is constructed, as far as it has been carried, of massive masonry with a granite facing, and is intended to defend the entrance to the Bay by the Main Channel, which is half a mile distant from it, and by the Swash Channel, which is a mile further to the northward. The main battery, or lower tier of guns, is completed, but the progress of the work has been arrested for more than half a score of years by the changes in modern artillery, which may yet require many modifications of the original plan.

Still nearer to the point of the Hook is the North Light. Close by are the two steam fog horns, called the Syrens, which in thick weather give out terrific blasts, six seconds in duration, at intervals of forty seconds.

On the east beach, near the Syrens, are the headquarters of the Ordnance Department, a model institution in all its details. Here are brought the heavy guns, and other ordnance introduced by the Government from time to time, to be tested. The guns are mounted on the platform near the beach, and are fired by electricity from the office, two hundred and fifty feet distant.

Close by is the station of the Western Union Telegraph Company, a tower seventy feet in height, with port-holes commanding every point of the compass. At the top is a small chamber, ten feet square, furnished with a desk, telegraph instruments, chairs, lamps, a stove, and telescopes and marine glasses of various kinds. It is a pleasant and breezy place in summer, but in winter it is bleak beyond description, and the stove is kept at a red heat, to render the room inhabitable. Here, year in and year out, is stationed an operator, whose business it is to report the approach of incoming ships and steamers. A wire connects the station directly with the principal office of the company in New York, and also with the office of the Maritime Association in Beaver street. By means of the "International Code of Signals" each vessel, by hoisting certain flags, or combination of flags, makes herself known to the lookout in the tower, who at once telegraphs the news of her arrival to New York. Vessels are reported only during the day.

CHAPTER VI

THE NEVERSINK HIGHLANDS

SITUATION OF THE HIGHLANDS—THE SHREWSBURY RIVER—RED BANK—ORIGIN OF THE NAME
OF THE HIGHLANDS—AS SEEN FROM THE SEA—THE LIGHT-TOWERS—A MAGNIFICENT LIGHT
—VIEW FROM THE TOWER—THE PICTURES IN THE LENSES—A GLIMPSE OF FAIRY LAND.

Along the New Jersey coast runs a narrow strip of sand, terminating at its northern end in the peninsula of Sandy Hook, which has already been described. On one side of it the waves of the Atlantic roll in white breakers upon the shore, and along the other the Shrewsbury River flows peacefully, and empties into Sandy Hook Bay. At its source in the interior of New Jersey, and as far down its course as the town of Red Bank, it is a mere streamlet, wandering lazily between high banks and through a rich and finely wooded country. At Red Bank it broadens into a wide estuary, and maintains this character until its waters find their resting place in Sandy Hook Bay.

As the river nears the bay, the left-hand shore increases in height, and finally rises into a line of bold verdure-clad hills known as the Neversink Highlands. They extend along the coast for several miles, commanding fine views of the Bay of New York and the ocean. They "have the post of honor among the American hills. They stand near the principal portal of the Continent, the first land to greet the curious eye of the stranger and to cheer the heart of the returning wanderer. The beauty of these wooded heights, the charming villas that stud their sides, the grace of their undulating lines, give to the traveler prompt assurance that the country he visits is not only blessed with rare natural beauty, but that art and culture have suitably adorned it. The delight with which the wearied ocean voyager greets the shores that first rise upon the horizon has often been described; but these shores have a rare sylvan beauty, that opens hour by hour as the vessel draws near. When, instead of frowning rocks or barren sands, he beholds noble hills clothed to their brows with green forests, fields, and meadows basking with summer beauty in the sun, cottages nestling amid shrubbery, and spires lifting above clustering tree tops, the picture possesses a charm which only he who first beholds it can realize. It is such a green paradise that the Neversink Hills offers to the gaze of every ocean wanderer who enters the harbor of New York."

The name of the Highlands is variously spelled. It is written sometimes *Navasink*, again *Navisink*, at other times *Nevisink*, and finally as *Neversink*. "The correct method can be determined only by a knowledge of its origin, and of this there appears to be some doubt. *Navasink* is supposed to be an Indian word, meaning fishing place; and, of course, applied to the river; but others claim that this is but a common instance of a natural desire to find an aboriginal verb for our nomenclature, and that the term is really *Neversink*, having been bestowed by sailors, as expressive of the long time these hills remain in view to the outward voyager. There is more romance in the Indian term, but, so far, the weight of authority does not appear to be in its favor."

However this may be, there can be no doubt that the

Highlands form one of the most interesting, as well as one of the pleasant features of New York Bay. They are easily reached from the city, as the Red Bank boat will land the visitor at the foot of Beacon Hill, near the mouth of the river. Once ashore, we follow the pathway up the steep bluff, and finally reach the twin lighthouses that crown its summit. These lighthouses form the chief feature in any view of the hills, and are very picturesque, from whatever point seen. The two towers stand wide apart from each other, on the brow of the hill, but are connected by a long structure, much lower in height, and at a point midway between the towers rises a massive castellated gateway, with an arched entrance, from which floats the flag of the Republic. One of the towers is square, and rises to a considerable height. It contains the finest and most powerful light on the Atlantic coast. Its rays can be easily seen at a distance of thirty-five miles, or as far as the height of the tower lifts the horizon. It is the first indication of land seen by vessels approaching the Bay at night. The light is of French construction, and secured the prize at one of the great International Exhibitions of France. It was afterwards purchased by the United States, for the sum of thirty thousand dollars. The light in the second tower is a duplicate of this one in construction, but is not so powerful. The two lighthouses constitute one station, and are kept in the most perfect order.

Through the courtesy of the keeper we are permitted to ascend to the lantern of the principal tower, and enjoy the superb view which it commands. To the eastward is the blue Atlantic, rolling lazily with its long, dreamy heave, for the day is bright and the wind is soft and fair. Clouds of white canvas glitter and nod in the sunlight, as scores of vessels, outward and inward bound, take their way over the waves. There is a large steamer just passing out to sea, plunging steadily into the blue water, and leaving a long, black trail of smoke behind. How many hearts beat hopefully in that black shell, soon to be to us a mere speck upon the water; and how many eyes are turned in farewell glances to the tower from which we look down. How lovingly they will watch it until it sinks down and fades away on the dim horizon. We wish God-speed and a safe voyage to the gallant vessel, whose long way across the deep has begun so happily. Directly below us the peaceful Shrewsbury flows gently, its bright bosom dotted with many smaller craft; and amid the trees along the river shore we can see the hotels and the white cottages of the little village of Highlands, one of the most popular summer resorts in the vicinity of the metropolis. Sandy Hook, with its tall lighthouse and the grim outline of the unfinished fort, are seen to the northward, seeming strangely near in this bright light of a summer afternoon; and within the cove are a score of vessels at anchor. Across the bay are Coney Island and Rockaway, and in the middle of the outer bay seem to float the substantial structures of the Quarantine. To the westward are the bold heights of Staten Island, and at the Narrows we can see the national ensign flapping from the tall flagstaff at Fort Richmond. The bay is full of shipping, some going and some coming, and several large excursion steamers are darting swiftly among them, laden with hundreds of the dwellers in the great city, who are seeking rest and recreation in the cool sea breeze on this warm afternoon.

Turning from this wonderful view we examine the lantern, which the genial light-keeper explains to us. As he raises the curtain that is spread over the lenses by day, we are startled at the picture which is reflected in the polished surface. The sky, the sea, the bay, every object within sight, is reproduced in excellent imitation upon the convex central crystal, and with a faithfulness and delicacy which the most gifted artist would despair of accomplishing. How wonderful the picture is, so small and yet so true, and giving out all the rare tints and shades of nature itself. It is like a scene of fairy land, and grows more beautiful as we continue to gaze upon it.

The keeper explains to us the construction and mode of working the light. We examine the delicate and costly machinery by which the bright flashes are sent far over the sea, and easily imagine how eagerly the homeward-bound seaman must watch for them as they shine out over the dark waves, telling him that port and rest are at hand. Then, as the afternoon is declining, we descend the tower and take our way down the hill back to the pleasant hotel at Highlands, to wait for the morning boat that is to convey us back to the city. When the night comes on we stroll out once more and watch the bright gleams as they dart out from the tall towers on the hill, and shine far over the waves, signals of hope and safety.

CHAPTER VII

MUNICIPAL GOVERNMENT

ORGANIZATION OF THE CITY GOVERNMENT—THE MAYOR AND BOARD OF ALDERMEN—THE COM-
MISSIONERS—DESCRIPTION OF THE VARIOUS MUNICIPAL DEPARTMENTS—POWERS OF OFFI-
CIALS—THE COURTS—POLICE JUSTICES—THE MEN BY WHOM NEW YORK IS GOVERNED—RESPON-
SIBILITY OF THE BETTER CLASSES—FROM THE GROG SHOP TO CIVIL POWER—WHO THE LEAD-
ERS ARE—THE " BOSS"—THE RING—HOW BOSS TWEED MAINTAINED HIS POWER—SPASMODIC
EFFORTS AT REFORM—MULHOOLYISM IN NEW YORK—AN INSIDE VIEW OF MUNICIPAL POLITICS
—THE SLAVE OF THE RING—LOOKING OUT FOR THE "BOYS"—THE INTERESTS OF THE CITY
NEGLECTED—THE POPULAR WILL DEFIED BY THE RING.

The City of New York is governed by a Mayor and
a Board of twenty-two Aldermen, with various Boards
of Commissioners. It is divided into twenty-four
wards and 557 election districts, and constitutes the
First Judicial District of the State. It sends 5 Senators
and 21 Assemblymen to the State Legislature, and 7
Representatives to Congress. The Mayor is elected
by the vote of the people for a term of two years, and
receives a salary of $12,000 per annum. The Alder-
men are chosen annually by the popular vote, and
receive each an annual salary of $4000, except the
President of the Board, who is paid $5000. "Six are
elected by the voters of the city at large (no one being
permitted to vote for more than four candidates), and
three from each of the four lower Senate districts (no
one being permitted to vote for more than two). The
upper Senate district with the 23d and 24th wards elects
four Aldermen (no one being permitted to vote for
more than three)."

The Mayor appoints the Commissioners and heads
of departments, with the consent of the Board of Alder-

men.   These hold office for periods varying from three
to six years, and receive salaries ranging from $3000
to $15,000 a year.

The principal department under the City Government is that of *Finance*.   It has charge of all the fiscal affairs of the corporation, and is presided over by the Comptroller, who receives a salary of $10,000 per annum, and occupies the most important position, from a political point of view, in the city.   He is generally the "Boss" of New York politics, and wields his power in a despotic manner.   Next in importance is the City Chamberlain or Treasurer.   He is appointed by the Mayor, and is confirmed by the Board of Aldermen. He receives a salary of $30,000, but out of this has to pay his office expenses, clerk hire, etc.

The Department of Taxes and Assessments ranks next in importance.   It consists of three Commissioners, appointed by the Mayor and confirmed by the Board of Aldermen.   They hold office for six years, and one of them is President of the Board.   The President receives $6500 a year; the others $5000. This Board fixes the rate of taxation upon real and personal property, and collects the taxes due the city. The Mayor, Comptroller, President of the Board of Aldermen, and President of the Department of Taxes, constitute a Board of Apportionment, which fixes the *amount* to be raised each year by taxation.   This Board also decides how much shall be spent by the City Government, and all appropriations for any branch of that government must receive its approval. It is thus really in possession of powers superior to those of the Board of Aldermen, and constitutes a check upon that body.

The President of the Board of Taxes and two others, appointed by the Mayor, are Commissioners of Accounts, whose duty it is to examine the accounts and expenditures of the various branches of the City Government. They are removable at the pleasure of the Mayor.

The Department of Public Works is presided over by a Commissioner, appointed by the Mayor and confirmed by the Board of Aldermen for a term of four years. He receives an annual salary of $10,000. The Department has charge of the Public Buildings, streets, sewers, water, gas, etc., and expends annually about $1,600,000.

The Department of Buildings is in charge of a superintendent, appointed by the Mayor and confirmed by the Board of Aldermen. He holds office for six years, and receives an annual salary of $6500. This department supervises the construction of new buildings, and additions to old ones within the city limits. All plans for new buildings, or alterations of old ones, must receive its approval. The department also has power to inspect all buildings in the city with regard to their safety, and to require all unsafe structures to be pulled down or properly repaired; and to compel owners of buildings to provide the proper fire escapes.

The Law Department has charge of all the law business of the city of New York. Its head is the Corporation Counsel, who is appointed by the Mayor and confirmed by the Board of Aldermen, for a period of four years. He receives a salary of $15,000 per annum. His principal subordinates are the Corporation Attorney, who receives $6000 a year; and the Public Administrator, with a salary of $5000. The first has charge of the prosecution of violators of city ordinances, etc.; the second administers upon the estates of persons who die intestate, and the estates of foreigners dying in New York.

The Health Department, or "Board of Health," as it is better known, consists of the President of the Board of Police, the Health Officer of the Port (who is a *State*, not a City Official), and two Commissioners, one of whom must have been for five years a practicing physician. The last two are appointed by the Mayor, and are confirmed by the Board of Aldermen, for a period of six years. The Commissioner, who is not a physician, is the President of the Board. The Board has charge of all matters relating to the health and sanitary condition of the city. It is divided into two bureaux: the sanitary bureau, the head of which is the Sanitary Superintendent, with a salary of $4800 per annum, and the bureau of records, over which is the Register of Records, with a salary of $2700 a year. The first bureau prepares the sanitary regulations of the city, and enforces them; the second records the births, deaths and marriages occurring within the city limits. It is sometimes called the Bureau of Vital Statistics. It gives all permits for burials or removals of bodies from the city.

The Department of Police will be referred to in another chapter.

The Excise Department consists of three commissioners, appointed by the mayor, and confirmed by the Board of Aldermen, for a term of years. It receives all applications for licenses to sell spirituous or malt liquors within the limits of the corporation; decides whether the applicant is a proper person to sell liquor, and his establishment a fit place to be licensed, and gives the license if the decision is favorable. Licenses are granted for one year only, and must be renewed annually.

"The courts of general jurisdiction in civil matters, are the Supreme Court for the First District, with five justices (salary $17,500), and the Superior Court and Court of Common Pleas, with six judges each (salary $15,000). The justices and judges are elected for a term of fourteen years. The Surrogate, Recorder and City Judge (salary $15,000 each), are elected for six years. The superior criminal courts are the Oyer and Terminer, held by a justice of the Supreme Court, and the General Sessions, held by the Recorder or City Judge. The Marine Court has civil jurisdiction to the amount of $1000, and consists of six judges (salary $10,000), elected for six years. For purposes of district courts, which have civil jurisdiction to the amount of $250, the city is divided into ten judicial districts, in each of which a justice (salary $8000) is elected for a term of six years. There are eleven police justices (salary $8000), appointed by the Mayor, with the consent of the Board of Aldermen, for a term of ten years, each of whom has power to hold a police court in either of the six police-court districts. Two police justices hold the Court of Special Sessions, with power to try cases of misdemeanor. The Sheriff, County Clerk, District Attorney and Register, are the principal other officials."

Such is the machinery by which the great American

metropolis is governed. Were it always possible to secure the best and most intelligent men of the city for the offices included within this vast system, the arrangement would certainly achieve the results for which it was designed—the good government of the city and the impartial administration of justice. But apart from the judges of the higher courts, who are men of great ability and unquestioned integrity, it must be confessed that the government of New York is not in the hands of either its best or its most thoroughly representative citizens. The majority of the office-holders of the great city are men whom a reputable citizen would not ask into his house. Under the shadows of the temples of justice, Mulhoolyism flourishes in all its glory. Go to the City Hall, or to any of the various departments, and you will find the majority of the persons present in official capacity, loud-voiced, big-handed, red-faced, sinister-eyed men, with coarse features, dull expressions, heavily-dyed moustaches, and all bearing in their personal appearance unmistakable evidences that they have risen from the slums to their present position by the power—not of intellect or ability, but of "politics."

The cause of this is not hard to find. The better class of New Yorkers have a holy horror of politics, and all things pertaining thereunto. They will not attend the primary meetings or the nominating conventions, and, in too many instances, will not even vote. Thus the wealth and intelligence, the two conservative classes of the city, leave the control of all the vast machinery we have described, with all the great and varied interests dependent upon it, in the hands of professional politicians and their followers.

This being the case, it becomes interesting to ask, who are the professional politicians, and from whom do they derive their support?

The professional politician is generally an Irishman, or of Irish descent. The immense Irish population of New York, which constitutes at least one-fifth of the total number of the inhabitants of the city, comprises the ruling element in metropolitan politics. It is also the most ignorant, as well as the most reckless class in the great city. It is blindly devoted to its leaders, and obeys their orders implicitly, and without care of consequences. It controls the primary meetings, the ward conventions, and even the greater political bodies by which the electoral machinery of the city is governed. Its leaders are men who have risen from the grogshop, by the exercise of bribery and sheer knavery. Its headquarters are the numerous bar-rooms with which the city abounds; and votes are bought and sold; incompetent men are put in nomination and elected, and the whole system of free government in municipal affairs is thus placed at the mercy of a few leaders, who are in their turn subject to the control of a central authority, who is commonly known as "the Boss."

The author of that inimitable satire upon American politics, "Solid for Mulhooly," thus sums up the system:

"When one man owns and dominates four wards or counties, he becomes a Leader. Half a dozen such Leaders constitute what is called a Ring. When one Leader is powerful enough to bring three or four such Leaders under his yoke, he becomes a Boss, and a Boss wields a power as absolute, while it lasts, as that which George III wielded over the thirteen colonies, until they ungratefully rebelled against him and commenced to murder his soldiers and take away their muskets and bayonets. The Leaders, the Ring, and the Boss combined, constitute the modern system of American politics, which has been found to work so successfully in all large cities, especially in those which are fortunate enough to have secured a working majority of Leaders from Ireland. It has also been tried with encouraging results in several of the oldest and largest States of the Union; and even with all the disadvantages of American birth and prejudices, some men have been found who could rule their own States, with a fair measure of success, for many years, by combining in themselves, at once, all the functions of the Leaders, the Ring, and the Boss."

It was such a system as this that enabled Boss Tweed and his confederates to hold the greatest city of the Union in their grasp for so many years, and to wring from the tax payers the enormous sums by which they built up their immense fortunes. Indignant outcries were raised from time to time by the Press, but the Boss found it easy in some cases to buy up dangerous journals, and where this could not be done, he felt safe in the indifference of the better class of voters, and above all in the strength of the solid Irish vote, upon which he could always rely. Since his downfall we have seen another Boss upheld by the same power, and so conscious of its support as to be able even to defy the better elements of his own party, and strong enough to defeat that party because it had dared to oppose him and his schemes. True, he is not tainted with the corruption of Boss Tweed, but his strength in political affairs is even greater; and this not because of his over-intellectual strength, or his lofty patriotism, but because of his undisputed control of the Irish vote.

Strong as is the Irish vote, it is made stronger by the accession of a large class of Americans and voters of other nationalities, who are drawn into alliance with it by the hope of sharing the plunder which falls into the hands of the successful party. "The Boss," who-ever he may be, finds these as devoted adherents as the Irish, and rewards them accordingly, only keeping the most profitable places for the Irish. Take the salary list of the city offices, and read the names opposite each office, and you will find nine out of ten pure Mile-sian. Go into the public offices, and you will hear the "rich Irish brogue" as purely and as plentifully as though you were in the Green Island itself. These are men who form the chairmen of the city, ward, and pre-cinct committees; who dominate the conventions, and name and secure the election of candidates of their choice.

To win success in any legitimate pursuit in New York requires the exercise of every power of intellect, shrewdness, industry, and perseverance. The whole man is brought out and developed to the full. Not so in politics. To win success in this line of life requires only an absence of principle, devotion to the Boss, and a careful cultivation of the Irish vote. It was by the exercise of these qualities that a certain well known ex-prize fighter and gambler mounted to a seat in the Congress of the United States, where for four years he disgraced that august body by his presence.

True it is, that once in a long while the better class of citizens, driven to desperation by the burdens laid upon them, arouse from their indifference, and combine in a great movement for reform. Sharp and vigorous work is done for a while, and the election results in the overthrow of the Ring and the defeat of the Irish vote. This done, the good citizens sink back into their former indifference, and leave political affairs to take care of themselves. Then matters fall back into their old channels; a new Ring is formed, a new Boss is created, or rather creates himself, the Irish vote reasserts itself, and a new era of corruption opens.

The author we have before quoted, in describing the experience of Mr. Michael Mulhooly in his successful rise in political life, thus records the results of that Honorable Gentleman's observations of the system as applied to municipal politics, and the observations, though made in another city, apply with equal force to the New York system:—

"He saw that the party organization was composed primarily of Precinct Committees, Ward Committees, and the City Committee, and secondarily of Conventions to place in nomination candidates for various offices to be chosen at elections held by the people; and that all these various members or parts of the organization were provided for and governed by a system of laws called Party Rules, which operated like the Constitution and laws of a great Commonwealth. He saw that while this perfect party organization was ostensibly created to insure the success of the party, and thereby the good of the people, it had been so ingeniously devised as to compel obedience on the part of the great body of voters, while it placed the entire control of the whole machinery in a central head or master spirit, composed of one man, or two men, or half a dozen men, according to circumstances; or in other words, of the leaders, the Ring, and the Boss. He saw also, that however the party rules might be modified from time to time, in the apparent interest of the great body of voters, in their practical operation, they would still be found to contribute only toward strengthening the power of those who, by the natural tendency of party organization toward centralization of power, might, from time to time, constitute the Leaders, the Ring, and the Boss.

"He saw that by this system the Leaders, the Ring, and the Boss practically nominated all candidates, and as—where the party is largely in the majority, and the voters can be kept in the traces—a nomination is equivalent to an election, they, therefore, practically appointed all public officers, under the form of an election by the people * * * He saw that one who would enter the lists as a candidate must give satisfactory proofs that he had already rendered valuable services to them; that no other man could fill the place with such advantage to them; and that he would at all times, and under all circumstances, implicitly obey their orders, irrespective of consequences, legal, moral, social, or political. He saw that if, for instance, one desired to be a candidate for judicial honors, he must be able to give undoubted assurances, either by his past record, or by some satisfactory pledges, that he would hold his office as of their gift, and might be at all times safely and privately conferred with by them, so as to be instructed how to further their interests in matters falling within the scope of his judicial functions.

"He soon saw that this whole system was founded on (*a*) the tendency of every voter to work in the traces, and vote for any man ostensibly nominated by the party; (*b*) the strict enforcement of party rules ; and (*c*) the judicious distribution of the regularly-salaried offices in the various departments of the city government * *; the various municipal, State, and national offices to which only perquisites and *aliunde* profits are attached; the various appointments which may be, from time to time, controlled in the various State and national offices * * * *, and of the various contracts for public work, involving the outlay of millions of dollars, given to contractors who are willing not only to rebate, but also to properly control, at all times, the thousands of workmen whom they employ in the public service * * * *

"His examination, though imperfect, had been carried far enough to show him these important results:

" 1. That nearly every member of the City Committees, and of the various Ward Committees, held a lucrative position by the appointment of some Leader, whose orders he was compelled to obey.

" 2. That as these committees fix the times and places for holding conventions, select the temporary chairmen to organize them, and decide all disputes and appeals, they practically control all conventions.

" 3. That every one of these * * department employees is presumed to be able to go to a convention when ordered to do so, or to send in his place a person who will obey orders; and that these appointees, as well as the thousands of others in other offices and employments, are so distributed through the different wards as to be able, when acting in concert, to control a large majority of all the wards.

"4. That the Leaders had, in one way or another, obtained control of one department of the city government after another, until more than four-fifths of all the men employed directly and indirectly in the public service, and paid by the public money, were under their immediate orders.

"5. That the Leaders were themselves subject to the orders of the Boss, who had made most of them, and without whose favor they would be comparatively powerless.

"6 *That the Boss was the Great Supreme.*"*

Thus the reader will see that it is a very simple system after all.   The Boss names the candidate he wishes elected to some city office, and the ward leaders act as his lieutenants in the execution of his orders.   The man so chosen is one upon whom absolute reliance can be placed, to stand by the party under any and all circumstances, and to yield implicit obedience to the orders of the Boss.   Intellectual qualifications are not sought after, high moral character and fidelity to the interests of the city are not desired.   The candidate must be true to the party, and obedient to the Boss.   The primary meetings, under the orders of the Leaders, send delegates to the Convention pledged to vote for the candidate named by the Boss.   The Convention is held, the candidate is nominated, and is announced to the world as the choice of the party, when in reality he is the

* "Solid for Mulhooly." G. W. Carleton & Co. New York. pp. 51-54; 57-58.

choice of one man, the Boss. The election is held, the candidate is triumphantly returned by the Irish vote, or, if there are not legal votes enough to elect him, the returns are skillfully manipulated, and he secures his certificate of election. It is all very simple; the choice of the Boss once made, the Irish vote does the rest, and does it thoroughly.

Once elected, the candidate is the slave of the Boss and the Leaders. It is useless to think of independence. He has sold himself, body and soul, to his political masters, and henceforth must think as they think, and act as they dictate. Now what is expected of him is simply this: that he shall use his official power to further the passage of all and any schemes the Boss or the Leaders may desire to succeed, whether he knows them to be corrupt or not. As a rule he does know them to be corrupt, but he must vote for them. Such schemes are carried through by bribery, and the Boss does not object to his faithful servant receiving his share of the spoils, and growing rich thereby. That is the reward held out to him at the beginning. Measures in which the Boss and the Leaders are interested become very numerous, but each and all receive his vote, and little by little the *aliunde* profits of the legislator swell to greater proportions, and finally he grows rich, becomes a Leader in his turn, and secretly cherishes the hope of one day becoming Boss. Meanwhile the true interests of the city suffer, the property holders are burdened with useless and unjust taxes. The "City Fathers" have no time to attend to such matters; they are too busily engaged in looking after the interests of the Boss and the Leaders, and accumulating fortunes for themselves. Then they must look out for the interests of "The Boys," as the voters who supported them are affectionately termed. Offices must be provided for them—without regard to their competency to fill them—the bar rooms in their respective districts or wards must be looked after, and the proper amount of money expended at each in treating "The Boys" who cannot be provided with office, and a thousand and one other similar things so occupy the time of the office holder, that the business of the city, to which he has sworn to give his time and best efforts, cannot be attended to. Thus it happens that the public service of New York, apart from one or two departments, is the most inefficient, and the most shamefully neglected, of any city in the land.

In the summer of 1881 the streets of New York were filthy beyond precedent. Disease and death stalked through the metropolis. Suffering and sorrow clouded many an otherwise happy home. Great piles of refuse, which had accumulated during the heavy snows of the previous winter, lay heaped in the streets, rotting in the fierce heat of the sun and scattering their poisons on every hand. The press teemed with descriptions of the horrible scenes to be witnessed, and called for the proper execution of the health laws ; the physicians of New York warned the city authorities of the dangers of a serious pestilence ; mass meetings of indignant citizens were held and redress demanded. Yet for months nothing was done. The city officials had their wine-parties, went on excursions where they could find purer air, and deliberately turned a deaf ear to the appeals of the great city. Secure in the strength of the Irish vote, they laughed to scorn all threats against their official existence.   All the while the boss, the leaders, and the ring went on with their corrupt schemes, careful only of their own interests, and sublimely indifferent to the real welfare of the people.   What had they to fear?   Were they not strong in the power of the Irish vote?

CHAPTER VIII

BROADWAY

EARLY HISTORY OF BROADWAY—UNDER THE DUTCH AND ENGLISH RULE—PRIMITIVE NAME OF THE STREET—IT COMMENCES TO GROW—THE GREAT FIRE OF 1776—THE BROADWAY OF TO-DAY—APPEARANCE OF THE STREET—A STROLL ON BROADWAY—THE LOWER STREET—TRINITY CHURCH—THE INSURANCE COMPANIES—THE TELEGRAPH WIRES—MAGNIFICENT BUILDINGS—SCENE FROM THE POST-OFFICE—A BROADWAY JAM—LOWER BROADWAY BY NIGHT—CHARACTERISTICS OF THE VARIOUS PORTIONS OF THE STREET—VIEW FROM CANAL STREET—THE HOTELS—AMONG THE PUBLISHERS—" STEWART'S "—GRACE CHURCH—BROADWAY AT UNION SQUARE—THE NARROWEST PART—MADISON SQUARE—A GRAND SIGHT—UPPER BROADWAY—A STREET OF MARBLE—THE GREAT HOTELS—THE CENTRAL PARK REACHED—STREET CARS AND OMNIBUSES—THE NIGHT LIFE OF BROADWAY—SCENES ON THE STREET—THE STREET WALKERS—THE ELECTRIC LIGHT—THE MIDNIGHT HOUR—BUSINESS ON BROADWAY.

To the dweller in New York, Broadway is what the Boulevards are to the Parisian. It is the centre of life, gayety, and business; the great artery through which flows the strong life-current of the metropolis. From the Bowling Green to the Central Park, a distance of five miles, it is lined with stately edifices and thronged with an endless crowd of busy workers, restless pleasure-seekers, the good and the bad, the grave and the gay, all hurrying on in eager pursuit of the objects before them. To the stranger it is the great "show street" of the city, and certainly no more wonderful sight can be witnessed than this grand thoroughfare at high noon.

The history of the street is the history of the city. It has grown steadily with it, shared its vicissitudes and good fortune, and, like a true mirror, has reflected every phase of the wonderful progress of New York.

Broadway was laid out as a street by the original

Dutch settlers of New Amsterdam, and was called by them the "Heere Straas," or "High Street." In the days of the Dutch colony it was lined, especially on the east side, with rows of pleasant mansions, the gardens of which ran back to the marsh, on the present site of Broad street. Under the Dutch rule it was extended to Wall street, where the city wall terminated it; and beyond this were pleasant fields and pastures, where the portly "mynheers" turned out their cows to graze, and dreamily smoked their pipes under the wide-spreading trees.

When the English came into possession of the city, and changed its name to New York, Broadway took a step forward. The character of the buildings was improved, and Bowling Green became the centre of a thickly settled and fashionable district. Mr. Archibald Kennedy, His Majesty's Collector of the Port of New York, built the house now known as No. 1 Broadway, a stately mansion in its day, and at one time the headquarters of the British General Sir Henry Clinton. The great fire of 1776 greatly damaged the street, but it was afterwards rebuilt in a more substantial manner. By the opening of the nineteenth century, Broadway had advanced from the Old Dutch Wall to a point above the present City Hall Park, and by 1818 it was built up beyond Duane street. In 1830 it had passed Canal street, and the portion between Chambers and Canal streets was the fashionable shopping quarter of the city. By 1832 it had reached Union Square, and by 1841 had been extended to Madison square. Since that year the growth of the street to the Central Park has been steady and rapid. Year after year its various portions

have changed their character. Business has steadily
driven out the residences, until now along the whole
distance of five miles there is scarcely a dwelling house
proper left.

The first thing that strikes the stranger in looking

BROADWAY, LOOKING NORTH FROM EXCHANGE PLACE.

at Broadway, is its narrowness. The early citizens
never dreamed of the future greatness of their favorite
thoroughfare, and laid off a street with an average
width of sixty feet. For many years past, numerous

plans have been offered for widening certain portions of the street, but each has been abandoned because of the immense expense attendant upon the enterprise. The probability is, therefore, that Broadway will retain its present width for all time. Through this narrow street pours an unending throng of vehicles of every description, which fairly choke it, and cause it to resound with the thundering roar of their wheels. The sidewalks are filled with handsomely dressed ladies, with men of wealth and fashion, with people in plainer clothes, representatives of all classes and conditions of the people of the city, hurrying on—for everybody walks rapidly on Broadway—jostling each other good humoredly. Over all pours the bright radiance of the sunlight, which seems to shine more beautifully here than elsewhere, and on all sides are evidences of the wealth and prosperity of the great city.

A stroll along Broadway, we mean along its entire length, is one of the most interesting occupations to which the stranger in New York can devote himself. It requires considerable "leg power," for the distance is five good miles, but the scene is so full of interest, and there is so much to divert one's thoughts from fatigue, that we invite the reader to accompany us.

We start from the Bowling Green, a small park lying between the lower end of Broadway and the Battery Park. Here we are in a region once the home of wealth and fashion, but now occupied by the offices of the foreign consuls, and the headquarters of the great European steamship lines. Among these are the familiar names of the "Cunard," "Inman," "White Star," and other leading companies, whose palatial steamers ply over the great ferry between New York and Liverpool. Higher up are the heavy importing houses, dealing chiefly in wines, and above these are

MUTUAL LIFE INSURANCE BUILDING.

the main offices of the great Express Companies. Opposite Wall street is the stately edifice of Trinity

ST. PAUL'S CHURCH.

Church, lying back among the grand trees of its church-yard, and surrounded by the time-worn grave stones of the old New Yorkers who lie sleeping peacefully amid all the turmoil and strife going on around them. The tall spire points solemnly heavenward, as if to lift the soul above the vulgar worship of mammon in the city below, and at intervals the sweet tones of the chimes come floating down into the street, telling that wealth is not all, folly is not all, pleasure is not all, business is not all, but that there is something purer, nobler, waiting high above the golden cross which the sunlight bathes so lovingly. Looking down Wall street one sees an equally busy throng, and catches a glimpse of the stately edifices with which the street is lined.

Passing Trinity Churchyard we notice the immense brick building which forms its upper boundary. This is the headquarters of the coal trade, not only of the city, but of a large portion of the Union, and here fortunes are made and lost by wise or unwise dealings in "black diamonds." Insurance offices now begin to multiply on both sides of the street, and on the right we notice the superb structure of the Equitable Life Insurance Company, above which is the marble building of the Mutual Life. These are very Towers of Babel, and dwarf the neighboring structures, which are themselves buildings of large proportions. On the left, at the corner of Dey street, the tall tower of the Western Union Telegraph Company rears its lofty head, and from it a bewildering network of wires stretches away in all directions, high overhead, and looking like a gigantic spider's web drawn against the sky. Across the way, at the corner of Fulton street, is the

ASTOR HOUSE, BROADWAY. NEW YORK POST OFFICE.

office of *The Evening Post,* eight or nine stories in height, a massive structure of brick. On the same side, above Fulton street, is the beautiful white marble building of the National Park Bank, its front elaborately ornamented with statuary, cne of the most sumptuous bank edifices in the city. Next door is the "Herald Building," also of white marble, in which is published "the King of American Dailies," the world-famous New York *Herald.* Opposite these two buildings, on the west side of Broadway, occupying the entire block from Fulton to Vesey streets, is St. Paul's churchyard, with its rows of crumbling tombstones. In it stands the venerable St. Paul's Church, one of the few ante-Revolutionary buildings remaining in the city. In this church the "Father of his country," in the early period of the War of Independence, heard himself denounced by the Royalist clergyman as a "Traitor to his King and his God." The square above the church is occupied by the Astor House, once the most famous hotel in New York, and even now, though reduced in size, an excellent and well-patronized establishment. Opposite stands the great Post Office, running far back into the City Hall Park, of which it now forms the southern boundary. At the southern end of the Post Office, Broadway and Park Row come together at an acute angle, and the porch of the great building constitutes one of the best points from which to view the lower part of the former street. Nothing in the street life of New York is more striking than the scene before us. "From morning till night there moves by an ever-changing procession of vehicles, that have poured into the great artery from a thousand tributaries, and to cross Broadway, at times, at this spot, one must needs be a sort of animated billiard-ball, with power to carom from wheel to wheel until he can safely 'pocket' his personal corporacity on the opposite walk. The crush of vehicles here is sometimes so great as to delay movement for ten minutes or more, and it requires the greatest energy on the part of the police to disentangle the dense, chaotic mass and set it in progress again. For those who are not obliged to cross the choked-up thoroughfare, the scene is full of a brief amusement—hack-drivers, truckmen, omnibus drivers, swearing vehemently at each other, or interchanging all kinds of 'chaff'; passengers indignantly railing at the delay, and police officers yelling and waving their clubs in their attempts to get the machinery of travel again running smoothly. If, at such a time, a fire-engine comes rattling up the street, post-haste for the scene of a fire, and attempts to enforce its right of way, the confusion becomes doubly confounded, and the scene a veritable pandemonium. Ordinarily, however, such tangles of traffic do not occur, for this locality is fully supplied with policemen, whose main business is to facilitate the passage of travel and prevent such a blockade as we have described.

"The outlook down Broadway from the Post Office is in all respects picturesque and impressive, and fills the mind with a vivid sense of the immense activity of New York life. In the distance the towers of Trinity Church and the Equitable Life Insurance Building lift themselves as landmarks, and noble buildings thickly studding the squares between the New York Evening Post Building and the Western Union Telegraph

Building, attract the eye by their massiveness and dignity; and directly opposite the spectator, but standing diagonally to each other, the Astor House and Herald Building demand the attention, as representing institutions which have been household words in New York for the last forty years or more. Up and down this vista roars and streams an ocean-tide of travel and traffic, and the eye can find food for continual interest in its changing kaleidoscope. Well dressed men and women are brushed in the throng by beggars and laborers grimed with the dust of work; and grotesquely attired negroes with huge advertising placards strapped to the front and back, pace up and down, in happy ignorance of the inconvenience they give to others by taking up a double share of room. Fruit and flower stands offer their tempting burdens on every corner, and retail venders of all kinds peddle their goods, and add fresh discord to the din by their shrill crying of their wares. About six o'clock in the afternoon, however, the feverish activity of this region begins to abate, and it is not long before the appearance of the scene becomes lethargic and quiet. Down town, New York has now begun to go to sleep, and it will not be many hours before the silence and emptiness will be alone relieved by the blaze of lights in the newspaper establishments of Printing House Square and the Western Union Telegraph Building, by the occasional tramp of the policeman or reporter, or the rattling of a casual carriage over the stony pave. This busy part of the city will not begin to waken again till about five o'clock in the morning, when the numerous street car lines which terminate in this vicinity commence to run their cars, bringing down porters, mechanics and laborers as the vanguard of the great army whose thronging battalions will make the new day the repetition of the one before."

Continuing our stroll up Broadway, we pass on our right the City Hall Park, the only open space in this section of the city.   Here are the City Hall and the new Court House, both handsome buildings, and across the Park looms up the tall tower of the New York Tribune Building, surmounted by an illuminated clock. On the west side of Broadway the buildings are handsome, large, and generally of iron or marble.   The upper floors are devoted mainly to offices, and here the lawyers congregate, because of their proximity to the courts.   Fireproof safes, firearms, and the lighter articles of machinery have their headquarters here. At the northeast corner of Broadway and Chambers street is an elegant marble structure, once the wholesale house of the great firm of A. T. Stewart & Co., but now devoted to other purposes.

Above Chambers street we enter a region devoted mainly to wholesale dry goods and kindred establishments, such as ribbons, fancy goods, boots and shoes, clothing, etc., and these establishments give character to the street almost to Union Square.   The buildings are large and elegant, marble and iron being chiefly used.   Some of the iron structures are fancifully ornamented in gay colors, and present a pleasing contrast to the long rows of solid colored edifices.   Glancing down the cross streets we see long rows of equally imposing business structures, stretching away as far as the eye can reach, all telling of the immense amount

of trade and wealth embraced in this section of the
city. Not one of these buildings would shame Broadway, and the little narrow lane, lying just west of and
parallel with it, and known as Church street, fairly
rivals the great thoroughfare in the splendor of its
business edifices.

At the corner of Leonard street is the marble building of the New York Life Insurance Company, one of
the finest structures ever erected by private enterprise
in America. It is a model of taste and elegance, and
forms one of the most imposing features of the street,
being of pure white marble on both the Broadway and
Leonard street fronts. Its interior decorations and
arrangements are magnificent.

Canal street is now reached. This is a broad, handsome thoroughfare, extending from the Bowery to the
Hudson River, and crosses Broadway at right angles.
It was once the bed of a stream, which has since been
converted into a sewer. At the southwest corner stands
the Brandreth House, a monument to the success of the
"Patent Medicine" trade. From this point a fine view
is had of Broadway in both directions—from Trinity
Church on the south to Grace Church on the north.
The eye takes in the long lines of stately buildings, the
constantly moving throngs of pedestrians and vehicles,
and the ear is deafened by the steady roar which goes
up unceasingly from the streets, for this is one of the
busiest parts of Broadway.

Higher up the street, between Broome and Spring,
is the St. Nicholas, once the most famous, and still one
of the most thoroughly comfortable hotels of New
York. In the square above is Tony Pastor's Theatre;

and at the corner of Prince street, on the east side of
Broadway, is the imposing brownstone structure of
the Metropolitan Hotel, in the centre of which is the
handsome entrance to Niblo's Theatre, which lies immediately in the rear of the hotel. Above Houston
street, on the west side of Broadway, is the marble
front of the Grand Central Hotel, rising to a height
of eight stories, and surmounted by a Mansard roof—
a monster establishment. Above this the buildings for
several squares are not as handsome as those lower
down the street, but improvements are being constantly made, which will soon render this portion of
Broadway equal to anything above or below it. The
square between Washington and Waverly Places is
occupied by the simple but aristocratic-looking red
brick front of the New York Hotel, one of the most
ultra fashionable houses of the city, and the favorite
resort of the Southerners who visit the city. Immediately opposite is Harrigan & Hart's new theatre, the
most attractive variety show in the metropolis. A
square above, Astor Place opens to the eastward, and
we catch distant views of the Cooper Institute and the
Great Bible House, with the elevated railroad rising
beyond them. The western side of Broadway here is
largely devoted to the book trade, several of the leading publishing houses of the country being quartered
in magnificent buildings, erected especially for their
uses. At 9th street, and extending on Broadway to
10th, and from Broadway back to Fourth avenue, is
the immense iron structure occupied by the house of
A. T. Stewart & Co.—probably the largest establishment of its kind in the world. Long rows of private

carriages are always standing in front of it, and an unbroken throng of purchasers is constantly entering and departing from its doors. Immediately above is Grace Church, a handsome edifice of white marble, with a pretty rectory of the same material; and just opposite, at the corner of 10th street and Broadway, is the fine building of the Methodist Book Concern, the street floor of which is occupied by one of New York's monster dry goods stores. Here Broadway turns slightly toward the northwest, and pursues a straight course to Union Square, about a quarter of a mile distant. This portion of the street is handsomely built, and improvements are being constantly made in it. The stores are mainly devoted to the retail dry goods business, millinery, fancy goods, and jewelry. At the northeast corner of 13th street is Wallack's Theatre, for many years the favorite place of amusement with the dwellers in the great city. In the course of a few months the house will be deserted by its present occupants, and a new "Wallack's" will be opened higher up town.

At 14th street, a noble thoroughfare, stretching across the entire island from east to west, we reach Union Square, a handsome park of three or four acres, which breaks the continuity of Broadway. This is one of the handsomest of the smaller parks of New York, and is tastefully adorned with shrubbery, statuary and fountains. We shall refer to it again elsewhere. Broadway passes around Union Square in a northwesterly direction, and is lined with large and elegant buildings of marble and iron. At the southwest corner of 14th street is the splendid iron building of the Domestic

Sewing Machine Company. Just above 14th street is Brentano's News Depot, the great literary rendezvous of New York; and on the southwest corner of 15th street is the famous jewelry establishment of Tiffany & Co., the largest of its kind in the United States.

Union Square is left at 17th street, and we pass once more into Broadway proper. This is the narrowest portion of the great street, and plans are being constantly presented for widening it on the east side. Consequently, while the west side of the street is built up with magnificent structures of marble and iron, the east side is lined with small, unpretending buildings. The entire block on the west side, from 18th to 19th streets, is occupied by a row of magnificent marble buildings, used as retail dry goods and fancy goods stores. The 19th street end is occupied by the great dry goods house of Arnold, Constable & Co. At the southwest corner of 20th street is another of these monster dry goods houses, a beautiful iron building, owned and occupied by the firm of Lord & Taylor. The show windows of this establishment constitute one of the prettiest sights of Broadway, and are filled with the richest and rarest goods of every description, amounting in value to thousands of dollars. In the square above, on the east side, is the Park Theatre, one of the prettiest, as regards the interior, in the city.

At 23d street Broadway crosses the Fifth avenue, going obliquely to the northwest. From the southwest corner of Broadway and 23d street we obtain one of the finest views in the city. 23d street, one of the widest in the metropolis, stretches away east and

LORD & TAYLOR'S DRY GOODS STORE.

west, lined with stately buildings. On the right is Madison Square, the handsomest of all the smaller parks, beautifully shaded with noble trees, and adorned with shrubbery, fountains and statuary. On the east side of the Square is Madison avenue, one of the stateliest and most fashionable streets of the metropolis. The Fifth avenue leads away to the northward, a splendid mass of brownstone buildings, broken at intervals by numerous church spires. To the northwest is Broadway, lined with superb marble edifices as far as the eye can reach. The throng of vehicles and pedestrians is very great here, coming and going in all directions, and all the streets which centre here present a gay and animated appearance, and the whole scene constitutes a panorama unequaled by anything in any of the great capitals of the Old World.

Crossing 23d street and Fifth avenue at the same time, we come to the Fifth Avenue Hotel. This immense building occupies an entire square, from 23d to 24th streets, and fronts on both Fifth avenue and Broadway. It is built of white marble, and is six stories in height. The block from 24th to 25th streets is occupied by the Albemarle and Hoffman Houses, in the order named. Both are of white marble. Immediately opposite, at the intersection of Broadway and Fifth avenue, is a handsome granite monument, erected to the memory of General W. J. Worth, a gallant soldier of the Seminole and Mexican wars. Facing this is the New York Club House, a tasteful red brick building, fronting on Broadway and Fifth avenue. Above this, and also fronting on both streets, is the famous restaurant of Delmonico. At the southwest corner of 26th street stands the St. James Hotel, also of white marble; and just across the way is the Victoria Hotel, formerly known as the Stevens House. It is an immense pile of red brick, with light stone trimmings, and is five stories high, with a Mansard roof containing three stories more. It was the first of the monster "Apartment Houses" erected in New York, and was built by the late Paran Stevens. On the northwest corner of 27th street is the Coleman House, and at the southeast corner of 29th street is the Sturtevant House. On the opposite corner of 29th street, also on the east side of Broadway, is the Gilsey House, one of the most magnificent hotel edifices in the city. It is built of iron, is highly ornamented, and is painted white. Diagonally opposite, on the west side of Broadway, is Daly's Broadway Theatre, formerly known as Wood's Museum. At the southeast corner of 30th street rises Wallack's New Theatre, one of the most perfectly appointed and beautiful establishments of its kind in New York. Immediately above this is the marble building of the Grand Hotel. On 32d street, between Broadway and Sixth avenue, is the superb marble structure of the Union Dime Savings Bank, facing northward.

At 34th street Broadway crosses the Sixth avenue obliquely, still pursuing its northwesterly course. Above this point the street is poorly built up. At 42d street are two handsome hotels, the Rossmore, on the southwest corner, and the St. Cloud, on the southeast corner, immediately opposite. Continuing its northwesterly course, Broadway crosses the Seventh avenue at 44th street. This portion of the street is sparsely built, and is uninteresting until the neighborhood of the

Park is reached, where immense blocks of "Apartment Houses" line it on both sides.

Below 14th street there are no street railways on Broadway. From Union Square to the Central Park there is a single horse-car line, which passes into University Place and thence southward below 14th street. From Union Square to the lower end of the street Broadway is traversed by several lines of stages, which monopolize the street traffic in this section. On all portions of the street the travel, as we have stated, is very great. It is estimated that at least 20,000 vehicles traverse Broadway every twenty-four hours. All day the roar and the rush are continuous, and the scene is brilliant and attractive. In the morning the throng pours down town, and in the afternoon the tide changes, and flows back northward to the upper portions of the city.

As night comes on, the lower portion of Broadway begins to be deserted. But few persons are to be seen on the sidewalks, and the omnibuses and carriages have the roadway to themselves. By eight o'clock Broadway below Canal street is almost deserted, save in the immediate neighborhood of the Post Office. Gradually this region becomes silent also, and below Union Square but little of interest is to be seen. The true night-life of Broadway is to be witnessed chiefly between 23d and 34th streets. From Union Square to 34th street the great thoroughfare is ablaze with the electric light, which illumines it with the radiance of day. Crowds throng the sidewalks; the lights of the omnibuses and carriages dart to and fro along the roadway like myriads of fire-flies; the great hotels, the theatres and restaurants, send out their blaze of gas-lamps, and are alive with visitors. The crowd is out for pleasure at night, and many and varied are the forms which the pursuit of it takes. Here is a family—father, mother, and children—out for a stroll to see the sights they have witnessed a hundred times, and which never grow dull; there is a party of theatre-goers, bent on an evening of innocent amusement; here is a "gang of roughs," swaggering along the sidewalk and jostling all who come within their way; here a party of young bloods, out for a lark, are drawing upon themselves the keen glances of the stalwart policeman, as he slowly follows in their rear. All sorts of people are out, and the scene is enlivening beyond description. Moving rapidly through the throng, sometimes in couples, sometimes alone, and glancing swiftly and keenly at the men they pass, are a number of flashily-dressed women, generally young, but far from attractive. You would never mistake them for respectable women, and they do not intend that you shall. They do not dare to stop and converse with men on the street, for the eyes of the police are upon them, and such a proceeding would be met with a sharp order to "move on." These are the "Street Walkers," one of the most degraded sections of the "Lost Sisterhood." The men of the city shun them, and their prey is the stranger. Should they succeed in attracting the attention of a victim, they dart off down the first side street, and wait for their dupes to join them. Woe to the man who follows after one of these creatures. The next step is to some of the low dives which still occupy too many of the cellars along Broadway.   Here bad or drugged liquors steal away the senses of the luckless victim, and robbery, or even worse violence, too often ends the adventure. These women have gone so far down into the depths of sin, that they scruple at nothing which will bring them money.

The throng fills the street until a late hour of the night.   Then the theatres pour out their audiences to join it, and for an hour or more the restaurants and cafés are filled to their utmost capacity.   Then, as midnight comes on, the street becomes quieter and more deserted.   The lights in the buildings are extinguished, and gradually upper Broadway becomes silent and deserted.   New York has gone to bed; and Broadway enjoys a rest of a few hours, only to begin at daybreak a repetition of the scenes of the previous day.

The upper part of Broadway constitutes, as we have said, the fashionable shopping quarter of New York. Here are the finest stores, the richest and most tempting display of goods.   New Yorkers prefer to shop here, for they know that Broadway prices are no higher than those charged in other sections, while the stock of goods to choose from is larger and better. You pay here only what an article is worth, and no more, and you can rely upon the representations of the employees in the leading houses as truthful.   Yet it must not be understood that all the Broadway merchants are models of honesty and fair dealing.   The street reflects the good and the bad qualities of New York, and there are many establishments along its length where the purchaser must use his wits and keep his eyes open. The greatest scoundrels deal right alongside of the most reputable merchants. In one thing only does Broadway maintain a uniform standard. It represents the cheerfulness and success of the great city. No struggling merchants are seen along its miles of palaces of trade, and failure has no place in the street. Successful men alone deal here, no matter by what methods the success has been won. Poverty is banished to the back streets, and Broadway glitters in the sunshine of prosperity.

CHAPTER IX

THE BROADWAY STAGES

POPULARITY OF THIS MODE OF CONVEYANCE—A CHEAP PLEASURE—DESCRIPTION OF THE VARI-
OUS LINES—THE STAGES AS REGARDS COMFORT—THE OUTSIDE SEATS—"KNOCKING DOWN
IN BY-GONE DAYS"—THE PATENT CASH BOX SYSTEM—THE "SPOTTERS"—A NIGHT RIDE
WITH JEHU—THE "BOSS" ON THE WATCH—MYSTERIOUS SIGNALS—SKILL OF THE STAGE
DRIVERS—A STAGE DRIVER PHOTOGRAPHED—SUFFERINGS OF THE DRIVERS—UPS AND DOWNS
OF THE CRAFT—THE MUTUAL BENEFIT ASSOCIATION.

In spite of the success of the elevated railways, and of the large number of passengers carried by the street car lines, the stages or omnibuses still manage to hold their own. Until a year or two ago the fare on all the lines was ten cents, but since the completion of the elevated railways it has been reduced to five cents. The low fares and the fact that, except for a short distance on upper Broadway, the stages pursue routes free from the presence and competition of the street cars, enable them still to command a very large share of the street travel of the city. In Broadway, below Union Square, and in Fifth and Madison avenues, they are the sole dependence of those who wish to ride cheaply along those thoroughfares. The principal lines now are as follows:—

The Broadway and Fifth Avenue, starting from the Fulton Ferry, on the East River, passing up Fulton street to Broadway, along which it continues to 23d street, where it enters Fifth avenue, and follows that thoroughfare as far as the Windsor Hotel.

The Broadway, Twenty-third Street and Ninth Avenue, running along Broadway from the South

Ferry to 23d street, thence along that street to Ninth
avenue, and up that avenue to 30th street.

The Madison Avenue Line, running from the Wall
street ferry on the East River, up Wall street to Broadway, thence to Madison avenue at 23d street, and up
that avenue to 42d street.

The stages are clumsy, uncomfortable vehicles,
inconvenient to enter, fatiguing to ride in, and dangerous to leave.   They are neither as commodious nor
as comfortable as those of the great European cities,
and unlike them, have no seats on top.   There is room
on the driver's seat for two passengers, one on each
side of him, but to reach these one must be expert at
climbing.   They are, by far, the best places from which
to view the street, and if the driver is inclined to be
talkative, many a pleasant half hour may be spent in
chatting with him.

Uncomfortable as they are, the stages are an institution of New York, and are liberally patronized.   One
reason of this is that they constitute, as has been stated,
the only means of cheap travel on the streets they
frequent; and another is that from them one can enjoy
one of the best views of Broadway and the magnificent
avenues, with their wonderful sights, for the insignificant sum of half a dime—certainly one of the cheapest
as well as one of the most genuine pleasures the city
affords.

In former days the driver of a stage was furnished
with a cash-box, which was securely fastened to the roof
of the coach, at his left hand.   All the money received
passed through his hands, and he had frequent opportunities of " knocking down," or appropriating a modest

sum to his own use. This led him to be very zealous in picking up passengers, for the larger the receipts the greater his chance of " knocking down " without detection. It was in those days a well-established fact that those who were the most skillful in helping themselves always made the largest returns to the office.

Now, however, each coach is provided with the Slawson patent cash-box, which is placed inside, at the front end of the vehicle. As he starts on his rounds the driver is furnished with little envelopes containing various sums, ranging from ten cents to two dollars. Each envelope contains a stage ticket and the balance of the amount, whatever it may be, in money. Passengers entering the coach, if they have the amount in change, deposit it in the Slawson box, which is so placed that the driver can see whether the correct fare is paid or not. If change is desired, the money is handed to the driver through a hole in the roof in the rear of his seat, and he returns an envelope containing a ticket and the remainder of the sum given him in change. The ticket is then deposited in the cash box by the passenger. As he must return the envelopes given him at starting, or their equivalent in money, the driver has no opportunity of "knocking down." His only opportunity for practicing the old game lies in the fares paid him by the outside riders, who cannot make use of the cash box. This has its risks, however, for he is closely watched, and the number of " outsiders " is carefully counted by " spotters " or spies placed along the route by the proprietor. Sometimes the " boss " takes this office upon himself, to the great disgust of the driver.

One night, not long since, a Fifth avenue stage was

passing the Fifth avenue Hotel, on its downward trip. Among the passengers was an outsider, who sat on the driver's right, enjoying the beautiful panorama of the lighted streets, and chatting socially with the knight of the whip. As they came opposite the great hotel, with its blaze of gas and electric lights, the driver turned suddenly to his companion, and exclaimed:—

"Do you see that old duffer with a slouched hat— that one just sneaking out of sight? He's my boss. If I was worth as much as he is, I wouldn't stand around all night watching stages."

"How much is he worth?"

"'Bout four million."

"Who is he?"

"He? Why, he's old Andrews, who runs the whole outfit. Thought everybody knew him. We know him. He runs seventy 'busses on this line and scoops in three'r four hundred a day, clean money. He's been offered's high's $200,000 cash for the line, but he wouldn't have it."

"What keeps him around here at night?"

"Just'er see that we don't 'knock down' the fares of passengers on top. We have to make a special return on the last trip for all top fares. The old chap hangs around to catch the boys."

Just then an up-town stage of the same line was passed. There was a mysterious interchange of signals between the two drivers. The upward bound had been warned by the downward bound that the "boss" was on duty.

"Sometimes," continued the driver, in his slow, scornful way, "he's there by the Fifth Avenue, where you saw him; next trip he'll be down to Bleecker street; maybe he'll jump in and ride a few blocks. He's a sly one. He thinks more of a cent with a hole in it than I do of a good dinner. He hangs around every night till one o'clock, when the last 'bus goes up. He's got an awful grip on his gold, but some day somebody'll have his money to spend." The thought of it gave an extra snap to the whip.

"He does look pretty old, that's a fact."

"Don't you worry about his dying off-hand. His father is alive now, up in Delaware county. No, sir; if I had his stamps I wouldn't hang around nights to catch a five-cent fare. When he finds a driver short a fare he docks him fifty cents."

"How do the receipts now compare with the ten-cent days?"

"We do more than double the business. A stage averages $3 more a day since they cut down to five cents. We used to take in $6 or $7, and now we count on from $9 to $11."

It requires the nicest skill to drive a stage on Broadway. Not only must the driver guide his ponderous vehicle safely through the crowded mass, but his quick eye must be all over the street, on the watch for passengers, and he must be ready to stop to take up or let them down at any moment, and in such a manner as will not block the already crowded street. The ease and accuracy with which a stage will dart through a crowd of Broadway vehicles, never colliding with or in any way touching them, shows that Jehu has a firm hand and a quick eye.

The stage drivers constitute a distinct and peculiar

class. Their work is hard, their pay small, and they show signs of the hard lives they lead. From six o'clock in the morning until midnight they are coming and going, in all weathers and in all seasons—Sunday, on which day the stages do not run, being their only time of rest. They are generally middle-aged men, and some are far advanced in years. They are corpulent, heavy-limbed, and large-handed men, with faces seasoned by the weather, to which they are constantly exposed; and when on their feet, walk with an unsteady, rolling gait, caused by their being so constantly on the box. They have no distinct dress, and get themselves up according to their own fancies; and it must be confessed, that while their costumes may be artistic, they are not neat or attractive. The odor of the horse-blanket clings to them always. The majority of them have driven their routes for years, and have witnessed all the changes along them for the past twenty-five or thirty years. Some have been on the lines longer, and have seen their routes gradually lengthen, year by year, as the city has grown northward. They can tell you many an interesting tale of the streets through which you pass, for the local histories of these thoroughfares are as household words to them. With strangers they are silent and uncommunicative, but an offer of a chew of tobacco or a cigar will unseal their lips, and they grow eloquent over the hard life they lead, and will impart to you more interesting information concerning the localities through which you are passing than you can obtain from any other source. They are masters of the science of "chaffing," and the eloquence with which they assail drivers of rival lines is sublime in its way. They suffer greatly from exposure to the weather. In the hot days of summer they protect themselves from the fierce rays of the sun by large cotton umbrellas, securely fastened to the roof of the vehicle ; but it is no uncommon thing for them to fall victims to sunstroke. In the winter, when the snow and sleet swirl about him, and lash his face and head with their pitiless fury, the driver wraps his lower limbs in a mass of blankets, and protects the rest of his body with a succession of overcoats. His sufferings, in spite of these precautions, are often terrible, and his first care, upon arriving at the end of his route, is to hurry to the nearest saloon and comfort himself with a tumblerful of hot whisky or gin. Who shall blame him? Without this, even his iron constitution would be powerless to withstand the terrible exposure to which he is subjected. Oftentimes the horses will drag the coach into the stable in the midst of some wild winter storm, while the driver sits motionless on his box. The stable men lift him down, to find him frozen almost stiff. Yet, in spite of its hardships, the life has a fascination for Jehu. Once a stage driver, always a stage driver, is the motto of the craft, and it would be a powerful inducement, indeed, that could cause him to surrender the reins that he has handled so long, and betake himself to some other mode of life. He fears two things only— the loss of his place on the box and falling into the hands of the stalwart policemen who guard the most crowded portions of Broadway. He submits in humble silence to the reprimands, and meekly and promptly obeys the orders, of these stern guardians of the street, for well he knows that trouble with "the cops" means a month for him on "the Island," and probably a permanent loss of place. The latter would be ruin to him. He has no other resource, is fit for no other employment. His beggarly wages do not allow him to lay up any money, and he knows he must stick to his box as long as he can. Fortunately his iron constitution enables him to hold his place far on into old age, and, as a general rule, he leaves it only for the long rest in which wages can avail him nothing.

The stage drivers have a Mutual Benefit Association, which looks after them when they are sick or disabled. They are generally a healthy set, and do not find it necessary to call on the Association often.

CHAPTER X

THE FIFTH AVENUE

FIFTH AVENUE THE CENTRE OF FASHION AND WEALTH—DESCRIPTION OF THE STREET—A
GRAND PANORAMA—LOWER FIFTH AVENUE—ENCROACHMENTS OF BUSINESS—FOURTEENTH
STREET—THE "SWALLOW-TAIL" DEMOCRACY—AMONG THE PIANO MAKERS—CHICKERING
HALL—CHURCHES—CLUBS AND ART GALLERIES—TWENTY-THIRD STREET—DELMONICO S—
THE ASTOR RESIDENCES—STEWART'S MARBLE PALACE—A REGION OF BROWN STONE—UPPER
FIFTH AVENUE—THE HOTELS—THE CATHEDRAL—THE VANDERBILT MANSIONS—ALONG
THE CENTRAL PARK—THE LENOX LIBRARY—THE FIFTH AVENUE MANSIONS—HOMES OF
WEALTH AND LUXURY—HOW THEY ARE FITTED UP—FIFTH AVENUE ON NEW YEAR'S NIGHT—
LIFE IN FIFTH AVENUE—THE WHIRL OF DISSIPATION—WHAT IT COSTS—THE STRUGGLE FOR
SHOW—THE " NEWLY RICH "—DARK SIDE OF FIFTH AVENUE LIFE—THE SKELETONS—FIFTH
AVENUE HUSBANDS AND WIVES—THE CHILDREN—" ALL IS NOT GOLD THAT GLITTERS."

Fifth avenue is the fashionable street, *par excellence*, of New York. It commences at Washington Square and extends to the Harlem river, a distance of nearly six miles, and is a broad, well-paved, and superbly built street for the first three miles of its course. To live and die in a Fifth avenue mansion is the dearest wish of every New Yorker's heart. Though the lower squares are being rapidly encroached upon by business edifices, the street as a whole maintains its character as the most magnificent avenue of residences in the world. The buildings along its course are mainly of brown-stone, though in the upper section, near the Central Park, marble and the lighter-colored stones are being used with pleasing effect.

The avenue begins at Waverly Place, the northern boundary of Washington Square, and runs in a straight line to 59th street, the southern boundary of the Central Park, after which it skirts the eastern side of the Park to 110th street. At 120th street its continuity is broken by Mount Morris Park, around which it passes, and commences again at 124th street, and pursues an unbroken line to the Harlem river. From Washington Square to the Central Park, a distance of three miles, it is built up solidly, with magnificent residences, splendid hotels and imposing churches. From 59th street, along the eastern side, it is being built up rapidly. and before many years have elapsed this section will be an unbroken line of buildings. It will be a very pleasant section, too, for the western boundary of the street will be the open expanse of the Central Park, and the occupants of the houses will have before them one of the loveliest landscapes in the world, as a source of perpetual enjoyment. From the upper end of the park to Mount Morris there are, as yet, no improvements. Passing Mount Morris and entering the Harlem section of the avenue, we find it rapidly growing, the houses here being equal in splendor to those below or opposite the park.

Starting on our tour of inspection from Washington Square, we find the first blocks of the avenue occupied by stately, old-fashioned mansions, and shaded by fine trees. At the corner of Clinton Place is the Brevoort House, one of the most exclusive hostelries of the city, and largely patronized by English visitors. At the northwest corner of 10th street is the Episcopal Church of the Ascension, a handsome brownstone structure, and on the southwest corner of 11th street is the First Presbyterian Church, equally handsome, and also of brownstone. Fourteenth street is a busy, bustling, thoroughfare at its intersection with the avenue, and here are a number of fashionable "Apartment Houses," which form quite a feature of the avenue. Here the electric lamps begin, and extend along Fifth avenue to 34th street. At the southwest corner of 15th street is the splendid building of the Manhattan Club. This is the headquarters of what is known in New York as "the Swallow Tail Democracy," and the club consists of the better elements of the Democratic party. Business is largely invading this section of the avenue; and here are the warerooms of the most famous piano makers, such as Chickering, Weber and Knabe. The Chickerings have a magnificent hall attached to their establishment, which is used for concerts, lectures, and other entertainments. It stands on the northwest corner of 18th street. At the southeast corner of 19th street is the Fifth Avenue Presbyterian Church, formerly in charge of the Rev. Dr. John Hall. At the southwest corner of 21st street is the South Reformed Dutch Church, a beautiful edifice of brownstone. On the opposite side of 21st street is the Union Club, generally known as "The Rich Man's Club," since it embraces a greater aggregate of wealth among its members than any club in the city. Across the avenue is the Lotus Club, the chief rendezvous of the art and literary professions. On the southwest corner of 22d street is Knoedler's Art Gallery, a branch of the famous establishment of Goupil & Co., of Paris. It is always open to visitors, and is filled with an interesting collection of works of art. There is no pleasanter place in New York in which to pass an idle hour.

At 23d street, Fifth avenue crosses Broadway, and passing along the western side of Madison Square pursues its northward course. On the left is the Fifth

Avenue Hotel, with the magnificent vista of Broadway extending beyond it, and on the right is Madison Square, with its fine trees and noble statues. The Worth Monument, already described, is passed on the left, and at the corner of 25th street is the New York Club, beyond which is "Delmonico's," extending through the block to Broadway. At the southeast corner of 27th street stands the Victoria Hotel, while immediately opposite, occupying the entire block on the east side of the avenue, from 26th to 27th streets, is the Hotel Brunswick, well known for its splendid restaurant and high prices. Business is encroaching upon this portion of the avenue, and bids fair to monopolize it in a few years. At the northwest corner of 29th street is a handsome church of white granite, belonging to the Dutch Reformed faith. Its tall spire is surmounted by a gilt-wreathed vane in the shape of a game chicken, and this has caused irreverent New York to dub the edifice "the Church of the Holy Rooster." The block on the west side of the avenue, between 33d and 34th streets, is occupied by two stately brick mansions, one at each corner. These are the residences of John Jacob and William Astor, sons of the late William B. Astor. At the northwest corner of 34th street stands the marble palace of the late A. T. Stewart, now the residence of his widow. Its interior decorations and arrangements are sumptuous, and in keeping with the exterior. At the time of its erection it was regarded as the most magnificent in the New World. On the opposite corner is a noble brownstone mansion, for many years the residence of Mr. Stewart. "We are now in a region of an unbroken line of architectural beauty; handsome churches and mansions abound, and the wonderful changes that are taking place in the upper portion of New York are written on every side. Superb mansions are continually being pulled down to make way for structures still more palatial, and the rage for surpassing each other in the splendor of their domiciles seems to have taken possession of our merchants, bankers and railroad princes." The window fronts in this section of the avenue present a pretty sight during the summer months, when they are "decorated with tiled flower boxes, laden with a perfect glory of blooms in all the colors of the rainbow. This is a charming characteristic of the leading residence streets in the aristocratic portion of the city, and speaks volumes for the taste and love of beauty inherent even among those who may have made their money so suddenly as to be without the social and æsthetic culture which makes wealth the most enjoyable. Fifth avenue is exceptionally noticeable for this lavish display of flowers on the window ledges, that seem to be literally blossoming out of the brown stone a little distance away."

At the northwest corner of 35th street is a plain dwelling of brick, with light stone trimmings. This was the residence of the late William B. Astor, and here he died, a few years ago. Immediately across the avenue is Christ (Episcopal) Church, and on the northwest corner of 37th street is the Brick (Presbyterian) Church, for so many years under the pastoral care of the Rev. Dr. Gardiner Spring. At the northeast corner of 39th street is the new building of the Union League Club, a palatial structure, and the most perfectly-appointed club-house in America. The west side

of the avenue, from 40th to 42d street, is occupied by
the old Distributing Reservoir, a massive, fortress-like
structure, of stone, from the summit of which a fine
view of the noble thoroughfare may be enjoyed. Immediately opposite is Rutger's College, a handsome
castellated structure in the Gothic style. The northwest corner of 42d street is occupied by "The Flor-
ence," the finest specimen of the palatial "Apartment
House" in the city, and a noticeable feature of the
avenue. The northeast corner of 43d street is occupied by the superb Jewish Temple E-manu-el, and
diagonally opposite, on the southwest corner of 45th
street, is the Church of the Divine Paternity, of which
the late Dr. E. W. Chapin was for many years the
pastor. Nearly opposite, between 45th and 46th
streets, is the pretty Church of the Heavenly Rest.
On the east side of the avenue, occupying the block
from 47th to 48th streets, is the massive red-brick
front of the Windsor Hotel, one of the most elegant
and costly houses in the city. Opposite, on the northwest corner of 48th street, is the Collegiate Dutch Reformed Church, an elaborate structure of brown stone.
At the southeast corner of 50th street is "The Buckingham," a fashionable hotel, built upon the principle
that "land is cheap up stairs." The block above, from
50th to 51st street, is taken up by the magnificent
Cathedral of St. Patrick. This is, in all respects, the
most superb church in America. It is built, within and
without, of pure white marble, and occupies the most
commanding position on the avenue. The next block,
on the east side, from 51st to 52d, is occupied by the
Roman Catholic Male Orphan Asylum and its grounds.

The block on the west side of the avenue, immediately opposite the Asylum, contains two superb mansions of brown stone, connected by a covered gallery, into which the main entrance leads. On the northwest corner of 52d street is another elegant and artistic mansion, of light gray stone, elaborately ornamented. These are the famous Vanderbilt mansions, and constitute the finest residences in New York. At the northwest corner of 53d street is the massive brownstone Church of St. Thomas (Episcopal), one of the noblest church edifices on the continent. Between 54th and 55th streets, on the same side of the avenue, is St. Luke's (Episcopal) Hospital, standing in the midst of handsomely ornamented grounds. On the northwest corner of 55th street is another of the grand churches of New York. It is built of brown stone, with a lofty spire, and belongs to the Presbyterian faith. It is under the pastoral care of the Rev. Dr. John Hall, one of the most eloquent divines of the day. At the northwest corner of 57th street is a large mansion of red brick, with gray stone trimmings, the property of another member of the Vanderbilt family. A row of fine houses, of white marble, occupies the block on the east side, from 57th to 58th streets.

At 59th street the avenue reaches the Central Park. It is handsomely built along the east side of the street for a considerable distance, and new houses are constantly going up. There is nothing of special interest to be seen, however, until 70th street is reached. Here stands the Lenox Library, a massive building of granite. From this point to the Harlem River the street is without interest apart from its handsome residences.

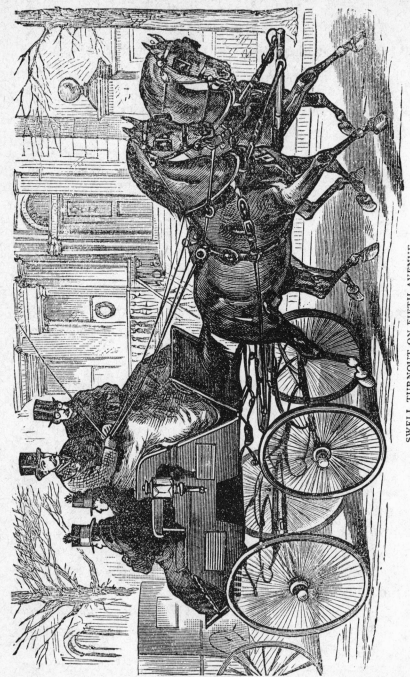

SWELL TURNOUT ON FIFTH AVENUE.

The principal material used in the construction of the buildings on the avenue is brown stone. This gives to the street a sombre look, but of late years, white marble, brick, and the lighter-colored stones have been used to a great extent, and the upper portion of the avenue presents a much lighter and more attractive appearance than the regions below it. In spite of the general uniformity of the street, however, it is a grand sight upon which the eye rests from any point of view.

The interior of the houses is in keeping with their external grandeur. They are decorated in magnificent style by artists of ability and taste, and are furnished in the most superb and costly manner. Rare and valuable works of art abound in all, and everything that luxury can devise or wealth provide is here in abundance. The softest and richest carpets cover the floors and deaden every foot fall, the windows are draped with curtains the cost of which would provide an average family with a home in other cities, and which shut out the bright daylight and give to the apartments a soft, luxurious glow; costly chandeliers shed a flood of warm light through the elegantly furnished rooms, and through the half open doors you may catch a view of the library, with its rows of daintily bound books in elaborate cases, its works of art scattered about in tasteful negligence, and its rich and cosy furniture. The "Library" forms quite a feature in a Fifth avenue mansion. Whether the books are read or not, it is the correct thing to have. The chambers and upper rooms are furnished with equal magnificence, the cost of fitting up one of these houses sometimes exceeding the amount paid for the building. Everything is perfect in its way, each appointment being the most sumptuous that wealth can purchase. Some of these mansions are furnished with rare taste and good judgment, but many, on the other hand, are simply vast collections of flashy and costly furniture and decorations, their owners lacking the culture necessary to make a proper disposition of their riches. There is no more attractive sight to the stranger in New York than a stroll along Fifth avenue about dusk on New Year's Day. It is the custom of those who receive calls on that day to leave window curtains partly drawn, and through these openings one can see the richly furnished, brightly lighted drawing rooms, with their elegantly dressed occupants, and can thus enjoy a succession of "pictures from life" unequaled in any part of the world.

The dwellers in the Fifth avenue mansions represent all the various phases of the wealthier class of New York. You will find here many persons whose fortunes are so secure and great that they can amply afford the style in which they live; and also many who are sacrificing everything in order to shine for awhile in such splendor. Men make money very quickly in New York. A Fifth avenue mansion is either purchased or rented, and then commences a life of fashion and dissipation to which neither they nor their families are accustomed. Everything is sacrificed to maintain their newly gained position; money flows like water; the recently gotten wealth vanishes, and in a few years the family disappears from the avenue, to begin life anew in an humbler sphere. The history of the street abounds in such cases. No wonder so many men living in these palaces have weary, careworn faces, restless glances, and quick, nervous ways. The strain they are living under to keep their places in the avenue is too great. They are not able to keep pace with those whose firmly-secured millions justify them in a lavish style of living, and they know it. They dread the day that must inevitably come, when they must leave all this luxury behind them and go out into the world again to begin life anew. Even if they maintain their places, they cannot resist the conviction that their splendor has been bought at too dear a price.

The avenue mansions contain many families of wealth and culture, many whose names have been household words in New York for generations. These live elegantly, and in proportion to their means, but avoid show and vulgar display. They are courtly in manner, hospitable and warm-hearted, and constitute fine specimens of the cultured American. They do not make up the majority of the dwellers in the avenue, however. These latter represent mainly the newly rich families, that have risen to affluence through the lucky ventures of the husband and father, and have come to their new honors without the refinement or culture necessary to sustain them with dignity. You may know them by their loud voices, vulgar countenances, flashy dressing, and coarse ways. They plunge headlong into the dissipations of society with a recklessness unknown to persons accustomed to such pleasures, and their fast life soon tells upon them. The men go to their business heavy and jaded in the morning, after a night of fashionable dissipation, and the women sink into an indolence from which nothing can rouse them save a renewal of the excesses which caused their lassitude.

They greatly err who imagine that the possessor of a Fifth avenue mansion is, as a matter of course, to be envied. These splendid palaces hide many aching hearts, and could tell many a tale of sorrow, and even of shame, could they speak. The master of the house goes often to his business in the morning with knit brows and a tragedy lurking in his heart, and returns with reluctant steps to his splendid palace in the evening; and madame, for all her gorgeous surroundings, fails to wear a happy or contented look, and sighs as she thinks of the price she has paid for such luxury. Generally the skeleton is kept securely within the closet, but sometimes it will break forth, and then Fifth avenue is startled for a moment by its revelations. Sometimes the scandal is hushed up, but frequently the divorce courts are called in to straighten matters out.

One does not see home life in its truest sense in the avenue. The demands of fashion are too exacting to permit an indulgence in this richest of pleasures. Day and night are spent in a ceaseless whirl of gayety, and in many cases the only times husband and wife are really in their home for more than a few hours at a time, is when their parlors are crowded with guests in attendance upon some grand entertainment given by them. Thus it happens that they lead different lives, with but little common interest between them. The husband has his "affinity," and seeks in her society the pleasures his wife will not share with him; and madame has her "lovers," who are as much of a grief as a happiness to her, as she lives in constant terror of being compromised. Fortunately, children are scarce in the avenue; the necessities of fashion forbid large families.

Such as come receive little of a mother's care until they are old enough to be put on exhibition, to accompany "mamma" in a drive through the Park, or to occupy the front seats of the opera-box, when they should be soundly sleeping in their beds. They are dressed to death, are always in charge of a maid when out for a walk, and know little of the pure, free joys of childhood. So they grow up to be premature men and women, fitted only to imitate the follies, and, alas, too often to repeat the bitter experience of their parents.

After all, in spite of its splendor, in spite of its wealth, and its mad round of pleasures, Fifth avenue does not hold the happiest homes in New York. You can see the glare and the glitter of the false metal all around you; but if you would find the pure gold of domestic happiness, you must seek it in more modest sections of the great city.

CHAPTER XI

THE ELEVATED RAILROADS

INCONVENIENCES OF OLD-STYLE TRAVEL—PLANS FOR RAPID TRANSIT—THE FIRST ELEVATED RAILROAD—THE PRESENT SYSTEM—THE METROPOLITAN AND NEW YORK ELEVATED ROADS—THE MANHATTAN COMPANY—DESCRIPTION OF THE ROADS—HOW THEY ARE BUILT—MODE OF OPERATIONS—STATIONS—EMPLOYEES—RAPID TRAINS—ADVANTAGES OF THE SYSTEM—ITS DRAWBACKS—IMMENSE TRAFFIC—RESULTS OF THE ELEVATED SYSTEM—RAPID GROWTH OF THE UPPER PART OF THE CITY—A RIDE ON THE ELEVATED RAILROADS—THE NIGHT TRAINS —FROM THE BATTERY TO HARLEM BY NIGHT.

The peculiar conformation of Manhattan Island rendered it impossible for New York to grow but in one direction—from south to north. As the lower portions of the city were taken for business purposes, the population moved northward. In the course of time this state of affairs came about: the majority of the dwellers in the city had their places of business down town, at a distance of several miles from their residences. To reach the former in the morning, and return to the latter in the afternoon, they were dependent upon the horse-cars and stages. These trips consumed a great deal of time, and imposed upon the people an immense amount of fatigue. Early in the morning and late in the evening the cars and stages were crowded, so that often the entire journey had to be made standing; the vehicles were dirty and badly ventilated, and every discomfort was encountered. During heavy snows, hours would be sometimes consumed in making the journey, and at all times street blockades caused the loss of much valuable time. Altogether, the whole system of street travel was badly arranged, uncom-

ELEVATED RAILROAD STATION, SIXTH AVENUE AND TWENTY-THIRD ST.

fortable, and entirely unsuited to the needs of a city like New York.

This led to many plans for "rapid transit;" that is, for a system of roads running the length of the city, and operated by steam, which should shorten the time between given points and increase the comforts of the traveler. At first these plans were for underground roads, but they were rejected almost as fast as proposed, as it was found that they would cost several million dollars per mile, and require a generation for their construction. After various other plans had been proposed, a company was chartered and began the construction of an elevated railroad on Greenwich street and Ninth avenue, from the Battery to the Central Park. It was proposed to operate the road by means of an endless wire rope, worked by stationary engines at stated points along the line. This proved a failure, however; the endless ropes would not work, and the stationary engines had to be abandoned. The road was then strengthened, dummy engines placed on it, and about 1870 it was opened for travel. After experiencing various changes of fortune it passed into the hands of the New York Elevated Railroad Company, and has since been rebuilt and strengthened. It now forms a part of the western division of the New York Elevated Railroad.

The next project was the Metropolitan Elevated Railroad, to run from Rector and New Church streets, by College Place, West Broadway, South Fifth avenue, Amity street and Sixth avenue to the Central Park. This scheme encountered a great deal of opposition from property holders along the route, but this was at last overcome, the road was built, and was opened for travel about three years ago.

At present there are four lines of Elevated Roads in successful operation in New York. These are the Sixth and Second avenue lines, belonging to the Metropolitan Elevated Railroad Company; and the Third and Ninth avenue lines, belonging to the New York Elevated Railroad Company. They all run from south to north, in the direction of the length of the city. Both of the above named companies have leased their lines to the Manhattan Elevated Railroad Company, and all the lines are thus consolidated under one management.

The Metropolitan Elevated Road begins at Rector street, in the rear of Trinity Church, and pursues the following route: Along New Church, Church and Murray streets to College Place, thence to West Broadway, to South Fifth avenue, which it follows to Amity street, along Amity street to Sixth avenue, and along Sixth avenue to 59th street and the Central Park. At 53d street a branch leads off to Ninth avenue, along which the line is carried to 110th street, where it crosses to Eighth avenue, and continues along that street to the Harlem River at 155th street. Here a bridge over the river enables the road to connect with the "New York City and Northern Road," for High Bridge, Fordham, and other points on the mainland. The latter road will eventually be carried through to Yonkers and Tarrytown, and will thus form, with the Elevated Road, a direct route from the lower part of New York to the pleasantest points on the Hudson River.

The Metropolitan Road occupies the centre of the streets it traverses, and is built in the most substantial manner, combining both lightness and solidity. The foundations for the supports are laid in concrete, stone, and brick work. Four long rods pass up through the heavy foundation stones, and around these is built up the brick work, inclining gradually inward from the base to the top. The rods extend several inches above the brickwork, and fit into holes at the four corners of the heavy iron castings, in which are the sockets for the reception of the supporting columns. These castings are secured to the rods by means of screw nuts. The columns, light in appearance, are calculated to bear a strain more than double that to which they are subjected, so that the margin of safety is large. Stout iron girders are laid across the street from column to column, and these are joined and strengthened by stays and beams of iron running in every direction. Above this is built the road bed, also of iron, firmly fastened together and strengthened in every possible manner, and on this is laid the road, consisting of a double track of steel rails. The whole structure forms a sort of arcade in the middle of the street, above the tracks of the horse railways. It seems a light and graceful affair, and, when viewed from below, appears scarcely capable of sustaining the immense strain put upon it. As a general rule the roadway is on a level with the second-story windows of the houses by which it passes. At 110th street, however, it reaches the height of sixty-three feet, and presents one of the most audacious and skillful specimens of engineering to be found on the globe. It makes a gigantic curve here, from Ninth to Eighth avenue, and from the street the trains passing over it seem to be running in mid air. Even the coolest person cannot resist a feeling of nervousness in passing over this portion of the road for the first time. Massive as it is, the structure seems too light for its purposes; but it stands firm and unshaken, and trains rattle over it daily with scarcely a jar.

The stations along the route are of iron, and are painted a light and dainty green. They are fitted up in elegant style, and are provided with every convenience for passengers and the employees of the road. They were designed by the celebrated landscape artist, J. F. Cropsey, and are tasteful cottages, provided with ticket offices, waiting rooms for gentlemen and ladies, and toilet conveniences for each. They are lighted with gas, as are also the platforms, and in winter are heated. The platforms extend beyond the station houses at each end, and are covered with a light and graceful iron pavilion roof. The stations are reached from the street by light iron stairways enclosed at the side and roofed over. The up stations are on the east side of the streets, and the down stations on the west side. Passengers purchase their tickets at the office on entering the station, and drop them in a patent box in charge of an attendant upon passing out on the platform.

The equipment of the road is excellent. The cars are built after the style of the Pullman palace cars. The seats have spring cushions, and are placed two by two in the centre of the car at each side of the passageway; at the ends they are ranged longitudinally around the car, thus affording ample space near the doors for the ingress and egress of passengers. The windows are unusually large, are of plate glass, and are provided

ELEVATED RAILROADS, CHATHAM SQUARE.

with adjustable rep blinds. The cars are painted a delicate shade of green, and are among the handsomest to be found on any road in the Union. The platforms are enclosed with iron balustrades, with gates at the sides. The locomotives used are small and of a peculiar construction. They make an average speed of twelve miles an hour, including stoppages. All trains are provided with air-brakes, and can be stopped in a little more than their own length. The road is operated by means of electric signals, and every precaution for safety is taken.

The conductors and brakemen are handsomely uniformed, as are also the attendants at the stations. They are dressed in blue flannel or cloth, with ornamental braidings on the shoulders, brass buttons on the coat and vest, and cap encircled with two gold cords and marked with silver letters in front above the peak, with the title, "conductor," "brakeman," etc. They have an air of extreme importance, and hustle passengers on and off the trains with a haste that amounts to recklessness, and which has, in more than one instance, led to serious accidents. It is said that many of the employees of this company were appointed for political reasons, and have had but little experience as railroad men.

The Second avenue line is owned by the Metropolitan Company, and is built in a manner similar to the Sixth avenue road. Its trains start from the South Ferry, and run through Pearl and Fulton streets and Franklin Square to Chatham Square, the junction of the Third avenue line; thence through Division street to First avenue, along that avenue to 23d street, through 23d street west to Second avenue, and along that street to the Harlem river. It is proposed to bridge the river at this point and extend the road into Westchester county. Passengers by this line are transferred to the Third avenue line at Chatham Square without extra charge. In its equipment and management it is similar to the Sixth avenue line.

The Ninth Avenue Line is owned by the New York Elevated Railroad Company. It is built on columns of iron set in concrete and masonry along the outer edge of the sidewalk on each side of the streets it traverses. These columns are connected by stout iron girders, and the structure, although so light in appearance, is as solid and firm as could be desired. It begins at the South Ferry, and runs across the Battery Park to Greenwich street, along which it continues to 14th street, where it enters Ninth avenue, and follows the line of that street to 59th street, where it joins the extension of the Metropolitan Road. Passengers going above 59th street are transferred to the Metropolitan cars without extra charge. The road runs, as has been said, along the sidewalks on each side of the street, the middle of the street being thus unobstructed. The cars of this line are painted a handsome brown color, very much like those of the Pennsylvania Road, and though neatly upholstered and decorated are not as ornamental as those of the Sixth avenue line.

The Third avenue line is also owned by the New York Elevated Railroad Company. It commences at the City Hall, immediately opposite to the stone causeway of the Brooklyn Bridge, and runs direct to Chatham Square, and thence by the Bowery and Third

avenue to the Harlem River at 129th street. At 42d
street a branch diverges westward to the Grand Central Depot. It is built on rows of pillars, like the Ninth
avenue road, and varies according to the character of
the street in which it is located. The Bowery being
wide the tracks are carried on separate pillars on each
side of the street; while on Third avenue they are
erected upon lines of columns at each side of the street
car tracks, and connected at the top by light, open
elliptic arch girders.

The cars on this line resemble those of the Ninth
avenue road. The officials are uniformed like those
of the Sixth avenue line, and are, as a rule, more efficient men. The New York Elevated made it its business at the outset to secure men who were thoroughly
accustomed to railroading, and who knew their duties.
The stations on the Ninth and Third Avenue lines are
alike in design. They are smaller than those of the
Sixth Avenue line, but are very handsome, are constructed of ornamental iron, and are reached from the
street by stairways.

From five o'clock until seven in the morning, and
during the same hours of the evening, the fare on all
the lines is five cents; at all other times it is ten cents.

There is no pleasanter way of seeing New York
than from the elevated railways. The following trip,
which may be made within three hours, will show the
visitor more of the great city than can be seen in two
days by any other means: Take the Third avenue
line at the City Hall and ride to 130th street—the Harlem river. It is but a step from the station to the landing of the East river steamers. Embark on one of

these and ride to the end of the route, at Peck Slip, near the Fulton Ferry, on the East river. The sail down the river is superb. A short walk along South street, from Peck Slip, brings the traveler to the terminus of the West Side Elevated Road at the South Ferry. Take the Ninth avenue line here and ride to 155th street. Return by the Sixth avenue line, and ride to the terminus at Rector street. This leaves out the Second avenue line, but the Third avenue road commands very much the same view, and nothing of importance is lost.

The elevated roads have been of the greatest service to New York, in spite of the complaints that they have injured property along their lines. The question of damage is still an open one, but there can be no doubt that the problem of rapid transit has been effectually and quickly solved. Travelers are independent now of the weather. The trains run on time and with ease in the heaviest snow storms, blockades are impossible, and time is saved and comfort secured to the passenger. In good weather and with a clear track the horse-cars took from three-quarters of an hour to fifty minutes from 59th street to the City Hall. The elevated trains make the same distance now in twenty-eight minutes, including stoppages. The Metropolitan Road runs over 1000 trains a day, and the New York Elevated about 900, making between 1900 and 2000 in all. An average train on either road in the busy hours will carry 350 passengers on the round trip.

Great complaints were made at first of the noise made by the trains passing over the roads, but these are not so numerous now as formerly. The peculiar construction of the New York Elevated Company's lines renders them less noisy than those of the Metropolitan Company. The posts of the latter roads are hollow tubes of boiler-iron, and each possesses the resonant qualities of a drum. On the New York Company's roads the posts are open ones, two sides of each being made of stout lattice-work, and give forth less sound.

During the five-cent hours the trains on all the lines are crowded, the seats, aisles, and even the platforms being filled to their fullest capacity. The station platforms are black with a struggling crowd, each individual of which is striving with all his powers to be the first on the train when it arrives. At such times the jam is dangerous. The seats are usually occupied before the train leaves the end of the line, and the throngs who wait at the way stations rush on board only to find standing room, and sometimes hardly that. Passengers leaving the trains at such stations have literally to fight their way out of the cars, and the stop is so brief that they are often carried one or two stations beyond their destination before they can reach the platform of the car. The conductors crowd as many into a car as can be packed into it during these hours, and the air soon becomes foul, and the danger of contracting contagious or infectious diseases, from being jammed in too closely with all sorts of people, is very great. Trains often start while passengers are in the act of getting on board, and men are frequently dragged some distance before they can be rescued from their perilous positions. The dense throngs on the narrow platforms of the stations afford a rich harvest for pickpockets, and a free field for bullies and ruffians,   When the platforms are so heavily crowded there is actual danger of being pushed over into the street, or under the wheels of the approaching trains. The over-crowded trains which run so frequently during the five-cent, or "commission" hours, are exceedingly liable to accident.   Engines not infrequently become disabled, causing the train to stop, and at such times there is danger of one of the rear trains crashing into the disabled one.   Should the breaks of the rear train give way such a disaster would be inevitable. Several accidents have occurred, and serious collisions have taken place.   It is urged that a reduction of the fare to five cents at all hours would remedy the trouble, and that such crowds would not collect for the early and late trains if the fare were the same at all hours.

Such are some of the drawbacks to the system; but it cannot be denied that these roads are, on the whole, a great gain for the city.   The upper sections of the Island being brought within rapid and easy reach of the business quarters are attracting large numbers of inhabitants, and property is rapidly appreciating in value above and along the Central Park.   Many persons who were forced to live in Brooklyn or some other suburb, are returning to the city, and taking houses in Harlem and the neighboring localities, and it is confidently expected that a few years will see a vast change for the better in this section of the city—thanks to the facilities offered by the Elevated Roads.   In the first place the city will push its grand streets and its rows of substantial dwellings rapidly northward until the Park is surrounded with a tolerably dense population. In a few years the fine country seats on the west side, as far up as Washington Heights, will have to give place to solid blocks of brick and brownstone, because the land will become too valuable to be used for lawns and gardens, and by the end of the century those who are now living may expect to see the whole of the upper part of Manhattan Island as closely built over as are now the districts immediately below the Park. Of course this rapid increase will not proceed from the ordinary process of a city's growth. Thousands of people who have taken refuge in the suburban towns to secure cheap rents and to avoid the miseries of street car travel, will return to New York. It will be a great deal more comfortable to step into a train a few blocks from the City Hall and be whirled in half an hour up to 100th street, than to walk to a ferry, wait five or ten minutes for a boat, submit to the jostling crowds, and occasionally miss a train on the other side of the river. Added to the inducements to draw people from the suburbs back to the city will be the facility for attending evening amusements, for hearing good Sunday sermons, and for getting easy access to the many attractions that the denizen of the Metropolis can enjoy, if he will, in his leisure hours. Already the Elevated Roads are beginning to affect the tenement houses, and many of the dwellers in these vast rookeries have moved up to Harlem and its vicinity, where they can obtain entire houses for a little more than the price paid for a few rooms in their former habitations.

To the stranger the Elevated Roads offer a pleasure not to be experienced in any other city. You mount the stairway to the station, purchase your ticket, deposit it in the box at the gate, and take your place

on the platform to await the arrival of the train. Here
it comes, puffing and snorting, and draws up to the
station as leisurely and quietly as if there was no hurry
about the performance. You step on board, and find
yourself in a handsome, airy, and comfortable car.
Then follows a ride which will be always remembered.
You whirl along the streets on a level with the second stories of the houses, and looking down can enjoy
all the sights in the roadway and on the sidewalk
below. Underneath you the horse cars pass and repass,
and you hear the pleasant jingle of bells. The grand
panorama of the streets traversed spreads out before
you; distant views of the rivers and their shipping are
caught, and at last you reach your destination, feeling
that you have had an experience to be remembered.
You have enjoyed New York's latest wonder; you
have made a trip on the Elevated Railroad.

The Third avenue line runs its trains all night.
They start from each end of the road every fifteen
minutes, from midnight to a quarter of five in the morning. These are "the Owl Trains," and carry home the
late workers in the great newspaper offices, belated
travelers, and the "b'hoys" who have been making a
night of it. Let us take the trip on one of these trains
in company with a reporter of the *New York Herald*,
starting from the South Ferry an hour after midnight.

"Puff! Puff! On we go, slowly at first, over the tangle
of switches, and then as the gleaming track stretches
out before, we gain headway, and go rushing into the
shadow of the silent tenements and the deserted work
shops of down town. A couple of passengers join us
at Fulton street, three more at Hanover Square, and

COENTIES SLIP.

then we sweep along toward the east side thoroughfare, where the flare of light before us shows that the
denizens are still astir.   We are rattling past the odd
clusters of houses that swarm down to the river's edge
—oddly enough they look in the darkness—these
human hives crowded together in so many uncouth
shapes, with a stray light struggling through the panes,
and the lines of the narrow streets broken and almost
lost among them.   On past this region of dark abodes,
from which even now the sound of a street broil reaches
us, and then there is a rattle of switches as we sweep
about the curve into the light and find ourselves
at Chatham Square.   A group of passengers come
aboard here, and there is a show of activity in the station.   Doubtless there is a certain animation imparted
to it by the sounds of life, loud enough and sufficiently
varied for the broadest kind of day, that float up to it
without ceasing from the Bowery beneath.   There is
nothing in this glare of light, nothing in this swarming
pavement, to indicate that midnight has passed.   The
windows gleam, the saloons are all aglare, a half-score
pianos and violins send as many airs floating into the
night to blend into an instrumental discord that attunes
itself fitly to the roysterer's song, the brawler's oath and
the hundred strange voices of the night.   We go on
now over all these, with the rattle of the wheels drowning the noise, and only the darkened and apparently
deserted stories of the houses on a level with our eyes.
It seems as though we were driving over a troubled
sea, but in an atmosphere becalmed.

"Grand street and then Houston are reached.   We
receive few accessions at either.

"The vehicle that will reduce the lateness of arrival by some minutes, and depreciate by a corresponding percentage the rancor of the waiting wife or the observant mother-in-law, is a boon sure to be appreciated. This sentiment received free expression at the hands of a professor-like body in the car, who, alone of all the passengers, opened communication with his fellow men, and who himself seemed a trifle anxious to bring his latch key into speedy communication with the front door.

"In fact, most of the passengers seemed very impassive and preoccupied. Several of them were conspicuously so, and the trip up town was quite uneventful until the advent of the ubiquitous small boy. He was a good specimen of the class—spry, saucy and mischievous. He was projected into our midst from the Houston street station, at which he flung a parting comment on some one's freshness. For a time he edified us by performing a sort of double-shuffle in one end of the car, and then fell into conversation with the professor-like person, to whom he confided that he was "a mechanic in a feather foundry," together with much other valuable and equally reliable information. A few popular airs, rather discordantly whistled, and an active passage at words with the brakeman, made up the sum of the small boy's entertainment, when, in a charitable effort to close the gate on the conductor's fingers, he retired at 68th street.

"We were now well up town, and running between the rows of flats and tenements on either side the street. Here all was repose. Closed shutters, draped windows,

darkened rooms—everywhere a recognition of the
hours of slumber.   Only the street lamps beneath, and
only a semi-occasional by-passer.   Here the din of
the cars seems louder than before, and strangely at
variance with the dead silence of the slumbering homesteads.   The pace of the engine seems quickest now,
and as we leave 86th street a sudden belt of darkness
is thrown upon the windows.   We have passed from
the tenanted portions of the avenue and are flying
across the Harlem flats.   How dim, how gloomy they
lie in this moonless night.   A medley here of roofs and
gables; there the flash of a whitewashed wall all down in
the hollow, with only a fitful glimmer in some window-
pane.   Even the street lamps gleaming by the way look
dim, and the twinkle of the lights of Astoria, away across
the water, are distant and uncertain.   Suddenly a great
yellow eye opens down towards the river and glows
like a full moon in the darkness.   It is the clock on the
Second avenue railroad depot, which we are whirling
past.   Only that sign of life in all the dark landscape,
from the line of the river to the sky on the other side,
where the hills and trees of Central Park stretch like
an undulating belt.   Yet we are going over scores of
little homesteads instinct with life.   And at such a pace!
The train seems to fairly spin along.   One thinks, going through the air at this rate, of the phantom hunts-
man of the Hartz tearing over the hamlets and forest
lands, and the witches of old whirling across the sky
astride their broomsticks.   But when one comes back
to the prosaic, cosy seats of the elevated road, he feels
that he has a much more substantial and comfortable

conveyance than the phantom steed, and one which has many points of superiority over the witches' favorite vehicle.

"106th street! We are going into Harlem. We have dropped all our passengers but two. Naturally, in these high local latitudes we take on no more. We keep the pace for a time from station to station, then 'down brakes' is whistled, we slow up and come rolling up to the end of the route in dignified fashion. There are a good many people at the station as we reach it, and while the engine waits others arrive. About double as many passengers board the train to go down as came up."

CHAPTER XII

SOCIETY

THE VARIOUS CLASSES OF SOCIETY—THE BEST OF ALL—THE "OLD KNICKERBOCKERS"—A HEAVY SET OF SWELLS—RICHES AND CULTURE COMBINED—THE NEWLY RICH—THE CONTROLLING ELEMENT—HOW SHODDY GETS INTO SOCIETY—THE POWER OF MONEY—FASHIONABLE SNOBBERY—FROM THE TENEMENT HOUSE TO THE FIFTH AVENUE MANSION—MANIA FOR COATS OF ARMS—HOW BOSS TWEED WAS VICTIMIZED—SUDDEN APPEARANCES AND DISAPPEARANCES IN SOCIETY—" RICHES HAVE WINGS "—A FAILURE AND A TRIUMPH—WHAT IT COSTS— MONEY THE ONE THING NEEDFUL—EXTRAVAGANCE OF NEW YORK SOCIETY—LOVE OF DRESS —A FASHIONABLE LADY'S WARDROBE—FOLLIES OF THE MEN—PASSION FOR THE LEG BUSINESS—FASHIONABLE ENTERTAINMENTS—THE END OF EXTRAVAGANT CAREERS—THE SKELETONS SOMETIMES COME OUT OF THEIR CLOSETS—FASHIONABLE BALLS AND PARTIES—HOW THEY ARE GIVEN—INVITATIONS—BALL ROOM SCENES—THE SUPPERS—A SWELL CONVERSATION —FASHIONABLE THIEVES—AN ARISTOCRATIC SNEAK THIEF—HOW A BROKER KEPT HIS PLACE IN SOCIETY—A DETECTIVE'S EXPERIENCE IN FASHIONABLE LIFE—THE PRETTY WIDOW AND THE LACES—FASHIONABLE RECEPTIONS—WEDDINGS IN HIGH LIFE—ARRANGED ON A PECUNIARY BASIS—MONEY THE ATTRACTION—HOW HEARTS ARE BOUGHT AND SOLD—THE WEDDING FESTIVITIES—GUARDING THE BRIDAL PRESENTS—WHAT IT ALL COSTS—FASHIONABLE DEATH—ONLY THE RICH CAN AFFORD TO DIE IN NEW YORK—COST OF A FASHIONABLE FUNERAL—INTERESTING DETAILS.

I

CONSTITUENT PARTS

Society in New York is made up of many parts, a few of which we propose to examine.

The first class is unfortunately the smallest, and consists of those who set culture and personal refinement above riches. It is made up of professional men and their families—lawyers, clergymen, artists, authors, physicians, scientific men, and others of kindred pursuits and tastes. Compared with the other classes, it is not wealthy, though many of its members manage to attain competency and ease. Their homes are tasteful, and often elegant, and the household graces are cultivated in preference to display. The tone of this

class is pure, healthful and vigorous, and personal
merit is the surest passport to it. It furnishes the best
specimens of manhood and womanhood to be met with
in the metropolis, and its home-life is simple and attractive. In short, it may be said to be the saving
element of the society of the metropolis, and fortunately
it is a growing element, drawing to it every year new
members, not only from the city itself, but from all
parts of the country. It is this class which gives tone
to the moral and religious life of the city, which supports
the lectures, concerts, oratorios and scientific entertainments which form so pleasant a feature of city life, and
it is seen in force at Wallack's and other leading theatres on the first night of some new play. Its members
are generally sufficiently well-off in this world's goods
to render them independent of the forms to which
others are slaves. Travel and observation, added to
natural abilities, enable them to estimate persons and
things at their true value, and they maintain their positions without caring to imitate or enter into competition
with their wealthier neighbors. They are always ready
to recognize and lend a helping hand to struggling
merit, but sternly discountenance vulgarity and impos-
ture. They furnish the men and women who do the
best work and accomplish the greatest results in social
and business life, and their names are honored throughout the city.

The next class is composed of the descendants of the
original Dutch settlers of New York, and style
themselves "the Old Knickerbockers." They are
clannish, and cling together, looking down with a
lofty contempt upon all who cannot show a Dutch

ancestor, or produce a long line of family portraits as proof of their descent. Many of these people are highly educated, refined, and would be a credit to any society, were it not for their ridiculous affectation of superiority to their neighbors. This affectation of superiority often exposes them to unmerciful ridicule, but they bear it with true Dutch phlegm. Each one has his coat of arms, and all seem to rely more upon their descent from the hard-headed old Dutchmen of New Amsterdam than upon their own merits. You could not insult them more deeply than to intimate that the venerable mynheer from whom they boast descent was, in the palmy days of New Amsterdam, a butcher, a fish vender, or a tanner down in the swamp, and knew little of and cared less for stately escutcheons and armorial bearings. Many of the members of this class are large real estate owners, their property being among the most valuable in the city. The little farm of the Dutch ancestor is now a succession of valuable building lots, and instead of bearing cabbages and onions is covered with stately edifices, and has enriched the descendants far beyond the "ancestor's" wildest dreams. They are a heavy and solemn class, these "Old Knickerbockers," even the very young ones. They are not overburdened with brains, as a rule, and try to atone for this deficiency by assuming the most pompous and heavy bearing. Many, perhaps a majority, of this class are undoubtedly what they claim to be as regards descent, but it must be confessed that there are those among them whose names are not to be found in the lists of the people of New Amsterdam. No matter, they have wealth, they affect the Dutch style, have a "Van" to their names, and somehow have a line of old, yellow "family portraits" to show, and if pressed for their pedigree, is there not a "college of heraldry" in the city to make one for them?

The third class consists of those who have inherited large wealth from one or more generations of ances- tors, but who make no claim to aristocratic descent. They are generally people of culture, with nothing of shoddyism or snobbery about them. They have traveled extensively, and are free from the narrow provincial ideas that characterize so many of the New York "Upper Ten." Their houses are filled with valuable works of art and mementoes of foreign travel. Having an abundance of leisure, they are free to cultivate the graces of life, and they constitute one of the pleasant- est portions of the society of the city. The class is not large, but it is constantly receiving new members in the children of men who have made their way in the world, and have learned to value money at its true worth. They make good citizens, with the exception of an easy going indifference to political affairs, are proud of their city and country, and do not ape the airs or customs of foreign lands.

The fourth and largest class, that which may be said to give New York fashionable society its peculiar tone, consists of the "Newly Rich." These are so numer- ous, and make themselves so conspicuous, that they are naturally regarded as the representative class of New York society. They may be known by their coarse appearances, and still coarser manners, their loud style, and ostentatious display of wealth. Money with them is everything, and they judge men, not by their merits, but by their bank accounts. They are strangers to the refinements and "small, sweet courtesies" of life, and for them substitute a hauteur and a dash that lay them open to unmerciful ridicule. Without education or polish, they look down upon those who are less fortunate than themselves, and fawn with cringing servility upon the more aristocratic portion of society. To be invited to an entertainment of some family of solid repute in the fashionable world, to be on visiting terms with those whose wealth and culture rank them as the true aristocracy, is the height of their ambition. This they generally accomplish, for money is a passport to all classes of New York society. The better elements may laugh at the "Newly Rich," but they invite them to their houses, entertain them, are entertained in return, and so do their share in keeping "Shoddy" firm in its position in the avenue. The "Newly Rich" know the power of their money, and they use it accordingly. The wealthy Mr. McGinnis, uncouth as he is, unrefined as his family are, can give handsomer and more costly entertainments, and in mere matters of richness and display, can far outshine the aristocratic Mr. Van Bomp, whose ancestors run back to the days of the Half Moon and New Amsterdam. So Mr. Van Bomp, meeting McGinnis in society, learns to put up with his rough ways, though he may laugh at them in private, exchanges hospitalities with him, and in many ways helps the new rich man up the social ladder, and the dream of McGinnis' life is realized.

The "Newly Rich" look down with supreme contempt upon the institutions which have enabled them to rise so high in the social scale. It is from them one

hears so many complaints of the degeneracy of society,
and it is they whose frowns chill the ambitious hopes
of rising merit.   Lacking personal dignity themselves,
they ridicule it in others.   They are ashamed of their
origin, and it is a mortal offence to one of these new-
fledged fashionables to remind him that you knew him
a few years back as a hard-working mechanic or shop-
keeper.   His better-half may have been a dressmaker,
a shop-girl, or have risen from some humbler position
in life ; but that is all forgotten now, and it would be
not only bad taste, but a mortal offence, to refer to it.
Some strange changes of names are brought about by
a translation to the upper circles.   Plain John Smith
becomes John Smythe, and perhaps, Smyythe.   Sam
Long, who began life by driving a dray, is now Mr.
Samuel Longue ; Mc'Ginnis becomes MacGuennesse.
A coat of arms suddenly makes its appearance, for the
establishment in the city which deals in such matters is
equal to any emergency, and oftentimes a pedigree is
manufactured in the same way.   As for family portraits, " Sypher's," or any of the old curiosity or bric-
a-brac stores, can provide any number of these.   Some
years ago, when the late Boss Tweed was at the height
of his power, he thought his new dignity required a
coat of arms, which was duly engraved upon his silver
and emblazoned on the panels of his equipages.   It
was a superb design, and tickled the Boss immensely;
but his joy was cut short when he found that the
" Herald's College " had bestowed upon him the armorial bearings of the Marquis of Tweedale, one of
England's proudest peers.   Of course there was a
broad laugh throughout the city at the honorable William's expense.

Some of the fashionables appear very suddenly in society. For the better part of their lives they have lived very modestly, perhaps in a tenement house. A series of fortunate speculations in Wall street, or in other branches of commerce places the husband speedily in possession of great wealth. The family is ambitious, and it has now the one thing necessary to enable it to shine in New York society. A mansion in Fifth or Madison avenue, or one of the aristocratic cross streets intersecting those thoroughfares, is secured; the newly acquired wealth is liberally expended in fitting up the new home; and then the fortunate owners of it suddenly burst upon society as stars of the first magnitude. They are ill adapted to their new position it is true, rude and unrefined, but they have wealth and are willing to spend it, and money is supposed to carry with it all the virtues and graces of fashionable life. This is all society requires, and it receives them with open arms, flatters and courts them, and exalts them to the seventh heaven of fashionable bliss.

Lucky are they who can manage to retain the positions thus acquired. It too often happens that this suddenly gotten wealth goes as rapidly as it came. Then the stars begin to pale, and finally the family drops out of the fashionable world. It is not missed, however; new stars take their places, perhaps to share the same fate. Thus this class of society is not permanent as regards its members. It is constantly changing. People come and go, and the leaders of one season may be conspicuous the next only by their absence.

Sometimes even this class of society takes a notion

to be exclusive, and then it is hard to enter the charmed circle.   Some years ago a gentleman, a man of brains and sterling merit, who had risen slowly to fortune, feeling himself in every way fitted for social distinction, resolved to enter society, and to signalize his entree by a grand entertainment.   At that time he lived in a not very fashionable street, but he did not regard this as a drawback.   He issued his invitations, and prepared his entertainment upon a scale of unusual magnificence, and at the appointed time his mansion was ablaze with light, and ready for the guests.   Great was his mortification.   Not one of those invited set foot within his doors.   In his anger he swore a mighty oath that he would yet compel New York society to humble itself to him.   He kept his word, became one of the wealthiest men in the city, indeed, one of the merchant princes of the land, and in the course of a few years society, which had scorned his first invitations, was begging for admission to his sumptuous fétes.   He became a leader of society, and his mandates were humbly obeyed by those who had once presumed to look down upon him.   It was a characteristic triumph; his millions did the work.

II

WHAT IT COSTS

Poverty is always a misfortune.   New York brands it as a crime.   Consequently no poor man, or even one of moderate means, can hold a place in New York society.   Indeed, it would be simply impossible for any one not possessed of great wealth to maintain a position there, as to do this requires an almost fabulous outlay of money.   As money opens the doors of the charmed circle, so money must keep one within it.

Thus society in New York has become the most extravagant in the world. Nowhere on the globe are such immense sums spent. Extravagance is the besetting sin of Metropolitan social life. Immense sums are expended annually in furnishing the aristocratic mansions, in dress, in entertainments, and in all sorts of folly and dissipation. It is no uncommon thing for a house and its contents to be heavily mortgaged to provide the means of keeping its occupants in proper style. The pawnbrokers drive a thriving trade with the ladies of position, who pledge jewels, costly dresses, and other articles of feminine luxury, to raise the money needed for some "high-toned" folly. Each member of society strives to outshine or outdress his or her acquaintances, and to do so requires a continual struggle, and a continual drain upon the bank account. Men have been led to madness and suicide, and women to sin and shame, by this constant race for social distinction; but the mad round of extravagance and folly goes on, the new comers failing to profit by the experience of those who have gone before them.

The love of dress is a characteristic of the New York woman of fashion. To be the best dressed woman at a ball, the opera, a dinner, or on the street, is the height of her ambition. To outshine all other women in the splendor of her attire or her jewels, is to render her supremely happy. Dresses are ordered without regard to cost, and other articles of luxury are purchased in proportion. Nowhere in the world are seen such splendidly dressed, such gorgeously bejeweled women as in New York. A recent writer, touching upon this topic says:—

"It is impossible to estimate the number of dresses a fashionable woman will have. Most women in society can afford to dress as it pleases them, since they have unlimited amounts of money at their disposal. Among females, dress is the principal part of society. What would Madame Mountain be without her laces or diamonds, or Madame Blanche without her silks or satins? Simply common-place, old women, past their prime, destined to be wall-flowers. A fashionable woman has just as many new dresses as the different times she goes into society. The *élite* do not wear the same dresses twice. If you can tell us how many receptions she has in a year, how many weddings she attends, how many balls she participates in, how many dinners she gives, how many parties she goes to, how many operas and theatres she patronizes, we can approximate somewhat to the size and cost of her wardrobe. It is not unreasonable to suppose that she has two new dresses of some sort for every day in the year, or seven hundred and twenty. Now, to purchase all these, to order them made, and to put them on afterward, consumes a vast amount of time. Indeed, the woman of society does little but don and doff dry goods. For a few brief hours she flutters the latest tint and *mode* in the glare of the gaslight, and then repeats the same operation the next night. She must have one or two velvet dresses, which cannot cost less than $500 each; she must possess thousands of dollars' worth of laces, in the shape of flounces, to loop up overskirts of dresses, as occasion shall require. Walking dresses cost from $50 to $300; ball dresses are frequently imported from Paris at a cost of from

$500 to $1000; while a wedding dress may cost from $1000 to $5000. Nice white Llama jackets can be had for $60; *robes princesse*, or overskirts of lace, are worth from $60 to $200. Then there are traveling dresses in black silk, in pongee, in velvet, in piqué, which range in price from $75 to $175. Then there are evening robes in Swiss muslin, robes in linen for the garden and croquet playing, dresses for horse-races and for yacht-races, *robes de nuit* and *robes de chambre*, dresses for breakfast and for dinner, dresses for receptions and for parties, dresses for watering places, and dresses for all possible occasions. A lady going to the Springs takes from twenty to sixty dresses, and fills an enormous number of Saratoga trunks. They are of every possible fabric, from Hindoo muslin, "gaze de soie,' crape maretz, to the heavy silks of Lyons."

This is no exaggerated picture. The sales of silks at Stewart's, alone, average about $15,000 daily, and each of the other monster dry goods establishments do a business in proportion. For the finer articles of dress, gloves, laces, velvets, shawls and the like, thousands are spent every day at these establishments; and the fashionable *modistes*, or dressmakers, have an enormous custom and soon grow rich. Some years ago a gentleman, whose residence had been consumed by fire, submitted to a leading insurance company a claim for $21,000 on his daughter's wardrobe alone. The claim was disputed. It was carried into court, where it was proved, item by item, and the company was compelled to pay the money.

Nor are the men one whit behind the women in their extravagance. They have their follies, their dissipations, their clubs, their fast teams, and a hundred other ways of getting rid of money, and they manage to spend it quite as lavishly as the ladies of their families. Yachting, the races and cards absorb large sums, and heavy amounts go to women whose charms are for sale to the highest bidder. The men are coarser than the women, and their pleasures and dissipations are of a lower grade. They have not the tact which enables the female members of their families to get along in the fashionable world, and seek amusement elsewhere. They are liberal patrons of the drama, especially the ballet and "the leg business." Many do not make any attempts to accompany their wives and daughters to fashionable entertainments. They are out of their element there, and prefer to seek pleasure in their own way.

Entertainments are given in the most elaborate and costly style, and thousands of dollars are paid out in a single evening for this purpose. A fashionable party will consume from fifteen hundred to two thousand dollars worth of champagne alone. It is no uncommon thing for an elaborate ball to cost from ten to fifteen thousand dollars, or even more, or for a dinner party to cost from five thousand dollars upward. There are many things to be provided besides the entertainment itself, and these all go to swell the bill. At some of these entertainments costly presents of jewelry are given to each guest, delicately enclosed in the folds of rich bouquets.

Now this is well enough for those who can afford it; but the majority of the New York fashionables cannot stand the strain long. As we have said, their wealth,

great though it be, melts steadily under such demands
upon it, until there is nothing left, and bankruptcy and
ruin end the story.   From time to time the business
community is startled by the failure, perhaps the suicide, of some nominally well-to-do merchant or banker.
The affair causes a brief sensation and is soon forgotten.   The cause is well known.   "Living beyond his
means," or "ruined by his family's extravagance," is
the stereotyped reason given.   Men suffer the tortures
of the damned in their efforts to maintain their commercial standing, and at the same time to provide their
families with the means of keeping their places in society.   They are driven to forgery, defalcation, and other
crimes, yet they do not achieve their object.   Ruin
lays its hand upon them, and the game is played out.

As for Madame, she must have money.   The husband may not be able to furnish it, and there may be
a limit to even the pawnbroker's generosity ; but money
she must have.   Fashionable life affords her the means.
She sells her honor for filthy lucre ;   she finds a lover
with a free purse, and willing to pay for her favors.
She acts with her eyes open, and sins deliberately, and
from the basest of motives.   She wants money and she
gets it.   Sometimes the intrigue runs on without detection, and Madame shifts from lover to lover, according
to her needs.   Again there is an unexpected discovery;
an explosion follows; Madame's fine reputation goes
to the winds; and there is a gap in society.   No
wonder so many fashionable women look jaded, have
an anxious, half-startled expression, and seem weary.
They are living in a state of dread lest their secrets be
discovered and the inevitable ruin overtake them.

III

FASHIONABLE BALLS AND PARTIES

The fashionable entertainments of New York are noted for their magnificence and their great cost. During the season, which comprises the late fall, the winter, and the early spring, scarcely a night passes that does not witness one or more balls or parties. Sometimes these are inconveniently close to each other, and the arriving and departing carriages are uncomfortably crowded in the street. Sometimes the host and hostess prefer to give their entertainment at one of the establishments—Delmonico's, or one of his rivals—specially fitted up for that purpose. This saves an immense amount of trouble at home, for the whole affair is then placed in the hands of the fashionable caterer, who provides everything, attends to all the details, and the givers of the entertainment have only to dress at home and repair to the appointed place in time to receive their guests. The plan has its advantages. Others, especially those who have large and elegant mansions suited to such gatherings, prefer to give their balls and parties at their own houses. Whichever method be adopted, the entertainment is sure to be a costly one. Anywhere from $5000 to $20,000 must be expended on a fashionable party. The details are generally left to the mistress of the house; the liege lord's share in the affair is to do what he can towards making the evening pleasant, and pay the bills without grumbling.

Having decided to give a party, the hostess summons to her aid the sexton of the fashionable church she attends, and gives him a list of the names of

the guests she wishes invited.   He has *carte blanche*
to add to this the names of any desirable young men
he may think worthy of the honor, and of any distinguished strangers, foreigners especially, who may be
in the city at the time.   The late lamented Brown, of
Grace Church, during his day enjoyed almost a mo-
nopoly of this business, and amassed quite a snug fortune therefrom.   The fashionable sextons all keep lists
of the eligible young men in town, and are literally besieged for invitations.   Some of them turn a pretty
penny by "giving" these only to the young men who
can afford to pay for them, even going so far as to re-
vise the list of the mistress of the house, when it is to
their interest to do so.

The invitations out, and the preparations for the ball
being made, the hostess turns her attention to her own
costume, and to those of the members of her family.
This requires much thought and many consultations
with the *modiste*.   Society, on its part, is engaged in
similar preparations, and the dry goods stores and
dressmakers reap a harvest.

Upon the night of the entertainment a carpet is
spread from the doorway to the edge of the sidewalk,
and a temporary awning is erected over this.   A policeman is provided to keep off the crowd of lookers-
on which such an occasion invariably draws, and the
sexton in charge takes his place at the door to receive
the cards of invitation as the guests arrive.

Between nine and ten, handsome carriages, with servants in livery, drive up and deposit their inmates at
the awning, through which they pass into the house,
delivering their cards of invitation to the pompous

sexton at the door. Thence they pass to the dressing-room, to divest themselves of their wraps, after which they descend to the drawing-room and pay their respects to their host and hostess. When there is to be dancing, a fine orchestra is provided, and if the German is to be danced during the evening, the fact is announced by placing a row of chairs around the room and tying them in couples with pocket handkerchiefs. But little dancing is engaged in during the earlier hours of the evening, this time being generally taken up by the arrivals of the guests, and in promenading. By a little before midnight the parlors are filled with a brilliant and richly-dressed throng; conversation and laughter rise confusedly on the heated air; and the enlivening strains of the musicians fill the place with entrancing melody.

At midnight the supper rooms are thrown open, and the parlors are at once deserted for the tables. Fashionable New York dearly loves these suppers, and responds cordially to the invitations of those who have the reputation of giving good ones. The service is excellent; the waiters are either French or colored, are attired as faultlessly as the gentlemen guests, and in exact imitation of them, and are adepts at their business. All one's wants are quickly and courteously supplied, without confusion or delay. The table groans with the choicest delicacies of the season, served in the most tempting manner. Wine flows freely; as many as several hundred bottles often being consumed during the evening. The ladies drink as heartily as their partners, and one wonders how they can stand it so well.

Supper over, the ball-room soon fills up again and the dancing begins in earnest. If the German is danced, the better part of the small hours of the morning are devoted to it. As the dance is generally familiar to our readers, we shall attempt no description of it; but will merely remark that it seems to owe its popularity to the fact that it permits liberties to be taken with the fair sex which would not be tolerated under other circumstances.

During the intervals of the dances conversation, such as it is, goes on unflaggingly. The following is a verbatim report of a part of a conversation between a young lady of high position in society and an equally "high-toned" young man. It is given as it was overheard :—

He. "Aw, Miss Jay, saw you 'joying the races to-day."

She. "Yeth; they're awfully jawly, ain't they? Right fun to bet, ain't it?"

He. "Ya-as, rawther jawly to bet when you win, you know; but beastly, awfully beastly, to bet and lose, you know."

She. "Did you lose? Well, that wan't so offly jawly. Lost myself, yest'day. Dare say you'll win 'gain to-morrow, and then you'll think it jawly fun, you know."

He. "O! dare say shall; but caunt help feelin' beastly 'bout losin' yest'day, you know. Do you like boating? Think its right fun, and offly jawly, you know."

But we will not weary the reader. Towards daylight the guests depart, worn out with fatigue, and sometimes a little hazy from the fumes of the champagne that has gotten into their heads, and the ball is over. Night after night, during the season, the same performance is repeated at other houses. No wonder, then, that society is so sorely in need of rest and change when the summer comes and the watering places open their doors; it is literally worn out.

Some strange things happen at these fashionable gatherings. Often the host or hostess is startled by the news of a robbery in the very midst of the festivities. In most instances the articles taken are of value, such as jewelry, and are such as can be easily secreted about the person. The criminal, as a rule, is no vulgar thief, but is one of society's privileged and envied members. Two instances, taken from real life, will illustrate this. *The New York Tribune* of July 16th, 1877, contained the following account of one of these fashionable thieves. We give it in the words of that journal, not wishing to be thought guilty of exaggeration :—

"The dingy back office of a New York detective was the scene of an impressive spectacle several weeks ago. In the presence of the gentlemen—one a well-known detective, the other a prominent merchant—knelt a fashionably dressed man of middle age, confessing a shameful story of crime, and imploring mercy.

"'I admit all,' he cried. 'I stole the property, but I cannot restore it. I was driven to the deed in order to maintain my position in society. My means had largely left me, and I could not resist temptation.'—

"This statement fell like a thunderbolt upon the merchant, who had known the speaker long and favorably. To the detective, however, it was not at all unexpected, as he had already satisfied himself as to the guilt of the man.   The stealing which was here confessed is one of those crimes in the higher circles of society which are generally kept hidden from the public.

"In the early part of last December the family of a prominent lawyer living on Fifth avenue gave a social entertainment, to which only persons of high standing in society were invited.   The following morning it was discovered that rings, watches, and jewelry worth several hundred dollars, were missing.   The most careful search and close examination of servants forced the conclusion upon the family that the robbery had been committed by some one of the guests, although this seemed incredible, as every name upon the list of those present seemed to forbid the thought of suspicion.   The affair was put into the hands of private detectives, who were unable, however, to obtain the slightest clew to the thief or to the property.

"A few days later a wealthy merchant entertained a large number of friends, and the following day a wedding ring and other jewelry, in value about $1000, but prized far more on account of family associations, were missing.   Every nook and corner of the house was searched, and detectives watched the servants, but mystery continued to surround the matter.   Meanwhile, another merchant held a reception in his brownstone house on a fashionable up-town street, and also suffered a loss during the evening of jewelry, watches, and other property, valued at from $200 to $300.   The articles in this case were in a room where the gentlemen assembled, and the theft lay between some one of them and an old servant, whom the master of the house immediately exculpated, declaring that he did not suspect him in the least. The investigation of this theft also was given to detectives, who visited the pawn-brokers' shops of this and other cities, but none of the property was discovered. An entertainment at the residence of another well known citizen resulted in the disappearance of more jewelry, and a mystery deeper than any of those already in the hands of detectives.

"One of the detectives at work upon these cases, becoming convinced that the thief in each case was one and the same person, and moreover, that this person was a member of the company at each party, began a systematic course of action, which was finally crowned with success. The names of the ladies and gentlemen attending all four of the parties were obtained, and were entered in his note-book. The list presented a formidable array of judges, lawyers, editors, physicians, brokers, and other professional and business men, and their wives and daughters. Upon investigating the reputations of these persons the detective was at a loss to know whom to suspect, all of them having the full confidence of their friends and the public. At length his attention was attracted to a gentleman whose expensive social habits and recent reverses in business made the detective think that he was on the right track. This man is a down-town broker, now a member of a well-known firm. His name and family are well known in this city, and he has long enjoyed a position in the very best society. For years he has been a prominent club and society man, always dressing in the height of fashion, and rendering himself very agreeable to his numerous acquaintances. He is an unmarried man, and having a handsome personal appearance and at-

tractive manners, he is popular with ladies. He is a
member of one of the leading regiments of New York,
and has sporting tastes.

"It was discovered that the broker was in the rooms
in the houses in which the thefts were made, and in the
case of the $1000 robbery, he and one of the judges of
the Supreme Court were the only persons who were
seen in the apartment containing the property. With
this and other clews the detective, and the families by
which he was employed, became convinced that the
broker was the thief, and an anonymous letter was sent
to him, charging him with the stealing, and informing
him that unless restitution of the property was made
immediately, the circumstances would be given to the
public, and he would be handed over to the police.
This letter had the desired effect, as the broker at once
appointed a meeting with the detective, and, in the
presence of one of the merchants whose residence he
had robbed while enjoying his hospitality, made a clean
breast of the entire matter. The broker, in telling his
story, said that he had not been doing so well, finan-
cially, as in former years, and it was necessary for him
to get sums of money from some source in order to
meet his obligations and social expenses. The jewelry
he had sold for cash, and it was now impossible to
recover it."

The broker was arrested at the instigation of one of
the merchants whom he had robbed, but through the
influence of his relatives and friends he was released
on bail, and the matter was finally hushed up, the value
of the stolen property being paid.

The following incident was reported by the late

Samuel McKeever, for one of the city journals to which he was attached :—

"Investigation has shown me that no experienced lady gives a party now without having among her black-coated gentlemen guests a regular detective, whose duty it is to look as if he were enjoying himself intensely, and to watch all the others at the same time.

"You can't blame the practice, although it does take the bloom off of hospitality, and makes the amenities of fashionable life a rather ghastly farce. If those you invite to your house number among them men and women with the instincts of footpads, it becomes the duty of the entertainer to protect his or her property, and the property of the guests, at all hazards.

"One of these detectives was introduced to me, and I had quite a talk with him upon the subject. It is new work for him, and he is mightily pleased with it. His first capture was a woman, a handsome, accomplished widow, who was invited as regularly to every swell affair as they happened.

"This is how he caught her:

"'It was about the first of October,' he said 'that a lady living on 61st street issued cards for a very elegant reception, on the occasion of her daughter's marriage. She had been one of the sufferers from the fashionable stealing we have been talking about, and she resolved this time that she would set a trap for the mice.

"'So she drove down to our office the day before— I belong to a private firm of detectives—and asked that some one be detailed at her residence for that evening.

"'I was selected by the head of the firm, who presented me with regular cards of invitation that the high-toned lady had brought with her. I was not a little embarrassed, you can well imagine, for ten years' knocking about among dangerous characters, and being constantly engaged in putting up jobs on the most brilliant members of what we call the 'swell mob,' had rather unfitted me for contact with members of the upper ten thousand.

"'And I didn't have a dress suit!

"'But that was easily managed, thanks to a costumer on the Bowery, and when I presented myself at the brownstone mansion at about half-past nine, I flattered myself I was quite the correct thing in my get-up.

"'Necktie, kid gloves, suit, boots, all proclaimed me the proper kind of guest. One thing I am certain of; I wasn't half as awkward as some of the gawks about me, and I hadn't been in the parlors ten minutes before I felt perfectly at my ease.

"'The hostess introduced me as a friend of her late husband, and passed me over to a heavy old swell, who turned out to be in the grain trade. He got me in the corner, and kept buzzing me for nearly an hour about the crop failures in England, and the immense exporting advantages it would be to this country.

"'All this time, while I was listening to the aged cove, and trying to do my level best in replying to him, I didn't forget what I had come for. My eyes went up and down the room like a patrolman, studying each face and watching keenly if any of the guests disappeared from the rooms, after formally entering them. There was no reason for anticipating any dishonest operation, and my position was looked upon, both by myself and the lady of the house, as a sinecure; but, nevertheless, I could not drive it from my mind that something of a sensational nature would turn up during the course of the evening.

"'And it did.

"'There was a very stylish, vivacious, handsome widow present, to whom I had been introduced. It struck me then that she talked too much; that she surrounded herself with a cloud of conversation which concealed from every one but myself a certain restlessness, which was a sure indication of a project being evolved in her brain.

"'The wedding presents, which were very handsome, were all arranged in a brilliantly illuminated room up stairs, which, when the survey of them was finished, was left in charge of a faithful negro servant belonging to the establishment. Among the collection was a handsome, rare old point lace fichu. This was very valuable, and in proportion to its size, really the most valuable of all.

"'It was shortly after we entered the refreshment room that the widow complained of feeling ill. A chocolate ice had not agreed with her, and the apartment was too hot. She would go into the parlor and rest awhile. The time she chose was when every guest was more or less occupied with the cheerful task of eating and drinking, when all the servants of the house, excepting the one guarding the presents, were employed down stairs.

"'I looked steadily at the lady of the house, and with all the significance that I could command. This was to prepare her for what I was about to say, which was:

"'Hadn't I better take Mrs. —— a glass of wine?'

"'Certainly; it is very kind of you,' she replied, 'and tell her I will be there in a moment to see if she needs anything else.'

"'As I had anticipated, the parlor was empty, and what was more remarkable, the front door was open.

"'I went up the stairs as swiftly and as silently as I could. When I reached the door of the room containing the presents, I detected the odor of chloroform.

"'The door was partially closed. I pushed it open, and it was easily seen from whence the scent came. There sat the darkey, insensible, in his chair, his head thrown back, his face covered with a handkerchief. The widow was in the act of pocketing the fichu, the position of the two parties in the room clearly showing how she had stolen on the negro unawares. I could have arrested her then, but I had a great curiosity to see what her future movements would be like; so when she made a motion to turn, I stepped closely back in the shadow of the landing. She brushed past me, and floated down the stairs like a silken sigh, I after her.

"'All this hadn't taken more than five minutes. Instead of going straight into the parlor, she passed to the front door, which, as I have said, was open. I crouched down, but still sufficiently in range of vision to see her beckon her coachman, who was, singularly enough, in the neighborhood at so early an hour. He came to the stoop, and she passed him the fichu.

"'Then she entered the parlor again, and when I, in about ten seconds, followed her, she was the most beautiful sick woman, lying among the satin cushions of a sofa, that I ever saw.

" 'I went to the mantel where I had placed the glass of wine, and said, in my most engaging manner, 'Mrs. —— sent me to you with this, and her compliments. Try it; it will do you good.'

" 'There was no deceiving her. She saw at once that something terrible had happened. How came the wine to be in the parlor? I must have been there during her absence. Still, she did not give herself up to confusion. She shivered a little, and said, 'Is there not a door open somewhere?'

" ' 'Yes,' I replied, 'the front door. Since you did not close it just now when you spoke to your coachman, I thought you desired it open. Fresh air is a good thing after chloroform.'

" 'This ended it. She looked up at me and swooned. In the meantime the hostess and the guests began to arrive. They crowded about the widow, and I, taking advantage of an opportunity which presented itself, told the lady of the house what had occurred. Just as I did so, a servant discovered his chloroformed companion, and came shouting down the stairs.

" 'All was confusion. Four or five other ladies fainted in convenient corners, and in a few minutes the theory was that the establishment had been entered by means of a skeleton key, and that perhaps even now every closet was jammed with burglars and murderers. I know that we had a jolly good search all over the house. The bride was at first terribly annoyed at the loss, but when her mother told her the circumstances, dumb horror and surprise took possession of her.

" 'If I hadn't been there the plan would have worked beautifully. The front door was opened for three reasons—to communicate with the coachman, to start the theory of a sneak thief, and to have blown away whatever delicate traces of chloroform may have clung to the widow's dress.

"'I saw the pretty widow home that night in her own carriage. When we were a block away from the house, I made her get the stolen article from the driver. He was thunderstruck at the request, and was very much worried at my presence. I returned the loot, and that's all there is to the story.'

"'Didn't they prosecute her?'

"'No; what was the use. They got the fichu—the fish-hook, as I always call it—but they let the fish off. Such things are not stealing among the way up—it's kleptomania.'

"'But the coachman,'—

"'He wasn't a real coachman, any more than she was a real widow. They were man and wife, but he could work better as coachman.'

"'Then this was their regular business.'

"'Been at it for years. I squeezed Mr. Coachman on my own account, and got over one hundred pawn tickets from him, making quite a neat 'spec' by offering to return goods to parties if no questions were asked. Altogether, my first evening among the 'lum-tums' panned out well.'

IV

FASHIONABLE RECEPTIONS

Every lady of fashion in New York has a certain day of the week set apart on which she receives her "dear five hundred friends." At such times she is "at home" to all her acquaintances of both sexes, who may wish to call. These are very select affairs, and are occasions for the display of magnificent costumes by the lady visitors. Few gentlemen are present, the hours being generally from four to six, a period of the day when the male creature is occupied with other matters; so the ladies usually have the field to themselves. On such occasions any man who may happen to be present is pretty sure of being the centre of a circle of attraction, not because of any particular merit in himself, but simply because he is a creature who does not wear petticoats. A correspondent of *The Queen*, the London "Lady's Newspaper," thus describes one of these gatherings:—

"Of course the awning is up, and it is something better than a roof on poles, being a completely enclosed passage, sides, roof, floor and all, complete, running down to the curb, so that no wind or rain can penetrate it. The crowd of curious ragamuffins is thus dispensed with, and the kid boots and the front hair—which, by the way, is always frizzled, or crimped or curled in some loose way, on the American female head—protected from the ravages of the elements. The first figure we see is a remarkable one. Standing on the steps is a portly man, with pompous aids, the sexton of some fashionable temple, who by virtue of his office holds an unassailable position in New York society. He is a kind of social factotum at all parties of consideration.

"New York houses are mostly somewhat narrow—three or four rooms on the ground floor, one behind the other and with folding doors thrown open, and perhaps one or two rooms on the first floor, form the reception apartment, into which, without individual announcement, we are ushered. It is an inconvenient but very general custom here, even if you are making a call, for the man to say, 'Step right into the parlor, sir,' indicating the room and leaving you to obtrude your unannounced presence on its occupants. This may be awkward, but any young lady who doesn't like it can remedy it. Possibly this reception is given, as is the custom here, in addition to a ball, to celebrate the 'coming out' of a daughter of the house. If so, she has some of her friends to receive with her, who have their bonnets off and move round the room, introducing where it is necessary—always called 'presenting' in this country—and performing all those little offices which are almost too much for one hostess. It is a good plan, and quite frequent here, for the hostess to have other ladies to receive with her, as besides the air of comfort and familiarity, it gives a certain 'go' to what would otherwise be rather a slow and formal affair. The cards have 'four to six' on them, and, of course, in the winter gas is necessary all over the house. The effect of the brilliantly lighted and decorated rooms is enriched by a throng of women dressed up to their eyes and full of gayety. Over all these is an aspect of high spirits and animation, which would strike an English visitor more than anything else.

"The air of general animation over a party here, composed of a different class of people, is, perhaps, not excepting beauty, its most charming element; it is the aggregate effect of the individual vivacity and piquancy of the American female character, which, in its best representatives, seems to add these traits to all that is

estimable in English women—a tolerably bold statement, I fear, for your columns. Observe this young
lady here, on the sofa, a belle, and considered 'bright,'
but there are many like her in the room. Her beauty
and grace, her complexion and dress, we will put on
one side or wont mention, as the Irish writer puts it;
but mark her sparkling face and genial good humor as
she talks, the felicity of her language, the readiness of
her repartee, always delicate, but generally with a
delicious little dash of satire; the clearness of her
ideas, the tact with which she draws out her companion,
to show his best points, and the generally unaffected
ease with which she sustains a lengthened conversation
on any subject under the sun, with fool or wise man.
Mr. Editor, they are a wonderful race are these American women; but one word about the flowers, this afternoon, and I shall have done. The rooms are covered
with them in every shape and variety of tasteful
arrangement. Wreaths of the fresh and graceful
smilax—a fern which I have not seen in England, but
which is admirably adapted to decoration—interspersed
with flowers, depend from the chandeliers, cornices,
and mantelpieces. A magnificent cornucopia of all
kinds of flowers, perfect in formation and in the blend-
ing of color, stands in one corner of the room. In the
next, where the chandelier is hung, is a large, loosely
made ball, nearly a yard in diameter, of different-colored
flowers, and embedded in it on either side, also formed
of flowers, is a graceful H, the initial letter of the
daughter's name for whom the reception is given.
Plateaus of flowers stand against the walls and hang
from the pictures, while the mantelpieces are buds of

moss and fern, in which rare exotics are growing, or drooping plants form a natural fringe toward the effect of freshness, light, and nature's beauty that this floral wealth gives to rooms which, without it, have nothing to depend on but art. It is the great forte of American entertainment. Flowers are very dear in winter, but no cost is spared to secure their display."

V

FASHIONABLE WEDDINGS

The Roman Catholic Church teaches that the "holy estate of Matrimony" is a sacrament, and the Protestant Churches hold that it is "honorable among all men; and therefore is not to be entered into unadvisedly or lightly, but reverently, discreetly, advisedly, soberly, and in the fear of God." New York fashionable society regards it as a financial matter, to be regulated and arranged upon strict business principles. True, there may be affection on one or both sides, and many happy marriages are contracted in this class; but it may be laid down as a general rule that fashionable marriages are arranged with regard to the amount of money on one or both sides. Men who have risen to wealth often make the marriage of a son or daughter the means of getting their families within the sacred pale of fashionable society. Again, there are many aristocratic families, genuine Knickerbockers, who have run down in wealth, and are unable to provide for a son or daughter. With all their blue blood, they know they cannot maintain their places in society without money. That must be had, and the only way to procure it is to arrange a marriage for their child with an offspring of one of the " Newly Rich." It may be a bitter pill to swallow, but it has to be done. The money that will thus be brought into the family will enable their child to keep his or her accustomed place in society, and, of course, Papa and Mamma will not be allowed to suffer. So a desirable partner is sought. Personal qualifications, such as beauty, intelligence, education, or refinement, are not considered; money is the sole desideratum, and every effort is made to secure as rich a match as possible. The acquaintance of some wealthy shoddy family is formed; every social attention is showered upon them; the intimacy of the Knickerbockers opens the way for them into the most exclusive circles of fashionable life, and they are made to taste the sweets of this seventh heaven to their utmost. The "Newly Rich" are delighted; their proudest hopes are realized; they rank among the most select families of New York, and at last are at the very summit of fashionable fame. When the proper moment arrives, Knickerbocker squarely proposes to Shoddy that the two families, already so intimate, shall be bound to each other by a still stronger tie, in the marriage of their children. Shoddy, in delight, accepts the proposition, and the matter is arranged by the heads of the respective families before the young people are informed of the good fortune in store for them. The parents have too much confidence in the good sense of their children to apprehend any opposition. Young as they are, they will be sure to see the advantages of a match which will bring with it fortune to one and a secured social position to the other. The young fashionables of the great city are very wise in their generation, as regards money. They have been taught and appreciate its power. The one cannot afford to throw away such a brilliant chance for social distinction, and the other shudders at the thought of stepping down from the place so long occupied, and giving up the power and distinction that wealth brings with it. Tender ties may have been formed by one or both, in some other direction; but these are remorselessly severed, and the "sensible" young people fall into the arrangement of their parents, and meekly submit to the inevitable. After all, what matters it. The marriage yoke, as they see, sits loosely upon those of their acquaintance who bear it. Why should it be different with them? So the matter is arranged, the marriage is solemnized, and society is delighted with the splendid match.

Again, fashionable marriages are often arranged with regard to the business advantages that will follow them. Two fortunes combined are more powerful than either could be singly, and as wealth is the great power in New York, it is well to concentrate as much as possible in one family. So the sale of hearts and hands goes on from year to year, and paves the way for more of the domestic infelicity that makes fashionable life so hollow and empty.

Oftentimes one of the Newly Rich deliberately seeks out some man of assured position, and offers him the hand of his daughter, and a handsome fortune with it. The condition of the bargain is that the gentleman, on his part, shall do all in his power to secure every social advantage for the family of the lady. The girl may be handsome and clever, or the reverse, but if the sum tendered is sufficiently large, the offer is rarely refused.

When an engagement is contracted, it is promptly announced in one of the "Society journals," of which there are several in New York. Then the marriage is hurried forward with as much speed as is consistent with propriety. The ceremony, of course, is celebrated at a fashionable church. To be married from St. Thomas' or Grace Church is to enjoy the highest social distinction on such occasions. Invitations are sent out to fashionable friends, and at the appointed time the church is filled with a throng of magnificently dressed ladies, and gentlemen in the regulation full dress. Two or more clergymen are present to tie the knot, and a reporter of one of the city dailies is on hand to "write up" the wedding in the most glowing terms. Evening is generally the time chosen for the ceremony, as gaslight is more favorable than daylight for showing off the toilettes of the bridal party and the invited guests.

The English style is now the "correct thing" at fashionable weddings. At the appointed hour the organ breaks forth into the exquisite strains of the "Bridal Chorus," from Lohengrin, and the bridegroom enters from the vestry room, accompanied by his "best man," and takes his place before the altar rail, while the clergy file into the church and stand ready to perform their functions. Then the great doors of the church are thrown open, and the bridal party enters, led by the bride, in full dress, on the arm of her father. The places are taken at the altar rail, the groom receives the bride from her father's hands, and the ceremony begins, the organ all the while filling the church with a low undertone of delicious harmony.

The ceremony over, the bridal party returns to the residence of the bride, where the intimate friends of the two families quickly assemble to offer their congratulations, inspect the wedding presents, and partake of the banquet that is generally served. The presents are displayed in a room set apart for the purpose, and are always handsome, and sometimes magnificent. Experience has taught the master of the house that even fashionable New York cannot be trusted alone with so many costly articles, and a detective is generally on hand to look after their safety.

Yet it is not professional thieves that those who get up fashionable entertainments chiefly fear. The most dangerous class, because the most numerous, are included among the invited guests, and are called, when detected, kleptomaniacs.

For almost every large and fashionable wedding there is a request made upon Inspector Byrnes, in charge of the Detective Bureau at the Police Central Office, for an officer to watch the array of presents, and in general to protect the house and its guests from loss by theft. Among the Central Office detectives on whom this duty frequently falls is George W. Lanthier. He is a young man of good address and appearance, who wears a fine diamond in his shirt front, and whose clothes fit him. His fellow detectives say that when he is arrayed in a Prince Albert coat, with silk facings, for an afternoon wedding, there is nothing left to be asked for by the most critical observer, but when he appears attired in full costume for an evening wedding or reception, language fails. Mr. Lanthier was sought out recently. He said his duties were simple, and for the most part agreeable.

"The first thing I do," he said, "when I go to a reception, is to take a look through the house, up and down stairs, in order to acquaint myself with the different rooms as well as with the position of valuable articles. For this reason I usually go a short time before the guests are expected. While the guests are arriving I usually stand in the hall to watch them as they enter. I am very apt to know a professional thief by his face. Where the presents are very numerous and valuable I generally have the smaller ones, such as the diamonds and other jewelry which a person could pocket and carry away readily, put on a table by themselves. Then I take a seat near them. I am supposed, by most of those who see me, to be a guest. If anybody guesses otherwise, I am contented they should have their opinion. I inform myself about the presents, and when guests come up to inspect them, they naturally fall to talking, to express their admiration. I am able to tell them about the presents. One guest, therefore, sees me talking with another, and he is not likely to remark that I remain in one part of the room all the afternoon or evening. If I sat still and said nothing, I would soon become an object of notice.

Stories are told by detectives, of ladies, whose families are of the highest respectability, whom they have pointed out to the givers of entertainments as having stolen valuable presents. In several cases related by the detective, the valuables were recovered under threats of arrest, and scandals resulted. In others, the host was unwilling to make accusations, preferring to avoid the scandal that would follow an exposure. In one case a lady fainted when she was accused. She would not confess, and she was not searched, but it was afterwards said a diamond ring was returned by her father, an action which the detective who told the story criticised as inexcusably simple on the father's part, if he had in view merely the reputation of his daughter. It is said that several series of thefts have been committed by young men so fascinated with society life that they lived beyond their means, and at last were driven by what appeared to them necessity, to steal.

A fashionable wedding is a costly affair, not only to the families immediately concerned with it, but also to their friends who are honored with invitations. Thousands of dollars are spent upon the outfits of the "happy pair;" and the fees to the clergyman, the sexton, the organist and attendants at the church, and the cost of the festivities after the ceremony, make up an enormous sum. The friends of both families are expected to send handsome presents, and as these are always put on exhibition with the cards of the givers attached, they are always elegant and costly. A few years ago, at the wedding of one of the daughters of a leading politician, the wedding presents amounted in value to more than $250,000. When it is remembered that marriages in fashionable life are numerous each year, it will be easy to understand what a tax upon the friends of the happy pair this present-giving amounts to. It is a sort of fashionable "black mail" which society levies upon its members.

FASHIONABLE DEATH.

As only the rich can afford to live in New York society, so only the rich can afford to die in it. Death is an expensive luxury in the great city, and a fashionable funeral generally costs as much as a comfortable dwelling in one of our smaller cities. In nothing, probably, is the law of fashion more rigorously enforced than in the burial of the dead. Music and flowers are as necessary at a funeral as at a wedding, and the body must be attired for its final resting-place with the utmost care. The best of kid gloves must be furnished to the pall bearers, and carriages must be provided in which the relatives and friends may ride to the cemetery. If the funeral ceremonies be held at a church, and it is one of the strictest laws of fashion that they shall be, the sexton must not be neglected, nor the organist and choir go unrewarded, and unless a handsome fee is given, the personal attendance of the undertaker cannot be secured. Lots in first-class cemeteries are costly, and it is indispensable that a handsome and expensive monument of marble or granite should be erected over the grave. And besides all these expenses, mourning apparel is absolutely necessary; each member of the family of the deceased person, and all of his or her near relatives, must be clad in black, for in society, crape is both an indication and a measure of fashionable grief. These various items swell the bill for funeral expenses to an enormous aggregate.

The undertakers' charges are very high. Rosewood caskets vary in price, according to the trimmings, from $90 to $150; those trimmed with black or blue velvet are worth as much as $250, $300, and $400, or even more. A wooden casket, covered with cloth, costs $125. Coffin handles are an additional expense; eight handles are worth from $10 to $20, while full extension handles, extending along both sides of the coffin, are worth $30. Coffin plates of a variety of shapes— shields, crosses, square and oval—cost from $1 to $12, including engraving.

The box in which the coffin is inclosed before it is placed in the grave costs $5, and when this is taken to the cemetery in advance, in order that the beauty and richness of the casket may be seen through the glass plates of the open hearse, an additional charge of $3.50 is made. From $9 to $12 is charged for the use of the hearse, and the price of a carriage to Calvary Cemetery is $6; to Greenwood, $7; and to Woodlawn, $11. The charge for ice-coffins varies from $12 to $18. Scarfs are worth $7 or $8, and gloves for the pall-bearers cost $2.50 a pair. Shrouds are made of lawn or merino, and vary in price from $3 to $40. When a body is deposited in a vault, an engraved copper plate is usually procured, the price being about $2. The personal attendance of an undertaker is worth from $1 to $50, and porters to carry the coffin from the house to the hearse are paid $1.50 each; if they also accompany the friends to the church, their services are worth $2.50 for each. For his services in opening the church, tolling the bell, and attending to his duties as usher, the sexton is paid from $10 to $20, and the choir and organist are paid from $40 to $50 for the funeral march and other music. The amount of money expended for flowers is very large in many cases. Large wreaths and crosses cost from $5 to $10, and large crowns from $15 to $20. It is not an unusual thing for from $600 to $800 to be expended in procuring and preserving flowers, and more than $2000 has been spent for this purpose on the occasion of a single burial. Grief most generally expresses itself thus extravagantly in the cases of young widows of rich old husbands.

The expenses which have been thus far enumerated include only those which enter into the undertaker's bill. At the cemetery the cost of a lot swells the expenditure, and it is no inconsiderable amount. At Greenwood each lot contains 378 square feet. Its form depends upon the surface of the ground, and may be circular, oval, oblong, square, or irregular. The situation determines the value; the prices vary generally from $500 to $800, although some in specially desirable places are valued at $1000. Half, third, and quarter lots are sold at $275, $200, and $155 each and upward, according to situation. Entire lots of a quadrangular form, fourteen feet by twenty-seven feet, admit fifteen graves each; half lots contain six graves, third lots four graves, and quarter lots three graves. At Woodlawn a somewhat different system is pursued. Ground in the cemetery is sold at prices ranging from 80 cents to $2 a square foot, and the shape and size of lots vary with the extent of the purchase and the formation of the ground. Half lots, however, are sold for $187.50 and $120, according to situation, and quarter lots for $60. But in all cases where fractional lots are purchased, granite corner posts must be procured, the prices for which are $9 for half lots and $4 for quarter lots.

The ordinary depth of graves is six feet, although some are dug seven, eight, nine, and even ten feet in depth. The usual charge for opening a grave is $5 for adults and $4 for children. At both Greenwood and Woodlawn the cost of an interment in the receiving vault is $25. If the body is removed in three months $20 will be returned, but it will be buried in a lot provided for that purpose if not removed in three months at Woodlawn, and in six months at Greenwood. This rule was made because a few years ago the receiving tomb at Greenwood became overcrowded on account of the low charge for depositing a body in it. But as the demand increased, prices advanced, and the market naturally corrected itself precisely as demand and supply regulate other markets. Single graves in either of these cemeteries can be procured for $25, but at the Cemetery of the Evergreens, and at Cypress Hills, the price of a single grave is $12. For opening a vault $4 is charged at Greenwood, and $3 at Woodlawn. In both these cemeteries a person who purchases but does not wish to use an entire lot, may sell a portion of it, but speculation and "corners" in lots are prevented by the fact that if an exorbitant price is demanded the purchaser will find it much cheaper to buy from the trustees of the cemetery than from an individual lot owner. At Woodlawn a receiving lot is provided for those who choose this method of sepulture in preference to the receiving tombs. The price of a grave in the receiving lot is $38 for an adult, and $30 for a child.

Another matter of expenditure closely connected with the funeral is the tombstone or monument. In these there is a countless variety in material and design, from the plain marble slab, entirely destitute of ornament, to the elegant and highly-polished shaft of Scotch granite. The material from which the majority of tombstones are made is Italian marble. The native American marble is not sufficiently firm to withstand exposure to the weather. Quincy granite is extensively used, as is also the granite from Aberdeen, Scotland. In localities adjacent to quarries of brownstone, that article is used for the construction of monuments, but it is objectionable, because it rapidly becomes covered with moss. Tombstones of marble can be obtained for $15, and from this the prices range to $450. Occasionally as much as $600 is paid for a tombstone, but generally when so large an amount as this is expended a monument is purchased. The tombstones are generally placed on a block of granite, and the foundation must be placed below the reach of frost. The price is affected by differences in the style of ornamentation, crosses, wreaths, anchors, urns, palls, and figures of many sorts being carved in the marble. A marble monument, fifteen feet in height, without any ornamentation, cannot be bought for less than $900. The price of monuments of Quincy granite is fifteen per cent. more than those of Italian marble, and Scotch granite is more costly still. The latter is greatly in demand, because of the high polish of which it is capable, but there is an ad valorem duty of twenty per cent. on it, which only the deepest grief consents to pay. In the vicinity of New York there are monuments of Scotch granite which cost $10,000, and a number of Quincy granite monuments varying in value from $500 to $20,000. The Canda monument is made of Italian marble, and cost $40,000. Vaults are also expensive. The prices of those in Greenwood and Woodlawn, and also in Calvary Cemetery, vary from $3000 to $15,000, and there is one in Trinity Cemetery which cost $50,000.

From these facts the following schedule of the cost of a first-class funeral on the American plan may be adduced:

1 Rosewood coffin, lined with velvet, - - - - -	$300
1 Coffin-plate (name, and all the virtues engraved gratis), - -	12
8 Full extension silver-plated handles, - - - - -	30
1 Coffin-box, to protect coffin, - - - - - - -	8
1 Ice-box (second-hand), - - - - - - - -	15
1 Shroud, - - - - - - - - - -	25
1 Hearse, - - - - - - - - - -	10
10 Coaches to Greenwood, - - - - - - -	70
8 Pairs gloves to pall-bearers, - - - - - - -	20
8 Scarfs for pall-bearers and one for the door, - - - -	10
1 Undertaker's fee for personal attendance, - - - -	25
4 Porters to carry out coffin, - - - - - - -	6
1 Sexton at church, - - - - - - - - -	15
1 Organist and choir, - - - - - - - - -	40
Flowers, - - - - - - - - - -	100
1 Lot in Greenwood, - - - - - - - - -	600
1 Grave-digger, - - - - - - - - -	5
1 Monument, home manufacture, of Quincy granite, - - -	900
Total, - - - - - - - - - -	$2191

Well, after all, the power of money, the might of fashion, cease at the grave. Beyond that dreary portal to the unknown world —; but society does not bother its head about these things.

After the funeral is over, none of the feminine bereaved ones can be seen for a certain length of time, the period of their seclusion being fixed by a rigid law.

CHAPTER XIII

THE STREET RAILWAYS

THR PRESENT STREET-RAILWAY SYSTEM—IMMENSE BUSINESS DONE BY THE SURFACE ROADS—
EXPENSES AND RECEIPTS—HOW THE ELEVATED ROADS HAVE AFFECTED THE HORSE RAIL-
WAYS—DISCOMFORTS OF THE STREET CARS—THE CONDUCTORS AND DRIVERS—STORY OF A
CONDUCTOR'S LOT—HARD WORK AND POOR PAY—KNOCKING DOWN—HOW IT IS DONE—BEAT-
ING THE BELL-PUNCH.

There are thirty-two lines of street (or surface) railways traversing New York.   Their general direction is
either from south to north, or across the Island from
east to west.   The fare, on all the lines but two, is five
cents.   On the Madison avenue line it is six cents, and
on the short line, from Vesey street to the South Ferry,
three cents.   Notwithstanding the enormous patronage
of the Elevated roads, the surface railways are still
liberally supported.   Many people have a nervous
dread of the aerial structures of which New York is
so proud, and remain faithful to the horse cars ; and
for those who wish to ride short distances only, the
surface roads are the most useful.   Then, again, during the hours when the fare on " The Elevated " is ten
cents, many persons, with whom time is not an object,
use the horse cars to save the extra half-dime.   The
peculiar shape of the city renders it possible for all the
various modes of travel—the Elevated, the surface
roads, and the stages—to be operated with profit.   The
majority of the lines run from south to north, and
centre in the neighborhood of the Post Office.   Before
the construction of the Elevated roads, the travel on the

street cars was enormous; the companies earned fabulous sums; and the stockholders received dividends
the true amount of which could rarely be ascertained.
It was known that they were extraordinarily large. In
1875, the year before the successful completion of the
Elevated roads, the street cars carried over one hundred and sixty million passengers. Over 1500 cars
and more than 12,000 horses were employed in this
work, and the cost of operating the 450 miles of track
included within the city limits, was $6,500,000. At an
average of five cents per passenger, the receipts of the
roads were estimated at over $8,000,000. The receipts
of the Third avenue road alone were $1,666,000, of
which $300,000 was clear profit.

There are many expenses attached to street railroads that travelers are not aware of. In addition to
the wages of conductors and drivers, there is the outlay for offices, clerks, watchmen, starters, switchmen,
changers for changing the horses at the termini, fore-
men of stables and stablemen, feed men, washers,
horse shoers, blacksmiths, carpenters, painters, road and
track men, and others. To pay all these, more than
one-half of the amount set down for operating the road
is expended. The feed of the horses requires nearly
a quarter of the total amount, while large sums are annually expended on fuel, gas, lights for cars, oil for
wheels, waste, the water tax, and other expenses.
Damages and law suits for accidents amount on the
average to over one per cent. on the gross receipts,
and insurance costs three-fourths of one per cent.
more. The expense of removing snow and ice is considerable every year, aggregating about $100,000 for

the season, if favorable, and often requiring double
that amount of money.   The clearing of the snow from
about half a mile of track during one winter cost the
Dry Dock Company nearly $2000.   The average cost
of cars is about $900, and of horses about $150.   A
car rarely lasts more than three years, the cost of repairing amounting to nearly the original outlay in that
time.   The average life of a railroad horse is about
five years, and very often several horses will be in hospital at a time, disease or accident rendering them
unfit for duty.   Horses have often been lamed by sew-
ing-machine needles and hoop-skirts, which were left
on the track.   In times of epidemic disease among
horses, the large numbers that are congregated in railroad stables cause it to spread rapidly, and to prevent
the regular running of the cars.   These are only a few
of the many difficulties which the managers of street
railroads must meet.   The open or excursion cars
have to be in the storehouse about seven months of
the year, as they can only be used during the warm
months.   About one-fifth of the entire stock of cars is
idle during the whole year.   The cost of shoeing horses
is also an important matter of expense, aggregating for
all the roads in the city over $500,000 per year.   The
number of nails used in shoeing amounts annually to
hundreds of millions.

Since the opening of the Elevated roads the receipts
and profits of the leading surface lines have been
greatly reduced, but still all continue to be operated at
a profit, and some of the horse roads which run along
the streets occupied by their aerial rivals are beginning to experience a return of their old prosperity.

As a rule, the horse-cars are not nice. Some of the lines run clean and handsome cars, but the majority of these vehicles are dirty, badly ventilated, and full of vermin. In the winter the floor is covered with straw, as a protection from the cold; but this soon becomes foul, and constitutes an intolerable nuisance.

All sorts of people are met on the street cars, and a crowded car is a favorite place for pickpockets to ply their trade. These generally work in parties of two or three, to render detection difficult and escape easy.

THE THIRD AVENUE DEPOT.

The drivers and conductors are often brutal wretches, and insult and maltreat their passengers in a manner that would be incredible, were not the facts so well attested. Many, on the other hand, are honest and courteous. All are overworked and poorly paid. They are on duty about fifteen or sixteen hours out of twenty-four, and have no holidays, unless they choose to forfeit a day's pay. The drivers receive from $2.25 to $2.75, and the conductors from $2 to $2.50 per diem.

The lot of a horse car conductor is a peculiar one, and his life stands apart from that of most men. While there is considerable monotony about it—and to the outsider who sees only the bell-punch and the bell-rope it seems all monotony—it is, after all, a decidedly novel career.   The conductor has his joys and sorrows; his life is made up of shadow and sunshine, and humor and pathos mark the round of his daily duties, as is the case with all of us.   The story of one conductor is very much the story of all.   While they fare better on some lines and worse on others, take them right through and the narrative has but slight variation.   Jump on any car and talk with any of them, and the similarity of their circumstances strikes you at once.   The story told by one of them not long since is the story of all, and his epitome of his accustomed association is an epitome of them all.   It was told amid the roar of the street and the jingle of the bells; it was interrupted by passengers and the collection of fares; it was renewed while waiting at the depot, but taken as a whole it was somewhat as follows:—

"You want a sort of running account of my daily work and what is required of us when we first go on the road? Well, we have to furnish our suits. If it is summer time the suit costs us from $14 to $16, while the winter apparel is worth several dollars more. Then we have to procure an overcoat, and some of us are required to make a deposit on the bell-punch. Of course that is repaid us whenever we leave.   Then we must have a watch, and one that will keep good time. We have to regulate our watches by the large clock in the depot, and any variation makes it all the more difficult for us to run on time.   Our clothes must be kept clean, and we are expected always to present a neat appearance and get down to the depot in the morning about five minutes before our car starts.   The mats, which I took up the night before and which the driver has shaken, I put in their places.   And just here let me say that we are compelled to keep our car clean and have the windows washed whenever they need it.   I sweep out the car the last thing at night and before running in with the other cars, in order to avoid scattering dust over them.   I am supposed to have full control over the car, and the driver is, to a certain extent, under me.   If there is any trouble between us we can make it unpleasant for each other, but I have the privilege to report any misconduct or disobedience, and the conductor is generally sustained.

"Before starting out I take a certain amount in change, which is charged against me by the cashier. Some men turn their cash in at the end of each trip, but most of us wait until night, and hand the account for the entire day in at once.   At the close of every trip I make out my report, specifying on this card the amount.   As a general thing, my account comes out square, but once in a while I find myself out a few cents. It is rare that I find a surplus in my favor.   Occasionally I will give too little change, or mistake one of those twenty-cent pieces for a quarter, thus cheating the passenger, but usually the other way.   For a long time we were sold on those twenty-cent coins, and learned to be cautious.   Then once in awhile, when the car is full and we are making change rapidly, a three-cent piece or one of those small half-dimes will get in between other change which we hand to a passenger. Of course we are 'docked' in those cases. The same way with counterfeit money—we have to run the risk and bear the loss. I got stuck on a five dollar note not long ago. The receiver handed it back to me the next day and charged me with it. I had to get rid of it as best I could. They are pretty lenient with us, however, and we do not often suffer.

"There is a difference as to the time given for meals and stops by the lines. I have about two minutes at the lower end of the trip and from seven to fourteen at the upper. In the evening we get from fifteen to twenty. About fifteen minutes is allowed us for meals— that is, we have that time between trips at noon and night, but if we are behind time that is taken off and we have so much less to eat in. We generally manage to have full time, however, for eating. Our meals are brought us by our children or wives, and are placed in the conductors' room at the depot. Some of the men live close enough to run home and get a bite. We get very little time to see our families, I tell you, except when we get our day off. Some of the roads let you have whatever day you ask for, and supply your place with one of the extras. An "extra" is a man who is substituted, and generally has been taken off the regular force for disobeying orders. Slight disobedience, such as neglect to clean your car, often places you on the extra list, while gross carelessness will discharge you. You get no pay on your holidays, while you are paid from $2.00 to $2.50 a day while on duty. The "trip-pers," as those men are called who only run three-quarters of a day, get $1.50. I know the pay is not so poor, compared with many other occupations, but then we have so little time to ourselves, or for sleep. I only get five hours a day sleep, and I am terribly tired when the work is over. It is very hard to awaken me in the morning, so soundly do I sleep. All the chance we get to sit down is between trips or on this board seat, which we pay for ourselves, and that is not over comfortable, as you can see.

"Our life is pretty monotonous, and yet all sorts of scenes occur to give it variety. If it was not for that, I could not stand it, and so most of the men say. We have all kinds of people, and articles of every description travel with us. The washerwoman gets on with her basket of clothes; the tailor brings in a bundle; the emigrant rides with a big bag or small trunk; the lady has a dozen small packages, and the caterer carries dainties for a party. Now and then a funny thing happens that sets the car in a roar of laughter. A man got in the morning after the election in Indiana and Ohio and purchased a paper. When he read the result, he rolled the paper up and fired it the length of the car, narrowly missing a dozen heads and striking a small boy with a pail of milk here on the platform. A German got on board the other day, who could not speak a word of English. Fortunately, I understand German a little, and was able to make out that he wanted to get out at Twenty-second street. When we reached there I told him, putting my hand up to pull the bell, as he had several immense bundles. He shook his head and drew my hand back, so we went on. I tried to find out what he meant, but he laughed and said nothing. Suddenly, when we were moving quite fast, he gathered up his luggage, shook hands with me, and before I could comprehend his movements, jumped off. He turned over and over, his bundles flew in every direction and his hat rolled into the gutter. At first I thought he was hurt, but he sat up in the street, kissed his hand to me, and laughed loud enough to be heard a block off.

"We conductors have our annoyances also. It is hard to tell who worry us the most, but I guess the women do. Some of them are so nervous and fidgety, never knowing where they want to go, and asking every minute if we have reached there. They get out on the platform before the car stops, and often have to be held back from jumping off. They start out to shop sometimes, and forget their purses. After riding a block or two they suddenly discover the lack of money, and either declare there are pickpockets in the car or else are in tribulation lest we will put them off right away. On rainy days we have to raise their umbrellas and wait for them to get their dresses adjusted. Then those of them who go marketing bring huge baskets, which we have to lift on and off. Still, we ought to be courteous, and I think most of us are, though the ladies do not often take the pains to thank us for any extra attention. The worst lot we have to deal with are the young clerks and store boys, who ride regularly back and forth from business. They put on any quantity of airs and try to occupy the entire car. One of them always sits out here on my seat, even though there is plenty of room inside. They smoke when they shouldn't, and then want to know when the rule was made prohibiting it. They get in the way, jostle the other passengers, declare we do not give them the right change, and make themselves disagreeable generally. The newsboys are forbidden on many of the cars after nine o'clock in the morning, yet persist in jumping on after that time. The small boy steals a ride while we are forward in the car, and rainy days we get thoroughly drenched, particularly if the storm beats down the street. Only now and then are we able to stand inside and avoid the wet. Then we have the chronic grumblers—men and women—who want the windows up and down at the same time. We put them up, and some lady begins to shiver and some man turns up his coat-collar and looks daggers at us; we put them down, and at once there are complaints that the air is stifling. Then there are those who annoy us by charging that they left articles in the cars, very valuable in most cases, which we have taken, but which, strange to say, are generally found at home or in some store. I might mention the drunken characters and the noisy ones who ride with us, but the list I have named embraces the majority of troublesome persons.

"We cannot complain generally of bad treatment by the companies. They relieve us when we are sick, allow us a day to ourselves, and pay what they promise. Many of us are sorry we ever took the position, for an entirely different reason, and that is, that the place is regarded as a degrading one by so many, and we are excluded socially because of our occupation. Some of us are of good families, but the hard times compelled us to do anything that would secure us a competence and was not actually disreputable. Yet we are mostly looked down upon."

The practice of "knocking down" is carried on very extensively on the horse car lines, and the companies suffer heavily by it. They take every precaution to secure good men, and have a thorough system of espionage at work to detect and stop the dishonest practice. Their spies are constantly traveling over the road and note the number of passengers carried on the cars they are appointed to watch, and when the conductor's report is handed in, they examine it, and report any inaccuracies. The conductor, it is said, often divides the stolen money with the spy, or "spotter," as he is called, and thus secures his silence. He has also to buy the driver's co-operation, and this costs him from $1 to $2 a day, and the driver has to pay the stablemen for a similar purpose. Even the bell punch fails to put a stop to the nefarious practice. Some time ago, coming down town on a car of one of the principal lines, a gentleman asked the driver after a conductor who formerly had charge of the car, and was a very popular man with the passengers on the road.

"Where is he now?" asked the gentleman.

"Discharged."

"What for?"

"Stealing," answered the driver, with complacency. "They don't keep a conductor a minute after they catch him at it."

"But I thought they had put a stop to that sort of thing."

"Bah! they can't stop it, and on a quiet road like this, it's worse than on the big roads. Half the conductors on this line make $3 or $4 a day above their wages. I know it, because I watch 'em. When a conductor gives a driver $1 a day, you can bet he has made three times as much. The bell punches, eh? They're no good. I'll tell you how it's done, and you can see it yourself if you watch. Suppose a man got off the rear platform just as you got on here. The conductor takes your fare and don't mark it on the punch. If there is a "counter" on the car at the time, the conductor knows it and he marks the fare. He gets to know most of 'em. But if he took your fare, as I said, and a counter got on afterward, the counter would not find out anything. There would be as many passengers in the car as the punch indicated, and that's the only thing the conductors have to look out for. Oh! it's easy enough when you know how to do it. Git up there!"

CHAPTER XIV

SIXTH AVENUE

RAPID ADVANCE OF SIXTH AVENUE IN PROSPERITY—DESCRIPTION OF THE STREET—THE LOWER PORTION—THE TENEMENT HOUSES—FRENCH FLATS—THE ELEVATED RAILROAD AND ITS STATIONS—A BUSY SCENE—SIXTH-AVENUE STORES—"MACEY'S"—THE JEFFERSON MARKET POLICE COURT—BOOTH'S THEATRE—THE MASONIC TEMPLE—"THE TABERNACLE"—SIXTH AVENUE BY NIGHT—A CHANGE OF SCENE—THE STREET-WALKERS—BRAZEN VICE—THE FRENCH WOMEN—SNARING A VICTIM—SHAMEFUL SCENES ON THE AVENUE—THE STREET A TERROR TO DECENT PEOPLE—THE ROUGHS—SIXTH-AVENUE OYSTER HOUSES AND BEER SALOONS—SCENE IN A FLASH SALOON—A YOUTHFUL CRIMINAL—THE DETECTIVE'S PRIZE—SIXTH AVENUE AFTER MIDNIGHT—A DRUNKEN SINGER—"IN THE SWEET BYE-AND-BYE"—NO EFFORT MADE TO CHECK THE EVIL.

Of late years Sixth avenue has come prominently before the public as one of the most noted streets of the great city. It commences at the northern end of Carmine street, and runs northward to 59th street. At this point it is broken by the Central Park, but commences again at 110th street, the northern boundary of the Park, and pursues its northward course to the Harlem River. It is traversed from its southern extremity to the Park by the Metropolitan Elevated Railroad, and below the arcade formed by this structure run the horse-cars of the Sixth-Avenue Railroad Company, the northern terminus of which is 59th street. The avenue is solidly built up below the Park, and ranks next to Broadway as a business street, being devoted to the retail trade. In the lower part are a number of tenement-houses, but above 34th street the upper floors of the buildings are laid off in "French flats," some of which are elegant and stylish. For miles on both sides of the street are handsome retail stores, some of which are elegant and extensive enough to merit a place on Broadway.   The sidewalks are always filled with throngs of purchasers, drawn here by the fine display of goods and the prevailing belief that Sixth avenue prices are lower than those of Broadway. All through the day the street is bright and lively, and the rapid passage of the trains on the Elevated railroad overhead adds greatly to the interest of the scene.   At 14th street is one of the handsomest stations of the Elevated road, and on the corners of this street and the avenue are "Macey's" and several other popular stores.   "Macey's" is a world in itself, the most perfect Noah's ark in the land.   You can find in it everything, from the simplest toys for children to dress goods of the most costly kind.   The crowd at this part of the avenue is always greatest, and is generally composed of richly and fashionably-attired ladies and children; and both streets are frequently almost blocked by the long lines of elegant carriages standing in them and awaiting their owners.

Several handsome buildings front on Sixth avenue. The first of these is the Jefferson Market Police Court, a new and unique edifice, constructed of red brick, with sandstone trimmings, in the Italian Gothic style. It is one of the most noted edifices in New York, and stands on the site of one of the most disgraceful rookeries that ever shamed the metropolis.   On the southeast corner of 23d street is a noble edifice, built of Concord granite, in the rennaissance style.   This is the superb theatre, built twelve years ago by Edwin Booth, as a fitting house for the drama in New York. It is still known as Booth's Theatre.   Immediately opposite, on the northeast corner of 23d street, is the Ma-

sonic Temple, also built of granite, and one of the most
elegant and tasteful buildings in the city. At the
northeast corner of 34th street is the Tabernacle Baptist Church, a handsome edifice of brownstone. Between 40th and 42d streets, on the east side of the
avenue, is Reservoir Park, a charming enclosure occupying the site of the famous Crystal Palace, which was
destroyed by fire nearly thirty years ago.

MASONIC TEMPLE, SIXTH AVENUE AND 23D STREET.

When the darkness settles down over the city, and
the lamps flare out along the street, and the broad rays
of light stream brightly into the open air from the
stores, restaurants, and saloons, Sixth avenue under-
goes a transformation. All day it has been crowded
with the best of New York's people, intent upon honest business. Now the crowd is almost as great, but
it is of a different character. The larger, and better
class stores are closed; only the smaller retail shops,

the drug stores, the saloons, restaurants, and tobacconists remain open, but these are numerous enough to give a brilliant coloring to the street with their bright lights and elaborately-decorated windows. The many-colored lights of the stations of the Elevated Railroad lend another attractive feature to the scene, and the whirl and roar of the brilliantly-illuminated trains, as they whiz by overhead, give to the street an air of life and bustle in keeping with the movements of the crowd on the sidewalk below.

Among the promenaders are scores of young women, flashily dressed, with bold, brazen faces, plentifully covered with rouge and enamel, which show plainly under the bright glare of the gas-lamps. They are simply street-walkers, of the worst class, and are boldly plying their trade in the very faces of the police. They do not conduct themselves here with the outward propriety they are forced to assume on Broadway, but are loud-voiced and foul-tongued. They do not hesitate to accost men, and too often succeed in inducing them to accompany them to one of the dance-houses, or "gardens," which abound in the side streets, and in whose pay these women are. Once there, the wretched victim is asked to treat, and begins a course of hard drinking with the girl, who, on her part, manages to drink but little, and this is kept up until he is in fit condition for her to lead him further on into the depths of sin, and perhaps to robbery and death. It is but a step from the dance-hall to one of the vile dens, where certain robbery, and perhaps violence, awaits the victim; and the girl is an old hand at her trade.

Many of these women are French, and can scarcely

speak English at all; yet, strange to say, they are among the most successful in the practice of their abandoned calling. They know enough, however, to say, "You come wiz me, my love;" "You treat me;" "I take a leetle beer;" "Fife dollar," and similar phrases. Some of the women have reputable employments during the day, but these pay them beggarly wages, and they supply their wants by resorting to their horrid trade by night. Of late years they have become so numerous on the avenue that decent people, especially females, cannot venture on the street unless accompanied by a male protector. Even then they are in constant hearing of vile oaths and foul expressions from the lips of members of their own sex. Should a woman, unaccompanied by a man, attempt to pass along the avenue between 14th and 34th streets, after night, she is almost sure to be insulted by some of the ruffians who parade the street, hang around the barrooms, or stand on the corners, and who are hand and glove with the street-walkers. You see them stand in groups around a party of abandoned women on the sidewalk, exchanging ribald jests with them, and should you pause to listen, you would hear words spoken openly and loudly that would make your ears tingle.

All along the avenue are saloons of more than doubtful character, and oyster-houses in which no decent person ever sets foot. These are favorite resorts with the street-walkers and their companions, and rallying places for the ruffians that lend the girls their protection and live upon the wretched earnings of the women. In these resorts, says a writer in the *Police Gazette*, "you see the rough, intoxicated elements of

METROPOLITAN ELEVATED RAILROAD STATION, SIXTH AVENUE AND FOURTEENTH STREET.

Sixth avenue. Girls lounge about in the midst of the smoke; do not hesitate to sit on the laps of gentlemen, and are always ready for one of the foaming glasses of beer which are pyramidally carried about by the ubiquitous waiters. There are many young men being ruined here. While we look on, an episode occurs that illuminates the whole subject as a flash of lightning does a gloomy wood.

"At one of the tables has been sitting, with two girls of the town, a handsome boy of about eighteen years. The rose of health is still on his cheek, and, although the gin and water he has been drinking have given his eyes a false lustre, you can easily see that he hasn't gone far on the road. His vital organs are healthy. How about his moral tone?

"Directly back of him sits a silent and apparently abstracted individual, who has gone to such depths in a brown study that the glass of beer before him is as yet untasted, although it has been there ten minutes.

"The youth gives the waiter a twenty-dollar bill, and his companions exchange glances. Just as the proprietor thrusts it into the drawer, the detective—for the abstracted man is none other—reaches over the bar, utters a few words, and takes the note and examines it. His suspicions are correct. It is a marked bill, marked that day in the down-town office where the unfortunate boy is employed. It is quite a tableau when the arrest is made. He turns pale as a ghost, and then goes out with an attempt at bravery and carelessness that is pitiable to behold. As for the women, in ten minutes they are drinking more beer, at the expense of some one else.

"At about two A. M. the avenue is not so crowded as at midnight, but its life is more intense. The old 'Argyle Rooms,' 'Cremorne,' and 'Buckingham' have vomited forth their crowds of dancers. They flood the oyster saloons, and fill the beer shops with the rustle of silken skirts.

"In one beer saloon a negro band is in full blast. When they stop to pass around the hat, a tipsy young woman, bantered to it by her companions, goes to the piano and sings, 'In the Sweet Bye-and-Bye.' It is a strange, sad scene. She is handsome, but undeniably drunk. Her hair is disheveled. As she sings, being at the maudlin state of drinking, the song overmasters her with its pathos, and she breaks off abruptly and begins to cry.

"At this the 'lovers,' petty gamblers, and 'strikers' gradually break into a coarse laugh. The poor girl falls, sobbing, with her head on the table, robbed even of the sympathy of her drunken companions, while the 'negro' band squares matters with the audience by giving 'I've Just Been Down to the Club, Dear.'"

These wretched scenes last until "the wee sma' hours" of the morning. Then there is a brief period of silence and darkness in the avenue, and with the dawning day all signs of sin and vice have disappeared. Sixth avenue puts on its respectable dress, and until sunset devotes itself to legitimate and reputable business. The avenue is strongly policed, both day and night, yet the "cops" have neither eyes for the shameful sights nor ears for the vile sounds we have described. The city authorities are perfectly aware of the character of the street, and the business

of its promenaders by night, but they make no effort
to correct the evil.   The ruffians who stand behind the
street-walkers as " backers," and who live upon their
wretched gains, have political influence, and can command votes.   Therefore the municipal authorities stand
aloof.   They are afraid to touch the fearful sore.
Their interference might lose votes for their party, and
so they permit one of the best and most attractive
thoroughfares of the Metropolis to remain the " stamping ground" of vice and crime.

CHAPTER XV

COACHING DAY

MEMORIES OF BYGONE DAYS—STAGE COACHING IN FORMER YEARS—REVIVAL OF COACHING IN NEW YORK—COLONEL KANE'S ENTERPRISE—THE "TALLY HO"—A HANDSOME SUCCESS—SOCIETY ADOPTS COACHING AS THE "CORRECT THING"—THE COACHING CLUB ORGANIZED—COACHING DAY—THE ANNUAL PARADE—A BRILLIANT SIGHT.

Many of the readers of these pages will remember the old fashioned stage coach, which, before the advent of the railways, was the sole means of travel between the various parts of the country. It had its disadvantages, but its pleasures were also numerous and decided. The time was slow, the company small, and the road often rough and tedious, but the passengers were generally sociable, and on long journeys pleasant acquaintances were made and lasting friendships often formed. The very slowness of the ponderous vehicle gave one an opportunity of enjoying to the utmost the beautiful scenery through which the route lay. And the inns at which the coach stopped for meals, what delightful, rambling old structures they were, and what tempting repasts they spread for the hungry passengers, with the hearty old landlord hovering about the table to see that his guests were well supplied and comfortable. Then the traveler was not worried out of his life by the announcement "twenty minutes for refreshments," and did not have to choke down a few mouthfuls of badly cooked eatables, with a certainty of the horrors of dyspepsia looming up before him; but instead he had abundant time to do justice to a repast fit for a prince, nicely and cleanly served, and could resume his place in the coach with a tranquil mind and a full stomach, and be prepared to enjoy at his ease the ride through the clear, fresh air and the smiling country. Well, they have all passed away, the coaches, the inns, the landlords, and the square meals. The iron horse and the railway restaurant have taken their places. Yet those who have enjoyed the pleasures of the past look back at them regretfully, and wonder, with a sigh, if we are any more comfortable, after all, than we were in those slow, old fashioned days.

Of late years New York fashionable society has undertaken to revive in some measure the memories of the past, and the result of the effort is seen in the "Coaching Club," whose annual parade is one of the sights of the great city, and an eagerly anticipated and much enjoyed feature of fashionable life.

The Coaching Club owes its existence to Colonel Delancey Kane, a New York gentleman of wealth. It has long been the "style" in London for the young gentlemen of the aristocracy to kill a part of the time that hangs so heavily on their hands, by becoming amateur Jehus, and driving four-in-hand coaches from designated points in the city to fixed destinations in the country. They carry passengers and parcels over the route at the regular coach fares, and as a rule manage to reap a neat little sum, as well as to extract a great deal of pleasure from the performance.

In 1875 Colonel Delancey Kane, being in the British Metropolis, adopted the practice of his "high-toned" associates, and during the summer of that year drove a coach regularly from London to Windsor Forest.

Returning home, he resolved to introduce the practice
into New York, and thus become a benefactor of society by giving it a new sensation. Accordingly, in
the summer of 1876, the "Tally-Ho," the first four-in-
hand coach, made its appearance in Fifth avenue, with
Colonel Kane, its owner, as driver. It was imported
from London, and was elegant and luxurious. Promptly
at eleven o'clock in the morning the "Tally-Ho"
started from the Hotel Brunswick, at Fifth avenue and
Madison Square, and took the route up the avenue to
59th street, through the Central Park, thence to Mc-
Comb's Dam Bridge, over the Harlem River to the
mainland, and from that point to Pelham Bridge, in
Westchester County, which was reached promptly at
one o'clock. At half past three the return trip began,
over the same route, and at five the coach drew up before the Hotel Brunswick. The fare for the round
trip was three dollars, with an extra charge of fifty
cents each way for a seat on the box. Passengers'
luggage, up to eighty-five pounds, was carried free.
Parcels were taken at moderate rates, and were delivered with care and punctuality. The fares for inter-
mediate distances were at proportionate rates, and the
coach took up and set down passengers and parcels
at any point except between Madison Square and the
Central Park. The route lay through a delightful
country, abounding in picturesque scenery, and the
drive was highly enjoyable.

The "Tally-Ho" was a success from the start.
Fashionable society greeted it heartily as a new diver-
sion, and patronized it liberally. Every day it was
filled with parties of gayly-dressed ladies and gentle-

men, representing the greatest wealth and the highest society of the city. Drawn by four magnificent brown steeds, the coach rattled along the avenue, through the Park, and over the pleasant country roads, and its occupants, in the highest spirits, found the drive all too short for their pleasure. It became the correct thing to ride on the "Tally-Ho," and its proprietor was literally besieged by applications for places. Seats were engaged weeks in advance, and the season·proved not only a brilliant one from a fashionable standpoint, but a very handsome financial success for its projector.

The success of Colonel Kane encouraged other gentlemen of wealth and fashion to attempt the same thing, and soon a number of four-in-hand coaches were to be seen bowling through the streets, the ribbons in the hands of "swells" who had never before known harder labor than treading the mazes of the German, or handling a billiard-cue. Four-in-hand driving became quite the rage, and in 1876 the owners of the coaches organized the "Coaching Club," which at present has a membership of twenty-six, representing twenty-one coaches.

The club is made up principally of young men of wealth and fashion. No one is eligible for membership unless he is the owner of at least one-fourth of a coach, or "drag," as the vehicle is called. Candidates must be proposed and seconded by two members of the club, and voted for by sealed ballot. One negative ballot in ten excludes. The club is very careful as to the admission of new members, for Plutus is the ruling divinity here.

The members of the club are uniformed. The dress

consists of a dark-green cut-away coat, with brass buttons, and a yellow, striped waistcoat. Pants are *ad
libitum*, though generally they are like the coat in color,
but a high white hat is the "tip of the style." The
evening dress is of the same materials and colors, cut
like the conventional evening dress. The annual dues
are ten dollars, and the ostensible object of the club
is to "encourage four-in-hand driving."

The annual parade of the club is held on the last
Saturday in May, and is known in society as "Coaching Day." It calls forth a general turnout of the fashionables, and the scene along the avenue and at the
entrance to the Park is brilliant and interesting. The
"meet" is always at the Hotel Brunswick, which is
gayly decorated for the occasion. The coaches are
drawn up in line, led by the "turn-out" of the president
of the club, and the route is up Fifth avenue to 59th
street; through the Park to Mount St. Vincent; back
to the avenue; down that street to Washington Square,
and then along the avenue again to the Hotel Brunswick, where the parade is dismissed. Then follows
the annual club dinner at the hotel. The avenue and
Park drives are lined with carriages and equestrians,
and the windows of the mansions along the route are
filled with bright and smiling faces. The fashionable
world is out in all its strength, and is reinforced by
crowds of dwellers in the less select circles of the city.
The throng is so great, that along the entire route the
procession is obliged to pursue a slow and stately
pace. This enables the richly-dressed ladies who fill
the seats of the "drags" to show their millinery to
greater advantage. Care is taken by the fair riders

COACHING DAY IN CENTRAL PARK.

to make the colors of their dresses harmonize with the prevailing tints of the coaches, and each turn-out, as it flashes by, is a study in form, color, and grace of movement. The avenue and the Park drives at such times are musical with the long-drawn notes of the horns of the outriders of the coaches, and the clear, soft sky of the May afternoon gives a glow to the scene that greatly heightens its beauty.

"Truly "Coaching Day" is an enjoyable occasion, both to those who take part in the performance and to the lookers-on. Colonel Kane well deserves the thanks of society for his efforts, for he has not only given it a new sensation, but a healthful and innocent pleasure.

During the season the "drags" may be seen daily on the avenue, or in the Park, and at the races they form a prominent feature of the scene.

CHAPTER XVI

THE STREETS OF NEW YORK

MADISON AVENUE—MILES OF BROWN STONE—PARK AVENUE—LEXINGTON AVENUE—THIRTY-
FOURTH AND FIFTY-SEVENTH STREETS—MAGNIFICENT RESIDENCES—THIRD AVENUE THE
GREAT HIGHWAY OF THE EAST SIDE—EIGHTH AVENUE THE SMALL TRADERS' PARADISE—THE
SATURDAY NIGHT MARKET—TWENTY-THIRD AND FOURTEENTH STREETS—DISAPPEARANCE OF
LANDMARKS—CHANGES IN THE CHARACTER OF THE STREETS—A GLANCE AT TWENTY-THIRD
STREET TO-DAY—"THE BEGGARS' PARADISE"—STREET CHARACTERS—A YOUNG IMPOSTOR—
KICKED FROM A HORSE CAR INTO A HOME—BLEECKER STREET—LIFE IN BOHEMIA—A STREET
WHERE NO QUESTIONS ARE ASKED—GRAND STREET—CHATHAM STREET—THE CHILDREN OF
ISRAEL AND THEIR WAYS—FULTON STREET—NASSAU STREET—A CROWDED NEIGHBORHOOD—
PECULIARITIES OF THE STREET—PINE STREET—AMONG THE MONEYED MEN—WEST AND
SOUTH STREETS—ALONG THE WATER SIDE—BUSY SCENES.

Elsewhere we have described the principal thoroughfares of New York at length. In this chapter we propose to glance briefly at some of the prominent streets
of the city, of which the limits of this work do not
allow such extended notice.

The street immediately east of Fifth avenue is Madison avenue, the fashionable rival of the former
thoroughfare. Begining at 23d street, it extends in an
unbroken line to the Harlem River. At the lower end
of the avenue, from 23d to 26th streets, is Madison
Square, described elsewhere. From 23d to 59th street,
a distance of about two miles, Madison avenue is built
up as handsomely as Fifth avenue. The dwellings are
chiefly of brownstone, and rival the Fifth avenue mansions in external and internal splendor. Stately
churches and splendid club houses break the line of
dwellings, and give an air of picturesqueness to the
street. There is not so much travel here as on Fifth
avenue, and the street, therefore, constitutes a pleasanter dwelling place than its more famous rival.

Immediately east of Madison avenue is Park avenue. This name is applied to the portion of Fourth avenue lying between 34th and 42d streets. It occupies the centre of Murray Hill, and is one of the most ultra fashionable sections of the city. The mansions which line the street are among the handsomest in New York, some of them being especially noted for the beauty of their designs. Park avenue is built over the tunnel by which the line of the Fourth avenue railroad is carried through Murray Hill from 34th to 42d street, and is the widest of all the fashionable thoroughfares. In the centre of the street is a succession of small, handsome, enclosed parks, from which the avenue takes its name, planted with flowers and shrubbery, which give to the street a pleasant and somewhat rural aspect. Each of these individually is a city square in length, and is pierced with a grated aperture, through which light and air are supplied to the tunnel below. A fine roadway runs on each side of the enclosures, and affords ample room for the travel of the street. The avenue is noted for its exclusiveness. Being so short, and being already occupied, there is no room for new comers.

Lexington avenue, commencing at 14th street and lying midway between Third and Fourth avenues, is the next street east of Park avenue. It is broken at 20th street by Grammercy Park, which extends to 21st street, but above that street the avenue extends in an unbroken line to the Harlem River. From 14th street to Grammercy Park it is known as Irving Place. It is handsomely built, brownstone being the prevailing material. The lower part, around and above Gram-

COOPER INSTITUTE AND ELEVATED RAILROAD. THIRD AVENUE.

mercy Park is occupied by the residences of families of wealth and fashion, but the upper part makes little claim to social distinction. It is a pleasant residence street, and one of the cleanest in the city.

34th and 57th streets are lined for several squares, east and west of Fifth avenue, with palatial mansions, and are among the ultra fashionable thoroughfares. Indeed, nearly all the cross streets above 34th, and between Lexington and Sixth avenues, are magnificently built, and are included within the limits of the world of fashion. Many of these streets, within the boundaries named, are built up solidly with splendid mansions which would do credit even to Fifth avenue.

The Third avenue begins at 9th street, where it joins the Bowery, and runs in a straight line to the Harlem River at 130th street. It is six miles in length, and has always been the principal thoroughfare of the east side of the island. It is now traversed by the Elevated Railroad and a line of horse cars, each of which transport enormous numbers of passengers daily. It is almost entirely built up from end to end, and is devoted to small retail stores, whose aggregate business represents a gigantic traffic. Along its entire length it has not a single building of prominence, and the street has an aspect of sameness and monotony that is not to be found in the west side thoroughfares. But saloons and tenement houses abound, and the upper portions of the houses are occupied by several families, each having but a single floor. Of late years a number of cheap apartment houses have been erected along the upper part of the avenue, and are occupied by families of small means.

The Sixth avenue has been noticed elsewhere.

The Eighth avenue is to the west side, what the Third is to the east. It commences at Greenwich street and Abingdon Square, and extends to the Harlem River, about six miles distant. Like Third avenue it is devoted to small retail dealers, whose transactions, though insignificant in themselves, make up an enormous aggregate. It is the paradise of the Jews, and cheap jewelry and clothing stores abound. It is poorly built, the only building of prominence on the avenue being the Grand Opera House at the corner of 23d street. In many portions of the street the stock in trade of the dealers overflows the stores, and is displayed in stands along the sidewalk. The street is always crowded, and the sidewalk dealers appear to drive a thriving trade. On Saturday night the avenue at 42d street presents a curious sight. Numerous wagons are ranged along the curbstones, and stands are erected along the sidewalk. These stretch out into 42d street to the westward, and each is brightly illuminated with blazing lights which even a strong wind cannot extinguish. Fruits, oysters, fish, game, provisions of all kinds, are sold here by licensed venders, and for this one night of the week a general market is held, which is patronized by vast numbers of the people living near, especially the poorer classes. In the neighborhood of 59th street a number of large "Apartment Houses" are springing up. From 59th to 110th street Eighth avenue forms the western boundary of the Central Park, and above the park it is sparsely built up, being lined mainly with market gardens. It is traversed along its entire length by a line of horse cars, and from about 112th street to 155th, at the Harlem River, the middle of the street is occupied by the Metropolitan Elevated Railroad.

Twenty-third and 14th streets are broad, handsome thoroughfares, extending across the island from river to river. Twenty years ago they were the chosen seats of wealth and fashion, and from Broadway westward were lined with superb mansions. Now they are busy, bustling marts of trade. The old mansions have disappeared, and in their places stand huge iron, marble, and stone structures, devoted to the various branches of the retail trade. Dry goods, furniture, millinery, sewing-machines, and musical instruments, are the trades chiefly to be found on 14th street. Scarcely a vestige of the old street remains, and those who, twenty years ago, thought it the perfection of a residence street, would fail to recognize it, so thoroughly has it gone over to trade.

Twenty-third street retained its private character longer than 14th. In bygone days it was one of the most fashionable promenades of the city. On sunny mornings, nurses with infants in their arms, and children with hoops, go-carts and toys, monopolized the sidewalks; elegantly-attired ladies sauntered along; and splendid equipages stood before the stately mansions, while their mistresses paid calls within. There was no haste, no bustle. Although so near Broadway, the street was peaceful and quiet. Now the omnibuses and the street cars, and countless wagons, trucks, and peddler's carts make the place a very Babel.

Twenty-third street presents quite a bizarre appearance, from Broadway to Eighth avenue. Here are hotels, express offices, theatres, beer saloons, restaurants, rum shops, French flats, dry goods stores, stables, churches, undertakers' warehouses, and a large music garden, where concerts are given and beer drank nightly.   The high rents of Broadway have done much to bring about this condition of things ; but, more than this, the gradual progress of trade, and the overcrowding of the stores along the line of the surface roads, have effected the changes.   Most of all, however, it is due to the establishment of the Elevated Railroads, which bring the two extremities of the city within half an hour's distance of each other, and make 23d street the natural half-way stopping-place for shoppers and sight-seers.

There are nearly a score of refreshment saloons in Twenty-third street, between Broadway and Eighth avenue, ranging from the pretentious hotel and club house to the simple bar for beer.   Billiard rooms and Masonic lodges abound, boot-black stands decorate every corner, and dry goods are exhibited in the modest thread and needle shops as well as in palatial warehouses that cost half a million of dollars.   Trotting stables and theatres are near neighbors, and some of the finest residences in the city have been turned into flats for milliners, dentists, and barbers.   For some reason the theatres in Twenty-third street have always had but a shaky existence.   Two of them will live in local history; one as the scene of a monumental dramatic failure, the other as the place where financial giants fought for supremacy in one of the great railroads of the world.

Twenty-third and Fourteenth street constitute the

"Beggars' Paradise," the former by day and the latter
by night. The same cripples, hand-organ men, Italian
men and women, and professional boy beggars who
infest Twenty-third street by day change their quarters
to Fourteenth street, when the darkness settles down

PLEASE GIVE ME A PENNY.

over the city, and the blaze of the electric lights bursts
forth over the latter thoroughfare.

These beggars constitute an intolerable nuisance,
and some of them are characters in their way. It is
noticeable that nearly all the professional beggars

have watchers and guardians near them. One very
old man, with a head as bald as a billiard ball, takes
his stand every day, hat in hand, near the residence of
a prominent city official on Twenty-third street, while
he challenges every passer by with the most piteous
looks. On the opposite side of the street, and generally in the calm retreat of a church, stands his "pal."
If business is good, the two now and then adjourn to
a cheap beer saloon in Sixth avenue, and lay out a
part of the receipts in drink. Another is a hideous
looking fellow with St. Vitus' dance, and a terribly
scarred face and mutilated hand. He pays more attention to ladies than to men. As one approaches he
begins to bow. Fastening his evil eyes upon her, he
bows and bows until she has passed. If she gives him
a coin, he returns a ghastly grin of gratitude. If she
bestows no notice upon him, the look of entreaty in
his face changes to a scowl of positive malignity. This
beggar's pal is a female, and the two can be seen frequently counting their spoils on Seventh avenue near
Twenty-second street. The most systematic beggar
of all is a man paralyzed from his waist downward.
He sits in a four-wheeled wagon, and is drawn to a
fresh station each day. He works the thoroughfare
between Fourth and Eighth avenue, on both sides.
He is a large, fine looking man, and so successfully
imposes an expression of melancholy into his large
eyes that the ladies cannot resist the impulse to pity
his misfortunes and reward his pertinacity. The
creature who wheels the wagon and watches the
contributors, is an elderly man with a vicious face.
He makes his companion settle up three or four times

a day, and is liberal with his oaths if his share does not equal the amount he expected.

The worst feature is the begging of children. They follow the passers-by with the greatest persistence, urging them to buy hair-pins, shawl-pins, matches, and a dozen other things for which they have no use. There are three well-known workers of the Twenty-third street cars, who are not over ten years old, one of them, in fact, being under seven. They adopt all manner of dodges and tricks and constitute a sore annoyance to the passengers. One rainy night, a little six year old child leaned against a tree between Sixth and Seventh avenues, and began to cry bitterly. His grief attracted the attention of a kind-hearted lady, who stopped and asked him what was the matter. His only reply was a fresh burst of tears. A crowd soon gathered, and the little rascal saw his opportunity. Taking from under his arm a package of evening papers, soaked through with the rain, he stated, in a voice choked with sobs, that he must sell these papers or be beaten when he returned home, and now the rain had ruined them, and nobody would buy them. Some generous person in the crowd at once took the papers, gave the lad a quarter, and told him to go home in peace. The young beggar was off like a flash as soon as he received the money, and was immediately joined by a companion who had been waiting for him, and together they proceeded to a cheap oyster house to enjoy a stew, and laugh over the tender-heartedness of the philanthropist who had so easily taken the bait.

Now and then a case of real distress occurs among

these professional child beggars, but not often, as the routes are carefully watched and guarded by the old hands, and intruders on "claims" are as summarily dealt with as they are in a western mining camp. One night last winter, when the keen wind whistled around the corner of Fifth avenue and Twenty-third street, a bob-tailed car was jolting along. On the little rear platform, curled up like a rat, was a very small boy, with a visorless cap. He was sound asleep, and the driving sleet was fast stiffening his ragged coat. With a slam and a bang, a well-dressed young snob inside shoved back the sliding door, and as he endeavored to get off, his foot unwittingly struck the drenched waif on the platform. With an oath at the delay, he kicked the sleeping child into the street, where good fortune rolled him beyond the track of the Broadway line, on which a Broome street car was bounding along. Before the lad had rubbed his sleepy eyes, the fine young gentleman was caught by the collar of his fur-lined ulster, and hauled to the corner where the stalwart policeman, who had seen the outrage, had laid the boy. The little fellow, more frightened by the "cop" than hurt by the fall, glanced around in alarm, and the offender was dismissed with a severe and well merited rebuke from the officer. The policeman eyed the lad quietly for awhile, and then asked what he was doing on the car platform. "I wa'nt doing nuthin," was the reply; "I was only sleepin'." "Why didn't you go home to sleep?" "Ain't got none." "Where do you live?" "Anywheres." "Have you had any supper?" "No." "Any breakfast?" "Plenty." "Where did you get it?" "In the box on Eighth avenue, just round the corner of Twenty-third street." "What did you eat?" "Tater peelins and a piece of sausage." "Have you a father or mother?" "Father's dead, and mother's on the Island. They never warn't no good, nohow." "Would you like some dinner?" "No, you don't. You can't catch me, my covey." "I don't wan't to catch you, I want to help you. Would you like some dinner?" "Would I like a dinner? Would I like forty bloody dinners? You just try me." He was given a dinner, and afterwards a bed in the station house. Subsequent inquiry by the police proved the truth of the little fellow's story, and he was kindly cared for, and a home secured for him. He may live to be a useful man, and may yet thank the well dressed ruffian who kicked him from want and beggary into the hands of a kind-hearted policeman.

Bleecker street is another of the noted thoroughfares of the great city. From the Bowery westward it is lined with rows of comfortable old fashioned dwellings, all of which speak of former glory and present distress. The street was at one time the chosen seat of the fashion and wealth of the city, and it was then that these stately old houses were built. Until the march of trade drove the fashionable world into Washington Square and Fifth avenue, to be the owner of a Bleecker street mansion was to be at the heighth of fashionable felicity. Now the buildings have been converted into stores, restaurants, and beer saloons, and the street is known as the headquarters of the Bohemian element of the city's population. Struggling artists, musicians, actresses, ballet girls, sewing women, all sorts of people who live by their wits, find homes here, and it is a queer looking crowd one meets on the sidewalks. The street cannot be said to be bad or even disreputable, but it is at the best a sort of doubtful neighborhood, which people with reputations to lose avoid. Life here is free from most of the restraints imposed elsewhere, and so long as the denizens of the neighborhood do not actually violate the law, they may do as they please. It is emphatically a street in which no questions are asked.

Grand street east of the Bowery is one of the busiest and liveliest in New York. It is devoted to the cheap dry goods and millinery trades, and does a thriving business. Some of the establishments are large and elegant, but the customers belong chiefly to the humbler walks of life. Occasionally a west side lady in search of a bargain comes into the street, but such visitors are rare. On Saturday night the street is in its glory. The stores are open until a late hour, and the colored lamps of the stores and blazing torches of the sidewalk hucksters' stands give to it the effect of a partial illumination. Shops and sidewalks are all thronged, and the air is alive with the sound of voices.

Chatham street, extending from Chatham Square to City Hall Square, has long been famous in the local history of New York. It is about a quarter of a mile in length, and narrow and dirty throughout. Near the City Hall Square are several cheap hotels and fair restaurants, but the remainder of the street is taken up with old clothes stores, cheap clothing stores, pawnbrokers' shops, beer saloons, dance-houses of the lowest description, and establishments of various kinds. The dealers in the street are nearly all Jews, the sharpest and most unscrupulous of their class, who do not hesitate to swindle their customers before their very eyes, and then call on the police to arrest their victims if they resist. The streets leading to the right and left run off to the Five Points and other similar localities, to which Chatham street is a worthy neighbor. Respectable people in New York avoid making purchases here, and the stranger would do well to follow their example. A heavy tide of travel passes through this wretched street. Several prominent lines of horse-cars find their way to the City Hall Square and the Post Office through it, and overhead the Third-avenue branch of the Elevated road whirls its crowded trains to and from the terminus opposite the City Hall.

Fulton street is the great artery through which the enormous stream of travel and traffic between New York and Brooklyn ebbs and flows. From Broadway to the Fulton Ferry, on the East River, it is always crowded with vehicles and pedestrians. It is well built, and contains a number of handsome business structures.

Nassau street runs parallel with Broadway, immediately east of it, and extends from Wall street to Printing-House Square. It is one of the narrowest streets in the city, and is built up with lofty houses, which shut out the sunlight and give it a dark and gloomy appearance. The roadway is so narrow that two vehicles can scarcely pass each other, and the sidewalks afford such little room, that half the passers through the street are obliged to take to the roadway. The southern end of the street is taken up with handsome bank and insurance buildings, generally of marble. The northern part contains numbers of old book stores, and is a favorite locality with the stationery trade. Real estate men and diamond merchants like the street, and dealers in watches and jewelry also have their head-quarters here, generally in the second stories of the houses. Each house appears to contain a little world within its four walls. The front, the stairways, and the walls of the vestibules are covered with scores of signs, setting forth the nature of the various pursuits carried on within. Enter one of these "offices," and you will find it a mere closet. Yet enormous rents are paid for them, and their occupants remain in them as long as possible, or until a fortunate change in their business sends them to better-arranged quarters. It has been said that Nassau street is a good place to hide in, and it would seem that in the thousand and one "estab-lishments" with which the tall buildings on the street are filled, one might very easily slip out of observation and be forgotten. You wonder, indeed, how persons having business with the occupants of these dens ever find them. This characteristic of the street renders it a favorite place with persons who carry on unlawful trades, and do business by means of circulars, and un-der assumed names.

Pine street extends from Broadway eastward, imme-diately north of Wall street. It is a narrow thorough-fare, but between Nassau street and Broadway is lined with noble structures occupied by banks and corporate institutions. These buildings are so tall that the street is always in shadow. At the head of the street, in Trinity churchyard, rises the Martyr's monument.

Two of the busiest and most crowded streets in the

SCENE ON WEST STREET.

city are South and West streets, the former running along the East River, and the latter along the Hudson or North River. The great Brooklyn ferries have their landings on the former street, while on West street are the ferries which connect New York with the shores of New Jersey. Both are thronged throughout the day with a constant stream of heavily laden wagons and trucks. Along the East River front are long lines of sailing craft, from the huge Indiaman down to the little coasting sloop, and in the various slips which break the line of South street the barges which are brought down the Hudson from the Erie Canal have their headquarters. On West street are the piers of the various railway lines terminating in Jersey City and Hoboken, and here also are the wharves of the great European steamship lines. Each street has its peculiar characteristics, but both are alike in the dirt and filth with which they are covered, the roar and crash of vehicles, and the difficulties which beset the pedestrian in his efforts to struggle across them from the sidewalk to the ferries.

CHAPTER XVII

DIVORCES WITHOUT PUBLICITY

QUEER ADVERTISEMENTS—THE "DIVORCE RING"—ITS FIELD OF OPERATIONS—THE DIVORCE LAWYER—WHO HE IS—HEADQUARTERS OF THE MEMBERS OF THE RING—SCENE IN A LAWYER'S OFFICE—A RICH CLIENT—"OFF WITH THE OLD LOVE AND ON WITH THE NEW"—A CHARACTERISTIC CASE—"THE EASIEST THING IN THE WORLD TO GET A DIVORCE"—WESTERN DIVORCES—HOW A MERCHANT MADE A MISTRESS OF HIS WIFE—WHO ARE THE CLIENTS —COST OF A DIVORCE—HOW IT IS MANAGED—THE REFEREE SYSTEM—SPOTTING A HUSBAND—MANUFACTURING EVIDENCE—THE "OLD MAN" ENTRAPPED—PROFESSIONAL WITNESSES—THE DIVORCE LAWYER'S SYSTEM OF DRUMMING UP BUSINESS—DIRTY WORK FOR TEN PER CENT—SERVING A SUMMONS—A MOCKERY OF JUSTICE—POWER OF THE RING—THE COURTS AND BAR AFRAID TO BREAK IT UP.

A leading New York daily, of a recent date, contains the following advertisements :—

DIVORCES without publicity in 30 days ; all causes ; every State ; consultation free ; experienced lawyer ; success guaranteed.
SMITH, BROWN & Co., 86 — Street.

DIVORCES cheaply, without publicity ; desertion, incompatibility, non-support, intemperance, compulsory marriages ; parties any State ; explanatory blanks free ; always successful ; consultations free ; confidential.
LAWYER SMOOTHTONGUE, 105 — Street.

Similar advertisements are to be found in other journals, especially in those of "sporting" proclivities. They announce to the public that there is in New York a powerful and regularly organized "Ring," whose business it is to untie the marriage-knot, and they guarantee to do it with the ease and celerity with which it is tied. This would seem strange in a State where the laws regulating divorces are so rigid ; but the divorce lawyer knows how to set even these at defiance, and that his efforts are successful, is shown by the handsome income he enjoys and the elegant style in which he lives. He does not rely upon New York alone for his field of operations; other States are more liberal in this matter, and if the separation of husband and wife cannot be procured in the Empire State, he can easily accomplish it in some other part of the Union.

The divorce lawyer devotes himself to this branch of his profession exclusively. He is sometimes an ex-member of the Bar, who has been disbarred for dishonest practices, and cannot appear directly in the case himself. He hires some shyster lawyer to go through the formalities of the courts for him, and sometimes succeeds in inducing a barrister of good standing to act for him. His office is usually in the quarter most frequented by practitioners of standing, and is located in some large building with long halls, so that his clients may come and go without attracting special notice. The outer office is fitted up in regular legal style, with substantial desks and tables, and the walls are lined with cases of law books. The private consultation room is elegantly furnished, and is provided with the coziest arm-chairs, in which the clients can sit at their ease, and pour into the sympathizing ears of the "counsellor" their tales of woe.

Let us seat ourselves, unseen, in the private office of a leading divorce firm. They are located at the rear of a superb building on Broadway, and have elegantly fitted-up apartments. Counsellor ——, the head of the firm, conducts the consultations. He is a portly, smooth-faced, oily-tongued man, possessing great powers of cheek and plausiveness, just the man to lead a hesitating client to take the decisive step. A clerk from the outer office announces a visitor. A richly dressed, closely veiled lady is shown in, and the portly counsellor, rising courteously, places a chair for her. The seat is taken, the veil thrown back, and the counsellor finds himself face to face with a woman of beauty and refinement, and evidently of wealth—a most desirable client. In his blandest tones he invites her to state the nature of her business with him. Then follows a long tale of domestic unhappiness, the sum and substance of which is that she is tired of her husband, and wants a divorce from him.

"Upon what grounds, Madame?" asks the counsellor, settling down to business.

"Grounds?" is the startled, hesitating reply; "Why —I—that is—I am so unhappy with him."

"Is he unfaithful to you?"

"I do not know. I hope he is—I am afraid not, however. I thought you would ascertain for me."

"Certainly, Madame, certainly. Nothing easier in the world. We'll find out all about him. We'll learn the innermost secrets of his heart, and I've no doubt we shall find him grossly unfaithful. Most men are."

"Oh, not all, sir," the lady cries, a little startled, "I'm sure that——"

Good sense comes to her aid, and she pauses. She must not tell all, even to her "legal adviser." The counsellor smiles; he has seen such cases before. It is only an affair of exchanging an old love for a new.

"Has he ever maltreated you—struck you?" he asks

"Oh no."

"Never attempted any violence with you?"

"He once seized a paper weight on the library table, very much excited, while I was talking with him."

"Indeed! He tried to dash your brains out with a paper weight, did he? That is very important evidence, Madame, very important."

And the counsellor jots it down on a memorandum.

"But, sir, I did not say that he——."

"Oh, never mind, Madame. Wives are too ready to forgive their husbands' brutality. The fact remains the same, however. This infamous attempt upon your life will be sufficient evidence with the Western judge before whom the case will be tried. I congratulate you, Madame, upon the prospect of a speedy release from such a monster."

The lady is delighted, pays the retainer, which is a handsome one, agrees upon the amount to be paid when the divorce is granted, and the parties separate, mutually pleased with each other.

The counsellor now goes to work in earnest. Operations are carried on in some Western State. Witnesses are provided who will swear to anything they are paid for; the divorce is duly obtained; the fee is paid; and the Madame coolly informs her husband that they are no longer husband and wife.

A year or two ago the New York papers contained an account of a man who had gotten one of these patent divorces from his wife. Not caring to part from her just then, but wishing to be able to do so when he pleased, he locked the papers up in his desk, and said nothing to her about the matter, and for ten years she lived with him as his mistress, in total ignorance of her true relations to him. At last, becoming tired of her, he produced the decree of divorce, and left her.

All sorts of people seek the assistance of the divorce lawyers to free them from their matrimonial ties. Extravagant and reckless wives of men who are not able to meet their demands for money; dissolute actresses, who wish to break up an old alliance in order to form a new one; married women, who have become infatuated with some scamp they have met at a theatre matinee, or through the medium of a personal; married men who are tired of their wives and desire to be united to a new partner; lovers of married women, who come to engage fabricated testimony and surreptitious divorce for the frail creatures whose virtue is still too cowardly to dare the more honest sin; all who, with or without protest, seek a release from the marriage bond. For each and all the divorce lawyer has a ready ear and an encouraging word. Nothing is easier than to obtain a divorce, he assures them. If the cause assigned by them is insufficient, it can be made strong enough; if evidence is lacking, it can be obtained—manufactured, if necessary. He receives a retainer from each and all, and sends them away with the happy consciousness that their matrimonial troubles will soon be over.

A divorce costs anywhere from $25 to whatever sum the applicant is willing to pay for it, and can be obtained in New York, or any other State, according to the wishes of the party and the desire to avoid publicity. Any cause may be assigned; the lawyer guarantees that the evidence to support it shall be forthcoming at the proper time. It is a little more troublesome to obtain a New York divorce, but the machinery of the law is sufficiently loose even there to enable a

well-managed case to be successful. The divorce
lawyer has witnesses upon whom he can depend, for
they are regularly in his pay. They will swear as they
are instructed. The proceedings are private, the
courts turning the whole matter over to a referee, who
is frequently in collusion with the lawyer conducting
the case. Not a word about the affair is allowed to
get into the newspapers. The defendant has been
kept in ignorance of the proceedings, and naturally
does not appear in court, in person or by counsel, to
offer any opposition, and the case goes by default.
The referee hears the evidence, which has been carefully prepared, in the case ; submits a decision in favor
of the plaintiff; the court confirms the decision ; the
divorce is granted, and the first thing the defendant
knows of the whole affair is the triumphant proclama-
tion of the decree of the court, and the announcement
of the dissolution of the marriage.

Adultery is a favorite ground with the divorce lawyer, and, strange as it may appear, it is comparatively
easy to fasten such a charge upon the defendant, if that
person happens to be the husband. This is how it is
done : One of the "agents" of the firm makes the acquaintance of the husband, who is in total ignorance
of the plot against him, and after becoming somewhat
familiar with him, invites him to a quiet little supper at
some convenient restaurant. When the wine has done
its work, a party of ladies drop in, quite by accident,
of course, and are pressed by the agent to remain.
The innocent victim joins in the request ; he would be
an ill-bred fellow if he did not. A dead set is made at
the victim, whose wits are generally somewhat confused

with the wine he has drank, and the natural consequences follow. The agent coolly looks on, and takes
his notes, and the particular beauty who has won over
the victim to her charms becomes an important witness
in the case. There is no difficulty in proving the
charge.

Where the husband is a jolly, good-natured man,
and loves to take his pleasure, the agent's business is
greatly simplified. He has but to shadow his victim,
note down his acts, even his words, for the most innocent deed can be distorted by a shrewd divorce lawyer
into damaging evidence of guilt. The least imprudence
is magnified into sin, and little by little all the needed
evidence is obtained.

Sometimes all these arts fail. Then the lawyer has
but one resource, to employ paid witnesses to swear
to the husband's guilt, where no overt act has been
committed. The divorce must be obtained at any cost;
and the lawyer knows "no such word as fail."

Sometimes business becomes dull. People appear
to be satisfied with their partners, and applications for
patent divorces fall off. The divorce lawyer is equal
to the emergency, however, and sets his agents to work
to drum up business. They proceed upon a regular
system, and seek high game. They operate among
persons able to pay large fees, and seek women as
their victims in preference to men. A member of the
Metropolitan bar, conversing with a friend not long
since, thus explained the system pursued :—

"You understand, of course, that society is not
happy in all its honors. All the brownstone houses
have to have new closets put in every year in order to

accommodate the skeletons. Still, many a woman and man, if let alone, would bear his or her connubial burdens meekly, rather than face the scandal and publicity of a divorce trial. Our special divorce lawyers know this, and so they invade society. They transfer the base of operations to the drawing rooms. How? By using swell members of the fashionable world to first find out where there is a canker in the rose, and then to deftly set forth in a perfect Mephistophilian way how divorce is the only cure. Nine-tenths of this delicate diplomatic business is employed in persuading hesitating wives. Husbands could hardly be approached in their own homes with a proposition to break them up. Take an impressionable woman, already unhappy, who has once been thinking of divorce, and the case is different. She is clay for the moulder. The serpent whispers of how nice it will be to bank her alimony, tells her lies about the old man, induces her to believe that the firm down town will put in no bill if they don't succeed, and so the affair is arranged."

For this despicable service the agent receives ten per cent. of the fee paid the divorce lawyer by the wife, which fee, be it remembered, comes out of the husband's pocket.

Oftentimes the agent is called upon to personate the husband, especially in serving the summons of the court upon him, if the case is to be tried in New York. The lawyer in charge has the case quietly put on record in the proper court, and has a summons prepared for service upon the defendant. A boy is called in from the street, anybody will answer, and is paid a trifle to take the summons to the defendant's place of business or residence, and deliver it to him in person. Arrived at his destination, the boy is met by the agent of the divorce lawyer, at the door or on the steps. The agent sharply demands his business, and is answered by the boy that he wishes to deliver a paper to Mr. X——. "I am Mr. X——," replies the agent, sharply, "give me the paper." The boy, in perfect good faith, for he has never seen Mr. X—— in his life, delivers the summons to the agent, and goes back to the lawyer's office, where he signs an affidavit that he has served the summons upon the defendant in person. He is then dismissed, and plays no further part in the case. His affidavit is sufficient for this part of the proceedings, and the shameful mockery of justice proceeds to another stage.

This is no exaggerated description. The acts of these divorce lawyers are well known in New York, and every member of the bar is familiar with their mode of proceeding. Reputable barristers denounce them as a disgrace, not only to the profession, but to humanity. The judges on the bench know these men and their ways. Yet neither the bench nor the Bar Association make any effort to stop the evil or to disbar the wretches who thus prey upon the most sacred relations of life. The "Divorce Ring" is a powerful clique, intimately connected with and very useful to the whole referee system, and lawyers of standing are afraid to attempt to bring it to justice, lest they should draw upon themselves the vengeance of the "Referee Ring," and so injure their own professional prospects. So the evil continues to grow. It will flourish as long as there are foolish people to take advantage of it.

CHAPTER XVIII

CHRISTMAS IN NEW YORK

PREPARATIONS FOR CHRISTMAS—HOLIDAY APPEARANCE OF THE CITY—STREET SCENES—BUSINESS BOOMING—SCENES IN THE CITY BY NIGHT—A NOVEL SIGHT ON THE ELEVATED RAILROAD TRAINS—BUSY TIMES IN THE MARKETS—THE TURKEYS—TRINITY CHIMES—MIDNIGHT SERVICES—CHRISTMAS DAY—HOW IT IS OBSERVED IN NEW YORK—CHRISTMAS WITH THE POOR.

New York attests its Dutch and English descent by the heartiness with which it "keeps Christmas." For weeks before the great day of the Feast the city is in gala attire. The stores present a brighter and more attractive appearance than at any other season of the year, the streets are filled with larger throngs, and the stages, street cars, and trains of the Elevated roads are more crowded than ever. Every family in the great Babel is looking forward with eagerness to the period when happiness shall rule the hour, and dull care be banished from the household. The little folks are in their glory, for it is their season, *par excellence*. They look forward eagerly to the "day of days;" wonder what presents the good Saint Nicholas—for by whatever other name the tutelary saint of Christmas be called elsewhere, this is his true title in the Metropolis —will bring them; and scan with longing eyes the impenetrable wrappers of the parcels that daily find their way to their homes, and are put with haste under lock and key. As the festival draws nearer, the bustle and excitement increase throughout the city, and when Christmas Eve is reached New York is fairly crazed with enthusiasm.

The city presents an interesting appearance on the day before Christmas. The air is keen and crisp, and if the streets and the house tops are covered with a mantle of snow, so much the better, for to the lover of Christmas the season should always be a snowy one. The streets and stores are now packed to their utmost capacity. It is the money spending time of the year, and those who are out mean business. No matter if the weather is cold, and the thoroughfares are slushy, no matter if the wind whirls in fitful gusts along the streets, chilling the hands and noses of the passers by. Warm hearts beat under the warm clothing of the holiday makers. Broadway, from Bleecker street to Thirty-fourth, Sixth, Eighth, and Third avenues almost along their entire length, 23d, 14th, and Grand streets, and the Bowery are all driving a thriving trade. The display in the stores is something wonderful, and the proprietors are in high good humor at the rapid disappearance of their wares. The streets are filled with booths and stands at which a busy trade is going on. Articles which find no sale at other seasons of the year are now disposed of rapidly and at satisfactory prices. Men and women jostle each other on the sidewalks, and it is difficult in some places to force one's way through the throng. Huge piles of Christmas trees stand on the corners, and find ready purchasers, and wagons loaded with trees and evergreen decorations, wreaths, stars, festoons, and the like, pass along the up-town streets, disposing of their wares from house to house. Thousands of dollars change hands every minute. The clerks in the stores are as busy as bees, and extra help has to be engaged. It is marvelous to see how

rapidly and with what promptness purchases are delivered at the houses of the buyers.   Many, however, do
not trust to these deliveries, but take their purchases
with them, and all day the streets are filled with men
and women literally loaded down with parcels.

At night Broadway, 14th street and Fifth avenue
are ablaze with the electric light.   The stores are all
open and thronged with buyers.   The crowds in the
streets are even greater, for those who were at work
during the day are now out, busy with their purchases.
Men, women and children, loaded with merchandise,
struggle along the packed sidewalks, and the roar of
passing vehicles is as great as at any hour of the day.
Here is a woman with a bundle of toys in her arms,
surmounted by a huge turkey for the Christmas dinner.   There goes a man struggling under the weight
of a Christmas tree, and sweeping his way through the
mass with its thick, sharp branches.   Boys with penny
whistles, young men with tin horns, render the streets
discordant with their noise; half-dressed children of
both sexes stand on the sidewalks watching the throng,
or gaze into the brightly-lighted shop-windows with
wistful eyes, and wonder what Christmas has in store
for them.   They will not be forgotten on the morrow.
New York opens its great heart and its big pocket-
book at this blessed time, and to-morrow huge tables
will groan with good things, and tall Christmas trees
stagger under the weight of toys and trinkets, for the
children of the poor.   Lights gleam from every house
in the great city, and could you enter, you would find
in each and all nearly the same scene going on—the
elder members of the family dressing the Christmas

tree, and loading it with the toys and trinkets that are to gladden the eyes of the young folks when they wake on the morrow, and decorating the rooms with wreaths and festoons of green, amid which the bright holly berries shine out in their crimson beauty. Something of this may be seen from the cars of the Elevated roads, as you whirl by the second-story windows of the houses along the route.

These Elevated trains present a curious spectacle on Christmas Eve. At every station there are long lines of people going up and down the narrow stairways, laden with all manner of Christmas treasures. The stations themselves have the appearance of booths where toys of all kinds are disposed for sale. In the cars it is almost impossible to move, because of the great bundles of merchandise. You stumble over huge turkeys and market-baskets filled to overflowing with all manner of eatables, and at every step are warned by some anxious passenger to be careful not to step on his bundles. Throughout the day, and late into the night, each passing train presents the appearance of being a combination of a toy store and a Washington Market stall.

As for the markets, they seem the very incarnation of Christmas. They are thronged to overflowing, and the dealers can scarcely supply the demand upon them. The scene, especially at night, almost baffles description. Long rows of turkeys hang from the hooks of the stalls, and are arranged on counters and stands which usually groan beneath the weight of butchers' meats and sugar-cured hams. Wreaths and festoons of evergreens, mingled with holly-berries, decorate every stall, and the great sheds are aglow with hundreds of lamps of every description. Moving in all directions are people with huge market-baskets, filled with every luxury which can tempt the appetite, and the vast, surging, eager crowd acts as though there was but one hour in which to buy all that is necessary for the crowning festival of the year. Towards eleven o'clock business begins to slacken, the crowds of purchasers fall off, and soon the stalls are closed, the lights go out, and the dealers prepare to go home. The city becomes quieter, and by midnight the Christmas purchases are over, and New York prepares for a little rest. Yet not long does the silence continue.

When the bell of old Trinity tolls the last stroke of the hour of midnight, there is a momentary hush in the streets, and then rolling down from their lofty height, through the dark thoroughfares and over the silent waters of the bay, come the rich, glad tones of the chimes, filling the air with a burst of melody. "Christmas has come," they seem to say. "Awake and rejoice, ye dwellers in the great city. Banish your cares and lift up your hearts. For one day let sin and sorrow cease. 'Glad tidings of great joy' await you. Christmas has come: Christ is born." Lights gleam in the grand old church below, and soon the full, rich tones of the organ and the sweet voices of the choristers swell out on the midnight air.

Midnight services are held in many of the Episcopal and all of the Catholic churches of the city, and are well attended.

On Christmas day the city is full of gayety, its observance being very much the same as in other places.

Morning services are held at the churches of many of the denominations, and large congregations are in attendance. In the afternoon the Sunday schools generally distribute presents to their attendants, from huge Christmas trees.

The Christmas dinner is the great event of the day, and at such repasts the turkey always occupies the post of honor. Nor are these feasts confined to the family board alone. The numerous charitable and benevolent institutions spread bountiful tables for their inmates. The children of the poor, washed clean and neatly dressed, are gathered in from all quarters, at certain establishments, and are given the only hearty and enjoyable meal of the year. At many of these places Christmas trees are provided, and the hearts of the little ones are gladdened with toys, trinkets, and other presents suited to their needs and years. Even the prisoners in the Tombs and on Blackwell's Island are not forgotten, and the Christmas dinner spread for them sheds a little of light and hope into their otherwise gloomy existence. The charitable institutions are busy receiving and distributing clothing, food and other articles sent to them. New York gives bountifully at this season; even those whose pocket-books are tightly clasped at other times, open them now, and distribute their bounty with generous hands.

All the theatres give special performances, termed "Matineés," in the afternoon. The houses are thronged, and the managers pocket large receipts. At night, balls, festivals and entertainments of all kinds, close the day.

CHAPTER XIX

PUBLIC BUILDINGS

THE CITY HALL—THE GOVERNOR'S ROOM—THE COUNTY COURT HOUSE—REMINISCENCES OF THE
"TWEED RING"—THE HALL OF RECORDS—THE UNITED STATES SUB-TREASURY—THE GREAT
VAULTS—HOW UNCLE SAM'S MONEY IS GUARDED—THE ASSAY OFFICE—THE CUSTOM HOUSE—
A NOBLE EDIFICE—THE BUSINESS OF THE PORT OF NEW YORK—DUTIES OF OFFICIALS—THE
BARGE OFFICE—PASSING THROUGH THE CUSTOM HOUSE—CUSTOM HOUSE BROKERS—TAM-
MANY HALL—THE TAMMANY SOCIETY—POLITICAL ORGANIZATION—"BOSS KELLY"—THE
COOPER UNION—WORK OF THE INSTITUTION—THE BIBLE HOUSE—A GREAT WORK DONE—THE
NATIONAL ACADEMY OF DESIGN—HOW THE SCHOOLS ARE CONDUCTED—ANNUAL EXHIBI-
TIONS—THE YOUNG MEN'S CHRISTIAN ASSOCIATION BUILDING—THE LECTURE ROOM—A
REFUGE FOR YOUNG MEN—THE GRAND CENTRAL RAILROAD DEPOT—INTERNAL ARRANGE-
MENTS—THE CAR HOUSE—THE FOURTH AVENUE TUNNELS.

Apart from the great public edifices mentioned
separately in these pages, there are many which de-
serve special notice. Of the principal of these we
propose to speak in this chapter.

The most prominent of the public buildings is the
City Hall, the headquarters of the Municipal Government of New York. It stands in the City Hall Park,
in the rear of the Post Office, from which it is separated by a wide, open space, and between that
building and the County Court House. The front
and sides are of white marble, and the rear of brown
sandstone. It is built in the Italian style, and was
begun in 1803 and completed in 1812, at a cost of
more than half a million of dollars. It is 216 feet
long and 105 feet deep, and is surmounted by a cupola
containing a clock with four faces, which are illuminated
by gas at night. On the summit of the cupola stands
a statue of Justice. The building contains the Mayor's
office, the Common Council Chamber, the City Library,

FRONT VIEW OF THE CITY HALL, NEW YORK

and a number of the City offices. Some of its rooms are handsome, and are elegantly decorated. The principal chamber is called "The Governor's Room," and is used chiefly for official receptions. It is located on the second floor, and contains the portraits of a number of the Governors of New York, Mayors of the City, prominent officers of the army of the Revolution, and many other distinguished persons. These portraits are nearly all by celebrated artists. Here also are the chairs used by the First Congress of the United States, the chair in which Washington sat at his first inauguration as President of the Republic, and that in which he penned his first message to Congress.

The *County Court House* stands in the rear of the City Hall, and fronts on Chambers street. It was begun in 1861, and since 1867 has been occupied by the State Courts and several of the City Departments, though still uncompleted. When finished it will be one of the finest edifices in the Union. It is built in the Corinthian style of architecture, is three stories high, 250 feet long by 150 wide, and is constructed of white marble from Massachusetts. The dome, when completed, will be 210 feet above the sidewalk. "One of the most novel features of the dome will be the arrangement of the tower crowning its apex, into a lighthouse, which, from its extreme power and height, it is supposed, will furnish guidance to vessels as far out at sea as that afforded by any beacon on the neighboring coast." The building has already cost many millions of dollars. It was the chief means used by the Tweed Ring in carrying out their stupendous frauds upon the city. The better part of the money appropriated for its construction went into the pockets of the Ring.

At the northeast corner of the City Hall Park, and a few yards from the City Hall, stands a stone building covered with stucco. It was erected in 1757, as a city prison. It is known as the *Hall of Records*, and is occupied by the Registrar and his clerks.

The *United States Sub-Treasury* stands at the northeast corner of Wall and Nassau streets, and on the site of old Federal Hall, in which Washington was inaugurated first President of the United States. It faces Broad street, and extends back to Pine street. It is built of white marble, in the Doric style of architecture, and its fronts on Wall and Pine streets are adorned with noble porticoes, each supported by eight marble columns 32 feet high. The Wall street portico is approached by a massive flight of eighteen marble steps, extending the entire width of the building. As the grade on Pine street is higher than that of Wall street, the portico on that side is without steps. The main entrances lead into a rotunda sixty feet in diameter. The dome is very handsome, and is supported by sixteen Corinthian columns. The desks of the officials in charge of the various departments of the Sub-Treasury are arranged around the sides of the rotunda, and are separated from the public portion by a handsome counter provided with a glass screen similar to those used in banks. The rotunda always presents a busy scene, as the business of the Sub-Treasury is very great. Beneath the rotunda is an extensive basement arranged in a series of vaults, in which are kept the coins, notes and bonds belonging to the general government. The amount on deposit here is always enormous, and every precaution is taken to ensure its safety.   During the past year the vaults have been considerably enlarged, to accommodate the vast amount of bullion sent here for storage, and the great bags of coined money, and

UNITED STATES SUB-TREASURY.

new doors have been provided, with an intricate network of horizontal and perpendicular bars, operated by time locks of the most ingenious construction.

There have been many occasions when alarm has been felt lest an attack might be attempted upon the building by a mob. This apprehension is now over-come by the practical conversion of the building into a formidable fortress. Every window has been provided with heavy steel shutters, and these have been so perforated as to admit of very accurate firing by the defenders within, in case the building should be attacked by a body of rioters. Upon the roof strong steel turrets have been erected, fitted with loopholes for rifle firing, and larger ones for the destructive work of improved Gatling guns. There are four of these combination guns, so mounted as to sweep the neighboring housetops, or by being depressed scatter their score of bullets into the street. Above the apertures for the Gatlings are loopholes for riflemen, by which every angle of approach can be readily covered. The greatest secrecy is maintained respecting these means of defense, and no stranger is allowed to inspect them. Neither are visitors permitted to see the great vaults in the basement.

The Sub-Treasury was originally built for and used by the Custom House, but becoming too small for its purposes was remodeled for its present use.

Adjoining the Treasury is the Assay Office, which is practically a department of the Sub-Treasury. It is a much smaller edifice, and is constructed of granite.

The *Custom House* occupies an irregular square bounded by Wall street, Exchange Place, William street, and Hanover street. The Wall street front is 144 feet long, and the Exchange Place front, 171 feet long. The depth of the building is 200 feet. The height of the building is 77 feet, and from the ground to the top of the central dome, the distance is 124 feet.

The Wall street front is ornamented with a handsome portico supported by twelve front, four middle and two rear columns of granite, each thirty-eight feet in height. The building is constructed of Quincy granite, and was

CUSTOM HOUSE.

erected in 1835, at a cost, including the ground, of $1,800,000. It was used for a number of years as the Merchants' Exchange. It was subsequently sold to the United States Government for $1,000,000, and was converted to its present use. The main entrance is on Wall street, but there are entrances on every side of the building.

The Wall street entrance leads directly to the rotunda, the main hall of the building, lying immediately beneath the dome. Around the sides of this beautiful hall are eight lofty columns of Italian marble, the superb Corinthian columns of which were carved in Italy. They support the base of the dome, and are probably the largest and noblest marble columns in the United States. The immense building is divided into offices, which are used by the Collector of the Port, the Naval Officer, and the Surveyor of the Port, and their subordinates. The other departments of the Custom House are in different parts of the city. The Sample Offices are at 254 West street; the Appraiser's Stores at 486 Washington street; the Barge Office at 6 State street; and the Public Stores at the corner of Washington and Laight street. Large as it is, the Custom House building is too small for the business transacted within it, and the erection of a new Custom House has been strongly urged upon the Government.

The business of the port of New York is immense. Five-sixths of all the duties collected on imports in the United States are received here. The Collectorship of the Port is perhaps the best paying office within the gift of the National Government, and is eagerly sought after by politicians. The Collector is also possessed of great political influence and power, by reason of his being the chief of the vast army of employees of every description engaged in doing Government work

CUSTOM HOUSE INSPECTION.

in the city. In the Custom House proper there are about 1150 clerks, whose aggregate salaries amount to about $3,000,000 per annum.

The duties of the principal officers of the port are thus stated by Colonel T. B. Thorpe, a veteran employee in the Custom House :—

"The Collector shall receive all reports, manifests, and documents to be made or exhibited on the entry of any ship or vessel; shall record, on books to be kept for that purpose, all manifests ; shall receive the entries of all ships or vessels, and of the goods, wares and merchandise imported in them; shall estimate the amount of the duties payable thereupon, indorsing said amount on the respective entries; shall receive all moneys paid for duties, and take all bonds for securing the payment thereof; shall, with the approbation of the Secretary of the Treasury, employ proper personages, weighers, gaugers, measurers and inspectors, at the port within his district.

"The Naval Officer shall receive copies of all manifests and entries on all goods, wares and merchandise subject to duty (and no duties shall be received without such estimate), and shall keep a separate record thereof; and shall countersign all permits, clearances, certificates, debentures, and other documents granted by the Collector. He shall also examine the Collector's abstract of duties, his accounts, receipts, bonds and expenditures, and, if found correct, shall certify to the same.

"The Surveyor shall superintend and direct all inspectors, weighers, measurers, and gaugers; shall visit and inspect the ships and vessels; shall return in writing every morning, to the Collector, the name and nationality of all vessels which shall have arrived from foreign ports; shall examine all goods, wares and merchandise imported, to see that they agree with the Inspector's returns; and shall see that all goods intended for exportation correspond with the entries and permits granted therefor; and the said Surveyor shall, in all cases, be subject to the Collector.

"The Appraiser's department is simply for the purpose of deciding the market value and dutiable character of all goods imported, so that the imposts can be laid with correctness.   Other than this, it has no connection with the Custom House."

The Barge office is located at the Battery, and is a handsome granite edifice.   It is described in connection with the Battery Park, in another chapter.   It is the headquarters of the Inspectors connected with the Surveyor's office.   When the arrival of a steamer or vessel from a foreign port is announced by the telegraph operator at Sandy Hook, several Inspectors are sent down in a revenue tug to take charge of her. As soon as they go on board the vessel they have absolute control of her passengers and cargo.   Should the vessel be a steamer from abroad, they accompany her to her anchorage in the river, examine the baggage of the passengers, and take charge of all containing dutiable articles; see that the proper duties are levied and collected, and if the amount of the duties exceeds a certain sum, send the trunks or parcels to the public store for appraisement.   They remain on the vessel until she reaches her landing, and then turn her over to the Custom House officials appointed to supervise the discharge of her cargo.

The formalities of passing goods through the Custom House are tedious and vexatious. Merchants and others in the city having such matters on their hands employ a "Custom House Broker," who, however, has no official connection with the Custom House, to attend to the details for them. The broker is familiar with all the ins and outs of the great establishment, possesses peculiar facilities for the prompt despatch of his work, and is not subject to the delays and annoyances which await a private individual. His fee for passing an entry is five dollars, and on busy days he frequently earns several hundred dollars in this way.

The portion of the Custom House building most familiar to the general public is the rotunda. In the centre of this hall are the enclosed desks of the officials whose duties bring them in constant contact with merchants, shippers, captains of vessels, and all who have business with the establishment. They consist of four "Deputy Collectors," three "Chief Clerks," five "Entry Clerks," two "Bond Clerks," and a "Foreign-Clearance Clerk," and his assistant.

Tammany Hall stands on the North side of East Fourteenth street, between Irving place and Third avenue, and adjoins the Academy of Music. It is a large, plain structure of red brick with white marble trimmings, and possesses no architectural attractions. It is the property of the Tammany Society, a political organization, and the controlling element of the Democratic party in municipal affairs. It contains a fine hall on the second floor, used for public meetings, and formerly occupied as a theatre, and several other smaller halls, and a number of committee rooms.

One of the smaller halls, opening on Fourteenth street, on the ground floor, is used as a German variety theatre.

The "Tammany Society, or Columbian Order," was incorporated in 1789 as a benevolent institution, but at an early day degenerated into a political organization,

STEINWAY HALL.

and gave the name of its building to the ruling section of the Democratic party. The organization of the Society is still maintained distinct from the political party, but as a matter of fact, scarcely any one but a member of the Tammany General Committee is elected a member of the Society. The members are divided into two classes, known as "Braves" and

"Sachems." New members are admitted from time
to time, and the Society is self-perpetuating. The
Sachems constitute the governing class, and are the
trustees of the property of the Society. The chief
officer is called the "Grand Sachem," and his subordinates are designated by Indian titles. As a political
organization, "Tammany Hall" is said to be the best
disciplined body in the Union. It is governed by
a Central Committee of over 1100 members, under
which are City Committees in every ward of the Metropolis. In municipal politics it is all-powerful, and
controls fully one-half of the lawful votes of the city.
In its practical workings "Tammany Hall" is ruled by
one man, who is naturally the shrewdest and most
energetic of its leaders. He is popularly termed "The
Boss." In the days of his glory, this position was held
by "Boss Tweed." At present, Mr. John Kelly is regarded as "The Boss" of Tammany.

The *Cooper Union* occupies the triangular space
formed by the junction of the Bowery, Third and
Fourth avenues and 7th street, one square east of
Broadway. It is a plain but massive and imposing
edifice of brownstone, six stories high, with a large
basement below the level of the streets. It was erected by Peter Cooper in 1857, at a cost of $630,000, and
was endowed by him with $150,000, for the support of
the free reading room and library. The street floor is
let out in stores, and the floor above is occupied with
offices of various kinds. These floors and the great
hall in the basement yield a handsome revenue, which
is devoted to paying a part of the expenses of the
institution. The remainder of the building is devoted

to a free library and reading room, and halls for lectures and for study.

The institution was designed by Mr. Cooper for the free instruction of the working classes in science, art, English literature, the foreign languages, and telegraphy. Of late years there has been added to it a school of

COOPER UNION.

design for women. The course of instruction is very thorough, the ablest teachers being employed, and the standard of scholarship is high. Searching and rigid examinations test the proficiency of the pupils, and the graduates are sent forth into the world thoroughly prepared in the branches taught here. Mr. Cooper's plans have been ably carried out by the teachers in charge of the institution, and he has lived to see his noble work one of the crowning glories of the Metropolis. The library contains about 15,000 volumes of miscellaneous works, and the reading room nearly 300 daily and weekly papers and magazines, both domestic and foreign. During the winter months free lectures are delivered in the hall in the basement, on popular and instructive subjects, to crowded audiences. The annual cost of maintaining the institution is about $45,000. It is derived principally from the rental of the stores and offices, and the interest on the endowment fund.

The *Bible House* stands immediately facing the Cooper Union, and occupies the entire block bounded by Third and Fourth avenues and 8th and 9th streets. It is a massive structure of red brick, covers an area of three-quarters of an acre, and is six stories in height. It was erected in 1852 and 1853, at a cost of $303,000, but is to-day worth more than twice that sum. It is the property of the American Bible Society, and besides the portion occupied by that organization, contains fifty stores and offices, which return a rental of more than $40,000. Many of the stores on the ground floor are occupied by dealers in religious books, and the offices are mainly taken up by benevolent and charitable societies. The greater portion of the building is occupied by the offices, the printing establishment, and the bindery of the American Bible Society. Over six hundred persons are employed in these establishments, and six thousand Bibles are printed, and three hundred and fifty Bibles are bound and finished, and sent to the warerooms every day. The Bible is printed here in twenty-nine different languages, and portions of it have been published in other languages still. The Society possesses a magnificent library upon biblical subjects, among which is one of the largest and most complete and valuable collections of the Scriptures in existence. The receipts of the Society from 1816, the date of its organization, to 1876, exceeded $17,000,000. In the sixty-three years following its organization it printed and circulated 36,052,169 copies of the Scriptures.

The *National Academy of Design* is located at the northwest corner of Fourth avenue and 23d street, and is one of the most beautiful and artistic buildings in New York. It is built in the pure Gothic style of the thirteenth century, and is constructed of gray and white marble and bluestone, artistically blended, and producing a novel and pleasing effect. The 23d street front is eighty feet, and the Fourth avenue side ninety feet in length. A double flight of steps leads to the main entrance, and is ornamented with beautiful carvings and a drinking fountain, all of which blend harmoniously with the general design. The main entrance, on 23d street, leads to a handsome vestibule, paved with variegated marbles. From this a massive and imposing stairway leads to the exhibition galleries, which are located in the third story and lighted from the roof. The first and second stories are devoted to the reception room, offices, lecture rooms, art schools, and the library. All the halls and rooms are finished handsomely in white pine, ash, mahogany, oak, and black walnut, in their natural colors, no paint being used on the woodwork of the building.

The Academy is designed for the free instruction of

students in painting and sculpture.   The schools open
on the first Monday in October, and close on the first
of June in the following year.   Great care is exercised
in the admission of pupils, as it is designed to restrict
the schools to those who intend to make art the profession of their lives.   The course of instruction is
thorough, and is conducted by artists of national repu-

NATIONAL ACADEMY OF DESIGN.

tation.   An exhibition of new paintings is held in the
Spring of each year, and is open to the public upon
payment of a small admission fee.   Only the works of
living American artists are exhibited.   During the first
three days, known respectively as "Artists' Day,"
"Varnishing Day," and "Private View," no one is
admitted without a card of invitation from a member
of the Academy.   These days are noted events in

fashionable society, and invitations are eagerly sought after by the Upper Ten.

The *Young Men's Christian Association Building* stands opposite the Academy of Design, on the south-west corner of Fourth avenue and Twenty-third street. It is four stories in height, with a mansard roof, broken by three domes, containing a fifth story. The building is constructed of dark New Jersey sandstone, brought from the Belleville quarries, is in the French renais-sance style, and was erected in 1869, at a cost of $500,000. It is handsomely trimmed with light Ohio stone. It has a frontage of one hundred and seventy-five feet on Twenty-third street, and eighty-three feet on Fourth avenue. The Association occupies the second and third floors, while the fourth and fifth floors are taken up chiefly with artists' studios, and the ground floor is occupied with handsome stores. The leased portions of the building return a rental of about $13,000 per annum.

The main entrance is in the centre of the Twenty-third street front. A broad, handsome stairway leads to the second floor, on which is situated the main hall, which occupies the western portion of this and the third story. It is one of the largest and handsomest halls in the city, and will comfortably seat 1500 people. It is two stories in height, and is beautifully and taste-fully decorated. A broad gallery extends around three sides of the hall, and this and the floor below are provided with iron chairs, such as are used in the principal theatres. At the western end is a large plat-form upon which opens a retiring room. On the side of the platform opposite the retiring room is the great organ, one of the finest instruments in the city. The hall is used for lectures and concerts during the fall, winter, and spring, and on Sunday religious services are conducted here by eminent divines invited by a committee of the Association for that purpose.

The remainder of the second floor is occupied by the reception room, the social parlor, the office of the Secretary, who is the executive officer of the Association, and the reading room, which is liberally supplied with files of the leading American and foreign papers and magazines. A stairway leads from the reception room to the basement, in which are located the bowling alley and gymnasium. The eastern portion of the third floor is taken up with the library, containing about 13,000 volumes, and rooms for Bible class and prayer meetings and for instruction in modern languages and other studies. Bath rooms and other toilet conveniences are provided in the building. All the appointments are complete, handsome and elegant.

The building is the property of the New York branch of the Young Men's Christian Association, an organization too well known throughout the country to need a description here. It is open every day, from 8 A. M. to 10 P. M., except on Sunday, when the hours are from 2 to 7 P. M. It is a sort of moral oasis to young men in the great wilderness of New York; a refuge from the temptations and dissipations by which they are surrounded. While it has a fixed scale of charges, moderate in amount, for membership, it cordially opens its doors to all, especially to young men living in the city, away from their homes, and subject to the demoralizing influences of hotel and boarding-house life. Strangers sojourning in the city are especially welcome. The Association is also actively engaged in many noble works of charity. A writer in *Harpers' Magazine* styles the Association Building a "club house." "For such it is," he declares, "both in its appliances and its purposes, though consecrated neither to politics, as are some; to social festivities, degenerating too often into gambling and intemperance, as are others; nor to literature and polite society, as are one or two; but to the cause of good morals, of pure religion, and of Him who is the divine inspirer of the one and the divine founder of the other.

The *Grand Central Depot*, at the corner of Fourth avenue and 42d street, and extending from Fourth to Vanderbilt avenues, and from 42d to 45th streets, is one of the most imposing edifices in New York, and the most superb and complete railway terminus in America. With the exception of the old Hudson River Railroad Depot, at Ninth avenue and 30th street, now used for suburban trains only, it is the only railway station in the city. It is built of red brick, with iron trimmings, painted in imitation of white marble. Three massive pavilions adorn the 42d street front, and two the Vanderbilt avenue front, the central pavilion of each front being provided with an ornamental illuminated clock. The building is six hundred and ninety-six feet long, and two hundred and forty feet wide. The space devoted to the railway tracks under the great roof is six hundred and ten feet long and two hundred feet wide. Twelve trains, each consisting of a locomotive and twelve passenger cars, can be admitted side by side at one time in the depot. The tracks and platforms are sheltered by an immense glass and iron roof, of a single arch, with a span of two hundred feet and a height of one hundred and ten feet. The offices, baggage and waiting-rooms, etc., are located in the southern end and the western side. Besides these, the basement contains a police station, barber shop, and restaurant.

The depot is occupied by four important lines of railways. The 42d street front contains the offices, waiting and baggage-rooms of the New York, New Haven and Boston, and the Shore Line Railroads; and the Vanderbilt avenue, or western side, is taken up with the offices, baggage and waiting-rooms of the New York, Harlem and Albany, and the Hudson River and New York Central Railroads, the rooms of each road being entirely separated from those of the other. The upper floors of the building are occupied by the offices of the various railway companies. All the apartments in the great structure are handsomely frescoed, finished in hard wood, and provided with every convenience.

The car house, which comprises the principal portion of the depot, is very handsome. The roof is supported by thirty-one ornamental iron trusses, each one of which weighs forty tons and forms a single arch stretching from side to side. Eighty thousand feet of glass admit the light of day, and at night the place is brilliantly illuminated by gas jets supplied with large reflectors and lit by electricity. The platforms between the tracks and on the sides are constructed of a light-colored stone. Each road has its own tracks, and so perfect are the arrangements of the depot, that though

GRAND CENTRAL DEPOT. FRONT VIEW.

one hundred and twenty-five trains arrive and depart daily, there is no confusion. The running of the trains is regulated by the depot master, who occupies a lofty box or office at the north end of the station, from which he can command a view of the various roads as far as the entrance to the tunnels, half a mile distant. A system of automatic signals governs the movements of all trains from the depot to the Harlem River.

This great building was begun on the 15th of November, 1869, and was completed on the 9th of October, 1871. It was projected by and erected under the supervision of the late Commodore Vanderbilt.

In the yards to the north of the depot are numerous buildings for the shelter of cars and locomotives, coal sheds and repair shops. The tracks beyond the depot being for several squares on a level with the street, a number of bridges, built over the tracks, continue the lines of the various cross streets from one side of Fourth avenue to the other. Above the depot Fourth avenue is in a perfectly straight line, and along it the trains run to Harlem River, which is four and a half miles above the depot. For a mile and a half above the point where the trains pass entirely below the street level, the road bed, containing two tracks, is within an open cut flanked on each side by a tunnel, built of brick, and having within it another single track. The cross streets are carried over the cut on iron or brick arches, while iron railings extend all around the cut, fencing it off from the avenue, which is wide enough to provide a good-sized roadway for driving, and the usual sidewalks for pedestrians on each side of the cut. Above this mile and a half the street level gradually becomes much higher, and the road bed of the railways runs for half a mile through a partly brick built and partly rock cut tunnel, at the upper end of which the street level makes a sudden descent, and the road bed is carried over the Harlem Flats on a stone viaduct, the cross streets passing underneath, through arches. When the street level again ascends, about a mile and a quarter from the Harlem River, the road bed is again run through an open cut, like that just above the depot."

CHAPTER XX

NEW YEAR'S CALLS

NEW YORK'S GREAT FESTAL DAY—PREPARATIONS FOR NEW YEAR'S DAY—THE HAIR-DRESSERS'
ROUNDS—RECEPTION CARDS—HOW THEY ARE ISSUED—JOINT RECEPTIONS—THE CARD-BAS-
KET AND ITS MEANING—LADIES' TOILETS—A CHANCE FOR REFORM—THE FIRST CALLERS—
THE VETERANS—ADVANTAGES OF A LIST—SCENES TOWARD NIGHTFALL—TOO MUCH PUNCH—
MRS. B.'S RECEPTION—A SWEET FINALE—NEW YEAR IN THE KITCHEN—HOW THE SALOONS
CELEBRATE THE DAY—REFRESHMENTS AND PUNCH FOR ALL—NEW YORK WITH A HEAD-
ACHE—LADIES' DAY.

The Christmas festivities are scarcely over, when
New York again puts on its holiday attire, and prepares to celebrate in hearty style its own peculiar day
—the first day of the New Year. Since the settlement
of the colony by the Dutch, the first of January has
been set apart by the dwellers in the metropolis for
social observance, for renewing former friendships,
strengthening old ones, and wishing each other health
and happiness for the year just opening. The custom
is a pleasing one, but it is observed now in a manner
that would make the old Knickerbockers roll their eyes
in surprise could they but look upon it.

Among the middle classes and the steadier-going
citizens, New Year's Day is observed with heartiness, but also with characteristic good sense. It is
only after we enter the charmed realm of society that
we find the glare and the show that have given to the
day its peculiar characteristics. With the Upper-Ten-
Thousand it is made the occasion of displaying the
wealth and style of the family, and of impressing the

callers with a proper sense of its importance in the social world.

Long before Christmas preparations are begun for the great event, houses are cleaned, garnished, and put in apple-pie order. If new furniture is needed, its purchase is postponed until the last of the old year, in order that it may shine forth in all its splendor at the beginning of the new. The dressmakers are busy preparing magnificent costumes for the occasion, and the tailors have all they can do to provide the gentlemen with new outfits in which to make their calls. Carriages are engaged for weeks beforehand, and enormous prices are charged for them, as much as forty or fifty dollars being paid for a vehicle for the day. From five to ten dollars an hour is the usual charge. Hairdressers are busy going from house to house, arranging the *coiffures* of the ladies. They begin their rounds at midnight on the 31st of December, and are busy until noon the next day. Those who are so unfortunate as to be among the first served by these "*artistes* in hair," have a hard time of it. They cannot think of lying down, as to do so would be to disarrange their hair, so they must either keep awake all night, or sleep sitting bolt upright in a chair.

Ladies who intend to "receive," often club together at the residence of one of the party and hold a joint reception. This is rather hard on the average caller, especially towards the later hours of the day. A gentleman calls at a house, expecting to pay his respects to Mrs. A., the mistress of the establishment. He finds associated with her Mrs. B., Mrs. C., and perhaps Mrs. D., to each of whom he must pay his respects and get

off his prettiest sayings.   On such occasions the matters are wholly in the hands of the ladies of the house.
The male members of the family are out making calls
at other residences, and the ladies have things all their
own way.

Of late years, ladies who desire a long list of callers
—and the larger the list the greater the social *éclat*—
issue cards a week or so prior to the first of January,
a virtual invitation to the person receiving one to call
on New Year's Day.   The consequence is, that Tom,
Dick, and Harry pull the bells of houses they never
saw before, are greeted by ladies they may or may not
know, and are, as a rule, prepared to meet their hostess
on just such terms as her unsolicited acquaintance and
advances would apparently warrant.   This is on a par
with a habit some very young men have of "pooling
their lists."   Mr. A. knows twenty ladies, Mr. B. the
same number, Mr. C. thirty, and Mr. D. twenty-five.
The quartette hire a carriage together, put their lists in
one, and rush around frantically·from house to house,
each introducing the others to his friends in turn.
Nowadays the Elevated Railroads save the young men
considerable expense in carriage hire.   They can get
about the city very quickly by means of these rapid
trains, and as the lines run but a short distance from
the fashionable thoroughfares, the walk before them is
short.

It has become the custom for families who do not
intend to receive callers to close the front of the house
and suspend a small card-basket from the front door
knob.   Visitors at once take the hint, drop their cards
into the basket, and pass on.   Sometimes the mansion

thus closed is one famous for its bountifully-spread table. In such cases the visitor is not a little put out by the reflection that the failure of the family to observe "the time-honored custom" has cut him out of a "royal feed."

Ten o'clock is the earliest hour at which Society permits calls to be paid. The most exclusive do not open their doors until noon. Then the stream of visitors begins to set in, and continues until eight or nine o'clock.

The parlors of the mansions where calls are expected are lavishly adorned with flowers, and a handsome table is spread, provided with all the delicacies of the season, and rare and costly wines, and punch. In the more exclusive dwellings the curtains are down and the gas lighted. The ladies of the family, ravishingly dressed, take their stand in the drawing-room and await their visitors. The dresses are all new for the occasion—that is, what there is of them. They are full and elaborate below the waist, but above that there is a plentiful lack of dry goods, and a liberal display of neck, arms and shoulders. Gazing at these marvelously attired creatures, one cannot help calling to mind the words of the great Dr. Johnson to the equally great David Garrick: "Davy, I shan't come behind the scenes at your theatre any more—the silk stockings and white bosoms of your actresses excite my amatory propensities, and render me unfit for work on the dictionary."

Amid all the outcry for reform on these occasions, why does not some one propose a reform in the matter of feminine toilettes at New Year receptions? Is it

strange that some very young men, whose weak heads
have been dazed by the numerous healths they have
drank during the day, should, in the presence of so
many charms, occasionally forget where they are?

In a little while the first caller is announced by the
servant in charge of the front door. He divests himself of his hat and overcoat in the hall, and enters the
presence of the ladies. The first ones are generally
young men who are anxious to make as many calls as
possible, and start out early. The old stagers do not
come upon the scene until later in the day. The
visitor advances to the hostess, pays his respects to
her and the other ladies present, wishes them a happy
New Year, and utters a few common-places on the
weather. The hostess responds pleasantly, and invites
the gentleman to partake of some of the refreshments
spread before him, including a glass of wine or punch,
and smiles quietly at the eagerness with which he
responds to her invitation. The refreshments are
swallowed hurriedly, the visitor winds up with a few
complimentary phrases, which he repeats at every
house he visits, until the wine and the punch have
driven them from his memory, and bows himself out,
leaving the ladies to pick his character to pieces when
he is gone. Other callers follow in rapid succession,
and the same scene is repeated until the night ends the
farce. The young men eat little and drink much at
such visits. The veteran caller, however, knows where
the best tables are spread, and the hostess' heart
warms to see the ample justice he does to her good
taste. He drinks little, and so keeps his head cool,
and during the day manages to get three or four good

A VETERAN CALLER AT WORK.

square meals, under the pretence of partaking of refreshments.

Most of the men, in starting out on their calls, make
out a list of the houses they intend to visit. This is
given to the driver of the carriage occupied, and he
follows it in the order in which it is made out. Now
this is a wise precaution. Few men could trust their
memories with so many names, and towards the end
of the day, when the wine and the punch have done
their work, memory is incapable of performing any of
her functions, and the list becomes a necessity. Sometimes, when the list is almost used up, and the caller is
in the same condition, the driver leads him from the
carriage to the door of the next mansion to be visited,
rings the bell, and thrusts him inside. Be not too
quick, oh reader, to commend the tender care of said
driver. The door remains open long enough for him
to catch a glimpse of what follows, and you may be
very sure he is repaid by the fun that ensues.

The scene towards the close of the day, in some of
the splendid mansions of the upper ten, is one that
must be witnessed to be appreciated. The ladies are
worn out with fatigue, and bored to death by the stu-
pidity of their visitors. Carriages rattle up furiously;
young men in various stages of booziness are ushered
in. Some are dreamy and melancholy, and hold on
firmly to a chair or the corner of the table while
endeavoring to get out their set speeches; others are
merry and boisterous; others still are disposed to be a
little too friendly with the ladies. It may be that the
ladies themselves have had too much punch—such
things do happen. And then the scene is indescrib-

ably ludicrous. These late visitors leer vaguely at the hostess and her companions, mutter their compliments and good wishes in thick, unsteady voices, gulp down

A CALLER WHO HAS HAD "TOO MUCH PUNCH."

the liquors offered them, and stagger out into the hall, where the servant assists them in making their way out. Sometimes a gentleman who has paid a large number of calls falls helpless at the feet of the hostess, and has to be assisted by the servants to his carriage. They tell a story in New York of a certain Mrs. B——, one of the latest new comers in the avenue. Of her origin it is needless to speak; her peculiar brogue told the story of that. Having no daughters of her own, she induced two of her lady friends, like herself new stars in the firmament of fashion, to assist her at her first reception. They had scores of callers, and the reception lasted late into the evening. It ended with the servants closing the house, and leaving the hostess, her fair friends, and several gentlemen callers, comfortably settled in sofas and arm chairs—one was on the floor, where they passed the remainder of the night. It was the old story—too much champagne and punch.

No one loses caste in society for these little indiscretions, however. Society is charitable, and the parties are readily pardoned for "what might occur to any one."

While these things are going on above stairs, the kitchen is doing its full share in the proper observance of the day. Biddy sets a fine table for her own callers, and a travesty of the scenes in the drawing room is enacted in the kitchen below—all at the master's expense. Trust Biddy for looking after that.

Those who have no friends to call upon may be supposed to feel lonely on New Year's day. Not so. The free lunch tables of the bar rooms are bountifully spread, and are open to all comers. True, the liquors used must be paid for, and are not quite as good in quality as those provided gratis in the avenue mansions, but enough is dispensed to repay the saloon keeper for his outlay upon the lunch table. The fun is rather more uproarious than in the drawing room, and sometimes degenerates into a free fight, which the police are called upon to stop. But all who wish to be merry, and do homage to "the time-honored custom," can find ample opportunity to indulge their inclinations, in one way or another, on this festal day.

January the 2d finds Young New York with a head-ache, and the older part used up with fatigue. This is "Ladies' Day," and is devoted by the fair sex to calling upon each other, exchanging notes as to the receptions of the previous day, imbibing more punch, and swallow-ing more refreshments. The balance of the week is spent in recovering from the effects of two days of hard social work, and in preparing for the round of fashion-able dissipation, which fills up the balance of the winter.

CHAPTER XXI

AMONG THE BULLS AND BEARS OF WALL STREET

DESCRIPTION OF WALL STREET—VALUE OF REAL ESTATE—ENORMOUS RENTS—ORIGIN OF THE
NAME OF THE STREET—NOTABLE BUILDINGS—TRANSACTIONS OF THE STREET—THE SCENE
AT NOON—THE STOCK EXCHANGE—THE LONG ROOM—OUTSIDE DEALERS—THE REGULAR
BOARD—HOW BUSINESS IS CONDUCTED IN THE EXCHANGE—THE VICE-PRESIDENT—RULES OF
THE EXCHANGE—GOOD FAITH EXACTED OF ITS MEMBERS—THE GOVERNMENT BOARD—
CHARACTERISTIC SCENES—THE VAULTS AND THEIR TREASURES—THE TELEGRAPH INSTRU-
MENTS—THE "TICKERS"—LIFE OF A STOCK BROKER—SPORTS OF THE EXCHANGE—THE
CLEARING HOUSE AND ITS OPERATIONS—CURBSTONE BROKERS—RECKLESS TRANSACTIONS—
STOCK SPECULATIONS—BUYING AND SELLING ON COMMISSION—UNCERTAINTIES OF THE
STREET—HOW FORTUNES ARE MADE AND LOST ON WALL STREET—STOCK GAMBLING—WHO
ARE THE SPECULATORS—A DARING BROKER—"BLACK FRIDAY"—HOW AN OPERATOR WAS
RUINED—STOCK SWINDLERS—SHARPERS IN WALL STREET—THE COMBINATION SYSTEM—A
BAREFACED SWINDLE—ACTION OF THE GENERAL GOVERNMENT—HOW BOGUS OPERATORS
FLEECE UNSUSPECTING CUSTOMERS—AN INSIDE VIEW OF THE COMBINATION SYSTEM—
ENORMOUS PROFITS—THE SWINDLE EXPOSED—A WARNING TO WOULD-BE SPECULATORS.

I

WALL STREET

Wall Street, the financial centre, not only of New
York, but of the New World, is but half a mile in
length, and is one of the narrowest thoroughfares in
the Great City. It commences on the East side of
Broadway, opposite Trinity Church, and runs direct to
the East River, gradually sloping from its Western end
towards the water. It is handsomely built up along
the greater part of its course, and contains some of the
most elegant buildings in the city. Marble, brownstone and brick are the materials chiefly used, iron
finding no favor in the financial heart of the city. The
buildings are used for banks, brokers', lawyers' offices,
and as the headquarters of some of the greatest cor-

porations in the Union. The street contains the Stock
Exchange, the United States Sub-Treasury and Assay
Office, and the Custom House. All the buildings,
with the exception of those just named, are filled from
top to bottom with offices. Land is more valuable
here than in any other section of the city; even Broadway prices for real estate sink into insignificance when
compared with those demanded in Wall street. Rents
are in proportion, and the cost of a comfortable dwelling house is often paid for a year's use of a small
office in a desirable location. Landlords reap a rich
harvest here. Brokers must be close to the Stock
Exchange, and the lawyers doing business here must
be near their clients. These classes pay any rent
asked in order to hold their places.

The streets intersecting Wall street are lined for
several blocks with banks, bankers' and brokers' offices,
and are all included in the general term "Wall Street,"
in dealing with financial matters. Even Broad street
is absorbed in the term, and yields precedence to its
smaller rival.

Wall street derives its name from the fact that
under the rule of the Dutch, the northern wall of the
city followed the line now pursued by the street.
Long before the advent of the English, houses sprang
up on each side of the wall, and the open space between
them became a well traveled street, known as "Long
de Wal," which was afterwards changed to the present
name, Wall street. The wall was demolished in 1699,
and the stones were used to build a Town Hall, which
stood on the site of the present United States Sub-
Treasury. Prior to the Revolution, the lower part of

the street was occupied by rows of stores, from the river to Front Street, while the upper part, to Broadway, was taken up with dwellings. In 1791 the Bank of New York was erected at the corner of William street, and gave the signal for the removal of the residences and the conversion of the street into the centre of financial operations. The change was soon accomplished, and by 1825 the entire street was given over to the destiny which has since attended it.

On the south side of the street, a short distance below Broadway, is the Wall street front of the Stock Exchange, built of white marble and very handsome, but not so imposing as the Broad street front. On the northeast corner of Nassau street is the Sub-Treasury, a noble edifice of white marble, built in the Doric style of architecture, with an imposing portico reached from the street by a broad flight of marble stairs. Next door is the Assay Office, a branch of the Sub-Treasury, but a more modest edifice of granite. Immediately opposite is the finest private banking house in the Union. It is built of white marble, and fronts on both Wall and Broad streets. It is owned by the Drexels, who here conduct the New York branch of their enormous business. It is said that the ground on which it stands brought the highest price ever paid for land in New York. On the south side of the street, occupying an irregular block bounded by Wall street, Exchange Place, William and Hanover streets, is the Custom House, a stately edifice of granite, once known and used as the Merchants' Exchange. Just below, on the same side of Wall street, is the beautiful marble banking house of Brown

Brothers. All along the street are banks, with vaults stored with almost fabulous wealth, and offices occupied by men whose names are powers in the financial world. The transactions of "The Street" foot up an almost fabulous sum daily, and the mind fairly staggers under the weight of the figures which represent the aggregate of the business done here year by year. From 9 A. M. to 4 P. M. on week days, the financial transactions arranged here exceed those of all the financial exchanges in all the other cities of the Union.

The proper time to see Wall street in its glory is high noon. From the steps of the Sub-Treasury an admirable view is obtained of both Wall and Broad streets, with their busy, eager throngs, all bent on making money. Bank messengers, with bags filled with coin, greenbacks, bills of exchange, bonds, and stocks, hurry along, keeping a firm grip upon their bags and eyeing each person they pass warily; office boys, telegraph boys with yellow envelopes containing messages from all quarters of the globe, dart here and there through the throng, and quiet, unobtrusive detectives stroll leisurely along the sidewalks, on the alert to discover and prevent any attempt at street robberies. The great centre of attraction is the Broad street front of the Stock Exchange, where a stalwart policeman stands guard at the entrance, to keep out unauthorized visitors. The steps, the sidewalk and the street are black with a struggling, shrieking mass of "Curbstone Brokers," who are doing quite as lively, although not so reliable, a business as that which is going on within the Exchange. Long rows of cabs stand in Broad street awaiting customers. Men dart out from the Exchange or the neighboring offices, jump into these vehicles and are off like a flash. Fast driving is not noticed here, for time is everything. Overhead stretches a vast network of telegraph wires, looking like a gigantic cobweb, each and all throbbing messages that may affect the fate of millions. Over all come floating the sweet tones of the chimes of old Trinity, sounding clear and strong above the rattle and roar of the street, telling that time is passing, and eternity is drawing near for some of the busy schemers in this great realm of Mammon.

II

THE NEW YORK STOCK EXCHANGE

The Stock Exchange of New York is located on Broad street, and extends back to New street. It has also an L running through to Wall street, where the visitors' entrance is located. It is a handsome building of white marble, and the Broad street entrance is ornamented with a fine portico of iron. The building is occupied by the Stock Exchange proper, the Mining Board, and the Government Board. During the past year the internal arrangements of the building have been altered and improved, at great expense, and the Exchange is now one of the handsomest and most conveniently arranged edifices in the city.

The Broad street entrance leads directly to a large hall on the street floor. This is "The Long Room," and is devoted to the irregular sales of stocks which are not included among the transactions of the exchange proper. Any one, by paying $50, can purchase an annual ticket of admission to this room, and can engage

here in the purchase and sale of stocks without being
a member of the regular board. The hall is always
filled with a noisy crowd, yelling and gesticulating violently, and rushing about the room like a parcel of
lunatics. There is no regular order of proceedings.

NEW YORK STOCK EXCHANGE.

A dozen different stocks are being purchased and sold
at the same moment, and only an habitué of the place
can tell the meaning of the hideous cries and frantic
gestures of the half crazed mob. The crowd is not
overclean, and is in strange contrast with the natty,

sprucely dressed brokers operating in the Exchange above. Yet these men are equally in earnest with their more fortunate neighbors. Millions of dollars change hands here annually. No written and rigidly enforced code of laws governs the transactions of the Long Room, and you must know well the man you are dealing with here. Strange faces are constantly appearing here, for the ups and downs of the room are sudden and sharp. A few years hence you will see some of the men who are now dealing largely here begging a night's lodging at the station house, or you may find them seated in the Exchange above, among the financial magnates of the land.

The Stock Exchange occupies a spacious and lofty hall on the floor above the Long Room. It is handsomely decorated, well ventilated and warmed, and massive and elegant gas fixtures furnish the means of flooding the hall with a brilliant light. At one end is a gallery, with accommodations for about 200 persons, to which strangers are admitted during the sessions of the Board. A large platform at the opposite end of the hall is fitted up with handsome desks for the vice-president, the secretary, and the telegraph operator. On each side is a large blackboard on which the quotations of the day are recorded. Adjoining the hall are committee and cloak rooms for the use of the members.

The Stock Exchange Board is regularly incorporated under the laws of the State of New York, and is the only lawful association in the city for the purchase and sale of stocks and bonds. It consists of 1060 members, who are admitted by ballot, and no one but a man of well-known integrity and sound financial standing can obtain admission to the Board. The control of the organization is vested in a council of forty members, of which the President, Secretary, and Treasurer are members, *ex officio*. A seat in the Board costs about $6000, and is the absolute personal property of its owner. He may sell or otherwise dispose of it as he would any other property belonging to him, subject only to the approval of the Committee on Admissions. In case of the death of a member, the Committee disposes of his seat, and after paying all dues and other claims on the part of the Exchange against him, hands the balance to his heirs. A member who becomes insolvent or fails to meet his contracts is suspended, and cannot be readmitted until he has made a satisfactory settlement with his creditors. Should he fail to do this, his seat is sold, for their benefit. The Board requires from its members the utmost good faith in their transactions, and punishes any departure from the strictest commercial integrity.

All stocks and bonds offered for sale in the Exchange are closely examined by a committee, and none can be dealt in until it is found to be a *bona fide* security.

Two sessions of the Board are held daily, the morning session at half-past ten, and the afternoon session at one o'clock. The order of proceedings is the same on both occasions. Two lists of stocks, the Regular and the Free List, being called each time. The Regular List is made up in advance of the session, and must always be called, and called first. It is divided into five parts: 1, Miscellaneous Stocks; 2, Railroad Stocks; 3, State Bonds; 4, City Stocks; 5, Railroad Bonds.

The session is called to order by the Vice-president,

after which the Secretary reads the minutes of the previous meeting. The Regular List is then called, and the work of the day begins. Very little interest is manifested in the call, of miscellaneous stocks. Bids are quickly made and accepted, and there is an evident desire to get through with this part of the routine as quickly as possible. The offers and sales are repeated by the Vice-president to the Secretary as fast as they are made, and the transactions are recorded by him in the minutes, while a clerk registers them on the blackboard on the platform. Should a dispute arise as to the purchase or sale of a security, an appeal is made to the Vice-president, whose decision is final.

Railroad stocks are next called, and in an instant the Board is in an uproar. Offers to sell and to purchase come in rapid succession, sometimes a score or more at a time, and are all yelled out at the top of the brokers' lungs. The noise is terrific, and it seems as if the operators had suddenly gone mad. A stranger can make nothing out of this confusion, but the keen eye of the Vice-president is everywhere on the throng, and his quick ear catches the offers and bids, and notes the sales, which are promptly communicated by him to the Secretary, who writes them down. At the same time the clerk records them on the official blackboard, and the telegraph operator flashes them to all parts of New York, where they are noted on the long ribbons of the thousands of "tickers" in the offices, hotels, saloons, restaurants, and bar-rooms of the city. Thanks to these "tickers," or recording instruments, men can watch the market, and buy and sell, miles away from the Stock Exchange, for the "ticker" keeps them informed, minute by minute, of the transactions there, and the telegraph puts them in instantaneous communication with their brokers.

The railroad list completed, the excitement subsides somewhat, and the other portions of the regular list are called, arousing more or less interest, according to the popularity of the stock or the condition of the market. Then the Free List is in order, and the members can request the Vice-president to call such securities as they wish to deal in. At the close of the Free List members may ask for the call of some stock that has been hurriedly passed over in the call of the Regular List. This completes the work of the Board, and the session comes to an end. The afternoon session is but a repetition of the morning's proceedings.

The Vice-president's duties are very exacting. He must watch the proceedings with the closest attention, note every transaction, report it to the Secretary for record, settle disputes between buyers and sellers, repress all disorders, and punish all infractions of the rules of the Board. For the performance of these duties he receives a salary of $7000 a year. By his side sits the roll keeper, whose business it is to record the fines as they are imposed upon the members by the presiding officer. These fines are the source of a considerable revenue to the Exchange. The sessions of the Board are always marked by numerous violations of its rules by members, for the brokers are anything but a dignified or orderly body. The average broker pays annually several hundred dollars in fines, but he consoles himself with the reflection that the fine he has paid, or the objects he has accomplished by his practical jokes, are worth tne money. A member interrupting the presiding officer during a call of stocks is fined not less than twenty-five cents for each offence; smoking a cigar in the Exchange is punished with a fine of five dollars; to be absent from a special meeting is to incur a fine of not less than five dollars; standing on a chair or table costs one dollar; to throw a paper dart or ball at a member during the session of the Board is to incur a fine of ten dollars; refusing to be quiet when called to order by the presiding officer, smashing a hat over the eyes of a member while the Board is in session, and sundry other offences against good order, are punishable with fines ranging from twenty-five cents to ten dollars. The fines are charged against the members by the roll-keeper, and must be settled once every six months.

The Exchange watches carefully over the contracts made by its members. Its transactions are all open and made in good faith, and its members must live up to their agreements or leave the Board. This is not only a protection to the outside customers of the brokers, but also a safeguard thrown around the members themselves, as it teaches them to be cautious in their dealings, and to avoid risks that they cannot meet.

The proceedings of the Stock Board are generally exciting, and often indescribably ludicrous. Yet oftentimes the fun has a deliberate commercial purpose behind it. A sudden crushing of the hat over the eyes of some active operator may delay or change the character of an important transaction in which the offender is interested; a disturbance by a number of members acting in concert will prevent bids or offers from being heard until it is too late. In such cases the fines imposed are cheerfully paid, the purpose of the disorder being generally accomplished.

On the second floor of the Exchange building is a handsomely fitted up room known as "The Government Board." At the head of the chamber is a platform occupied by the desks of the officials and the telegraph instrument, and from this the seats of the members rise in tiers one above another. This Board is devoted exclusively to dealings in the bonds and securities of the General Government. Its organization and mode of procedure is similar to that of the Stock Board.

The Vice-president begins:—

"Sixes, '81 registered, '81 coupon; 5-20s '82 registered coupon. What's bid?"

Here and there from flanking chairs come sputtering bids or offers:—

"Ten thousand at ⅜, buyer three."

"I'll give an ⅛, seller three for the lot."

" ¼, buyer thirty, for fifty thousand."

" ¼, regular, for any part of five thousand."

First Voice.—"Sold, five hundred."

The presiding officer repeats the sale and terms, the Secretary makes his registry, and a new bond is started.

Sometimes when 5-20s are called, at first there is only one voice, which rings the changes on

"I'll give 115. I'll give 115 for a thousand; '15 for a thousand." Presently, however, before any response follows the offer, a member in a distant corner, either carelessly or maliciously, shouts out, "I'll give '14 for a thousand; '14 for a thousand."

The Vice-President plies his hammer: "Fine Irving—fine Irving, fifty cents." The roll keeper proceeds to make his little note of it, and Irving, who has violated the rule, founded on common sense, which forbids a member making a bid below or an offer above the one which has the floor, immediately subsides, amid the laughter of his neighbors.

Occasionally an interruption of a grosser character occurs, a member leaping from his seat on some slight provocation, and striking off the hat of the man who has offended. "Fine Harrison; fine Harrison again;" "*fine*, FINE him again." "FINE Harrison!" cries the Vice-president, repeating the word without cessation, until the broker's wrath has been appeased and he returns to his chair with the disagreeable reflection that a heavy score is against him for the semi-annual settlement day. Every repetition of that fatal monosyllable was a fresh mark of fifty cents or a dollar against his name. Generally, however, the Government brokers are more orderly than their neighbors in the Regular Board. Indeed, the whole proceedings are more decorous and respectful, the bidding, half the time, being carried on in a low conversational tone. At second call there is a brief excitement, but when things are dull throughout the street, this room peculiarly reflects the external influences.

Very different it is, however, on days when some special cause provokes great fluctuations. Then the members spring from their seats, arms, hands, excitable faces, rapid vociferations, all come in play, and the element or pantomime performs its part in assisting the human voice as naturally as among the Italians of Syracuse.   To the uninitiated the biddings here are as unintelligible as elsewhere, sounding to ordinary ears like the gibberish of Victor Hugo's Compachinos.   But the comparative quietude of this Board renders it easier to follow the course of the market, to detect the shades of difference in the running offers, and generally to get a clearer conception of this part of the machinery of stock brokerage.

In the basement beneath the room of the Government Board is a large vault containing 618 small safes, arranged in three tiers.   Each safe is a foot and a half square, and is rented by one of the brokers, who deposits in it for safe keeping, when the Board is not in session, a tin box containing his bonds and securities. It is said that the aggregate value of the securities kept here is over two hundred millions of dollars.   The vault is guarded day and night by four policemen specially detailed for that purpose.

The telegraph has very greatly simplified the business of Wall street, and considerably lessened its expense in one respect.   Previous to the introduction of the present system, the brokers were compelled to employ numbers of messengers to carry news of the transactions of the Exchange to their offices, and where time was of importance large sums were spent in cab hire.   The introduction of the Stock Telegraph has changed all this.   Every broker's office, all the principal hotels, restaurants, and bar rooms now contain an automatic recording instrument, connected by telegraph wires with the instruments in the various Boards at the Stock Exchange. The operator at the Exchange registers the quotations as they are made on his own instrument, and instantly they are repeated on every instrument in the city, the instruments printing the quotations in plain Roman letters and figures on a narrow ribbon of paper, where they can be easily read. Almost by the time the transactions of the Exchange are written down by the clerk at the blackboard they are known at every point in the city where a recording instrument is located. Thus both time and money are saved by this ingenious invention.

The life of a stock broker is one of constant excitement. Stocks go up and down so rapidly, so many changes occur, that he must be continually on the alert, watching the market eagerly, to take advantage of a lucky rise, or to guard against the mishaps of an unexpected decline. It is a wearying, wearing existence, and it is no wonder that in their amusements the brokers should be rather boisterous, or that they should seek to enliven the sometimes dull proceedings of the Boards with a bit of fun. The 15th of September is known as "White Hat Day," and is rigidly observed at the Exchange. Woe to the unfortunate broker who ventures to put in an appearance on that day with a straw or summer hat. It is ruthlessly knocked from his head, and the next moment the members are busy playing football with it.

III

THE CLEARING HOUSE

The Clearing House Association occupies a handsome building, erected for its purposes, at No. 14 Pine street, and owned by the Association. It is the medium through which the city banks exchange the bills and checks which each holds against all the others for the amount which all the others hold against it. The Association was organized in October, 1853, and now numbers as members fifty-nine banks, representing a capital of about $50,000,000.

The principal room is fitted up with handsome counters and desks for the officials. On the counters are placed fifty-nine desks, one for each bank belonging to the Association, each desk being marked with the name of the bank to which it belongs. The desks all contain fifty-nine pigeon-holes, each pigeon hole being marked with the name of the bank whose checks it contains. Each bank is represented by two clerks, one of whom remains at the desk, receives all the checks on his bank, and signs the name of his bank to the sheet which the clerks of the other banks present to him upon delivering his checks. The second clerk goes from desk to desk, and leaves with the banks on which they are drawn all the checks drawn upon them, deposited in his own bank on the previous day, and takes the receipts for the delivery of such checks. The city banks do not open their doors for business until ten o'clock, but the clerks are required to be on duty by eight, in order to arrange the checks collected on the previous day for delivery at the Clearing House.

At ten minutes to ten the bank messengers enter, and commence to take their places at the desks. As they come into the hall they hand to an official on duty at the door a paper containing the exact account of the bank they represent. These statements are transferred to a sheet prepared for that purpose by the Clearing House clerks, and must agree precisely with the checks received inside before the Clearing House closes its duties. If any error or discrepancy is discovered, the bank at fault is at once informed by telegraph, and its messenger is not permitted to leave the Clearing House until the mistake is corrected. The Manager of the establishment sits at a high desk on the side of the room nearest his private office, from which he can command a full view of all that is going on in the hall. At ten o'clock precisely he brings down his gavel, and opens the work of the day. The most perfect order and quiet are preserved. No loud talking or calling is permitted. A late bank is fined two dollars. A messenger violating any of the rules of the establishment is fined the same sum, and is reported to his bank. Should he repeat the offence he is expelled the Clearing House.

"The daily transactions of the Clearing House vary from \$65,000,000 to \$100,000,000. The system is so nicely balanced that three millions daily settle the difference. Each bank indebted to the Clearing House must send in its check before half after one. Creditors get the Clearing House check at the same hour. Daily business is squared and all accounts closed at half after three. Every bank in the city is connected with the Clearing House by telegraph. The morning work of clearing one hundred millions occupies ten minutes. Long before the clerks can reach the bank, its officials are acquainted with the exact state of their account, and know what loans to grant or refuse. Through the Clearing House each bank is connected with every other in the city. If a doubtful check is presented, if paper to be negotiated is not exactly clear, while the party offering the paper or check is entertained by some member of the bank, the telegraph is making minute inquiries about his financial standing. Before the conference closes, the bank knows the exact facts of the case."

The amount of the transactions of the Clearing House on the day it opened, October 11th, 1853, was $23,938,682.25. Its total annual transactions now amount to about $24,000,000,000. The largest amount for any one day since the organization, was $206,034,920.50, on November 17th, 1869. The largest balance paid to any bank was $10,585,471.31, on November 17th, 1869, and the largest balance paid to the Clearing House by any bank was $4,774,039.59, on the 5th of April, 1872. The operations of this Clearing House amount to over 65 per cent. of the total exchanges of the twenty-three Clearing Houses of the United States, and thus represent, to a certain extent, the magnitude of the daily business of the country at large. It is the boast of the Association that in spite of its enormous transactions, "no error or difference of any kind exists in any of its records;" and no bank belonging to the Association has "sustained any loss by the failure of any bank or otherwise while a member."

IV

THE CURBSTONE BROKERS

If the operations of Wall street were confined to the dealings of the members of the Regular Boards of the Stock Exchange, the business of the street would be

always conducted legitimately and safely. But a large
portion of these operations is in the hands of an entirely different set of men. The transactions of the
Long Room far exceed those of the Regular Boards,
and, as has been said, these are governed by no fixed
laws. Men must look out for themselves when dealing
with the frequenters of this room. Still another class
of operators exist. These cannot obtain admission
to either the Exchange or the Long Room, and so they
crowd about the doors of the Exchange, fill the sidewalks, and overflow into the street. They require
neither office nor capital for their operations. They
do business in the open air, and carry their capital in
their heads, or in their pocket-books. They are known
as "Curbstone Brokers," and are among the sharpest
and most unscrupulous operators on the street. The
only law that binds them in their dealings is that of
"honor among thieves," and they are often oblivious
to that obligation. So numerous are they, and so extensive and far-reaching are their operations, that in
times of excitement and distrust the combined power
of the Long Room and the Curbstone has made even
the Regular Boards tremble. They are men of the
coolest effrontery, and of the most unflinching nerve.
They know that fortune is even more fickle on the
Curbstone than in the gorgeous Exchange, and they
are always on the alert to profit by every chance that
comes in their way. They are gamblers, pure and un-
defiled, and are merciless toward those who fall into
their clutches. They have nothing to lose, and everything to gain; and as for compelling them to stand by
an unfavorable contract, why, he would be a wise man

indeed who could discover the means of accomplishing this feat. It is said that the daily operations of the Long Room sometimes reach the startling figure of $70,000,000, but there is no means of ascertaining the amount of the dealings of the Curbstone. That it is enormous, there can be no doubt.

V

SPECULATIONS IN STOCKS

In former years Wall street did a strictly legitimate business. Stocks were bought and sold on commission, and the broker was satisfied with his percentage on his transactions. He took no risk, and was in no danger of losing anything. Now-a-days a different state of affairs prevails. So great is the race for wealth, that many reputable houses not only buy and sell on commission, but speculate largely on their own account, taking all the chances of profit and loss. With such houses all is uncertainty. They may, by lucky ventures, reap large gains, but they are liable all the while to the losses caused by an unfavorable market, or a sudden crash in the securities they are operating in. No firm that does not confine itself strictly to a commission business can tell exactly from day to day where it stands. It is at the mercy of the market, and though prosperous at the opening of the day, the close may find it bankrupt.

The mania for speculation in stocks may be said to date from the close of the war. Then everything was in the flush tide of prosperity. Money was plentiful, and easy to be had, and men were led to engage in speculative ventures who, in former years, would have laughed to scorn the idea of their taking such risks. The petroleum discoveries added fuel to the passion for stock gambling. Securities of all kinds were dealt in with a recklessness that made the wiser heads of the street tremble for the future of the country. It was useless to offer advice, however. A. had amassed a fortune by some lucky speculation in Wall street, and B. was sure that he would be equally fortunate. What money he could raise was devoted to stock gambling. Often these ventures were successful, but very frequently they resulted in loss. Since those days the evil has grown, and has spread throughout the country. Men and women in all parts of the Union have their brokers in New York, who operate for them in their favorite stocks. Everybody longs for speedy and great wealth, and it seems so easy to find it in Wall street. Many win in the golden game, but many more lose their all. Nine out of ten who thus risk their money are ignorant of the street and its ways, and rely simply on the good faith and sound judgment of their brokers. But even if the broker is a model of honesty and business capacity, he cannot command success for his clients; he and they must take the chances of the market. They are playing an uncertain game. A sudden rise in the market may bring them wealth, or an unexpected depression may consign them to poverty. The only safe way for those who wish to get money is to keep out of Wall street, and seek a more legitimate and slower way of becoming rich. But, alas, like other forms of gambling, stock gambling holds its victims with a fearful power. They lose once, and venture again, but think that there must surely be a

THE BELL TELEPHONE EXCHANGE.

turn in the tide, and so they go on until they have nothing more to risk.

If fortunes are quickly made in Wall street they are lost there with even greater rapidity. You may see men in rags, so wretched that the Police Station is their lodging and the bread of charity their only subsistence, hanging about their old haunts in the street, watching the operators with wistful eyes, who were once high in the favor of the Exchange, and possessed of wealth and good commercial standing. They were ruined by stock gambling. Once they had palatial mansions on Fifth avenue, and were the favorites of fortune. Now they have no future, no hope. They have not the moral courage, even if they had the opportunity, to seek to regain their former positions. They have fallen never to rise again.

The best and most reputable firms in the street never speculate on their own account. They buy and sell on commission, and their only speculative dealings are for their customers. They take care in such cases to be protected by liberal "margins," which secure them against all possibility of loss.

All sorts of people come into the street to tempt fortune, and the brokers could tell some queer tales of their customers did they see fit to do so. When a person wishes to speculate in stocks, it is not necessary for him to buy the securities outright, though that is by far the safer way in dealing with first-class stocks. If he can satisfy the broker that he is a responsible person, he will be allowed to begin operations by paying down only ten per cent. of the value of the securities he wishes to deal in. Thus with $1000 he may buy

$10,000 worth of stocks. This percentage is called a *margin*, and the deposit of it is required to protect the broker from loss in case the stock should fall in value. If the stock advances the broker sells, and his customer makes a profit, out of which he must pay the broker his commission; if, however, the stock depreciates in value, the customer must either sell out at once, and bear the loss that attends the decline, or he must increase his margin to an extent sufficient to protect his broker should he decide to hold the security in hope of a turn of the market.

Of late years the control of the stock market has become centred in the hands of a few capitalists of enormous wealth. They move the market as they please, and their combined efforts will send stocks up or down, as they wish. They could ruin the whole street should they see fit to do so. That, however, would not be to their interest, so they content themselves with less sweeping operations, and on great "field days" in Wall street they fill their coffers remorselessly, at the expense of the smaller operators, scores of whom they coolly consign to ruin. Consequently these great operators are the objects of the most cordial hatred of the brokers in the street.

VI

STOCK SWINDLERS

If Wall street is the home of legitimate and honorable enterprises, it is also a chosen centre from which the worst of swindlers conduct their operations. From time to time advertisements appear in the city dailies and in the newspapers throughout the Union, announc-

ing that such and such a firm, the name of which is
given, is prepared to receive small orders for the purchase and sale of stocks on the "Combination System," and guaranteeing large profits to all persons
sending the firm their orders accompanied with remittances of from $10 upward. These firms announce
that they have peculiar facilities for operating in the
stock market, and that their system is so nicely arranged that persons entrusting them with their orders
cannot fail to receive a large return upon their investments. Money may be sent by express, or by postal
order or registered letter.

The country is flooded with these advertisements.
The religious press teems with them, and not long since
several of the leading religious weeklies warmly en-
dorsed a combination scheme, and commended it to
their subscribers. This particular scheme turned out
to be one of the most barefaced swindles ever attempted
in New York, and was broken up by the refusal of the
postal authorities of the United States to allow its proprietors to use the mails for their nefarious business.
It was proven that the names appended to the advertisements were bogus, and that all the various schemes
of the kind at that time in operation in New York
were owned and operated by one man; that no actual
operations of any kind were conducted by him in the
stock market, and that he coolly pocketed all the remittances sent to him, without any intention of making a
return of any description to the senders.

These advertisements do their work well. There
are always men and women ready to be caught by
cheap promises of sudden wealth, or handsome profits

on small investments. From all parts of the Union money is sent to the bogus bankers, who pocket it, and laugh at the innocence of their victims. Their mails are among the largest received at the New York Post Office, and every letter contains a remittance.

A little more than a year ago the attention of the postal authorities of New York was called to the operations of the bogus bankers. The matter was referred to the Postmaster General at Washington, and a special agent was detailed to investigate it, and in his efforts he was cordially assisted by the officials of the New York Stock Exchange, who were anxious to break up the infamous business. The investigations of the agent were directed towards several firms doing business under the following names: "Lawrence & Co.," 19 Broad street; "Adams, Brown & Co.," 28 Broad street; "Allen, Jordan & Co.," 54 Wall street; and "Barnes, Gibson & Co.," 11 Broad street and 55 Exchange Place. The investigation was thorough and satisfactory, and resulted in obtaining such conclusive evidence that the Postmaster General issued an order forbidding the Postmaster at New York to pay postal orders or to deliver registered letters to any of these firms.

It was ascertained by the special agent that all of the above named firms were bogus, and that they were all the property of one man, whom we shall term the proprietor, who had obtained control of them by recording, under the laws of the State of New York, fictitious articles of partnership. In order to carry on the business, he made an arrangement with two men, who were to assume the direct management of the various firms.

They agreed to pay the proprietor the sum of $12,500 a month, or $150,000 per annum, for the net receipts of the single firm of "Lawrence & Co.," and an equal amount for the privilege of transacting business under two of the other bogus firm names. The interests of the proprietor were guarded by his having confidential agents to be present at the opening of the letters containing remittances. These letters came in at such a rate as to make the profits of "Lawrence & Co." alone, for nine months, from March 1st to December 1st, 1879, from $17,500 to $20,000 per month, after paying all expenses, inclusive of very extensive advertising, and salaries of $100 a week to each of the two men employed by the proprietor. The profits of the other bogus firms were in proportion.

Now, this is no exaggerated story. The facts are given as stated by the special agent of the Post Office Department; they are known to the Post Office authorities at Washington and New York, and to the officials of the New York Stock Exchange, who can vouch for their truthfulness.

Schemes of this kind appear from time to time. The authorities discover them, and break them up, but in a little while others, under new names, take their places, and when investigated, are generally found to be in the hands of the old offenders.

The manner in which these bogus bankers, stock swindlers, or whatever one may choose to term them, conduct their operations, is very simple. They send out their advertisements, which appear in thousands of newspapers throughout the Union. Thousands of foolish people are attracted by them, and either at once send their remittances, or write for further information. In return, circulars are sent to parties making inquiry, setting forth the merits of the "Combination Scheme," and showing how even so small a sum as ten dollars can be used to advantage in the great operations of Wall street. "By combining your money with somebody else's," says the circular, "the probabilities of profit are far greater than by any other system, while the risk is diminished to the very lowest point and limited to the amount invested. Each customer has exact justice, and at the same time obtains all the advantages of the largest capitalist. By the combination system we concentrate our whole energies and capital on the most attractive stocks; keep the market well in hand; buy and sell at any hour; make quick turns; cover sales; and, above all, succeed, when others fail, from force of circumstances."

To the man or woman bent on making a successful venture in stocks, this seems perfectly clear, honest and above-board. The money is sent, and the return mail brings the sender a certificate of ownership of so many shares of stock in the "Combination Scheme." The firm promises to make a weekly report of its operations, and at the end of one month to close the combination and divide its profits, pro-rata, among the shareholders. It expressly stipulates, however, that no part of the profits or capital shall be withdrawn until the close of the combination. The certificate is accompanied by a pamphlet, containing testimonials (all bogus) from persons who have been benefited by the system; some showing how the writers have been saved from financial ruin by the investment of one hundred dollars in the combined scheme, and all testifying their delight at the immense profits realized from small investments, and thanking the firm for the fair and honorable way in which they have been treated.

In about a week or ten days a printed report is received by the certificate-holder, showing a handsome profit on the first week's transactions—the profit being generally about twenty-five per cent. The innocent victim is delighted. Surely he is on the royal road to wealth at last. Another week passes, and a second report is received, showing that the fortunate investor has gained fifty per cent. on his investment. This report is accompanied by a letter or circular, setting forth the merits of a new combination scheme, just forming, and urging the victim to send one hundred dollars, or as much as he feels justified in risking, in order to participate in its benefits. A large percentage of those receiving such circulars, delighted with the reports of their first venture, make a second investment. The third week arrives, and with it comes another letter, or circular, from the managers of the combined scheme. The victim opens it exultingly, but he has not read much of the communication before his hair begins to stand on end. The managers inform him, "with great regret," that they have no profits to report this week; that owing to the "unprecedented haste that had marked the efforts of a large number of small speculators to get rid of their holdings," the market had become completely demoralized, and the great operators bewildered. "A decline had been precipitated," they add, "that obliged us to make great personal sacrifices, in order to protect our patrons; and, although we have lived through the storm, we were obliged, most reluctantly, to witness the destruction of many a well-conceived and judiciously-executed combination."

The victim is now seriously alarmed, not only for the fate of his first investment and its fifty per cent. profits, but also for the second, from which he has, as yet, heard nothing. He sits down and writes to the managers, directing them to close his account, and forward him the amount sent them, with the profits to date, less their percentage. In reply he receives a few curt lines, calling his attention to the "contract" they sent him at the time they received his money, wherein it was stated that "no part of profits or original capital is to be withdrawn until the close of the combination." In other words, he is bluntly told that he has no control over the investment. For the next week the victim lives in suspense. Then comes the end. A circular is received from the managers, announcing the failure of the combination and the loss of all the money and all the profits. A melancholy preface alludes to a dastardly conspiracy headed by Jay Gould and some other well known speculators, which had so knocked the market to pieces that thousands had been ruined. In spite of their best efforts, say the managers, the combination has gone down with the rest, and they have suffered terrible losses themselves. "Trusting to appearances," they continue, "well calculated to deceive the most experienced veteran on 'change,' we, unfortunately, were caught in the same dreadful storm that has proved so fatal to many of the best known men on the street."

It is all over, the investor's dreams of wealth are rudely broken, and he must get over his disappointment the best way he can. This is not the end of it, however. In a few days he receives a letter from the managers asking another investment, and promising a return in thirty days that will more than compensate him for his previous loss. Strange to say, so fatal is the influence of stock gambling, thousands respond to this impudent request, and send their money, to be swindled a second time.

Pamphlets, circulars, and other publications are sent out through the country by the bogus bankers; the mails are burdened with tons of this matter, which is scattered broadcast throughout the land. Clergymen, country merchants, lawyers, mechanics, everybody who is supposed to be able to raise ten dollars, are plied with these printed appeals to try the wonderful combination system, and thousands from all parts of the country respond. None of these dupes ever receive a cent either of the money invested or of profits. They are simply fleeced. It is strange, but true, that men who in ordinary business transactions are regarded as sharp and shrewd, and not easily taken in, yield by thousands to the temptations of the stock swindlers, and risk their money as readily as the veriest greenhorn that ever lived.

Be warned, O! reader of these pages. What we have written is true, and carries its moral with it. If you want money, *work for it*. Keep out of Wall street, and have nothing to do with bankers and brokers who send you circulars and solicit your patronage in combination or other ventures.

CHAPTER XXII

ALONG THE WHARVES

WRETCHED CHARACTER OF THE WHARVES—PLAN FOR A NEW SYSTEM—THE NORTH RIVER FRONT—THE RAILROAD PIERS—THE FERRY HOUSES—THE FOREIGN STEAMSHIPS—THE FLOATING PALACES OF THE HUDSON AND LONG ISLAND SOUND—THE BETHEL—THE BOAT STORES—THE GRAIN ELEVATORS—THE EAST RIVER FRONT—SAILING VESSELS—THE SHIP YARDS—THE DRY DOCKS—THE CANAL BOATS—SCENES ON BOARD—THE FRUIT TRADE—THE FISH MARKET—SCENES ALONG THE WHARVES—ACCIDENTS—THE RESCUE STATIONS—THE VOLUNTEER LIFE-SAVING CORPS—" NAN, THE LIFE SAVER."

To the stranger the shores of the North and East Rivers present one of the most attractive scenes to be witnessed in the city. The wharves extend, in an unbroken line, along almost the entire water front of the city. They are, as a rule, wretched-looking piers of wood, thrown out into the water, and covered over with dilapidated sheds. The ferry-houses and the sheds of the great railway and steamship lines are well built, and often handsome structures, but they are the only respectable-looking buildings along the shore. It is hoped that at some future day the present system of piers will be replaced with substantial and handsome structures of granite and iron, which will enable New York to compete favorably with Liverpool and its other great rivals of Europe.

Beginning at the Battery, the North River front is taken up for some distance with the piers of the Pennsylvania Railroad, and several lines of steamers plying to ports on the coast of the United States. Above these are the ferry-houses of the New Jersey Central and the Pennsylvania Railroads, and at intervals higher

THE STEAMER BRISTOL.

up the river are other piers and the up-town ferry of the Pennsylvania road, the Pavonia and Erie Railroad ferry, the ferries to Hoboken and Weehawken, and the freight piers of the other lines of railroads terminating in Jersey City. All the great traffic and travel between New York and the South, and a large part of that to and from the West, enter and leave the city by the North River front. The foreign steamships lie thickly along this portion of the river. Here are the great floating palaces of the Pacific Mail Company, the In-

CUNARD STEAMSHIP "GALLIA."

man, White Star, National, State, Cunard, Anchor, and Guion lines, which are constantly arriving and depart-ing, bringing thousands of tourists and emigrants, and rich cargoes from far-off lands. "European steamers leave and arrive at the port of New York daily, some-times half a dozen in a single day; and in addition to these great ships that ply over the ocean ferry to Europe, there are lines to South and Central America, the West Indies, the Windward Islands, to Florida, New Orleans, Texas, Mexico, Cuba, and various other foreign and domestic destinations.   An ocean steamer is a vast floating hotel, where rich and poor find accommodations suited to their means and their tastes. When one of these great vessels, decked with flags, and crowded with people on its decks waving handkerchiefs to their friends ashore, moves out of the dock, it is one of the most striking and suggestive scenes to be witnessed on the water front of the city. The scenes consequent on the arrival of an ocean steamer have also their interesting phases, often mixed with a dash of the ludicrous, which grow out of the inspection of baggage by the Custom House officials."

The great steamers which ply the Hudson and navigate Long Island Sound also have their wharves on the North River.   These are the most magnificent vessels afloat, are fitted up with the greatest luxuriance and comfort, and well merit the name of floating palaces.   The grand saloon of these steamers extends the whole length of the boat, and is two stories in height. Massive columns support the roof, and around the entire saloon runs a broad gallery upon which the upper tier state rooms open.   The rooms are cozily furnished, and nothing that can contribute to the comfort of the passengers is neglected.   Some of the boats are now provided with the electric light, and present a brilliant spectacle as they glide along at night over the dark waters of the river or sound.   The table is provided with every luxury and delicacy of the season. The only drawback to these steamers is the constant

GRAND SALOON, SOUND STEAMER.

presence of numbers of women of ill fame, who make their homes on the boats, and boldly ply their infamous trade with men as shameless as themselves. These steamers cost immense sums, the price ranging from half a million to a million and a quarter of dollars. A night trip on one of these floating palaces is an experience never to be forgotten.

Right in among the shipping nestles the Bethel, or floating chapel for sailors, a neat little structure, with seats for several hundred persons.

Above Canal street the ice companies, whose houses are located along the upper Hudson, have their depots. The ice is brought down the river in barges, and distributed to city customers from this point.

In the neighborhood of Christopher street are the "boat stores," curious looking floating edifices devoted mainly to the sale of oysters and fish. They constitute one of the most singular and characteristic features of the river front, and carry on a busy trade.

At the foot of 54th street the telegraph lines which connect New York with New Jersey and the States beyond it are carried down to the river. The wires are enclosed in cables which rest upon the bed of the river. They reach the Jersey shore in the neighborhood of the Elysian Fields, in Hoboken.

Higher up the river are the grain elevators and docks of the New York Central Railroad, beyond which are the headquarters of the oil trade.

The East River front is devoted chiefly to sailing vessels, the California clippers, the great Indiamen, and the small craft that trade between the city and New England by way of Long Island Sound. Here also are the wharves of several lines of steamers running to points on the Sound, and the ferries to Brooklyn, Williamsburgh, and Long Island City. Several large ship yards, prominent among which is the establishment of John Roach, and a number of floating docks, lie along the upper part of the East River, and high over all rises the huge structure of the Brooklyn bridge. At the southern end of the East River front are the headquarters of the canal boats, "which receive the freight of the Erie Canal, and the locality is so deceptive that a stranger would never suspect the immense commerce which belongs to it. The turtle-like crafts, painted generally in the most grotesquely glaring colors, are so closely moored together that one can easily walk across them from wharf to wharf. Men, women, and mayhap children, may be seen from time to time on their decks, and strings of family washing flutter in the breeze, like ships' bunting. Here and there we may also see lace curtains at the windows, and flowers peeping from behind—in a word, all the signs of pleasant domesticity. If we could see through the decks, we should probably find the stern divided into three or four compartments, provided with all the comforts for a small family, even to parlor organs and sewing machines. The canal boatmen have their homes on board these vessels, and oftentimes show no little taste in fitting them up."

In the neighborhood of the Wall street ferry is the headquarters of the foreign fruit trade, and here are vast stores of the richest and most luscious productions of the tropics; lemons, oranges, dates, figs, bananas, grapes, and nuts of every description, for which the

Metropolis furnishes a profitable market. At the foot of Fulton street is the great Brooklyn Ferry, and the Brooklyn Market, and adjoining the ferry is the Fulton Fish Market, where dozens of small craft are discharging their finny cargoes.

Both river fronts present a busy and bustling scene. The streets are thronged with heavily laden wagons and trucks, and at the wharves gangs of stevedores are busy loading and unloading vessels. The noise and confusion are very great, and it is difficult for pedestrians to cross the streets.

Accidents are very common along the river shore, especially cases of drowning. As a means of rendering assistance at such times, rescue stations have been established at various points along the docks, and in each ferry house. Ladders of a sufficient length to reach from the pier to the water at low tide, boat hooks attached to long poles, life preservers, floats and coils of rope, are placed at these stations, together with a printed code of rules for their use, and instructions for the treatment of persons rescued from drowning. Each station is under the charge of the policeman stationed on the beat in which it is located, and in the absence of a superior officer it is his duty to take charge of all attempts at rescue and to render all the assistance in his power on such occasions. In case of accident, any one may use the materials of the station, but interfering with or removing them at other times is punishable by law. These stations have been of the greatest service since their establishment.

One of the most efficient forces engaged in the work of saving life along the water front of the city is the

COURTLANDT STREET AND LIBERTY STREET FERRIES.

"Volunteer Life Saving Corps," consisting of three boys, headed by William O'Neill, better known as "Nan, the Newsboy," or "Nan, the Life Saver;" the other two are named Gilbert Long and Edward Kelly. These three young heroes began their good work in the summer of 1878. At that time Nan was twenty years old, and Long and Kelly about eighteen. Having heard a great deal of the many lives lost by falling or jumping off the wharves, they resolved to start a life saving corps, and quietly went to work. They fitted themselves out with the necessary apparatus, rude, it is true, but effective, and after their labors of the day were over, devoted themselves to patrolling the East and North River fronts, from Grand street on the East River to Pier 28 on the North River, taking in seventy-one piers in all. They went on duty at seven o'clock, and continued their rounds until half-past ten or eleven. They received no public encouragement, no assistance of any kind from any quarter, but within six months from the date of their organization they saved twenty-five lives, some of them at the risk of their own. Only the policemen, whom they encountered in their rounds, knew of their noble work. Often they met with the blackest ingratitude from those whom they rescued. They did not hesitate to plunge into the river in the darkest nights, or to brave any danger, in their self-appointed task. Two years ago Captain Paul Boyton became much interested in Nan and his companions, and brought them before the public. Since then assistance has been rendered to the young braves, and they have been enabled to prosecute their work in a more thorough manner.

CHAPTER XXIII

THE MUNICIPAL POLICE FORCE

ORIGIN OF THE NEW YORK POLICE FORCE—THE OLD TIME POLICEMEN—"OLD HAYES"—
INCREASE OF CRIME—GEORGE W. MATSELL—THE FIRST REGULAR POLICE FORCE—OPPOSITION
TO IT—THE METROPOLITAN POLICE FORCE ORGANIZED—THE MUNICIPAL POLICE—POLICE
HEADQUARTERS—THE COMMISSIONERS—SUPERINTENDENT WALLING—THE SUBORDINATE
OFFICERS—THE PATROLMEN—QUALIFICATIONS OF A POLICEMAN—THE BROADWAY SQUAD—
DUTIES OF THE FORCE—OMNIPRESENCE OF THE POLICE—POWER OVER THE ROUGHS—DAN-
GERS OF A POLICEMAN'S LIFE—DARING EXPLOITS OF CAPTAINS WILLIAMS AND ALLAIRE—
FIGHTING A MOB—FEAR OF THE " LOCUSTS "—UNIFORM OF THE FORCE—HOW THE CITY IS
PATROLLED—HOURS OF DUTY—A SINGULAR POLICEMAN—HOW PETE JOINED THE FORCE—
HIS SERVICES—ARRESTS—THE STATION HOUSES—INTERNAL ARRANGEMENTS—THE " BUM-
MERS' ROOMS "—HOW VAGRANTS ARE LODGED—THE SERGEANT IN CHARGE—A NIGHT IN A
POLICE STATION—A FEMALE TRAMP—" DRUNK AND DISORDERLY "—A CASE OF DISTRESS—A
FRUITLESS ERRAND—A NEW WAY TO GET HOME AT NIGHT—SEARCH FOR A MISSING HUSBAND
—A POLITICAL ROW—YOUNG BLOODS ON A LARK—COSTLY FUN—A WOULD-BE-SUICIDE—
BROUGHT BACK FROM THE GRAVE—A JOLLY TRAMP—A GHASTLY SPECTACLE—MASKERS IN A
STATION HOUSE—THE MOUNTED POLICE—A SENSIBLE HORSE—THE HARBOR POLICE—A HARD
LIFE—PROVISION FOR DISABLED POLICEMEN AND THEIR FAMILIES.

In the year 1658 Peter Stuyvesant was Governor
of New Amsterdam, and the town had attained considerable proportions. The portly burghers, careful
for the safety of their lives and property, came to the
conclusion that it was dangerous to leave the town
unguarded at night, and so in that year a night watch
of eight men was organized, properly armed, and
provided with formidable looking rattles. This was the
origin of the splendid force of which New York is now
so justly proud. When the English came, in 1676, they
changed the name of the town to New York, and also
made a material change in the night watch. They
required all able-bodied citizens to keep watch by turns,
and punished a disregard of this duty by a fine. These
citizens were required to provide themselves with good
muskets and six rounds of ammunition. The head-

quarters of the watch were at the Town Hall, then located at Coenties Slip, and in the basement of this building cells were provided for the prisoners arrested. These were few in number, however, being mostly unruly negro slaves and drunken sailors from the ships in the harbor. New York was a very orderly town at that time, and the citizens gave the Night Watch but very little trouble. In 1697 a regular watch of "four good and honest inhabitants of the city" was appointed to patrol the streets by night. Each was provided with a bell, and was required to call out the hours of the night and the state of the weather. During the British occupation of the city, in the war of Independence, military patrols kept the streets at night, extending as far up the Island as the present line of 14th street. After the close of the war a patrol of civilians was appointed. They were generally men who pursued some humble and laborious occupation during the day, and watched on alternate nights, a good part of which they spent in dozing on their posts. They also called the hour for many years. They wore a leather hat with a wide brim, something like a fireman's hat, and this won for them the name of "Leatherheads." Their only badge of office was a stout club about 33 inches long.

During all this time the city had no day police. The first guardian of the peace by daylight was the High Constable, Jacob Hayes, generally known as "Old Hayes," who came into office more than forty years ago. His exploits were regarded as something wonderful by the New Yorkers of his time, though to the average policeman or detective of to-day they are simple enough. Yet, though he was a terror to evil doers, he was but one man against many, and even his zealous efforts could not keep the ruffianly class in order.

In 1840 New York had a population of about 400,000, and it was in the enjoyment of a commercial prosperity that then seemed marvelous. The lack of a police force was keenly felt. Crime was rampant, and in certain districts of the city respectable persons walking along the street were insulted, robbed, and beaten in open daylight, by gangs of ruffians who infested these quarters. At night the streets were absolutely unsafe. Burglaries and murders were of almost nightly occurrence. So bad did this state of affairs become, that the citizens with one accord declared that New York must be provided with a proper police force.

One of the four police justices of the city at this time was George W. Matsell, a young man of high character and great energy. He at once applied himself to the task of providing a proper force. He selected half a dozen good men, and placing himself at their head, nightly patrolled the wealthier districts, where burglaries were the most frequent. In a short time he was authorized by the other justices to increase his force, and a number of squads were organized and placed under the command of picked men, one of whom was the present superintendent of the force, George W. Walling. The force was regularly uniformed, and with Matsell at its head did good work. Mayor Harper lent it a vigorous support, but the uniform, which was copied from that of the London police, gave great offence to the Irish, who were very numerous then, as now, in the city, and the police encountered a stubborn resistance, which assumed its greatest proportions in the troubles at the burning of the Bowery Theatre. This brought matters to a crisis, and the Legislature of the State passed a law in March, 1844, abolishing the old night watch and organizing a regular police force, which was not to exceed nine hundred members. The city was divided into separate patrol districts, station-houses were provided, and the police force was systematically organized. In the spring of 1845 Mayor Havermeyer appointed Mr. Matsell Chief of Police, and from the first the force began to give a good account of itself, although its usefulness was sadly hampered by political influence, which has ever since been its curse. In 1857 a change was made. The Legislature consolidated New York, Brooklyn, Westchester, King and Richmond (Staten Island) counties into a Metropolitan police district. This district was under the control of a Board of Commissioners, seven in number, including the Mayors of New York and Brooklyn, who were *ex-officio* members. The consolidated force was under the command of a superintendent with headquarters in New York. The first superintendent under this law was John A. Kennedy. In 1860 the law was considerably modified, and the number of the commissioners was reduced to three. Superintendent Kennedy raised the efficiency of the Metropolitan Police to a high state. During the terrible "Draft Riots" of 1863 the magnificent courage with which the police held the city against the mob won them a proud and lasting reputation. Three days of incessant fighting proved them to be men who could be relied upon in the most trying emergency.

The charter of 1870 abolished the Metropolitan district so far as New York was concerned, and provided for the creation of a Municipal Police. All the old force doing duty in New York was retained, and the organization was placed under the control of four Commissioners, appointed by the Mayor with the consent of the Board of Aldermen. The command of the force was vested in a superintendent. This is the present police force of New York.

The Police Headquarters of New York are located in Mulberry street, between Houston and Bleecker street. This is known as "The Central Office." The building is a handsome structure of white marble, and extends through the block to Mott street, the front on that street being of pressed brick, with white marble trimmings. The entire building is elegantly fitted up, and is provided with every convenience for the prompt and proper discharge of the duties of the officials located within it. Here are the offices of the Commissioners and their clerks, the Superintendent, the Street Cleaning Bureau, the Detective Squad, the Chief Surgeon, and the "Rogue's Gallery." The building is connected with every station house by special telegraphic wires.

The control of the force, as has been said, is vested in a Board of four Commissioners. They receive an annual salary of $6000 each, except the President of the Board, who is paid $8000, and hold office for six years. They may be removed "for cause" by the Mayor, with the concurrence of the Governor of the State. They appoint the Superintendent and all the members of the force, make promotions, and have power to dismiss an offender after he has had a fair hearing before them. All complaints against policemen are laid before them, and they alone have power to try the members of the force. They also appoint the Inspectors of Election, about eleven hundred in number, select the five hundred and fifty polling places, and count the votes cast. The law requires that the Commissionerships shall be equally divided between the two leading political parties. This is an element of weakness in the organization, as it opens the door to political influence in the distribution of appointments.

The Superintendent is the immediate commander of the Police force. His duties are onerous, and only a man of high moral as well as physical courage and undoubted integrity can fill the position worthily. The members of the force receive their orders from him, through his subordinates, and are responsible to him for the proper performance of their duties, he being, in his turn, responsible to the Commissioners for the discipline and good conduct of the force. His office is connected with every station house in the city by telegraph, and he is in constant communication with all parts of the immense field over which he keeps watch. In this way he can spread the news of a robbery, trace a lost child, or track a criminal all over the city, and in fact throughout the Union, without leaving his desk.

The present Superintendent is Mr. George W. Walling, who has been connected with the force for forty years. He is a fine-looking, well-preserved man, and one of the most satisfactory officials New York has ever had. He is firm, but just, in the enforcement of the discipline of the force; brave as a lion, and deservedly popular with his men and with the citizens generally.

Under the Superintendent are four Inspectors of Police, one of whom must always be on duty at the central office. Each inspector has charge of one of the four inspection districts into which the city is divided, and is responsible for the preservation of order in his district. He must examine the police stations under his control, making his visits at times when he is not expected, and see that everything connected with it is conducted properly. Complaints made by citizens against members of the force are investigated by him, and he reports the result to the Superintendent, who, in his turn, lays the matter before the Commissioners, if the evidence submitted by the Inspector warrants him in doing so. The Inspector must also visit the patrolmen on their beats at uncertain hours, to ascertain if they are faithfully performing their duties.

The city is divided into thirty-five precincts, in each of which there is a station-house. Each precinct is commanded by a Captain of Police, under whom are several Sergeants, one of whom must be on duty at the station-house at all hours of the day and night. The Captain is responsible for the proper conduct of the station, the correct performance of their duties by the men under his command, and the general good order of his precinct. The Sergeants are the Captain's Lieutenants, and perform such duties as he may assign them. Below the Sergeants are the Roundsmen, who "go the rounds" in certain specified districts, to see that each patrolman is on his post, and to receive such reports as the patrolmen may wish to make.

The Patrolmen are the privates of the force. Each has a certain "beat" or route assigned him, which he must patrol faithfully during his hours of duty. He is responsible for the preservation of order on his beat, and is required to summon assistance when needed.

The present police force consists of about three thousand men. Their pay is not large, considering the arduous and dangerous duties required of them, and the great responsibility resting upon them. A Captain receives $2000 a year, a Sergeant $1500, a Roundsman $1200, and a Patrolman $1000.

Besides the force employed in patrolling the city, special detachments guard the City Hall, the Grand Central Depot, the Banks, the theatres, and public meetings; act as a Sanitary Police exclusively; do duty as a Mounted Police; watch over the neighboring waters as a "Harbor Police," and are assigned to special duty as detectives. For these special services they receive no extra pay.

Naturally, among so large a body of men, there will always be considerable sickness. When a Patrolman falls sick from "unusual exposure, exertion, or injury, while in the discharge of police duty," he is put on half-pay until he returns to duty. The Commissioners have power to award full pay to meritorious officers thus afflicted, and claim that such a course is usually pursued.

The Regulations of the force thus prescribe the qualifications of applicants for admission to the force:

"No person will be appointed a Patrolman of the Municipal Police Force unless he

"First.   Is able to read and write the English language understandingly.

"Second.   Is a citizen of the United States.

"Third.   Has been a resident of this State for a term of one year, next prior to his application for the office.

"Fourth.   Has never been convicted of a crime.

"Fifth.   Is at least five feet eight inches in height.

"Sixth.   Is less than thirty-five years of age.

"Seventh.   Is in good health, and of sound body and mind.

"Eighth.   Is of good moral character and habits.

"Applicants for the office must present to the Board of Commissioners a petition signed by not less than five citizens of good character and habits, and verified by the affidavit of one of them."

The applicant is subjected to a rigid medical examination, by one or more of the most competent surgeons of the force.   The standard of physical capacity is very high, and not more than one in ten of the applicants ever come up to it.   Only sound and perfectly healthy men are wanted.   Applicants must also state, under oath, their parentage, nationality, education, personal condition in every respect, their present business or employment, and physical condition.

The force is regularly drilled in military tactics by competent instructors, and the strictest discipline is maintained.   Thus, in times of emergency, the force is capable of acting as a body of veteran soldiers.   As a rule, the men are large, fine-looking fellows, and at their annual parades their martial bearing, steadiness and admirable discipline, never fail to win them hearty applause.   The largest and finest-looking men are assigned to duty on Broadway. Nor is this for show only. The duties of a Broadway patrolman are arduous and exacting, and scarcely a day passes that does not add its testimony in favor of the wisdom of the rule that governs their selection.

That many of the members of the force are brutal wretches, and are only kept in their positions by political influence, is unfortunately true; but taken as a whole, the police of New York are a credit to the city. They have never failed in their duty in any emergency, and instances of individual courage and heroism are of daily occurrence.

The duties of a Patrolman are numerous and difficult. Each has a certain "beat" or district assigned him, which he must patrol and watch faithfully during his hours of duty. In some sections of the city these beats are very extensive, and it takes the Patrolman a considerable length of time to walk around his district. In such cases more is required of the man than he is capable of performing, for a crime may be committed in some part of his beat, when he is far away on another part, faithfully doing his duty. The Patrolman is expected to use the utmost vigilance to prevent the occurrence of crime or wrong-doing along his beat, or, at least, to use such vigilance as will render the commission of it difficult. He must keep an eye on all persons passing along his route after dark, examine frequently the doors, lower windows, cellar doors, and gates of the houses he guards; peer through the peepholes into the stores in which the gas is left burning, to see that all is quiet and safe; to have a general knowledge of the occupants of the houses along his beat; to report to the officer in charge of his station "all persons suspected of being policy dealers, gamblers, receivers of stolen property, thieves, burglars, or offenders of any kind;" to watch all disorderly houses or houses of ill-fame, and observe and "report to his commanding officer all persons by whom they are frequented;" to give the alarm in case of fire; to aid persons appealing to him for protection; to stop all undue noise or disorder on the street; and to make arrests for certain offences which are named in the book of Regulations, of which each member of the force is required to have a copy. He is not allowed to stop and converse with strangers or acquaintances, except for the purpose of giving them such information as they may ask for; nor to converse with any other Patrolman, except to impart or receive information. He must not stop on his post, but must diligently patrol it, except when some suspicious light or person causes him to linger to watch it or him. He must be exceedingly careful in making arrests, so as to take into custody the actual offender, and not an innocent person; and he is forbidden to use violence, unless it shall be necessary in order to overcome the resistance of his prisoner. If he cannot make the arrest alone, or if he has good reason to believe that assistance is necessary, it is his duty to summon another officer, by rapping with his club upon the pavement, and in the meantime to call upon the bystanders for aid. A refusal to assist an officer when called upon constitutes a misdemeanor, and the offender is liable to arrest.

"It is common cant, that a policeman is always present—except when wanted. In the lower part of New

York this is an unjust charge. How far will you
walk in the region of Canal street, for instance, before
meeting a policeman—that is, if you look for one, for
it is his policy to remain inconspicuous?   Lower
Broadway, dim and gloomy at midnight, is full of police, furiously shaking at the handles of the doors, to
be sure that all are securely locked, peering through
the little peep-holes of the iron shutters, to see that no
burglars are at work in the stores where lights are left
burning all night, or that an incipient fire is not working insidious destruction; lurking out of sight in shady
doorways, while they watch suspicious loungers; or
standing in groups of two or three on the corners
where two posts intersect, and a Roundsman has happened to join them.   Leaving Broadway, and glancing
down dark and fearful back streets, like Bayard or Eliza-
beth, West, Houston or Sullivan, you are sure to see
the flickering light of the street lamps, and the ruddy
glare of red-sign lanterns, reflected from the silver
shield and brass buttons.   Go where you may, you
meet these erect and wide-awake watchmen.   They
are strolling through the deserted avenues of Washington Market; they are keeping an eye on rogues in
Madison Square; they are pulling silently in and out
of the shadows of the great ships lying asleep at the
wharves; they are dosing as 'reserves' in the thirty-
four station-houses, ready on telegraphic summons to
go to the care of a fire or the subduing of a riot.   The
worshiper, coming from his weekly prayer-meeting,
finds the policemen at the door, enforcing his coveted
quiet.   The family that goes for a day's recreation at
Rockaway, is sure that its pleasure will not be spoiled

by rowdyism, for a group of officers stand on the deck, seemingly absorbed in the magnificence of the summer's morning on the Bay; yet ready, ready! The opera-glasses sweeping the audience at 'Faust' or 'The Shaughran' catch a sight of a blue coat or two behind the ranks of white ribbons and pretty plumes.

"Though honest men sometimes do not seem able to put their finger upon a policeman at the instant they want him, rogues find far oftener that the 'peelers' are on hand when *not* wanted. Go to Chatham Square some night, break a window, and run; how far do you suppose you would get? Or go to Broadway and Sixth avenue and fire a revolver; how long would you keep that pistol? Let me snatch an apple from an old woman's stand in Fulton Market, and she would have me under lock and key in twenty minutes, if she thought it worth the trouble. Wander where we will in this vast city, the ruffian or vagrant cannot get away from the law. It follows him into his home, waits at all his resorts for amusement, and can often tell him better than he knows himself what he has been doing for twenty-four hours. This constant surveillance exasperates bad characters. They chafe under the restraint, make feeble efforts to rebel, but it is useless. The power of the police over the lower and evil circles of society is enormous; they have a mortal fear of the force. They know that behind that silver shield there resides indomitable courage, and in that closely buttoned coat are muscles of iron and nerves of steel. The 'Bowery Boys' and roughs of New York are all cowards, and they know it. They dare not meet half their weight of righteous pluck. I have seen a great bully cringe and cry under a policeman's open-handed cuffing, who had always avowed himself ready to fight any number of persons on the smallest provocation. Very likely he has a bowie-knife, or revolver, or slung shot—or all three in one, as I saw one night in 28th street—in his pocket at the time; yet he does not attempt to use it on the officer of the law. The occasional exceptions to this are rare and notable. How many times have a single policeman arrested a man out of a crowd, and no one of his fellows raised a finger to help him! They dare not. They have too wholesome a respect for the law, for that locust, for that revolver in the pocket; most of all they are awed by the cool courage of the *man* who dares to face them on their own ground."

Yet, in spite of all this, the policeman's life is full of danger. He must patrol streets that are known to be dangerous, narrow alleys, without a light along their course, where a well delivered blow from a slung shot, a skillfully aimed thrust from a knife, or a bullet from a revolver would make an end of him before he could summon help. He is an object of hatred, as well as of fear, to the dangerous classes, and they do not hesitate to take any advantage of him. Often some brave fellow is set on by a gang of roughs, and beaten or wounded. Yet whatever the danger, however great the odds, the policeman must face it all, and, to the honor of the force be it said, he does not shrink. Whatever their faults may be, cowardice cannot be charged against the police of New York.

"In 1873," says the writer in *Scribner's Magazine*, from whom we have quoted above, "'Mulligan's Hall' was a basement saloon in Broome street. It had been growing worse and worse, and one evening, hearing a disturbance, Captain Williams and the officer on that post went in. There were thirty-eight persons, men and women, of every color and nationality, all of the worst character and some notorious in crime. The Captain took in the situation at a glance, and determined with a thought to arrest the whole party. Placing his back to the front door, he covered the back door with his revolver, and threatened death to the first person who moved. Then he sent the patrolman to the station for help, and for fifteen long minutes held that crowd of desperadoes at bay. They glared at him, squirmed and twisted in their places, scowled and grated clenched teeth, itched to get at their knives and tear him to pieces; but all the while the stern mouth of that revolver looked at them, and looked them out of countenance, and the steady nerve behind it held sway over their brutal ferocity. It was a trial of nerve and endurance. Captain Williams stood the test and saved his life. He wonders now why they did not shoot him a dozen times. Certainly it was not because they had any scruples, for the first two prisoners sent to the station killed Officer Burns with a paving stone before they had gone two blocks. Captain Allaire made an almost precisely similar single-handed raid on the famous 'Burnt Rag' saloon in Bleecker street, one winter night in 1875."

One Fourth of July morning, a few years ago, the writer of these pages was coming up Third avenue on a street car. Looking down East 35th street a singular sight presented itself. A platoon of police formed across the street was slowly retreating backward, with revolvers drawn and pointed, while two of their number held on to a rough looking prisoner, whom they carried along with them. Following them was a mob of several hundred ruffians, yelling, cursing, and occasionally throwing stones. Wishing to see the result, I sprang from the car and hurried to a livery stable just opposite the Police station in 35th street, and about a hundred yards from Third avenue, from which I could see the whole affair. The Police retreated slowly across Third avenue, and to the station house, into which they quickly disappeared with their prisoner. A cheer went up from the mob, and the ruffians thronged about the station as if intending to attack it. Immediately the doors were thrown open and the entire force on duty at the station dashed into the street, armed with their long night clubs, and headed by their Captain. "Give them the locusts, men," came in sharp, ringing tones from the Captain, and without a word the force dashed at the mob, striking heads, arms, and shoulders, and in less time than it takes me to relate it, the ruffians were fleeing down the street and dispersing in all directions. Not all escaped, however, for each officer returned to the station with an ugly looking prisoner in his grasp.

The uniform of the force is a long blue coat, of heavy cloth, buttoned to the throat, with a row of brass buttons. A silver shield is worn on the left breast, with the arms of the city and the number of the officer upon it. A stout cloth helmet covers the head, and is also adorned with the wearer's number, enclosed in a wreath. A baton of heavy wood is suspended from a belt at the waist, and at night a club of greater length takes its place. This is provided with an ornamental but stout cord, by means of which the officer secures the club to his wrist when using it. A loaded revolver is carried night and day in the hip pocket. In the warm season a light blue blouse is worn in place of the heavy coat. The members of the force are required to be neat in their dress, and must come on duty with freshly polished boots or shoes. Untidiness in dress is punished.

"A policeman's time is reckoned by periods of four days, but he has no Sunday or holidays, save his annual summer leave of absence. Beginning at six P. M. on Sunday, for instance, he goes upon duty, and paces his beat until midnight. Returning he remains in the station house on "reserve" duty until six A.M.; then goes out for eight hours, after which there is four hours rest, bringing the time to six P. M. on Monday. At that time he goes on duty again for six hours, followed by six hours' reserve duty, bringing it to six A. M. This is followed by two hours' patrol and five hours' reserve, ending at one P. M., Tuesday. Then begins five hours' patrol, six hours in the house, and six hours more of patrol, ending at six A. M., Wednesday morning, after which he is "off," and goes where he pleases until six o'clock that evening, when he begins six hours of patrol followed by eight hours of reserve duty, five hours of patrolling again, then a rest of eleven hours in the station house, then another six hours of post duty, and at six on Thursday evening he finds himself off once more for twelve hours. The following morning he begins it all over again. Thus, once in eight

days he can stay at home all day, and every eighth
night he can sleep at home. But he must not be
tardy in returning to his work.

"At six in the morning and evening, and at twelve,
noon and midnight, the Sergeant on duty in each office
taps his bell. The platoon which is to go on duty—
each company is divided into two sections of two
platoons each—files in from the waiting room, dresses
ranks, answers roll call, is inspected, to see that each
man is in proper uniform, has his club, his revolver, his
handcuffs, and his fire alarm key. Then such general
orders as have come from headquarters are read, and
at the words, 'Draw batons, right face, march!' the
blue coats pass out and scatter to their posts. As fast
as relieved, the men who have been on duty during the
previous six hours return to the station."

At the Church street station the force on duty have
a singular coadjutor, in a dog, named "Pete." Pete's
history is a remarkable one, and is worth relating.
Late on a warm afternoon, about six years ago, a dog
walked into the main room of the station and stretched
himself on the floor. All attempts to drive him out
were in vain, and he was suffered to remain. Later in
the day he roused himself and trotted into the room
where the patrolmen congregate when on reserve duty,
and stretching himself under the table went to sleep.
At midnight the fourth section of the second platoon
was rung up. The men marched into the main room,
and ranged themselves in line. The dog followed and
took his position at the foot. When the roll was called
the Sergeant named the dog Pete, and bade him go
with the men. He followed them out, went around

from one post to another, returned with the platoon in the morning, and went to sleep under the table.

Relays of men were called during the day, but the dog did not move. At six o'clock the fourth section of the second platoon was again called out. The dog marched in with the men and took up his position at the foot of the line.

"By George!" said the Captain, "there's that pup again. Well, don't feed him, doorman, and he'll soon go away."

But he did'nt go away. He has never been fed in the station, and he has always acted thoroughly at home.

"There's one peculiar thing about Pete," said one of the Sergeants, "he moves and acts exactly like a policeman. He never runs or jumps or plays, but simply strolls along. He's fond of janitors' daughters, and will stand stock still in a shadowy doorway for hours at a stretch. Not a man in the precinct has ever seen him eat, and I'm pretty sure that the general public never saw him drink. And then, what a clever dog he is! In the winter of '79, on the 10th of January, if my memory serves, Pete was walking along Greenwich street, on his way from post to post, when he saw three men at the basement door of the bonded warehouses, Nos. 98, 100, and 102. A moment later, and the men had forced the door, entered the building, and closed up their work so that a passing glance could not detect that anything had been tampered with. Pete lay down by the door and growled. After a while Officer Dougherty came along, and patting the dog on the head walked on, expecting the dog to follow him.

Pete never moved, but growled louder than before, with his eyes fixed on that door. Dougherty tried to get him to move, but it wouldn't do. At last the officer suspected that something was wrong. He examined the door, then rapped for assistance, and the building was searched. Two of the burglars were captured. The other one escaped. About three o'clock one morning last winter Pete was trotting along Broadway, when he discovered a broken pane of glass in a clothing store near Cedar street. He stopped at once and barked like mad. Every man in the precinct knows Pete's voice. Officer Donnelly ran to him and found that there had been a light robbery. Whether the dog frightened the thieves away or not, we never knew. Another time the dog discovered a fire at 240 Fulton street. Pete has never missed his turn on the second platoon, and has never gone out with any other than the fourth section in six years."

The number of arrests made by the police is from 70,000 to 75,000 annually, sometimes running as high as 80,000 to 82,000. Of these more than one-fourth are for intoxication.

Each police precinct is provided with a station-house, for the accommodation of the force on duty and the detention of prisoners. These are so located as to be central to their respective precincts. They are model buildings of their kind, being generally constructed of red brick, with stone facings. The entrance leads directly to the main hall, at one side of which is the Sergeant's desk, generally a handsome affair of black walnut, with a standard gas lamp at each side. Behind this desk sits the Sergeant on duty, and before him is the "Blotter," in which are entered the arrests, charges against prisoners, and other events of each twenty-four hours. The room is provided with substantial furniture, according to its needs. The telegraph instrument is placed at a distance from the windows and entrance, as a protection to it in case of an attack upon the station. It is of a peculiar kind, and is easily worked by any person of ordinary intelligence. Speaking tubes and boxes for papers communicate with the other apartments. In the rear of the main office is the waiting room, in which the men congregate when not on duty. On the same floor is the private room of the Captain commanding the precinct. It is handsomely furnished, and is fitted up as a chamber and office combined, for the Captain as often sleeps here as at home. The upper floors contain the dormitories of the Sergeants, Roundsmen, and Patrolmen. In some of the stations the cellar contains the cells of the prisoners, and the rooms for the accommodation of persons who have nowhere else to spend the night. Two such rooms are provided, one for men and boys, the other for women. The women's room is in charge of a female attendant. In other stations the cells and lodging rooms are located in an annex, back of the main building. Bath rooms and other conveniences are provided for the officials and men of the force, and the entire station is kept scrupulously clean and neat Each Patrolman has a private closet for his clothing and other possessions, and each bed is stamped with the section number of its occupant.

As prisoners are brought in by the Patrolmen, the Sergeant in charge hears the accusation against them,

notes it down in the Blotter, and orders the prisoner to
a cell, where he is confined until the next day, when he
is sent to the courts for trial.

The rooms set apart for lodging tramps, casuals, and
those who have no other place to spend the night, are
furnished with Spartan simplicity. A platform with
movable planks runs along the longest side, and sometimes there is a second similar platform on the opposite
side of the room. This is the only bed provided, and
the sleepers must make the best of it. They are aroused
at daylight and turned into the street, after which the
rooms are thoroughly washed by means of a hose, and
made ready for their next occupants. It is usually
after heavy snow storms, or long, cold rains, that the
number of persons who seek shelter at the stations is
largest, and an uncommonly severe winter will send
an extraordinary number of vagrants to these lodgings.
Sometimes they are so full that there is no more room,
and then hundreds are turned away. The average age
of the lodgers is over twenty-five, but some few boys
are to be found among them. The men outnumber
the women two to one. Very few young girls apply
for lodgings at police stations. Most of the female
lodgers are women past middle age, dissipated and lost
to all sense of decency, although occasionally a woman
of modest appearance is found among them. Both
men and women are, in the main, Irish, German, and
Italian, very few native Americans being among the
applicants for shelter.

The majority of the lodgers are professional vagrants,
and sleep regularly at the station-houses. They are
generally found to have been drinking, and are some-

times so drunk and disorderly that it is necessary to lock them up in cells. Their names are recorded in the station-house books, and they are said to show great ingenuity in inventing new names and new stories to account for their condition. The police place little confidence in what they say. They seldom lodge at the same station house two nights in succession, but go from one to another, hoping to be forgotten by the Sergeants and keepers before they visit the same place again. Many of them claim to have come from the country, having been driven to the city by the sudden setting in of cold weather, and the consequent impossibility of getting employment on the farms.

The lodgers fare roughly in the stations. When one of them comes in, he takes one of the planks which must be his bed, and places it on the frame of the platform so that it slants from head to foot, and lies down, with his boots for a pillow and his coat for a covering. If there are but few persons in the room he may have two or three planks, but after he is asleep he is likely to be rudely dropped to the floor by having the extra planks jerked from under him. On a cold night all are taken early, and fifty men or fifty women lie heaped on the long platform. Next, the aisle is occupied, and as more come in they will crawl under the platform, until a mouse could hardly tread his way through this mass of humanity. Such a lodging place at 12 o'clock on a "full night" is almost as vile as the "Black-hole" of Calcutta. The heat comes up through the gratings in the floor, and the presence of sixty or seventy unwashed, gin soaked bodies adds stenches indescribable; while the snores of stentorian breathers, the groaning of wakeful lodgers, and driveling of drunken ones, the scream of some frightened dreamer, and the querulous wail of a sick child, unite to make a Babel of horrible sounds. A single flickering gaslight sends feeble rays through the laden air, and every ray touches a pile of rags which in the morning will become a tramp.

The Sergeant who sits behind the railed enclosure in the main room of the station-house sees many strange phases of life in his hours of duty. This is especially so when the station-house is situated in a populous tenement house district, where wrangles between neighbors are constantly going on, and landlords and tenants are in perpetual hot water with each other. The differences always happening between these two sets of people make a prominent feature in the complaint business of the station-house. The Sergeant sees most of the sad, wretched and unwholesome side of existence, and very little of its brighter and more encouraging aspect. If he be a man of kindly, sympathetic nature, he must be greatly moved at times; but his official position and the effect of long familiarity with cases of distress and wretchedness, give an apparent callousness to his manner and address. He comes to act his part with an even mechanical method, and is the same to all classes and conditions of people. A man who considers himself grievously wronged will enter the station and point out to the Sergeant with earnest profusion the story of his woes, to be met only with a few laconic, cold responses, that chill him to the very marrow, and make him wonder if a police officer has any heart at all. An old officer who has sat at the desk for the course of a few years, and who has a shrewd and observant turn of mind, can quickly measure the importance of every complaint made before him. Some Sergeants become expert in this line, and are the moral barometers of their precincts. They can furnish as accurate a diagnosis of the moral health of their districts, by a reference to their entry books, as a doctor can tell the physical condition of a patient by feeling his pulse.

Let us take our seat beside Sergeant —— at one of the busiest stations in the city. It is ten o'clock, and the night is cold and keen without, but the room is brightly lighted, warm and comfortable. With the exception of a few early lodgers who have been given quarters, no one has put in an appearance, and we begin to wonder if it is to be a dull night after all. The Sergeant smiles, and remarks that there will be business enough in the next three hours.

The door opens as he speaks, and a woman in a faded black dress, a battered bonnet, and a very dirty face enters, and hesitatingly approaches the desk.

"Can I have a night's lodging, sir?" she asks.

The Sergeant makes no reply for a moment, but gazes at her with curious interest, and then asks, abruptly:—

"When did you wash your face last?"

"I washed it in Bridgeport, sir," she answers; "an' I've come from there to-day; and never a drop o' wather have I seen."

"Give her a lodging," says the Sergeant, nodding to an officer standing by. "But, see here," he adds to the woman, "what are you doing in New York?"

"Ah! it's a long story, sir," she begins. "It was a man that was the cause of it, an' bad luck to him. He left me, after deceivin' me, an' I've come to New York to find him."

"How did he deceive you?"

"Oh, the way they always do. He got the best of me because I was innocent, an' he promised to marry me. When he was tired of me he landed out, an' I've never seen him since."

"Where do you expect to find him?"

"Here, in this city. I'd know his skin on a bush, an' I'll find him or die."

"Well, you'd better take a rest for to-night."

The woman goes off to her hard bed in the lodging-room, and the office is silent again; but only for a short while. The door opens again, and this time with a crash, and an officer enters, with a prisoner in his vise-like grasp. The man's coat is pulled over his head, his hat is gone, the blood is running from his nose, and his gait is so unsteady that he would certainly fall to the floor but for the firm hold of the policeman. His shirt front is covered with blood and beer, and his eyes are frenzied and bloodshot.

"Well, officer, what is it?" asks the Sergeant, taking up his pen, as the Patrolman drags his prisoner to the desk.

"Drunk and disorderly, sir," replies the policeman. "Wanted to fight everybody he met on the street. He got pretty badly damaged in being put out of Schlossheimer's beer saloon, and I had to take him in charge."

"What is your name, and where do you live?" asks the Sergeant of the prisoner.

The man gives his name and address, in a sort of incoherent manner, and is sent back to a cell, while the Sergeant jots down the circumstances of the arrest in his "Blotter."

The door opens again, and a woman, neatly draped in mourning, and with a pale, sad face, enters timidly and approaches the desk. In a low voice she asks the Sergeant if he can tell her of any respectable place in the neighborhood where she can obtain a lodging at a moderate price. Her manner is that of a lady, and the Sergeant listens with respect to her request, and gives her the address of such a place as she desires. In the same low tone she thanks him, and disappears, and the stern face of the officer of the law for a moment has a troubled expression.

The door is thrown open violently once more, and two flashily dressed young women enter, and hurry forward to the desk. Their faces are flushed, they are greatly excited, and have evidently been drinking. They begin their story together, talking loudly and angrily. They will not stand it any longer, they declare. Madame —— owes them money, and they "are going to have it, or raise ——." The Sergeant, who has listened patiently, mildly interposes with the hope that nothing of the kind will be raised in the station-house, and then asks:—

"How much does she owe you?"

"Twenty-five dollars each," they reply, in one voice.

"And why don't she pay you?"

"Because she thinks by keeping herself in our debt we won't leave her," they respond together; "and we want a policeman to come along and make her fork over."

The Sergeant considers for a moment, and then declares that the matter does not come within the jurisdiction of the police, and that he can do nothing for them. They stare at him in blank amazement for awhile, and then flounce out of the room, loudly cursing the whole police force, and the Sergeant in particular.

The next comer is in charge of another officer. He is very dirty, and wretchedly drunk. His tall hat is mashed in, and there is mud sticking to his hair. He is placed before the desk.

"Drunk and disorderly, sir," says the patrolman. "I caught him climbing a Third avenue Elevated Railroad pillar. He said he always went up to his room by way of the fire escape when he came home late."

The prisoner is silent, but tries to listen to the officer, and fixes upon the Sergeant as solemn a look as his bleared eyes will permit. He is too drunk to give his name, and is sent to a cell, where he is soon in a drunken slumber.

Toward midnight a poor woman, shabbily dressed, with a thin, well-worn shawl around her head enters, and approaches the desk.

"Can you tell me if anything has been heard of my husband yet?" she asks—the same question she has repeated every day for the past week.

"No, ma'am, nothing," answers the Sergeant briefly; but his eyes as he glances at the poor, sorrowful creature, have a pitying look in them.

"What was your husband's business?"

"He was a stevedore, sir."

" And you were married to him how long?"

"Eleven years and over, sir. We had five children,

all dead now but the youngest. He was a good husband to me; but he took a drop too much now and
then, and was cross and noisy. He left the house three
weeks ago, and we have never seen him since."

"Did he leave you any money?"

"He left us nothing, sir. The child and myself lives
on the charity of neighbors; but we can't expect to
live that way always."

"Well, I'll speak to the Captain," says the Sergeant
kindly, "and see what can be done for you, and if a
dollar will do you any good, here it is." And the good-
hearted Sergeant passes a silver coin over the desk,
and sends the woman away sobbing out her expressions
of gratitude.

Loud voices are heard on the station steps as the
woman passes out, the door is thrown open, and six
well dressed men enter, accompanied by two policemen. They approach the desk, talking excitedly, and
charges and counter-charges, mixed with much slang
and profanity, are brought before the Sergeant, who
sits stolidly gazing at the party, waiting for a return of
something like order. There is a lull in the talking,
and one of the policemen states that two of the men
have been engaged in a drunken assault at a political
primary held in the neighborhood, and that the others
have come to prefer charges against them. The
charges are made and entered in the Blotter, and the
accused then prefer counter-charges against the other
four, but as the policemen do not sustain them, the accu-
sers are suffered to depart, and the accused are sent to
a cell, where they raise a tremendous racket.

As the officials are departing for their beats again,

AN ATTEMPT AT SUICIDE FOILED.

two more enter, this time having in custody two hand-somely dressed, fashionable looking youths, whose flushed faces show they have been drinking, but not enough to prevent them from feeling the shame of their position.

"Drunk and disorderly, sir," says the officer. "Kicked over an old woman's peanut stand in the street, knocked all her stuff into the mud, and then tried to run away."

"But, Sergeant," pleads one of the youths, "it was only for a lark, you see. We'll make it all right in the morning with the old woman."

"Your names and addresses?" asks the Sergeant, coldly.

They are given, but are evidently fictitious.

"It was only a lark, Sergeant," begins the young man who has spoken before. "We didn't mean——"

"Lock them up," says the Sergeant, cutting him short. "You can state all that to the court in the morning."

And they are led away.

The silence that has fallen over the room after the young men have been led out is rudely broken by the hasty entrance of an officer from the direction of the cells. He is pale and excited.

"Sergeant," he exclaims, "the woman in Number Ten has committed suicide. She's hung herself."

The Sergeant springs up, tells the officer to take charge of the room, and hurries to the cells. We fol-low him. The door in Number Ten is wide open, and the doorman is in the act of cutting down the woman, who has suspended herself by means of a line made of her garters. He lays her on the floor of the cell, and he and the Sergeant bend over and gaze into the bloated face. The woman is not dead, and exhibits signs of returning life. Efforts are made to restore her, and are successful. As she recovers her consciousness she raises herself on her elbow, and glaring around savagely, curses bitterly the men who have saved her from death, and begs for a drink of whisky. No liquor is given her, however, and when the officers are satisfied that she is out of danger, she is handcuffed, to prevent her from attempting further violence. The rest of the night she keeps the place lively with her yells and blasphemous cries.

We return to the desk with the Sergeant, who enters the occurrence in the Blotter. We are scarcely seated, when two of the worst-looking tramps to be found in New York enter, and come up to the desk.

"Cap'n," exclaims one of them, in a thick voice, "let's have a shake-down for me and my pard, for the night?"

"All right," says the Sergeant. "Show these men back."

The tramp who has spoken, encouraged by the ready granting of his request, says coolly:—

"You hain't got a chew o' tobaccer, Cap'n, you can let a fellow have?"

"No, I hain't," answers the Sergeant, imitating the voice and expression of the tramp; "but I'll send you in an oyster supper presently, with a bottle of Mumm's Extra Dry, and a bunch of Henry Clay's; and perhaps some of the other delicacies of the season, if they are to be had."

The tramps laugh at this sally, and follow the officer to the lodging room.

Half an hour later four policemen enter the room bearing a stretcher, on which is laid a badly wounded man, while two more lead in the assailant, who is securely handcuffed, and bears the marks of the officers' clubs. He had assaulted and stabbed the wounded man in a brawl in a saloon; had resisted the officers who attempted to arrest him; and had proved so dangerous that they had been compelled to club and handcuff him. A telegram is sent to the New York Hospital for an ambulance, and the statements of the wounded man and the officials taken down by the Sergeant. The name and address of the prisoner are also written down, and he is sent to a cell with the irons still on him. In a short while the ambulance arrives and the wounded man is taken away to the hospital.

Shortly after two o'clock another detachment of officers bring in a batch of about twenty prisoners, male and female. They are dressed in all manner of fancy costumes. Here are Dukes, Don Cæsars, Hamlets, Little Buttercups, Indian princesses and warriors, and the like. They have been to a fancy ball, and left it so very drunk that they fell to fighting among themselves in the street, and were taken into custody by the officials. They are a motley lot indeed, and lend a strange aspect to the station. They appear to feel the ludicrousness of their position, and beg to be let off; but the Sergeant has no discretion, for the testimony of the officials is positive, and the charge is a serious one. So they go back to the cells, and in the morning will appear in full costume before the Court of Sessions, to answer the charges against them.

So the hours of darkness pass away, and the remainder of the night is but a repetition of many of the scenes we have described.

The Mounted Police, though a part of the regular force, constitute a distinct squad, and have their station-house in East 85th street. They are assigned to duty in the upper part of the city and the suburbs; are handsomely mounted, and make a fine appearance on parade. They are twenty-two in number, are all picked men, who have served honorably in the army of the United States, and are therefore experienced horsemen.

Each officer has full care of his horse and equipments and is responsible for their proper treatment. Nine hours' patrol duty is required each day, but there is no night duty except in case of emergency. The horses are the best that can be had, are all bays, and are selected with special reference to this work. It takes about six months to break them in so that they can be safely used to catch a runaway team, or allowed to stand alone while the officer dismounts to make an arrest. Some of them are very intelligent animals, and become greatly attached to the men who ride them. The older ones, when an arrest is to be made, will stand with their front feet on the sidewalk waiting for the officer to come out with his prisoner, when they will gently follow on to the station-house. Some of them will not allow a citizen to approach or catch them during any excitement. One of the officers gives his horse the credit of saving him from a severe handling while making an arrest for assault and battery in a group of shanties on 72d street near First avenue. He was surrounded by a crowd of sturdy Irish women, armed with sticks, stones, and everything they could lay hands on. The prisoner fought desperately, and tore the uniform of the officer nearly to pieces while struggling to escape, and would have succeeded, but that the old horse, appreciating the danger, dashed in, and by prancing and kicking up his heels kept the women at a distance until the officer had gotten clear out of reach with his prisoner safely in custody. The number of arrests made by the mounted squad for felonies of various kinds will compare favorably with those of any other up-town precinct.

The Mounted Police have other and equally important duties to perform, besides making arrests. As their posts are laid out on the principal drives, they are required to look sharply after runaway teams. During the sleighing season runaways are of daily occurrence, but it rarely happens that the officer fails to stop the team. In case of fire the men do good service by riding speedily to the nearest signal box, and sending out the alarm, after which they hasten to the police station and give the particulars to the Sergeant.

Since the annexation of Morrisania and North New York, seven mounted men from the squad patrol that district every day, leaving their station in the morning looking very much like soldiers starting on a scout, with rations for their horses strapped on behind the saddle. They remain away all day, and feed their horses at gentlemen's places in the suburbs. In the summer time they eat their noon lunch by the roadside. They are the terror of tramps and vagrants in these regions, and a welcome protection to the families along their routes.

The Twenty-fourth Precinct consists of the Harbor Police, and its station is on the steamboat Seneca, which lies at the foot of 3d street, in the East River, when not on duty. The men live on the steamer, and patrol the water front of the city in row boats. One of these boats guards the North River front, and another the East River front. They go up with the flow of the tide and return on the ebb. They row along the dark and silent wharves, watching the shipping, look under the piers for the concealed boats of the river thieves, strain their ears to catch the sound of muffled oars, and sometimes have a sharp conflict with the river thieves, in which revolvers are freely used on both sides. It is hard work, and on the dark, tempestuous nights of winter, when the wind is whistling through the rigging of the vessels at the wharves, and the surface of the river is roughened into a considerable sea, it is dangerous. Yet these are the times when the Harbor Police must be most alert, for they are the nights on which the river thieves are the most industrious. The police do their work well, however. Millions of dollars worth of property are in their keeping, and they guard it faithfully. Considering all this, it does seem strange that they should be required to perform such arduous labors. Several silent, swift steam launches would greatly lighten their labors and add much to their proficiency. Yet New York, with all its wealth, has never seen fit to strengthen the hands of the men upon whose promptness and fidelity the safety of so much of that wealth depends.

The annual cost of the police force to the city is $4,000,000; a sum much larger than is expended in either London or Paris for police purposes. The citizens, however, do not grumble at this. So long as the police are faithful and efficient they are willing they should be well paid. Nor is the city altogether unmindful of the brave men who watch over its safety. The Police Law contains the following clause:—

"If any member of the Municipal Police Force, whilst in the actual performance of duty, shall become permanently disabled, so as to render his dismissal from membership proper, or if any such member shall become superannuated after ten years of membership, a sum, not exceeding $150, as an annuity, to be paid such member, shall be chargeable upon the Municipal Police Life Insurance Fund. If any member of the Municipal Police Force, whilst in the actual discharge of his duty, shall be killed, or shall die from the immediate effect of any injury received by him, whilst in such discharge of duty, or shall die after ten years' service in the force, and shall leave a widow, and if no widow, any child or children under sixteen years, a like sum by way of annuity shall become chargeable upon the said fund, to be paid to such widow so long only as she remains unmarried, or to such child or children so long as said child, or the youngest of said children, continues under the age of sixteen years. In every case the Board of Municipal Police shall determine the circumstances thereof, and order payment of the annuity to be made by draft, signed by each trustee of the said fund. But nothing herein contained shall render any payment of said annuity obligatory upon the said Board, or the said trustees, or chargeable as a matter of legal right."

CHAPTER XXIV

THE FERRIES

NEW YORK'S ONLY MEANS OF COMMUNICATION WITH THE MAIN LAND—NUMBER OF FERRIES—
THE FERRY BOATS—CROSSING IN A FOG—ANNOYANCES OF FERRY TRAVEL—THE FERRY
HOUSES—A MOONLIGHT RIDE ON A FERRY BOAT—A SUICIDE—ACCIDENTS.

The situation of New York being upon an island, with a large portion of its population residing upon the opposite shores of the waters which surround it, with two large cities and several important towns lying opposite or near it, and with almost all of its principal railway lines terminating on the New Jersey shore, one of the chief needs of the city is an extensive and well-arranged ferry system. The system has grown with the necessities of the city, and now comprises about twenty-six lines, plying between New York and the shores of Long Island, West Chester County, New Jersey, and Staten Island. Of these lines, fourteen are to Brooklyn and adjacent points on Long Island, seven to Jersey City and points on the New Jersey shore, one to Harlem, one to Mott Haven, and two to Staten Island. Ten lines cross the North River, and sixteen the East River, and transport about 125,000,000 persons annually, besides a vast number of vehicles of every description.

As a rule, the ferries are well managed. The fare to the Jersey shore is three cents, to Brooklyn two cents, and to Staten Island ten cents. The boats run regularly at frequent intervals, from six o'clock until

PAVONIA AND ERIE RAILWAY FERRY.

midnight; and on some of the lines, half hourly from midnight to six o'clock in the morning. They are large and powerful side-wheel steamers, constructed on the double-end system, with a pilot-house at each end. The centre is devoted to vehicles and horses, and on each side is a comfortable cabin, with seats extending the whole length of the boat; one for ladies, the other for men. They carry as many as 1000 passengers at a single trip, at certain hours of the day, with a proportionate load of vehicles. They are handsomely fitted up, and on the principal lines are lighted with gas and heated by steam.

The passage of the rivers is made quickly and without difficulty in fair weather, but when the rivers are filled with floating ice, or shrouded in heavy fogs, one or more hours are sometimes consumed in a trip which usually requires but a few minutes. During a fog the trip is exciting beyond description. The dense mist hides the entire river and the opposite shores from view, and the pilots must trust to their compasses for the accuracy of their course on such occasions. On every hand is heard the hoarse whistle of steamers in the river, and the tolling of the bells at the landings on the shore. The boats proceed slowly and cautiously, stopping frequently, and the passengers crowd to the forward end, silent and anxious, and peering eagerly into the gloom. A steamer glides by like a phantom in the mist, and the next instant is lost, and oftentimes grazes the side of the ferry boat sharply, narrowly escaping a collision. At last, when the opposite shore looms up dimly, and the boat glides slowly but surely into her dock, the passengers breathe freely, thankful that danger has once more been passed, and glad to set foot again upon *terra firma*.

With the exception of a single line (the New York Central), all the great trunk lines from the West and South terminate in Jersey City, and few visitors to New York enter the city without making the acquaintance of the ferries. Thousands of persons doing business in the city and residing in New Jersey, Brooklyn, Long Island, or Staten Island, are dependent on them daily, and are often subjected to vexatious delays in seasons of fog, ice, or snow.

The ferry houses are handsome structures as a rule. They are built of wood, and are provided with comfortable waiting rooms for the accommodation of passengers. At the water's edge are slips with floating bridges which can be lowered or raised with the ebb and flow of the tide, and in these the boats lie securely moored until the moment of departure arrives.

A constant stream of travel ebbs and flows across the great rivers. From early morn until noon the rush is towards New York, and in the afternoon and until late at night the throng pours out of the city.

No greater pleasure can be enjoyed by the visitor to the Metropolis than a ride over one of the ferries by night. The river is alive with the lights of the vessels lying in the stream, at anchor along the shores, or gliding swiftly by over the dark waters. The long rows of lamps on the opposite sides of the river stretch away in unbroken lines of light. The boats are brilliantly lighted, and are filled with lively throngs. Vessels glide swiftly and silently by, exchanging signals by sharp blasts of a whistle or the tolling of bells.

A party of strolling musicians enliven the scene with the sounds of music, and the sharp click of the machinery of the boat blends harmoniously with the rush of the water as the steamer pursues its onward course. Suddenly there is a rush to the side of the boat, and a cry of alarm. A ghostly figure gleams for a moment on the surface of the water and then disappears. Some unhappy soul has sought refuge from the sorrows of the world "in the hush of the rolling river." The boat is stopped, a careful lookout is kept, but the suicide is seen no more, and the steamer resumes its course.

Accidents are common on the ferry boats, especially during fogs. Sometimes the loss of life is great; again the only damage is that sustained by the boat. Once or twice a steamer has taken fire in mid stream, and the disaster has been appalling. The boats are so crowded, that in case of trouble a great loss of life is inevitable.

CHAPTER XXV

THE PRISONS OF NEW YORK

THE TOMBS—DESCRIPTION OF THE BUILDING—THE INTERIOR—THE "BRIDGE OF SIGHS"—
PLACE OF EXECUTION–THE MALE PRISON—THE CELLS—THE WOMEN'S PRISON—THE
"BUMMERS' HALL"—THE WARDEN'S OFFICE—THE "SWELL CELLS"—THE BOY'S PRISON—
RELIGIOUS SERVICES—GOVERNMENT OF THE TOMBS—WARDEN FINN—THE MATRON—A
PRISON OF DETENTION—NOTED ESCAPES FROM THE TOMBS—"BLACK MARIA"—THE
POLICE COURT—HOW PRISONERS ARE DISPOSED OF—THE COURT OF SPECIAL SESSIONS—
THE "TOMBS SHYSTERS"—LUDLOW STREET JAIL—THE SHERIFF'S PRISON—IMPRISONMENT
FOR DEBT—CAPTIVE MILITIAMEN—FEDERAL PRISONERS—EXTORTIONS PRACTICED UPON
PRISONERS—HOW THE DEPUTY SHERIFFS BLEED THEIR VICTIMS.

I

THE TOMBS

In official circles the principal prison of New York is known as "The Halls of Justice," but the popular name of the edifice is "The Tombs." It is a massive structure of granite, in the Egyptian style of architecture, and occupies the square bounded by Centre, Elm, Franklin and Leonard streets. It was erected between 1835 and 1838, and occupies the site of the old Collect Pond, from which the city was once supplied with drinking water, and which was filled up in 1835. The building is one of the most imposing structures of the Metropolis, but its wretched situation, which is in a deep hollow, sadly mars its appearance. It is constructed of granite, in the shape of a parallelogram, 253 feet long by 200 feet deep. From the street it appears but a single story in height, the lofty windows being carried from a point a few feet above the ground, almost to the cornice. The principal entrance is in

Centre street, and is reached by a broad flight of dark stone steps, which lead to a massive and gloomy portico, supported by four immense Egyptian columns. Projecting entrances and columns break the outer walls on the other three sides, and give variety to the otherwise monotonous style. The site of the prison is

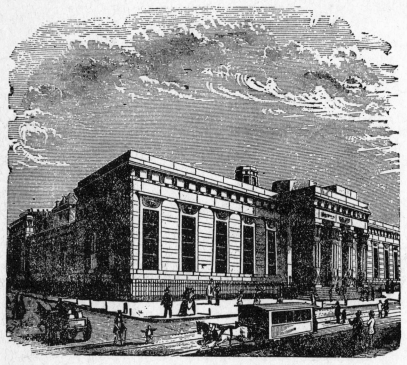

THE TOMBS.

low, damp and unhealthy, and successive Grand Juries have repeatedly condemned the building as unfit for its purposes. It was built to accommodate about two hundred prisoners, but of late years more than double that number have been confined in it. The foundations have settled in some places to a considerable extent, owing to the marshy character of the ground, and the building has been pronounced unsafe.

Passing in through the gloomy entrance, the visitor finds himself in a large courtyard, in the centre of which stands a second prison, one hundred and forty-two feet long by forty-five feet deep, containing one hundred and fifty cells. This is the male prison, and is entirely separated from the prison for females. It is connected with the outer building by a bridge, known as "the Bridge of Sighs," since all condemned prisoners pass over it on the way to their death. Executions are always conducted here in private, and are witnessed only by the officers of the law and such persons as they see fit to admit. The gallows is set up in the courtyard, near the Bridge of Sighs, and is taken down as soon as the tragedy is over.

The male prison contains a lofty but narrow hall, with four tiers of cells, opening upon the floor and upon three iron galleries, one above another. Two keepers are placed on duty in each gallery, to guard the prisoners. The cells are intended for two occupants, but are often forced to accommodate three. Each tier has its particular uses. In some of the ground-floor cells are placed the convicts or prisoners under sentence; the second tier is devoted to prisoners charged with grave offences, such as murder, arson, and the more serious crimes; the third tier is for the accommodation of prisoners charged with burglary, grand larceny, and like crimes; and the fourth tier is devoted to persons accused of light offences. The cells on the ground floor are the largest, while those of the fourth tier are the smallest; the former are very commodious, but the latter are scarcely large enough for two inmates.

The woman's prison occupies the Leonard street side of the Tombs, and contains fifty cells. It is in charge of a matron.

The Franklin street side of the buildings was formerly fitted up as a station-house for the police of the district, but it has lately been converted into a single large hall. This is known as "the Bummers' Hall," and here are confined the tramps, vagrants, and persons arrested for drunkenness and disorder in the streets. They are kept until the morning after their arrest, when they are brought before the courts for trial. Persons sentenced to confinement for ten days, or for a shorter time, are also imprisoned here.

The Centre street side contains the offices and residence of the Warden, the Police Court, and the Court of Special Sessions. Over the Centre street entrance are six comfortable cells, for the use of prisoners who can afford to pay for them. The windows of these cells look out upon the street, so that the inmates are not entirely separated from the world about them. Forgers, defaulters, and criminals who have moved in the higher walks of life, are the occupants of these cells. The Boys' Prison is also located in the Centre street side.

The Women's and Boys' Prisons are in charge of the Sisters of Charity, who endeavor to minister to the spiritual wants of the inmates. One of the rooms of the prison is fitted up as a chapel, and religious services are regularly held in it. The week is divided among the various religious denominations, as follows: Sunday and Tuesday mornings are given to the Roman Catholics; Sunday and Tuesday afternoons to the Episcopalians; Monday to the Methodists; and the other days of the week to such other denominations as may wish to avail themselves of them. Sometimes a Protestant clergyman will hold religious services in the corridor of the male prison, so that the prisoners may listen to them in their cells. But little is accomplished in this way, however, as the men pay no attention to the service, and often drown the preacher's voice with shouts, yells, and blasphemous cries.

The Tombs is in charge of a Warden, who is appointed by the Mayor of the city. Under him are two Deputy Wardens, a Matron, and a sufficient force of keepers to watch and guard the prisoners. The work of the kitchen, and the cleansing and repairing, are done by the boy prisoners, about thirty being so employed all the time. An abundance of good, plain food is provided, and prisoners are permitted to purchase provisions outside, or to receive them from their friends. Changes of clothing are supplied by the families of the inmates, but where these are too poor to make such provision, the Warden furnishes the necessary clothing at the expense of the city. Prisoners are allowed to receive visits from their friends, who are permitted to provide them with books and other reading matter; and are required to exercise themselves by walking for an hour every day around the gallery of the tier on which their cells are located. They are allowed to smoke, and to occupy themselves as they please during the day, but are constantly kept locked in their cells, except when out for exercise. No lights are allowed in the cells at night, as a precaution against fire. The sanitary arrangements are admirable, and are rigidly enforced, and it is said that, in spite of the unhealthy location of the prison, no case of disease has ever originated in it. This is remarkable, when one considers the wretched condition in which many of the captives are brought into the Tombs, saturated with alcohol, or broken down from destitution or exposure.

The excellent condition of the prison is due chiefly to the efforts of the Warden, Mr. James Finn, who has held the position for many years. He is ably seconded in the Women's and Boys' Prisons by the Matron, Miss Flora Foster, who has been in the service of the prison for thirty years. These admirable officials acquire an influence over the prisoners which is simply wonderful when the desperate character of the inmates is considered.

The Tombs is simply a prison of detention, where persons charged with crime are confined until sentence is passed upon them, after trial, by the Courts. About 50,000 prisoners are annually confined in it. As soon as sentence is passed upon the prisoners, they are sent to the prisons in which their terms are to be served, unless the sentence is a capital one, when they are detained here until execution. A constant watch is kept, day and night, over those sentenced to death, to prevent attempts at suicide; but in spite of all the vigilance exercised, the condemned sometimes succeed in putting an end to their lives and cheating the gallows. The greater number of suicides are insane persons, unhappy lovers, and ruined and deserted women.

Strong as it is, the Tombs has not always been able to retain the prisoners immured in its cells. Previous to the appointment of Warden Finn escapes were common. On the 1st of December, 1851, Henry A. Clark made his escape, but was recaptured; on the 2d of August, 1864, James Hampton sprang through the open window of the Police Court room, and got away safely; later on Robert Green escaped from the second tier of cells by using a forged visitor's ticket, in broad day; on the 11th of April, 1859, six boys escaped at four o'clock in the afternoon, from a window on the Franklin street side; on the 6th of July, 1860, Henry Hawk escaped by answering to the name of another prisoner who was summoned to receive his discharge; on the 19th of September, 1863, Conrad Smith escaped through the window of a second tier cell, after which he scaled the outer wall and leaped from the top into the street; and on the 19th of November, 1873, William J. Sharkey, imprisoned for murder, escaped in daylight, disguised in woman's clothes provided by his mistress, who also gave him her visitor's ticket for the purpose of passing the guards. These are the most noted escapes, but since Sharkey's performance, no prisoner has ever succeeded in passing the gates of the Tombs except in a legitimate manner.

In the service of the Tombs is a peculiar vehicle, known as "Black Maria." It is a strong, enclosed wagon with a door at the rear end, and with wooden blinds around the upper part of the sides, for light and ventilation. It is used for conveying prisoners from the police stations to the Tombs, and from that prison to the steamer on which they are transported to Blackwell's Island.

II

THE TOMBS COURTS OF JUSTICE

The Police Court sits in a hall in the Centre street side of the Tombs, and is presided over by a Police Justice, who administers the law in a sharp, decisive way. It is opened every morning at an early hour, and on Sunday morning at six o'clock. The Justice is well acquainted with the class of offenders brought before him, and often startles some old sinner by suddenly bringing up some portion of his life that will not bear examining. His time is precious, and he despatches each case with a promptness and celerity that astonish a stranger.

They are a queer set who come before the Justice at his morning session. Some are old offenders and are well known; a few are on trial for the first time. They started out the night before to see the sights and have a good time, and now find themselves called to answer to the law for their conduct. Drunk and disorderly is the charge against the majority of the prisoners. Some of the offenders are women, and others mere children, arrested for vagrancy or minor offences. The Justice hears each case as it is brought before him, disposes of it promptly, and either releases the prisoner with a fine or a warning, sends him on for trial in a higher Court, or commits him to the Tombs for ten days or to one of the institutions on Blackwell's Island for a longer period. First offences are dealt with as leniently as the law will allow, but old offenders receive severe punishments. Though a stern foe to vice and crime, the Justice is disposed to be as lenient as possible with those who are unfortunate, and often sends

SCENE IN A POLICE COURT.

a prisoner away with sound good advice, when the unfortunate has expected a harsh sentence. It is impossible for a criminal to deceive him, and he sternly puts down all attempts at sham innocence or mock penitence. During the sessions of the Court, many persons come to him with complaints against other parties. He listens to them patiently, and where their cases are not provided for by the law, kindly advises them as to the proper course to pursue. By ten o'clock the business of the Court is generally over, and the Justice is off duty until the next morning.

The Court of Special Sessions is held in the large Egyptian hall on the right of the Centre street entrance to the Tombs. It is devoted entirely to criminal matters, and here are tried the cases which are too important to be settled by the Tombs or other Police Courts. Two judges constitute the Court, but its sessions are often presided over by a single judge. Prisoners are defended here by counsel, and are allowed to introduce witnesses in their own behalf. The Court has jurisdiction over all misdemeanors, and as there is no jury trial in this Court, the accused has his choice of a trial here before the judges, or a trial in the Court of General Sessions, before a jury. His decision must be made in writing, and he cannot retract it when once made. Capital cases, burglaries, and the more serious charges are sent to the higher Courts for trial.

Hovering around the Special Sessions and the Police Court, is a species of lawyer known as "The Tombs Shyster." These men are licensed practitioners, but are without standing in their profession. They accost prisoners awaiting trial, and offer to defend them for any sum, from fifty cents to whatever amount the person is willing to pay. If the prisoner has no money the shyster will take his pay out in any kind of personal property that can be pawned or sold. He is not particular. He earns a precarious living, and is glad to receive anything for his services. He rarely succeeds in procuring the acquittal of his client, but collects his fee all the same.

III

LUDLOW STREET JAIL

Just north of Grand street, and in the shadow of the Essex Market, from which it is separated by a narrow alley, is a gloomy looking brick edifice, fronting on Ludlow street, and extending back to Essex street. This is Ludlow Street Jail, the prison of the county of New York. It is sometimes called "The Sheriff's Prison." All persons arrested under process issued by the Sheriff of the county of New York are imprisoned here.

The majority of the prisoners are arrested for debt. Although imprisonment for debt is forbidden by the Constitution of the State, it is easy for a creditor to consign a debtor to the cells of this prison. He has only to appear before the proper Court and make oath that his debtor is about leaving the State without paying him the amount due him. An order of arrest is at once issued by the Court, and the unfortunate debtor is arrested by the Sheriff, or by one of his deputies, and consigned to Ludlow Street Jail. Members of the National Guard arrested for violations of the laws governing that organization are also confined here, and these constitute a large class of the inmates. The United States Courts also send their prisoners here, the General Government paying the county a certain sum per day for the accommodations furnished such persons. The prison contains a number of excellent rooms, which prisoners who are willing to pay liberally for such comforts are allowed to occupy.

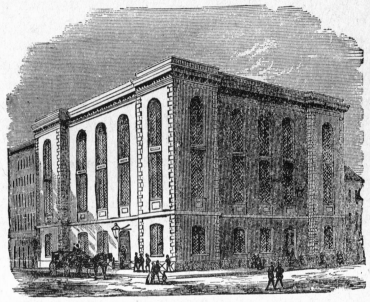

LUDLOW STREET JAIL.

The charges are extortionate, but the ordinary accommodations provided by the county are so wretched, that those who have the means will pay any price to obtain better quarters.

Perhaps no class of prisoners in New York are subject to such extortions as the unhappy persons confined in Ludlow Street Jail. Before reaching the prison they are obliged to pass through the hands of

the Sheriff's deputies, who receive no salaries, and are
dependent for support upon the sums they can extort
from their victims.   No favor will be granted unless
liberally paid for, and persons unacquainted with the
lawful charges of the establishment are fleeced un-
mercifully.

When a man is arrested by a deputy sheriff and desires to give bail, he is taken to the Sheriff's office, and
his friends who are likely to become his sureties are
sent for. The law requires that a reasonable time shall
be allowed him in which to find bail.   If, however, he
wishes to leave the Sheriff's office, he can do so only
by feeing a deputy, and the amount demanded is in
proportion to the prisoner's probable means.   A man
of wealth, if his bail be fixed at a large amount, not
infrequently pays several hundred dollars a day for the
privilege of being at large in the company of a deputy
Sheriff.   When the bondsmen appear, a charge of
$11.75 is made for giving a bond.   The law fixing the
Sheriff's fees says that the charge for giving a bail
bond shall be 37 cents; but this is interpreted to mean
simply for signing the bond, and by making charges
for drawing the bond, for a searcher's work in ascertaining the standing of the bondsmen, and for several
notary fees, the above amount is reached.   Lawyers
assert that as high as $21.75 has been charged, depu-
ties making any charge they think will be paid, failing
to pay which the defendant is incarcerated in Ludlow
Street Jail.   In many cases it is expected that the defendant's attorney, if he has one, will make no objection
to the extortionate charge, and will not enlighten his
client as to the legal fee.

It is also alleged that the Sheriff's deputies refrain from serving an order of arrest if $10 to $20 is forth-coming, and if the defendant shows a willingness to submit, the deputy repeats the process, until finally the plaintiff in the action compels the arrest to be made. Another common practice is to delay serving an order of arrest until after four o'clock, at which hour the Sheriff's office is closed. The arrested man is then willing to pay a considerable sum to have the order withheld until the next day, or to have his bonds taken at the deputy's house. Lawyers also say that no bail bond will be accepted at the Sheriff's office except one drawn there, the reason given being that the bond must be "satisfactory to the Sheriff." This is under-stood to mean that no bond will be considered "satis-factory" unless it is drawn in the Sheriff's office and can be charged for.

Efforts have been made by the Bar Association to put a stop to these abuses, but so far without success.

CHAPTER XXVI

PUBLIC SQUARES

THE BATTERY PARK--ITS HISTORY--THE BATTERY IN OLD TIMES--ITS PRESENT CONDITION--A
DELIGHTFUL BREATHING PLACE--THE BARGE OFFICE--THE BOWLING GREEN--THE CITY
HALL PARK--TOMPKINS SQUARE--SQUANDERING THE PUBLIC FUNDS--A FINE PARK RUINED--
WASHINGTON SQUARE--UNION SQUARE AND ITS SURROUNDINGS--THE "SLAVE MARKET"
--STUYVESANT SQUARE--MADISON SQUARE--A DELIGHTFUL PLEASURE-GROUND--MAGNIFI-
CENT SURROUNDINGS--GRAMMERCY PARK--RESERVOIR SQUARE--MOUNT MORRIS SQUARE--
MORNINGSIDE PARK--RIVERSIDE PARK.

Besides the Central Park, New York contains a
number of smaller pleasure grounds, all of which, with
one exception, are tastefully laid off and handsomely
ornamented with shrubbery, and some with statues and
fountains.

Beginning at the lower end of the city, the first of
these is Battery Park, which comprises an area of
twenty-one acres, and occupies the extreme southern-
most point of Manhattan Island. It derives its name
from the battery, built on the site by order of the English authorities, in 1734. The old Dutch fort, built by
the original settlers of Manhattan Island, was erected
on the spot now occupied by *the Bowling Green*. At
this time the point of the island was rocky and swampy,
but in 1792, after the independence of the country had
been won, measures were begun for filling up the site
and laying it off as a public park, and since then it has
been used for that purpose. Until about thirty-five
years ago, it was the favorite, as well as the handsomest, pleasure ground in the city, and was surrounded
by stately residences, occupied by wealthy and leading

citizens. Trade at length invaded this region, and the Upper Ten were driven higher up the island; the stately residences gave place to warehouses and offices, and the Battery was neglected. It became a rendezvous for tramps, and the favorite dumping-ground for all sorts of rubbish. What was once the pride and boast of the city became one of its greatest nuisances. Such a state of affairs could not continue long, however, and in 1869 the park was redeemed. The General Government built a massive sea-wall some distance into the water, and the park was extended to it, thus greatly enlarging its area. The rubbish which had accumulated here was carted away, and further deposits were prohibited under severe penalties; the old rookeries and street-venders' stands which had accumulated about Castle Garden were removed, and the Battery was laid off into a handsome and well-arranged park.

The Battery is handsomely planted with shade trees, flowers, and shrubbery, and is provided with broad stone walks, which traverse it in every direction. In the centre is a tasteful music pavilion, where concerts are given by the city band at stated times in the warm season; and close by is a tall flag-staff, from which the national ensign floats proudly in the breeze. A massive sea-wall of granite forms the water front, and is provided with broad stairways leading down to the water. At the northern end, projecting into the Bay, is Castle Garden, the famous emigrant depot, of which more elsewhere; and at the southern end, on the water's edge, is the barge office of the Custom House, an elegant granite edifice in the Byzantine style of architecture. This is the headquarters of the various boats used in the revenue service of the United States in these waters, and when completed will also be devoted to the reception of passengers from the European steamers and their baggage, during the examination by the Customs officials. The eastern portion of the Park is traversed by the line of the New York Elevated Railroad, which has one of its principal stations at the South Ferry, just beyond the limits of the grounds.

The Battery is by far the coolest place in New York in summer. Here one may escape from the heats of the city, and enjoy the delicious sea-breeze which sweeps in unobstructed from the blue water, which can be faintly seen beyond the Narrows. The Inner Bay, a portion of the East River, the Hudson, with Brooklyn, the islands of the Bay and their fortifications, and Jersey City, and the shipping in the harbor, and the wharves, are full in sight, and make up one of the grandest views to be seen on earth.

The Bowling Green is the name given to a small, circular space at the lower end of Broadway. It is well shaded, is filled with pretty shrubbery and flowers, and is ornamented with a fountain in the centre. It was the first public pleasure-ground laid out in New York, and dates from 1734. In 1711, a leaden statue of George III, of England, was erected where the fountain now stands. It was pulled down at the outbreak of the Revolution, and the metal was run into bullets for the use of Washington's army.

The *City Hall Park*, or "The Park" as it is termed by old residents, is located about a mile above the

Battery, and contains the City Hall and the County Buildings. It originally comprised eleven acres of ground, and was shaded with fine old trees. The city, about ten years ago, ceded to the General Government the extreme southern portion of the Park, as a site for a new Post Office, and this grand edifice has now considerably reduced the size of the Park. What is left is a large open space of several acres, laid out with walks, a fountain, trees, and shrubbery. It is the main thoroughfare between Broadway and the streets lying east of the Park.

Tompkins Square constitutes the only breathing space in the terribly overcrowded tenement house districts of the eastern side of the city. It comprises an area of ten acres, bounded by Avenues A and B and 7th and 10th streets. It was presented to the city about half a century ago, by John Jacob Astor, as "a place of healthful recreation" for the masses. Since then it has cost the city more money than any public square within its limits. At the time it became public property it was adorned with noble shade trees and shrubbery, was laid off with pleasant walks, and the surface was perfectly level. Some years ago the city authorities were seized with a desire to diversify its surface with artificial hills, and laborers were at once set to work to make the so-called improvements. Half of the trees were cut down, and the work on the grounds, which was simply a political job, lagged. Then it was decided to convert it into a drill ground, or "Military Plaza," and the surface was again leveled, and the remainder of the trees swept away. By this time the Astor family had become disgusted with the manner in which their ancestor's wish to provide a place of pleasant resort had been set aside, and they brought suit against the city to recover the property, basing their claim upon the plain fact that it had been diverted from the use for which it was given. The authorities then inaugurated another change. The drill ground was to be changed to a park again, and the work was immediately begun. It is still in progress.

Washington Square lies at the lower end of Fifth avenue, three blocks west of Broadway. It is bounded by Waverley Place, McDougal street, West Fourth street, and University Place. It comprises an area of eight acres, and contains some of the noblest trees in the city. A handsome fountain occupies the centre of the Square, and the grounds are tastefully laid off. On the east side of the Square are a Lutheran Church and the Gothic edifice of the University of New York.

Union Square lies between Broadway and Fourth avenue, and extends from 14th to 17th streets. It is about three and a half acres in extent, and contains a number of fine shade trees. In the centre is a handsome ornamental fountain, and flowers and shrubbery give to the place an air of beauty in the spring and summer. Near the fountain is a pretty cottage, containing toilet rooms for ladies and children on the main floor, and accommodations for gentlemen in the basement. A broad plaza borders the Square on the northern side, along 17th street, and here is arranged a long row of ornamental gas-lamps, which on special occasions illuminate the Square. Along the southern border, or 14th street side, are statues of Washington, Lafayette, and Lincoln.

UNION SQUARE, FROM FOURTEENTH STREET.

Union Square lies in the centre of one of the busiest and brightest portions of New York. Broadway sweeps around it, with its rows of magnificent buildings, and the 14th street and Fourth avenue sides rival the great thoroughfare in their grand edifices. The southeast corner of Broadway and 14th street is marked by the Union Place Hotel, next door to which is the Union Square Theatre, and immediately opposite, across Broadway, towers the superb iron building of the Domestic Sewing Machine Company. On the east side, facing on Fourth avenue, are the Union Square and Clarendon Hotels; the Everett House faces the Square on 17th street, and on Broadway are Tiffany's and several of the finest stores in the city. Everything is bright and lively. Crowds line the sidewalks of the streets surrounding the Square, and pour along its broad walks, by day and night; and after nightfall the dazzling rays of the electric lights illuminate the pretty grounds, with a brilliancy almost equal to that of day. Several of the leading places of amusement are in close proximity to Union Square, and this causes it to be thronged until a late hour of the night. The neighborhood is also a favorite rendezvous with the members of the theatrical profession, to whom that portion of 14th street opposite the Washington statue is known as "The Slave Market," in consequence of the large number of actors always to be found hanging around there in summer, looking for engagements.

Stuyvesant Square lies to the east of Union Square, between 15th and 17th streets, and covers an area of a little more than four acres. It is bisected by Second avenue, and each of its two sections is enclosed with an iron fence, the gates of which are locked at night. The grounds are prettily laid out, and are filled with shrubbery and flowers. In the centre of each portion of the square is a tasteful fountain. The ground was presented to the city by the late Peter G. Stuyvesant. The streets surrounding it are occupied by elegant private residences, and on the west side is St. George's Episcopal Church, one of the handsomest religious edifices in New York.

Madison Square is the prettiest of all the smaller parks of New York, and is situated in the most attractive portion of the city. It lies between Broadway and Fifth avenue and Madison avenue, and 23d and 26th streets, and is six acres in extent. The iron fence which formerly enclosed it was removed some years ago, and this imparts to it an air of space, which is heightened by an open area in the midst of which it lies. It is well shaded by noble trees, and fairly smiles with gay flowers in the summer. A fine fountain in the centre is one of its chief attractions, and around it gather, on fair mornings, crowds of children and nurses from the neighboring fashionable streets. A bronze statue of William H. Seward ornaments the southwestern corner, while at the northwest corner is the noble statue of Admiral Farragut, also of bronze. At night the grounds are well lighted by the electric lamps on Broadway and Fifth avenue. The Fifth Avenue Hotel, and the Albemarle and Hoffman Houses face it on the west, while on the north is the Hotel Brunswick, opposite which, across Fifth avenue, is the towering Hotel Victoria. 23d street is lined with elegant stores, and superb private mansions and a

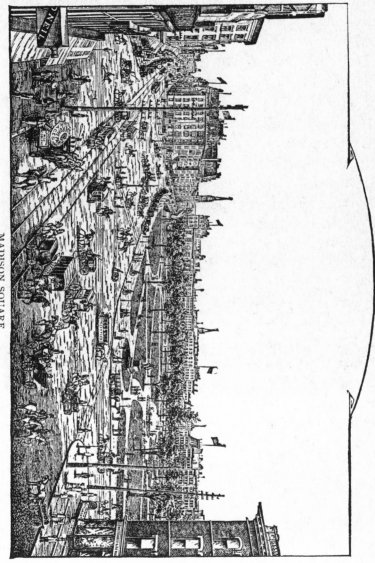

MADISON SQUARE.

Presbyterian Church rise along the Madison avenue side. So bright and beautiful are the park and all its surroundings, so full of life and gayety, so eloquent of wealth and splendor, is every object within view, that it is hard to realize that a little more than sixty years ago the pretty Square was used by the city as a Potter's Field, the last resting-place of the poor and wretched.

Grammercy Park lies between Third and Fourth avenues, and extends from 20th to 21st street. It separates Irving Place from Lexington avenue, and is a small enclosure belonging to a number of gentlemen of wealth living around it. It is a pretty spot, and being private property, is kept locked, and is used only for the recreation of its owners and their families. Peter Cooper, Cyrus W. Field, Moses Taylor, Ex-Governor Tilden, and a number of other well-known citizens reside here.

Reservoir Square is a small enclosure lying between Sixth avenue and the Distributing Reservoir on Fifth avenue and 40th and 42d streets. It occupies the site of the Crystal Palace, in which the World's Fair (the first international exhibition of America) was held, in 1853. The building was destroyed by fire in 1858.

Mount Morris Square covers an area of twenty acres, and lies on the line of Fifth avenue, which sweeps around it on the east and west sides, between 120th and 124th streets. It is a favorite resort for the residents of Harlem and the vicinity. In the centre a rocky hill, ornamented with an observatory, rises to a height of one hundred feet.

Morningside Park commences about five hundred feet from the northwestern corner of the Central Park, at 110th street, and extends to 123d street. It has an average breadth of about six hundred feet, and comprises an area of about forty-seven acres. It is one of the unfinished parks of the city, and will not be completed for several years at least.

Riverside Park lies between Riverside avenue and the Hudson River, and extends from 72d to 130th street. It is irregular in shape, is nearly three miles long, has an average breadth of five hundred feet, and contains one hundred and seventy-eight acres. It is still unfinished, though the walks and drives have been laid out, and afford fine views of the river and the picturesque heights of Weehawken, on the New Jersey shore. Real estate men confidently predict that its vicinity will become the most fashionable residence quarter of New York.

CHAPTER XXVII

THE PAWNBROKERS AND THEIR WAYS

THE SIGN OF THE THREE BALLS—LAWS RESPECTING PAWNBROKERS—HOW LICENSES ARE ISSUED—
DISREGARD OF THE LAW BY THE PAWNBROKERS—SOURCES OF PROFIT—EXCESSIVE INTEREST—
STORAGE CHARGES—SALES OF UNREDEEMED GOODS—WHO ARE THE PAWNBROKERS—THE
JEWS—A DISHONEST CLASS—SUCKING THE LIFE BLOOD OF THE POOR—HOW CUSTOMERS ARE
SWINDLED—CHARACTERISTIC SCENE IN A PAWN SHOP—THE JEWS' ONE PER CENT.—AN INSIDE
VIEW OF THE BUSINESS—DRUMMING UP CUSTOM.

The stranger in passing through East Broadway, the
Bowery, Chatham, Oliver, Division, Catharine, Grand,
Canal, Broome, or the neighboring streets, is struck
with the number of quiet, dingy-looking shops over
which are suspended the old sign of the Lombards—
three gilt balls. These shops and the three-ball signs,
all of the latter more or less dingy, may be seen in
many other quarters of the city, but they are nowhere
so numerous as in the streets named above, which are
centres of the abodes of poverty and wretchedness.
These are pawnbrokers' shops, and, as a rule, their
proprietors are harpies, who suck the life blood of the
poor, and grow rich upon their miseries. Of course,
in all large cities there must of necessity be a great
aggregation of poverty and misery. To the poor the
pawnbroker is a necessity. They must have some
place to which they can repair at once, and, by pledging
such articles as they possess, raise the pittance they so
sorely need. Municipal legislators the world over
recognize this necessity, and endeavor to throw such
safeguards around the business of pawnbroking that
the poor shall not be entirely at the mercy of the

brokers. In Great Britain the business is regulated by stringent laws, and in Continental Europe nearly all the Governments have taken it into their own hands, and have organized vast establishments, known as *Monts de Pieté*, where those in need of such assistance can obtain small loans on articles of almost every description. At these Government establishments the poor are treated fairly, the rate of interest charged is low, and every opportunity for the redemption of the property pledged is afforded.

In New York, the law requires that licenses to do business as pawnbrokers shall be issued to none but persons of known good character. The Mayor of the city alone has the power of issuing such licenses, and Mayors of all parties have been in the habit of putting a very liberal construction upon the law. None but those so licensed can do business in New York. "Mayors of all cliques and parties," says the Report of the New York Prison Association, "have exercised their power with, apparently, little sense of the responsibility which rests upon them. They have not, ordinarily at least, required clear proof of the integrity of the applicants, but have usually licensed every applicant possessed of political influence. There is scarcely an instance where they have revoked a license thus granted, even when they have been furnished with proofs of the dishonesty of the holders."

Section Eight of the Statute relating to pawnbrokers endeavors to impose some restraint upon their operations by declaring that "No pawnbroker shall ask, demand, or receive any greater rate of interest than twenty-five per cent. per annum upon any loan not exceeding the sum of twenty-five dollars, or than seven per cent. per annum upon any loan exceeding the sum of twenty-five dollars, under the penalty of one hundred dollars for every such offence."

As a matter of fact, none of the pawnbrokers pay the least attention to this law. They know that the great majority of their customers are ignorant of the provisions of the statute, and that those who are familiar with it will not avail themselves of its protection, as they fear to lose the favor of the pawnbroker. Consequently they fix their own rates of interest, which may be said to average about three per cent. for a month, or any fractional part of a month, or thirty-six per cent. a year. Some of the more unscrupulous members of the fraternity, whose dealings are exclusively with the poor, charge a much higher rate, extorting as much as fifty per cent. from those whose needs are very great.

Apart from the money received for interest, the pawnbrokers charge their customers exorbitant sums for storing in places of safety the articles left in their keeping. "On diamonds, watches, jewelry, silver-ware, opera-glasses, articles of *vertu*, ten per cent. on the amount loaned, over and above the interest, for what is called putting them away in the safes. On coats, vests, pants, dresses, cloaks, skirts, basques, from twenty cents to one dollar is charged for hanging up. On laces, silks, velvets, shawls, etc., from twenty-five cents to one dollar for putting away in bureau, wardrobe, or drawer. For wrappers, from fifteen to fifty cents is charged. Persons offering goods done up in papers are compelled to hire a wrapper, or the pawnbroker refuses to advance. The wrapper is simply a dirty piece of old muslin. The hire of one of these wrappers has been known to amount to over five dollars in one year. Upon trunks, valises, beds, pillows, carpets, tool-chests, musical instruments, sewing machines, clocks, pictures, etc., in proportion to their bulk, from one to five dollars is charged for storage."

Another source of profit to the pawnbroker arises from the sale of unredeemed articles. Advances are made at so low a rate that the property pledged is sure to bring more when put up for sale than the sum loaned upon it. The law requires that the amount received at such sales, over and above the pawnbroker's just claims, shall be returned to the depositor. The pawnbrokers, however, trouble themselves as little about this law as about that regulating interest. They coolly pocket the whole amount received, and the owner of the goods pledged loses the sum rightfully due him. Here, again, the pawnbroker trades upon his customer's ignorance of the law.

The majority of the pawnbrokers of New York are Jews, and are among the most rascally of that race. They do not monopolize the business, however, for there are a number of Englishmen, Irishmen, and even Americans, engaged in it. The more honest dealers are found among the Americans and Englishmen. The Jew pawnbroker is by nature a scoundrel, and so far as the observation of the writer goes, has not one redeeming quality. He advances the smallest amounts on goods pledged, extorts the highest rates of interest, and is the most merciless in his dealings with customers, of any of the fraternity. The Jews are so numerous in this business that they have given it its peculiar reputation. These wretches suck the very life blood from the poor, and having gotten possession of their property, do not hesitate to sell it for many times its value, when they see an opportunity of doing so. When the owner comes for his or her property, the pawnbroker declares, with well feigned regret, that it cannot be found, and either turns the owner out of doors, or buys up his pawn ticket at a heavy discount. He knows that the poor customer is in his power, and has neither the means nor the inclination to seek redress at law. These wretches do not hesitate to deck their families out in the clothing, shawls and jewelry pledged to them. Often the clothes are worn out, and the return of the pledge is either refused, or the articles are restored in such a damaged condition as to be useless. Sometimes a spirited depositor will demand full redress for the loss so inflicted upon him, and will threaten the broker with an appeal to the Courts. If the broker is convinced that the depositor is in earnest, he settles up promptly; but there is an end to his dealings with that person. He has no wish to have his transactions brought to the light of justice. Such a proceeding would bring unpleasant consequences in its train, and he does not desire such customers.

The majority of the pawn shops are dirty and repulsive in appearance. Before each hangs the sign of the three balls, and the windows are filled with unredeemed pledges for sale, and are adorned with signs stating that money is loaned here on all kinds of property at the most liberal rates. Pushing open the dirty door, we enter a dingy apartment. The air is close and stuffy, and the room smells strongly of garlic or onions. A man with an unmistakeably Jewish face and a villainous expression of countenance stands behind the narrow counter, the greater part of which is partitioned off from the public part of the room. We take our stand, invisibly, of course, and watch the proceedings.

A young man enters, well dressed, and rather dissipated in appearance. The child of Abraham watches him narrowly, and begins to shake his head and groan, as if in pain. The visitor approaches the counter, and lays a gold watch upon it. The broker clutches it eagerly, examines it, and groans louder than ever.

"Vat you vant on dis vatch?" he asks, mournfully.

"Fifty dollars. It cost me one hundred and fifty," is the reply.

"Fifty tollar! fifty tollar! Holy Moshish, vat you take me for!" Then, turning, he calls wildly, "Abraham! Abraham! you shust koom hier, quick."

A second Jew, dirtier and more disreputable looking than the first, makes his appearance, and the proprietor, passing the watch to him, and holding up his hands, shrieks out, as if in despair,

"Abraham! he vant fifty tollar on dat vatch. De man ish grazy."

"Ve shall be ruined," echoes Abraham, hoarsely. "Ve couldn't do it. 'Tish too much."

The proprietor waves his arms wildly, takes the watch from Abraham, and eyeing the owner sharply for a moment, says:—

"I tell you vat I do. I gif you fifteen tollar. How long you vant de monish?"

"Only for a month," replies the young man, evidently struggling between disgust and despair.

"I let you haf fifteen tollar for de month," says the pawnbroker, seizing a ticket, and commencing to make it out. "You pays me vone tollar for de loan, an you pays me fifty cent to put de vatch in de safe, you know. It might git shtole if I leaf it out hier. Dat shuit you, mine young frient?"

The young man has "been there" before, and knows that remonstrance is useless. He nods a silent affirmative, and the pawnbroker makes out a ticket for fifteen dollars, and hands him thirteen dollars and fifty cents, having deducted the interest and the charge for storage. The young man receives the money and the ticket, and goes out in silence.

"Dat ish peesness," says Abraham, admiringly, as the proprietor puts the watch away.

"Yesh," mutters the pawnbroker, with a satisfied air. "De vatch ish vort a hundred tollar. If he don't take it up, it vill bring us dat."

The next customer is a poor woman, who comes to pledge some article of household use. She is ground down to the lowest cent, and charged the highest interest; and so the proceedings go on until we become heart-sick, and leave the place as invisibly as we came.

The principal dealings of the pawnbrokers are, as we have said, with the poor. Life is hard in New York, and those who dwell under the shadow are obliged to make great sacrifices of comfort to keep body and soul together. Everything that will bring money finds its way to the pawn shop, and the miserable pittance received for it goes to provide food. Too often articles of household use or clothing are pawned to raise money for drink, and the possessions of the family are one by one sacrificed for this wretched purpose, until nothing is left.

The pawnbroker finds a very profitable class of customers in the respectable working people of the city. Many of these regularly pawn articles, sometimes of value, at the first of the week, and redeem them when they receive their wages on Saturday. It is to the broker's interest to be obliging to these people, since they are regular customers, and he reaps a rich harvest from them in the exorbitant interest they pay him.

It is the common belief that the pawnbrokers are also receivers of stolen goods. Some of the more unscrupulous may make ventures of this kind, but as a rule the brokers have nothing to do with the thieves; the risk of detection is too great, so they confine themselves to what they term their "legitimate business," and leave dealings in stolen property to the "fences," who constitute a distinct class, and to whom we shall refer in another chapter.

Another class of pawnbrokers do not own shops, or even offices. They conduct their business by calling at private houses, and asking if the ladies of the house wish any money advanced on jewelry or fine articles of clothing. Should they meet with a rebuff in the parlor they pass on to the kitchen, and rarely fail to find a customer in "Biddy." These dealers conduct large transactions; their customers are mainly ladies, who do not wish their dealings with them to be known; and the obliging pawnbroker usually adds one or two per cent. more to his charges to pay for his silence on the subject.

CHAPTER XXVIII

THE CENTRAL PARK

PLANS FOR A GRAND PARK—CHOICE OF A SITE—THE PARK COMMISSION ORGANIZED—DIFFICUL-
TIES IN THE WAY—THE WORK BEGUN—THE RESULT—THE CENTRAL PARK OF TO-DAY—COST
OF THE PARK—THE UPPER AND LOWER PARKS—THE ENTRANCES—THE POND—THE OLD
ARSENAL—THE MENAGERIE—THE METEOROLOGICAL OBSERVATORY—THE BALL GROUND—
THE DAIRY—AMUSEMENTS FOR CHILDREN—THE GREEN—THE SHEEPFOLD—THE SEVENTH
REGIMENT STATUE—STATUE OF WEBSTER—THE MARBLE ARCH—THE MALL—STATUES ON THE
MALL—THE PLAZA—THE VINE-COVERED WALK—THE ARCADE—THE TERRACE—THE ESPLAN-
ADE—THE BETHESDA FOUNTAIN—THE LAKE—BOATING—SKATING SCENES—THE CONSERVA-
TORY WATER—THE RAMBLE—THE CAVE—THE BELVIDERE—THE CROTON RESERVOIRS—THE
UPPER PARK—HARLEM BEER—THE OLD POWDER HOUSE—THE METROPOLITAN MUSEUM OF
ART—THE DI CESNOLA COLLECTION—THE OBELISK—A VENERABLE RELIC OF THE ANCIENT
WORLD—THE AMERICAN MUSEUM OF NATURAL HISTORY—THE TRANSVERSE ROADS— A TRI-
UMPH OF ENGINEERING—THE PARK COMMISSION—THE POLICE REGULATIONS—PARK TRAFFIC.

Thirty years ago the portion of Manhattan Island now occupied by the Central Park was a barren, rocky waste, broken by swamps, and as uninviting to the eye and dangerous to health as the most vivid imagination could fancy. It was an eyesore to the island, and the most enthusiastic speculator in real estate despaired of its ever being put to any useful or beneficial purpose. Great was the surprise of the whole city, therefore, when it was seriously proposed to convert this wretched looking tract into a grand park, which should be a lasting ornament to the Metropolis.

For some years the want of a place of public recreation larger than any of the existing squares or parks of the city, had been seriously felt. There was literally no place in which a large number of persons could assemble for pleasure, or to which they could resort on Sunday or holidays for a quiet day away from the cares of their homes and their work. All the pleasure grounds lay beyond the limits of the city. For owners of fine horses, or equipages of any kind, there was no driving place save the dusty Harlem Lane or Bloomingdale Road. It was universally admitted that a park must be provided within the city limits, at some point easy of access, and that such a pleasure ground must be in keeping with the splendor of the city, of which it must form for ages a principal ornament. The advocates of the scheme were perplexed, however, by the difficulty of finding a suitable site on Manhattan Island.

In April, 1851, Mayor Kingsland brought the subject before the Common Council, in a message in which he urged that a suitable site for a park should be chosen at once, before the upper part of the island should be covered with streets and buildings. The Council promptly considered the matter, and the Committee to which it was referred reported in favor of purchasing "Jones' Woods," a tract of about 60 acres lying between Third avenue and East River and above 66th street. It was well wooded, had a fine frontage on the East River, and in the opinion of the Committee was the most desirable site in the city for the location of a park. The scheme was warmly supported by numbers of leading citizens, and came near being successful. A bill for the purchase of "Jones' Woods" was introduced into the State Legislature, and was only defeated by a quarrel between two of the city members of that body. The Legislature then appointed a select Committee to ascertain whether a more suitable site could not be found. The attention of the Committee was directed to the rocky and swampy region between Fifth and Eighth avenues and 59th and 110th streets. It was

admitted that the location was the most central and
convenient of any on the island, but the enemies of
the scheme declared that it could never be converted
into an ornamental park, as the natural difficulties were
so great that it would require a fabulous sum to overcome them, and that trees and shrubbery could never
be made to grow there.   Nevertheless the Committee
were so much impressed with the location that they
reported a bill, which became a law on the 23d of July,
1853, authorizing the purchase of the land and its conversion into a Park.   The land was purchased between
1853 and 1856, and in May of the latter year the
Common Council appointed a Board of Commissioners,
to prepare and carry out a plan for the establishment
of the Park, satisfactory surveys of the land having
been previously made by Mr. Egbert L. Viele and a
corps of assistants.   The first Board was composed of
the Mayor and Street Commissioners, as *ex-officio*
members, Washington Irving, George Bancroft, James
E. Cooley, Charles F. Briggs, James Phalen, Charles
A. Dana, Stewart Brown, and several other leading
citizens.   Designs were presented by Frederick L.
Olmstead and Calvert Vaux, and being accepted, those
gentlemen were entrusted with the work of laying out
the Park.

   To the majority of the citizens of New York, the task
assumed by Messrs. Olmstead and Vaux seemed a
hopeless one.   The region selected for the Park was
wretched, barren and sickly.   Nature had done nothing more for it than to render it rugged and uneven.
It was covered for a considerable extent with wretched
shanties containing a squalid and filthy population, many

of whom pursued disgusting occupations, which being contrary to law, were engaged in only at night. The place had long been a dumping ground for rubbish of all descriptions, a low scrub underbrush grew rankly over it, and pools of stagnant water filled the hollows between the rocky bluffs. Scarcely a tree grew along the whole space, and the grass to be found there was of the poorest quality. The work of grading streets through the region had been begun, and the rude embankments and ragged rock excavations thus cre- ated added much to the natural irregularities of the sur- face. Nevertheless, Messrs. Olmstead and Vaux were confident of success. They went to work promptly, were liberally sustained by the Park Commission and the City Government, and the result of their labors is now seen in the magnificent Central Park, which occu- pies this once wretched site, and which is the admira- tion of the whole country and the especial pride of New York.

The Central Park derives its name from its situation in the centre of Manhattan Island. It is a parallelo- gram in shape, and is bounded on the south by 59th street, on the east by Fifth avenue, on the north by 110th street, and on the west by Eighth avenue. It is about two miles and a half long, half a mile wide, and comprises an area of eight hundred and forty-three acres. It ranks next to Fairmount Park, at Philadel- phia, as the largest in the Union, and is surpassed in extent by only three of the great parks of Europe— the Bois de Bologne, at Paris, the Prater, at Vienna, and the Phœnix, at Dublin. Nine miles of carriage drives, five miles of bridle-paths, and twenty-five miles

of walks, are laid off within its limits.   More than five
hundred thousand trees and shrubs have been planted
in the grounds with success, the soil being adapted to
the growth of almost any kind of vegetation.   The
rocky ridge which forms the backbone of the island
passes through the centre of the Park, and has been
made the means of rendering the scenery very beautiful and diversified.   The stagnant pools have been
converted into charming lakes, the ragged rocks have
been crowned with shrubbery and converted into picturesque adornments.   Every defect has been changed
into a beauty, and the admiration of the visitor is divided between the loveliness around him and the skill
which could convert such a waste into a fairy land.

The wooded portion of the Park covers about four
hundred acres, and is intersected in all directions with
walks, drives, and bridle paths.   Charming views greet
the visitor at every step, and lovely lawns stretch away
on every hand.

The total cost of the Central Park has been about
$15,000,000, including $5,028,884, expended in purchasing the land.   Large sums are spent annually in
improvements.

In the centre of the grounds, and upon the highest
point within the enclosure, stands the Croton Reservoir, which divides the Park into two sections, known
as the Upper and Lower Parks.   Up to the present
time the greatest number of improvements have been
bestowed upon the Lower Park, which contains the
Pond, the Mall, the Terrace, the Lake, the Ramble, the
Dairy, and a number of buildings used for Park purposes.   This portion of the grounds comprises one of
the most beautiful specimens of landscape gardening

in the world, and abounds in groves of noble trees, lovely lawns, walks and drives, and is ornamented with statuary, a lovely lake, beautiful fountains, and handsome buildings. The Upper Park is more rugged, and constitutes a sort of miniature mountainous region, which is being improved and beautified with each succeeding year.

The principal entrances to the Park are on 59th street. The Fifth and Eighth avenue entrances are for vehicles as well as pedestrians, while the Sixth and Seventh avenue entrances are for pedestrians only. Other entrances are on Fifth and Eighth avenues and 110th street. All these will eventually be ornamented with noble gateways and arches. The names of the various entrances are as follows, and convey some idea of the emblematical designs to be followed in the erection of the gateways:—

Fifth avenue and 59th street,				The	Scholars' Gate.
Sixth "	"	"	"	"	Artists' Gate.
Seventh "	"	"	"	"	Artisans' Gate.
Eighth "	"	"	"	"	Merchants' Gate.
Eighth "	"	72d	"	"	Women's Gate.
Eighth "	"	79th	"	"	Hunters' Gate.
Eighth "	"	85th	"	"	Mariners' Gate.
Eighth "	"	96th	"	"	Gate of All Saints.
Eighth "	"	100th	"	"	Boys' Gate.
Eighth "	"	110th	"	"	Strangers' Gate.
Fifth "	"	72d	"	"	Children's Gate.
Fifth "	"	79th	"	"	Miners' Gate.
Fifth "	"	90th	"	"	Engineers' Gate.
Fifth "	"	96th	"	"	Woodman's Gate.
Fifth "	"	102d	"	"	Girls' Gate.
Fifth "	"	110th	"	"	Pioneers' Gate.
Sixth "	"	110th	"	"	Farmers' Gate.
Seventh "	"	110th	"	"	Warriors' Gate.

The Park is easily reached by the Eighth avenue, Broadway, Sixth avenue, Madison avenue, and 59th street (Belt Road) Horse Cars, and by all the lines of the Elevated Railroads. From the entrances on 59th street charming pathways lead directly to the Marble Arch and the Mall.

A few yards from the Fifth avenue gate is a fine bronze bust of Alexander Von Humboldt, by Professor Blaiser, of Berlin. It was presented to the Park by the German citizens of New York, on the 14th of September, 1869, the one hundredth anniversary of the birth of the great scientist. Immediately back of this bust is The Pond, a small sheet of water, irregular in shape, and lying along the lower end of the Park from Fifth to Sixth avenue. It covers about five acres, and lies in a deep hollow, surrounded by steep and picturesque banks. The water consists of the natural drainage of the Park, and artificial means are provided for running it off into the city sewers should it rise too high. A beautifully shaded walk extends around the eastern and southern shores.

Just within the Eighth avenue entrance stands a fine statue of Commerce, in bronze, presented by Mr. Stephen B. Guion.

On the east side of the Park, opposite the Fifth avenue and 64th street entrance, is an old building which somewhat resembles the Cadet barracks at West Point. It was erected and used by the State of New York as an arsenal, but was purchased by the city in 1856, for the uses of the Park. In the lower stories and in several buildings around it is a fine collection of animals, birds, and reptiles, constituting the Menagerie of the Park. In the winter the collection is greatly enlarged by numerous animals and birds which are sent here for safe keeping by traveling shows which go into quarters in New York during the cold season. This is a favorite resort with visitors, especially with children, and is always crowded. The top floor of the Arsenal building contains the Meteorological Observatory, which is under the charge of Professor Daniel Draper. Some of the rooms are open to the public, and a number of self-recording instruments for measuring the velocity and direction of the wind, the fall of rain and snow, the variations of temperature, etc., may be examined. The remainder of the building is taken up with the offices of the Park Commission and officials, and a police station.

The southwest corner of the Park is occupied by the ball ground, a fine stretch of lawn, about ten acres in extent. It is set apart for the use of persons wishing to play base ball, cricket, croquet, or lawn tennis, and is provided with a comfortable brick cottage for the use of the players.

Immediately north of the Pond is the South Transverse Road, and on the high ground above it is the Dairy, a tasteful gothic structure of brick and stone. Here pure milk and refreshments may be had at moderate prices. Residents of the city can always purchase fresh milk or cream here, for sick children, and a great quantity is sold daily for this purpose. The proximity of the Dairy to the Transverse Road, on which a portion of it opens, enables that establishment to receive its supplies from vehicles in that road, and averts the necessity of bringing wagons and carts into the Park drives.

A few yards from the Dairy is the Children's Summer House, a large rustic pavilion for the special accommodation of children and their nurses, and close by is a cottage for the use of ladies and children. A number of patent swings stand near the Summer House, and are always filled with merry little folks. A few steps north of the swings is "The Carrousel," a circular building, fitted up with hobby horses and merry go rounds, for the amusement of younger children.

Immediately north of the Ball Ground is The Green, or, as it is usually called by visitors, the Common. It is a fine meadow of sixteen acres, and is occupied by a flock of imported sheep, in charge of a shepherd and his dog. Visitors are rigidly excluded from the Green, save on Saturday, and sometimes on Sunday, when they are permitted to roam over it at pleasure. The northwest portion of the Green terminates in a hill, on the highest part of which is a flashy looking building, in which mineral waters are sold.

Opposite The Green, and running along the Eighth avenue wall, is The Sheepfold, a range of picturesque buildings of red brick, in which the sheep are sheltered at night and during the bleak days of winter.

On the west side of the Park, a little way above the Sheepfold, is a bronze bust of the great Italian patriot and agitator, Joseph Mazzini. It is of heroic size, and stands on a pedestal of granite, ten feet in height. It was presented to the Park by the Italian residents of New York, in 1878.

A short distance above this bust, and also on the west drive, near 72d street, is J. Q. A. Ward's noble

statue of "A Private Soldier of the Seventh Regiment."
It is of bronze, of heroic size, and represents a soldier
in the uniform of the regiment, standing at rest, and
looking off into the distance.   The statue rests upon a
handsome pedestal of granite, and was erected by the
regiment to the memory of its members who fell
during the civil war.   The pedestal is ornamented with
trophies in bronze, near the base, and with bronze
shields on each side, emblazoned with the Stars and
Stripes of the National flag.   On the principal or east
front of the pedestal is the inscription, in bronze letters,
Pro Patria et Gloria.   Each face of the pedestal contains an inscription cut in the granite.   These are as
follows: On the east face, "The Seventh Regiment
Memorial of 1861-1865."   On the north face, "In
Honor of the Members of the Seventh Regiment, N. G.,
S. N. Y., fifty-eight in number, who gave their lives in
defence of the Union—1861-1865."   On the west face,
"Erected by the Seventh Regiment National Guard,
S. N. Y., MDCCCLXIII."   On the south face, the inscrip-
tion is similar to that on the north face.

At the intersection of the West Drive and the drive
from 72d street is a bronze statue, of heroic size, of
Daniel Webster, modeled by Ball, of Boston, and presented to the Park in 1876, by Gordon W. Burnham,
Esq.

A little to the northeast of the Dairy, and almost in
the centre of the grounds, from east to west, is the
Marble Arch, one of the most costly and beautiful
structures in the Park.   It is constructed of pure white
marble, and its office is to carry the carriage-drive,
in an unbroken line, to the Lake, and at the same time

to furnish easy access from the lower level of the south-western part of the Park to the Mall. All the paths from the Sixth, Seventh and Eighth avenue entrances on 59th street, converge here, and lead to a handsome and wide arch of marble, entering it at its western end. On each side of the arch is placed a marble bench, which furnishes a delightful and cool resting-place for visitors in the hot days of summer. At the eastern end of the arch is an open area, walled and paved with marble, and provided with a drinking fountain. Broad stairways of marble, at the northern and southern ends of the area, lead from the archway to the Mall above.

The Mall is the name given to the broad avenue, lined with four rows of American elms, and ornamented with statuary, extending from the Marble Arch to the Terrace. It is about one-third of a mile in length, about two hundred feet in width, is bordered on each side by lovely lawns, and constitutes the grand prome-nade of the Park. Along the southern end of the ave-nue are bronze statues of Fitz-Greene Halleck (by H. K. Browne), Sir Walter Scott (a copy of the statue in the Scott Memorial at Edinburgh), Shakspeare (by J. Q. A. Ward, the finest work of art in the Park), Robert Burns, and Alexander Hamilton. These give an air of dignity and beauty to this portion of the Park. A little to the west of the Mall is an ideal life-size fig-ure in bronze, representing an Indian hunter—the work of J. Q. A. Ward, the designer of the Shakspeare statue. Near the northern end of the Mall is the Music Pavilion, a handsome and gayly ornamented structure, from which concerts are given by a fine band on certain days of the week during the warm season.

These concerts are excellent, and draw large audiences, which are accommodated with seats placed near the music stand.

The Mall terminates at its northern end in a spacious and handsome Plaza, adorned with a couple of revolving fountains and a number of ornamental bird

VIEW OF THE LAKE FROM THE TERRACE.

cages placed on iron posts. Flowers and plants abound here in the season.

The northeastern side of the Mall is bordered by a pretty trelliswork of iron, forming an arbor, and raised about twenty feet above the promenade. This is called the Vine Covered Walk, and over it are trained roses, honeysuckles, and wisterias. It is a delightful resting place, from which one can listen to the music of the concerts or watch the crowds on the Mall and the Terrace. Both the Mall and this arbor command fine views of a large portion of the Park. The eastern side of the Vine-Covered Walk opens upon a circular space to which carriages are admitted. Across this circle is the Casino, a pretty cottage of stone, containing an excellent restaurant. Good meals are served here, but the charges are somewhat high. The grounds to the east of the Casino contain the famous group in brownstone, known as "Auld Lang Syne," the work of Robert Thompson, a self-taught sculptor, and formerly a stone mason.

At the northern end of the Mall a broad stairway leads down to the Arcade, or the hall beneath the Terrace. This hall is paved with handsome encaustic tiles, and the walls and ceilings are inlaid with encaustic tiles of a finer quality, ornamented with the most sumptuous designs. This magnificent apartment is used as an ice cream saloon.

The northern end of the Mall is separated from the Terrace by a massive and highly decorated screen of Albert stone, pierced with two large openings which give access from the Mall to the Terrace.

The Terrace is constructed of Albert freestone, of a soft yellowish brown color, and is one of the most imposing structures in the grounds. It is provided with a footway on each side and a carriage drive in the centre, and overlooks the Lower Terrace or Esplanade, and the Lake. At the northern end two grand flights of stone stairs lead to the Lower Terrace, and are ornamented with exquisite carvings of birds, animals,

fruits, etc., and beautiful tracery, cut in the soft stone
work. On the east and west sides of the stairways,
the adjoining grounds are lavishly ornamented with
flowers, and slope gracefully from the Terrace to the
Lake.

The Lower Terrace or Esplanade, is a large open
space extending from the stairways to the Lake. It is
paved with stone blocks, and at the water's edge is a
low stone wall with a seat running around the inner
side. Tall flag staffs rise along the water front, and
sustain handsome banners, which give to the place a
gay appearance.

In the centre of the Lower Terrace is a large stone
basin, in the middle of which stands the Bethesda
Fountain, the most beautiful ornament of the Park.

THE LOWER TERRACE IN CENTRAL PARK.

The figure and the pedestal on which it stands are of
bronze, as are also the four smaller figures beneath
the upper basin. The fountain is the work of Miss
Emma Stebbins, of New York; the design was executed in Rome, during the winters of 1864-67, and the
models were sent to Munich and cast in bronze. The

idea of the work was suggested by the account of the Pool of Bethesda, given in the 2d, 3d and 4th verses of the fifth chapter of St. John's Gospel, especially the 4th verse, which relates that "An angel went down at a certain season into the pool and troubled the water." The principal and uppermost figure of the group represents an angel with outspread wings, in the act of alighting on a mass of rock. The arms are extended in blessing, and the angel bears in her left hand a bunch of lilies, emblems of purity, and wears across her breast the cross bands of the messenger angel. From the left hand trickles a stream of water, and from the mass of rock over which she seems to hover the water gushes out into the upper basin, emblematic of Temperance, Purity, Health and Peace. At the feet of these figures is a second and larger basin, from which the water falls into the circular pool below. The fountain plays constantly during the mild weather, but in winter is covered over, to protect it from the severe frosts. It is exceedingly delicate and beautiful in conception and execution, and is deservedly admired by all who visit it.

The Lake is a lovely sheet of water bordering the Terrace, from which it stretches away to the east and west. It is irregular in shape, and is divided into two nearly distinct and unequal parts by a narrow strait, crossed by a graceful iron bridge. The larger and handsomer part sweeps away from the bridge to the west and north, with several arms. This lovely sheet of water covers an area of about twenty acres. The northern shore is high and rocky, terminating at several points in bold headlands, and is occupied by the Ram-

BRIDGE OVER THE LAKE IN CENTRAL PARK.

ble. To the east of the Terrace is a handsome boat house, where rowboats may be hired for a ride around the Lake for a small sum. In the winter this building is used for the accommodation of skaters. On fair days the Lake is covered with fleets of boats manned by expert rowers in sailor costume, and filled with gay parties of pleasure seekers. Landing places are located at various points on the shore, and are ornamented with rustic structures which command fine views of the water and surrounding grounds. Numbers of snow-white swans float dreamily over the edge of the Lake, waiting for food thrown to them by visitors.

No lovelier sheet of water is to be found on the globe than this beautiful lake, the larger portion of which lies west of the strait and the Bow Bridge. On the north side the shore rises up in steep bluffs; on the south is the magnificent Terrace, and the eastern and western shores slope gracefully in verdant lawns from the main carriage drives to the water. From whatever point on the shore you view it, the quiet lake stretches away, the very embodiment of peace and repose, its clear bosom gleaming in the bright rays of the sun, and reflecting the various objects which surround it. On a bright moonlight night in the summer the scene is indescribably beautiful. The waters lie gleaming in the golden light, breaking into myriads of flashing ripples as a ghost-like swan glides majestically by, or as they are broken by the dip of oars. Scores of pleasure boats, well filled, and each bearing a red or blue light, skim over the surface like so many fire-flies; the air is musical with the dash of oars and the sound of merry voices; and the breeze comes off the shore laden with the rich perfume of flowers. Above and below this magic realm the great city toils on, sending up its ceaseless roar heavenward; sorrow and care, mirth and recklessness, vice and crime, hold the dwellers in their resistless grasp; but here all is peace and beauty. This is a charmed world, and you can enjoy it regardless of the busy Babel by which it is surrounded. The sound of a distant bell tolling the hours, the scream of a locomotive, or the hoarse whistle of a steamer in the river, are the only sounds of the outer world heard here, and you scarcely heed them as you surrender yourself to the witchery of the scene around you.

During the winter the Lake presents a gay and brilliant sight. The large boat house near the Terrace is thronged with visitors, some of whom come to enjoy the skating and others to watch the sport. The water of the lake is covered to a depth sufficient to prevent serious accidents in case the ice should break, and every precaution is taken to ensure the safety of the skaters. The ice is carefully examined every day, weak spots are marked with danger signs, and every night the surface of the ice is scraped smooth, to render it fit for the next day's sport. Huge reflectors are placed behind the gas-lamps on the shore, and at night these shed a flood of light over the frozen surface, rendering it as bright as day, and enabling the skaters to enjoy their pleasure until midnight. Printed rules for the government of skaters are posted at conspicuous points, and all persons are required to conform to them on pain of being compelled to leave the ice. A large red ball is hoisted on the Arsenal building when the ice is in good condition, and the cars of the railway lines running to the Park are provided with small white flags, on each of which is printed a red ball, thus informing the public that their favorite winter pastime is the order of the day. Buildings for the accommodation of skaters are erected on the shore of the Pond and the Upper Lake, which also furnish their share of amusement. Thousands of skaters are on the ice daily, and the scene at such times is well worth witnessing.

To the east of the Terrace, along the Fifth avenue side of the Park, is a small, oval lake, covering about two acres and a half of space. This is the Conservatory Water, and is used principally by the young folks for miniature yacht races. At some future, and it is hoped not distant day, the grand Conservatory of the Park will be erected on the eastern shore of the water, and will front on Fifth avenue.

The high ground north of the Lake is known as the Ramble. This is one of the most charming portions of the Park, extends as far northward as the old Reservoir, lies between the East and West Drives, and covers an area of about thirty-six acres. It is a labyrinth of winding foot-paths, well shaded, and abounding in exquisite scenery, deep thickets, little brooks and picturesque waterfalls crossed by miniature bridges, small stretches of lawn, bits of rock work, and delightful views of the Lake. The grounds are well supplied with benches and rustic seats, on which the visitor may rest and enjoy the beauties of the scene at his ease. At several points winding paths lead down to rustic arbors on the Lake shore. At the upper end of the Ramble a path leads into a rocky glen, at the end of which is situated the Cave, a natural opening in the rocks, of considerable size. Here are kept a number of owls, whose solemn air of wisdom is heightened by the constant gloom in which they dwell.

The Ramble terminates on the north, in the highest point in the Park. Here is located the Belvedere, an open space walled and paved with stone, from which rises an ornamental tower of granite, fifty feet high. Visitors are admitted to this tower, and from it can command a view of the entire Park, the Reservoirs, the city and country to the northward as far as Harlem and the High Bridge, the entrance to Long Island Sound, and the portion of the city lying immediately below the Park. The Belvedere stands at the southwest corner of the Old Reservoir, and can be approached only on foot.

Immediately north of the Belvedere are the Croton Reservoirs, two in number, known as the Old and New Reservoirs. The former lies in the centre of the grounds, and extends from 79th street to 86th street, and the latter occupies almost the entire width of the Park, from 86th to 96th street. Together they cover an area of one hundred and forty-three acres. A bridle path and a walk encircle the New Reservoir and are much resorted to on account of the coolness of the location and the fine view.

Beyond the Reservoirs is the Upper Park, naturally the most beautiful portion of the grounds. But little has been done up to the present time in the way of improvement. Its principal attractions are Mount St.

Vincent, on the east side, above which is a pretty sheet of water, known as Harlem Meer, occupying the northeast corner of the Park, and covering an area of twelve and a half acres; the Pool, a small lake of two acres on the west side, just above 100th street; and the old Powder House at the extreme northern end of the grounds, near Sixth avenue and 110th street. A large part of what was once known as McGowan's Pass lies in the North Park. Through this pass the American army effected its retreat from New York after the disastrous battle of Long Island. Some of the old earthworks thrown up on this occasion are still to be seen here.

On the Fifth avenue, or east side of the Park, opposite 83d street, stands the Metropolitan Museum of Art, one of the greatest attractions of the city. The edifice, now completed, which is only one of a projected series of buildings, is constructed of red brick with sandstone trimmings, in the Gothic style, and is 218 feet long and 95 feet broad. The basement story contains the offices of the Museum and a hall devoted to the exhibition of works of industrial art. The next floor contains the main hall, a noble apartment, the roof of which rises in a graceful curve, held up by sweeping girders, the iron work being painted of an approved color. All the decorations of the building are handsome, but are subdued in tone, in order to render the collections more attractive than the rooms in which they are contained. "In the west entrance hall on this floor, which fronts the Park, are the modern statues. In the central hall are the loan collections, in numerous cases. Here are laces and embroideries.

At the east end are the Greek and Etruscan vases, with Kensington Museum reproductions at the west end. Right and left are numerous show cases containing the innumerable loans made to the Museum, such as Japanese and Chinese ivories, Egyptian antiquities, rare tomes, old books in their superb bindings, Limoges enamels, antique arms, with Dresden, Sèvres, and Majolica; Oriental and Japanese stuffs, silver repousseé, Venetian glass, miniatures, and an endless variety of artistic objects. In the north and south aisles of the east hall are the Cyprian antiquities, the vases, terra-cottas, bronzes, busts, and statues of the Cesnola collection. In this hall these Cypriote objects occupy quite three sides of the room, besides being placed in many additional cases. The most careful attention has been paid to their classification, which must be of the greatest advantage to those desiring to study them. The two sarcophagi, which are the capital pieces of the Cesnola collection, are at the back of the hall. On the left-hand side, facing the entrance, has been carefully placed the immense Cesnola collection of pottery. Mounting to the next floor is easy, as the steps have a comfortable rise. The visitor then arrives at the upper halls. Here are the pictures, in two halls, the east and west ones. Proceeding along the gallery taken up by the Avery collection of porcelain, the east picture gallery is reached. Continuing the circuit, the south gallery may now be traversed, which leads to the west hall. This south gallery contains the most precious of General Di Cesnola's discoveries, the Curium treasures, with the iridescent glass. Here, too, are all the bronzes, Venetian glass, a

collection of watches, and bibelots innumerable. The
Di Cesnola collection consists of a large number of
ancient art objects exhumed at Cyprus by General Di
Cesnola, United States Consul at that island, and is
regarded by archæologists as the most remarkable and
valuable in the world. The eastern picture gallery
contains a number of the best paintings by the old
Dutch, Flemish and Spanish masters; the western
gallery is devoted to pictures loaned to the Museum.
The public is admitted to the Museum, free of charge,
on Wednesdays, Thursdays, Fridays and Saturdays.

A short distance west of the Museum is the Obelisk,
or, as it is popularly, but erroneously termed, "Cleo-
patra's Needle." It stands on a slight knoll in one of the
most commanding situations in the Park, and constitutes one of the chief attractions of the grounds. It
was presented to the city of New York in 1877, by
Ismail Pasha, then the reigning Khedive of Egypt, and
was brought across the Atlantic in 1880, through the
remarkable engineering skill of Lieutenant-Comman-
der Gorringe, of the United States Navy. It was successfully removed from the vessel in which it made the
voyage, conveyed from the river, and set up on its present site in the autumn of 1880. The cost of the entire
undertaking was paid by William H. Vanderbilt, Esq.

The Obelisk stands upon a pedestal of massive
granite, built upon solid rock. It is a monolith, four
sided in shape, tapering to a point at the top, is sixty-
seven feet two inches in height, five and a half feet
square at the apex, and weighs about two hundred
tons. It is cut from a single block of granite hewn out
of the quarries at Syene, in Upper Egypt, and its four

THE OBELISK.

sides are all covered with inscriptions in hieroglyphics cut into the stone. It was one of two obelisks erected in front of the Temple of the Sun, at Heliopolis (or On, as it is termed in the Bible), a city of Lower Egypt, which stood not far from the present city of Cairo. These obelisks were erected by Thothmes III, to commemorate his victories. This king was one of the greatest conquerors in Egyptian history, and his dominions extended from India on the east to the isles of the Mediterranean on the north and west, and to the southern confines of Equatorial Africa. Three centuries after his death, another great king, Rameses II (believed to be the Greek Sesostris), caused these obelisks to be set up a second time at Heliopolis, and a new line of inscriptions full of his own more pompous titles and names was added, on the right and left sides of the central line, all along the four sides of the stone. Centuries afterwards, when Rome had brought Egypt to her feet, these obelisks were removed from Heliopolis to Alexandria. ' It is not certain by whom they were removed; some authors attribute the work to Julius Cæsar, some to Marc Antony, and others still to Augustus. The companion to this obelisk was presented to the British government by Ismail Pasha, and was conveyed to London in 1877, and set up on the Thames embankment.

It is no wonder that the Obelisk is the object of so much interest. It is one of the oldest existing monuments of the ancient world, and carries us back fifteen centuries beyond the Christian Era. It was venerable when Moses enjoyed the favor of the Egyptian court, as "the son of Pharaoh's daughter," and he must have

seen it frequently.   It witnessed all the various changes
in the destiny of Egypt, under its native rulers and
foreign masters, for three thousand years, and was
already fifteen hundred years old when it was removed
from its original site to Alexandria.   What changes it
shall behold in its new home in the metropolis of the
Western World the future alone can disclose.

Just without the limits of the Park, and between
Eighth and Ninth avenues and 77th and 81st streets,
but under the control of the Park Commission, stands
a massive and handsome building of red brick, with
yellow sandstone trimmings, erected in the modern
Gothic style.   This is the American Museum of Natural History, the present edifice being only a single
wing of the immense mass of buildings which is to be
erected for the uses of the Museum.   The building is
fireproof; the corner-stone was laid on the 2d of June,
1874, by President Grant, and the Museum was formally opened by President Hayes, on the 22d of December, 1877.   "The general interior arrangement is
probably the best that has been yet devised for the
purpose, and, indeed, leaves little to be desired.   The
collections are arranged in large halls, or in balconies
running around them; and at each end of these halls
is a large vestibule, containing stairways and offices
for the curator of the department to which the floor is
devoted.   The entrance is at present at the south end.
Each hall is 170 feet long by 60 wide inside the walls.
The lowest story is 18 feet high; the second, or principal story, including the balcony or gallery, 30 feet;
the upper story 22 feet; and the story in the mansard
roof 16 feet.   On the lower story, the desk cases, in

the centre of the hall, are filled with the Jay collection
of shells, presented by Miss C. L. Wolfe, as a memorial of her father, the first President of the Museum.
The remainder of the hall, excepting several cases filled
with building stones, marbles, woods, and wax fruits, is
devoted to mounted specimens of mammalia. The
floor of the second story hall contains specimens of
birds exclusively, arranged in geographical order.
The gallery is set apart for the archæological department, and contains specimens of the implements of the
Pacific islanders, spears and lances of various peoples,
carved war-clubs, Indian dresses and weapons, stone
axes, pottery, skulls, skeletons, etc., all in upright
cases; in the railing case is the De Morgan collection
of stone implements, from the valley of the Somme,
Northern France; the Bement specimens of the stone
age of Denmark; specimens from the Swiss lake
dwellings; Squier and Davis's collection, from the
Mississippi Valley, and several minor collections. On
the upper or third floor is the James Hall collection of
geologic specimens of New York State, recently purchased by the Museum, and a number of other specimens in the same department of science. The attic
story is set apart for work and study rooms for those
carrying on original researches. The peculiarity of the
arrangement for the different wall cases containing the
collections is, that they extend out at right angles to
the windows, so that the end against the wall is but a
small part of the whole, while the light, which, owing
to the large window space gained by this arrangement
is exceedingly abundant, is permitted to travel to every
nook and corner of the hall, so that there is not a spot

anywhere in the exhibition rooms where a shadow is cast." The public is admitted to the Museum free of charge on Wednesdays, Thursdays, Fridays, and Saturdays.

One of the problems presented to the engineers who laid out the Park consisted in devising a means of communication between Fifth and Eighth avenues, along its course. As it lay in the centre of the island for two miles and a half from north to south, it would prove a serious obstacle to the transaction of the business of the city unless some means of communication should be provided between the above-mentioned avenues. To carry the city streets through the grounds would be to destroy the Park, and to open the carriage roads to vehicles of trade would sadly mar the pleasure of visitors. The skill of the engineers and the natural formation of the land soon afforded a solution of the problem, difficult as it seemed. A system of transverse roads was devised and successfully carried out. These roads are among the "curiosities" of the Park, and constitute one of the most skillful engineering triumphs of the time. The transverse roads are four in number, and are used to carry 65th, 79th, 85th, and 97th streets across the line of the Park. They follow the natural depressions between the hills and rocks of the Park, are sunken far below the general level of the grounds, and are walled up on each side with massive masonry. The carriage drives and walks of the Park cross them by means of handsome bridges, which are so embowered in vines and shrubbery that the road below is entirely unseen. Visitors pass over them without being conscious of their existence. These roads are inaccessible from the Park, are paved like the city streets, and are lighted with gas at night.

The Central Park is under the control of the Department of Public Parks, which has its headquarters at 36 Union Square. The board consists of four commissioners, appointed for five years by the Mayor and Board of Aldermen. The President of the Board receives an annual salary of $6500, but the other members are not paid for their services. The Commissioners draw up and enforce the regulations for the government of the Park, and appoint the police force to which the care of the grounds and the property in them is entrusted. The Park police are uniformed in gray, and have the powers of ordinary policemen. Their headquarters are at the Arsenal building. A policeman is on duty at each entrance, and others of the force patrol the grounds, to prevent violations of the rules, to render assistance to persons in need of it.

The rules for the government of visitors are very simple. They are forbidden to pluck the shrubbery or flowers, to write upon or otherwise deface the seats, bridges, arches, or buildings, to feed the birds, or annoy the animals, and to walk on the grass except in such places as are marked by signs bearing the word "Common." Every convenience is provided for the comfort of visitors. More than ten thousand seats are scattered through the grounds, six hundred of these being under vine-covered arbors. Water closets for gentlemen, and cottages with toilet conveniences for ladies and children, each of the latter in charge of a female attendant, are placed at convenient points.

CHAPTER XXIX

TRINITY CHURCH

OLD TRINITY"—THE THREE CHURCHES—DESCRIPTION OF TRINITY CHURCH—THE INTERIOR—
THE ALTAR AND REREDOS—THE WINDOWS—THE SERVICES—FINE MUSIC—DAILY SIGHTS IN
TRINITY—THE SPIRE—THE CHIMES—VIEW FROM THE SPIRE—THE CHURCHYARD—NOTED
TOMBS—TRINITY PARISH—THE CHAPELS—WEALTH OF THE PARISH—ITS NOBLE WORK.

The most interesting church edifice in New York is
Trinity Church, or, as it is affectionately termed by the
citizens, "Old Trinity." It stands on Broadway opposite the head of Wall street, and forms one of the most
conspicuous objects on the great thoroughfare. The
present edifice is the third that has stood on the site.
The first church was completed in 1697, and was destroyed in the great fire of 1776. A second church
was built in 1790, and in 1839 this was demolished, and
the present stately edifice begun on its site. It was
completed and consecrated in 1846.

Trinity is one of the few specimens of pure Gothic
architecture to be found in the United States, and is
stately and beautiful within and without. It is built of
brownstone from the base to the summit of the spire,
and the interior is finished in the same material. The
walls are fifty feet high, and the arch of the ceiling is
sixty feet above the floor of the church. The roof is
supported by massive brownstone columns. The spire
is two hundred and eighty-four feet in height, and is
surmounted by a bright gilded cross. The church consists of a nave, choir, and aisles. On each side of the
choir are the vestry rooms. The south room contains

the offices of the clergy, and is also the robing room. The north room contains a fine tomb, with a full length effigy in stone, to the memory of Bishop Onderdonk. The chancel occupies the choir, and is beautifully fitted up. At the sides are stalls for the clergy and choristers, with a fine organ on the north side, and at the back are the altar and reredos, which were erected as a memorial to the late William B. Astor, by his sons, both of whom are active members of the church. They are very beautiful, and are of a soft colored stone, richly ornamented with sculptures. The windows of the church are of stained glass, those at the sides being very simple. The great window back of the altar is a magnificent work. Over the Broadway entrance is a gallery containing the grand organ, one of the most powerful instruments in the city.

Trinity is noted for its elaborate services. Morning and evening prayer are celebrated in simple style every day, but on Sundays and feast days the full choral service is used. The choir consists of men and boys, carefully trained by the Musical Director; they are surpliced, and are famous for their skill. No grander or more impressive service can be heard in the land than in Old Trinity on Sunday mornings. The church is always kept open during the day, and it is no uncommon sight, during business hours, to see numbers of persons kneeling in the pews of the church in silent prayer. A soft, subdued, holy light streams in through the colored windows, giving to the beautiful interior an air of solemnity, in harmony with its sacred character.

The spire of the church faces Wall street, and is

TRINITY CHURCH.

built of solid stone. It contains a clock, with three
faces, placed just above the roof of the church, and a
great bell, which strikes the quarters, half-hours, and
hours. Above these is the finest chime of bells in the
city. They are played by machinery, and their music
is well worth listening to. All through the day and
night the voices of the bells float down into the city,
solemn and sweet, reminding the heedless passers-by
that time is flying and eternity drawing nigh. The
view from the balcony at the base of the spire, two
hundred and fifty feet above the street, is sublime.
The gazer looks down upon Broadway and Wall
street, with their busy crowds, and over the city far
away to the northward. From this elevated point you
can see almost the entire city, Brooklyn, Jersey City,
and the suburban towns on the Jersey shore, back to
the Orange Mountains; the harbor, the East river, the
Narrows, the Lower Bay, Staten Island, Long Island
Sound, and the distant hills of Connecticut. Nearly
four millions of people are below you, with a dozen
cities and towns.

The church stands in the midst of a large open
space, filled with crumbling tombstones and monuments, shaded with noble trees and ornamented with
flowers. At the northern end, on the Broadway side,
facing Pine street, is "The Martyr's Monument," a
splendid structure of brownstone, erected to the
memory of the "Patriotic Americans who died during
the Revolution, in British Prisons."

Trinity Church is the "mother" of a vast corporation, embracing the following chapels: St. Paul's, St.
John's, Trinity Chapel, St. Chrysostom's, St. Augus-

tine's, and St. Cornelius's, the last being on Governor's Island. All these establishments are supported from the funds of the parish, with the exception of Trinity Chapel, which has a wealthy congregation, and is maintained by its members. These constitute what is known as "Trinity Parish," at the head of which is the rector of Trinity Church. Each church or chapel has its pastor and vestry, who are subject to the control of the rector and vestry of "Old Trinity." The salaries are liberal, and are promptly paid. Each clergyman with a family is provided with a furnished house; should any clergyman die in the service of the parish, a liberal provision is made for his family, and superannuated ministers are supported in comfort during their lives.

Trinity is the richest church in the United States. Its wealth consists almost entirely of real estate. In 1697 the English crown granted to it the land on which it stands, and in 1705 supplemented this grant with the gift of the immense tract known as "Queen Anne's Farm," embracing the entire district lying along the North River, from Vesey to Christopher street. Much of this was subsequently donated by Trinity to various institutions needing assistance, but the corporation still owns a large part of this valuable district, worth at present many millions of dollars. Much of this property is unproductive, however, so that the actual income of the corporation is only about half a million of dollars. It makes a good use of this, however, and besides paying its own expenses, lends a liberal support to many needy churches in the city, and maintains a number of benevolent institutions.

CHAPTER XXX

THE LOST SISTERHOOD

PREVALENCE OF PROSTITUTION IN NEW YORK—POLICE STATISTICS—FIRST-CLASS HOUSES—
THE PROPRIETRESS — THE INMATES — THE ARISTOCRACY OF SHAME — THE VISITORS—
VISITS OF MARRIED MEN—AVERAGE LIFE OF A FASHIONABLE PROSTITUTE—THE NEXT
STEP—THE SECOND-CLASS HOUSES—TERRORS OF THESE PLACES—THE GREENE STREET
BAGNIOS—GOING DOWN INTO THE DEPTHS—THE NEXT STEP—THE WATER STREET HELLS
—AVERAGE LIFE OF A PROSTITUTE—"THE WAGES OF SIN IS DEATH"—HOW YOUNG GIRLS
ARE TEMPTED INTO SIN—EFFORTS TO SAVE AN ERRING DAUGHTER—THE STREET WALK-
ERS—THE PANEL HOUSES—HOW MEN ARE ROBBED AND MURDERED IN THESE HOUSES—
THE CONCERT SALOONS—THE WAITER GIRLS—THE DANCE HALLS—THE "BUCKINGHAM"—
THE "CREMORNE"—BUCKINGHAM BALLS—ASSIGNATION HOUSES—PERSONALS—THE MID-
NIGHT MISSION — REFORMATORY ESTABLISHMENTS — ABORTIONISTS — THE WICKEDEST
WOMAN IN NEW YORK.

Prostitution is an appalling evil in New York. One
can scarcely look in any direction without seeing some
evidence of it. Street walkers parade the most prominent thoroughfares, dance houses and low concert
halls flaunt their gaudy signs in public, and houses
of ill-fame are conducted with a boldness unequalled
anywhere in the world. The evil is very great, but it
is far from assuming the proportions that some well-
meaning, but misinformed, persons have assigned it.
Some years ago Bishop Simpson, of the Methodist
Church, made the startling assertion, at a public meeting, that the prostitutes of New York were as numerous as the members of the Methodist Church in that
city. This drew from the Superintendent of Police a
statement, in which he showed that while the evil was
undeniably very great, it was not so bad as the Bishop
had reported it. The truth is that there are about 600
houses of prostitution and about 90 assignation houses

in New York. The number of women known to the police as professional prostitutes is about 5000, in which estimate are included several hundred waiter girls in the concert saloons. The Census of 1880 returned the female population of New York as 615,-815. This would give one professional prostitute for 123 females of all ages in the entire city. These figures are horrible enough to contemplate, but they are not so bad as the statement referred to above. Of the number of women who resort to prostitution as a means of obtaining money, or from other motives, and who yet manage to retain positions of respectability in society, of course no estimate can be made. They are, unfortunately, very numerous, and are said, by persons in position to speak with some degree of accuracy, to equal the professionals in numbers.

These things are sad to contemplate, and disagreeable to write about. The whole subject is unsavory; but no picture of New York would be complete did it not include an account of this terrible feature of city life, which meets the visitor at almost every turn; and it is believed that some good may be accomplished by stripping the subject of all its romance, and presenting it to the reader in its true and hideous colors.

The professional women of New York represent every grade of their wretched life, from the belle of the fashionable house of ill-fame to the slowly dying inmate of the Water street brothel. They begin their careers with the hope that they will always remain in the class into which they enter, but find, when it is too late, that they must go steadily down into the depths, closing their lives with a horrible death and a pauper's grave.

The first-class houses of New York are conducted with more or less secrecy. It is the object of the proprietress to remain unknown to the police as long as possible, but she finds at last that this is impracticable. The sharp-eyed patrolmen soon discover suspicious signs about the house, and watch it until their suspicions are verified, when the establishment is recorded at police headquarters as a house of ill-fame, and placed under the surveillance of the police. These houses are few in number, the entire city containing, according to police reports, not more than fifty. Large rents are paid for them, and they are generally hired furnished. They are located in some quiet, respectable portion of the city, and outwardly appear to be simply private dwellings. It often happens that the neighbors are in ignorance of the true character of the house, long after it is well known to the police. It is hinted that even Fifth avenue is not free from the taint. The houses are magnificently furnished, and every attraction is held out to lure desirable visitors to them. The proprietress is a woman of respectable appearance, and passes as a married woman, some man generally living with her, and passing as her husband. This enables her, in case of trouble with the authorities, to show a legal protector and insist upon her claim to be a married woman.

The inmates are women in the first flush of their charms. They are handsome, well dressed, generally refined in manner, and conduct themselves with outward propriety; rude and boisterous conduct, im-

proper language, and indecent behavior are forbidden
in the parlors of the house, and a casual visitor passing through the public rooms of the place would see
nothing out of the usual way.

It is difficult to learn the causes which induce these
women to adopt a life of shame. No reliance whatever can be placed upon the stories they tell of themselves. It cannot be doubted, however, that they are
generally of respectable origin, and some of them are
otherwise fitted to adorn the best circles of society.
Some are young women who have been led astray by
men who have failed to keep their promises to them,
and have drifted into sin to hide their shame; others
are wives who have left, or have been deserted by,
their husbands; others are widows who have been
left without any other means of support; others still
have deliberately chosen the life in the hope of escaping poverty, or to gratify their love of money and dress;
and others again appear to be influenced by motives
of pure licentiousness. Whatever the cause of their
adoption of such a life, it is evident that they have
seen better days. They are still fresh and attractive,
and for a while pursue their gilded career of sin and
shame, hoping that they may be fortunate enough to
retain their places in the aristocracy of vice. The
proprietress will have no others than attractive women
in her house; and as soon as the inmates begin to
show signs of the wretched life they lead, as soon as
sickness falls upon them, or they lose their beauty and
freshness, she sends them away, and fills their places
with more attractive women. She has no difficulty in
doing this, for she has her agents on the watch for

them all the time, and unfortunately new women are always soliciting admission to such places. Besides this, the proprietress knows that her patrons soon grow tired of seeing the same women in her establishment. She must make frequent changes to satisfy them, and she has no scruples about thrusting a woman out of her doors to begin the descent of the ladder of shame. Therefore, about one or two years is the average term of the stay of a woman in a fashionable house. A few manage to remain longer, but the number is so small as to constitute scarcely an exception to the general rule. As long as her "boarders" remain with her, the proprietress treats them fairly enough, apart from the fact that she manages to get out of them all the money she can. The women earn large amounts of money, but a considerable portion of this goes for board and other expenses in the house, and their extravagant habits and tastes exhaust the rest. They save nothing, and if taken sick must go to the Charity Hospital for treatment. Their dream of saving money lasts but a short time, and they leave the fashionable houses penniless.

The visitors to these houses are men of means. No one without a full pocket could afford such indulgence. Visitors are expected to spend considerable money for wine, which is always furnished by the proprietress at the most exorbitant prices, and at a profit of about 200 per cent. A large part of her revenue is derived from such sales, and she looks sharply after this branch of her business. The shamelessness with which men of standing and prominence, many of whom are husbands and fathers of families, resort to these houses, and display

themselves in the parlors is astounding.   Indeed, the
keeper of one of the most fashionable houses boasts
that married men are her principal customers.   Sometimes the visitor desires that his visit shall not be
known.   For such persons there are private rooms,
where they are sure of seeing no one but the proprietress and the woman for whom their visit is intended.
The fashionable houses are largely patronized by strangers visiting New York; these, thinking themselves
unknown in the great city, care little for privacy, and
boldly show themselves in the general parlors.   The
proportion of married and middle-aged men among
them is very great.   You will find among them lawyers, physicians, judges of courts, members of Congress, and even ministers of the gospel from all parts
of the country.   This may seem a startling assertion,
but the police authorities will confirm it.   If the secrets
of these places as regards their visitors could be made
public, there would be a terrible trouble in many happy
families throughout the land, as well as in the Metropolis.   Men who at home are models of propriety
seem to lose all sense of restraint when they come to
New York.   These same gentlemen would be merciless towards any female member of their families
who should display a similar laxity.

To return to the women:—The inmates of the first-
class houses rarely remain in them for more than two
years.   Their shameful and dissipated lives render
them by this time unfit for companionship with their
aristocratic associates.   The proprietress quickly detects this, and remorselessly orders them from her
house.   She knows the fate that awaits them; but her

only care is to keep her house full of fresh and attractive women.

Having quitted the fashionable house, the wretched woman has no resource but to enter a second-class house, and thus go down one grade lower in vice. The difference between this place and the house she has left is very great. The proprietress is cruel and exacting, and boldly robs her boarders whenever occasion offers. The visitors are more numerous, but are a rougher and coarser set than those who patronized her in the first stage of her career. Money is less plentiful, her life is harder in every way, and she seeks relief from the reflections that will crowd upon her in drink, and perhaps to drunkenness adds the vice of opium eating. Her health breaks fast. What was left of her beauty when she entered the house soon fades, and in two or three years she becomes unfit to remain even in a second-class house. She is turned into the street by the proprietress, who generally robs her of her money and jewelry, and sometimes even of her clothing, save what she has on at the time. The wretches who keep these houses do not hesitate to detain a woman's trunk, or other effects, upon some trumped-up charge of arrears of debt, when they have no longer any use for her. The poor creature has no redress, and is obliged to submit in silence to any wrong practised upon her.

The woman whose career opened so brilliantly is now a confirmed prostitute and drunkard, bloated, sickly, and perhaps diseased. She is without hope, and there is nothing left to her but to sink still lower. Yet it is only four or five years, perhaps less, since

A FANCY BALL AT THE BUCKINGHAM PALACE.

she entered the fashionable up-town mansion, beautiful and attractive in all the freshness of her charms, and little dreaming of the fate in store for her. She is not an exception to the rule, however. She has but followed the usual road, met the inevitable doom of her class.

From the second-class house the lost woman passes into one of the bagnios of Greene, Worster, or some similar street. Here her lot is infinitely more wretched. Her companions are the vilest of her class, and the visitors are thieves, roughs, and men who cannot gain admittance into places such as she has left. She finds herself a slave to the keeper of the house, who is often a burly ruffian, and even more brutal than a woman would be in the same position. She is robbed of her earnings, is beaten, and often falls into the hands of the police. She becomes familiar with the station-house, the Tombs, and Blackwell's Island, and whatever of womanly feeling remained to her is crushed out of her. She is a brute simply. She remains in Greene street and similar places a year or two—human nature cannot bear up longer against such a life—and is then unfit to remain even there. Would you seek her after this, you will find her in the terrible dens, sailors' dance houses, and living hells of Water street, or some kindred locality. She is a mass of disease, utterly vile and repulsive, steadily dying from her bodily ailments, and the effects of rum and gin. She has reached the bottom of the ladder, and can go no lower. She knows it, and in a sort of dumbly desperate way is glad it is so. Life is such a daily torture to her, hope has so entirely left her, that death only

offers her any relief. She is really a living corpse. The
end soon comes.   Some die from the effects of their
terrible lives, and, ah! such fearful deaths; others are
killed or fatally injured in the drunken brawls which
so often occur in this locality; and others still seek an
end of their miseries in the dark waters of the East
River.

I draw no exaggerated picture of the gradual but
inevitable descent of a fallen woman in New York.
Every detail is true to life.   Seven years is the average life of an abandoned woman in the great city.
She may begin her career with all the *éclat* possible,
she may queen it by virtue of her beauty and charms
in some fashionable house, at the beginning, and may
even outlast the average term at such places; it matters not; her doom is certain.   The time will come
when she must leave the aristocracy of shame, must
take the second step in her terrible career.   Seven
years for the majority of these women, and then death
in its most horrible form.   Some may, and do, anticipate the end of it by suicide; few ever escape from it.
"The wages of sin is death."   Some cherish the hope
that after a few years of pleasure they will reform;
but, alas, they find it impossible to do so.   A few, a
very few, do escape through the aid extended to them
by the Midnight Mission, but they are so few that they
but serve to emphasize the hopelessness of the effort.
The doom of the fallen woman is sure.   "The wages
of sin is death."   Once entered upon a career of
shame, the whole world sets its face against her.
Even the men who associated with her in her palmy
days would turn a deaf ear to her appeals for aid

after she has gone down into the depths. I would to God that the women who are about to enter upon this terrible life could walk through the purlieus of Water street and witness the sights that I have seen there. I would they could see the awful, rum-bloated, disease-scarred, despairing faces that look out from the bagnios of that terrible neighborhood, and then realize that, however brilliant the opening of their career may be, this must be the end of it. It is idle for them to hope to escape the terrible doom of the fallen woman. "The wages of sin is death." Would any one know what sort of a death? Let her come to New York and see.

Many of the women of the town never pass through the various gradations of vice that I have described. Many never see the inside of a fashionable house of ill-fame, but begin lower down the scale, as inmates of second-class houses, as waiter girls in concert saloons, as inmates of dance houses, or as street walkers. These meet their inevitable doom all the quicker, but not the less surely.

The city is full of people whose object is to lead young girls into lives of shame. Some of these are men, but the majority are women. They watch the hotels, and lure respectable girls away on various pretexts. Every inducement is held out to working girls and women to adopt the vile trade, and many fall willing victims. Hundreds of these women are from New England. They come to the city seeking work, and are sometimes successful. Often, however, they can find nothing to do, and, when poverty and want stare them in the face, they listen to the voice of the

tempter, become street walkers, waiters in concert
halls, or inmates of houses of ill-fame. Sometimes,
while they are in the first days of their success, they
will write home that they are pursuing honest callings
in the city, and earning reputable livings, and will
even send money home to their deluded parents.
After a while the letters cease—the writers have
gone down into the depths; they are lost. Said one
whose duties often brought him in contact with women
of this class: "It is strange to see how these women
cherish the memory of their homes even in the midst
of their shame. They will speak of the pleasant home,
of the old father or mother, in accents full of despair.
Often these memories will cause them to burst into
uncontrollable weeping. If I try to take advantage of
this moment of tenderness, and urge them to make
an effort to reform, I am met with but one answer,—
'It is too late.'" The keepers of the bagnios of the
city use every means to lure young women into their
power. Not long since a girl, who had managed to
escape from a Greene street brothel, told the following story to the magistrate at the Jefferson Market
Police Court. It reveals the system practised in such
places. "I watched the advertisements in the papers
to see something that would suit me. I learned that
a Mrs. Myers, of Greene street, wanted two young
girls to do light chamber work, and I hastened there,
with a friend, in quest of a job. We were received
by Mrs. Myers, who sat down and began to explain
to us the nature of the duties we were expected to
perform. It was an awful proposition, your Honor.
She kept a house of ill-fame. We fled. I was very

much discouraged. Not so my friend, who told me
there was another lady down the street, who was
really in want of girls to help her. We went to her
house. It was another of the same sort; but after I
got in there my own clothes were taken away from
me, and the lady furnished me with some sort of silk,
trimmed with fur, and tried to make me behave and
act like the other girls in her establishment. I
remained there from Saturday to Wednesday night,
because I could not get away. I had no clothes to
wear in the streets, even if I should succeed in reaching them, which was impossible, and the woman who
kept the house was angry with me, and treated me
brutally because I would not comply with her wishes.
I and another young girl tried to escape by climbing
over the fence of the back yard. The other girl got
away, but I was discovered by the barkeeper, who
drove me back into the house, with curses. On
Wednesday evening I was made to sit at the window,
and call a man, who was passing, into the house. He
turned out to be a detective, and arrested me, and
brought me here."

The girl's story proving to be true, the magistrate
restored her to her friends, and caused the arrest of
the keeper of the house.

The police are often called upon by the relatives of
abandoned women to assist them in finding them, and
rescuing them from their lives of shame. Sometimes,
in the cases of very young girls, these efforts are successful, and the poor creature gladly goes with her
friends. Others again refuse to leave their wretched
haunts; they prefer to lead their lives of infamy.

One night a young man called at the "Buckingham Palace," a dance-house, in West Twenty-seventh street, and inquired for his sister Dora, whom, he had learned, was in that place. The young lady came out, while he was speaking, in company with a well-dressed man. Instead of complying with her brother's entreaties, she entered a carriage, with her escort, and drove to the Thirtieth street Police Station to seek release from her brother's importunities. The brother followed, told to the sergeant the story of his sister's shame, and asked him to keep her there until he could summon their father. The sergeant complied with this request, and the father soon arrived. He was a respectable master carpenter. He confirmed his son's statement, and appealed to his daughter to go home with him. She answered him flippantly, and the indignant father cursed her for her sin, and would have attacked the man with her had not the officers prevented him. The woman was locked up for the night in the station house, and brought before the Jefferson Market Police Court the next morning. The father urged that she should be sent to some reformatory establishment, but the woman met him with the statement that she was twenty-three years old, beyond legal control, and therefore entitled to choose her own mode of life. Her plea was valid, and the magistrate was unwillingly compelled to discharge her from custody, though he endeavored to persuade her to return to her family. She then left the court room, was joined by several flashily dressed women, and departed in high spirits, completely ignoring her relatives.

One of the worst classes of abandoned women consists of the street walkers. On Broadway, Sixth avenue, and the Bowery these women are very numerous. They are generally well dressed, and as a rule are young. They pursue certain regular routes, rarely pausing unless they "pick up" a companion, when they dart off with him into a side street. On Broadway the police do not allow them to stop and accost men, but they manage to do so. The neighborhoods of the hotels and the places of amusement are their principal "cruising grounds," and their victims are mainly strangers to the city. Many of them have some regular employment during the day, and ply their wretched trade at night to increase their gains. They accompany their victims to the "bed-houses," which are conveniently at hand, and if an opportunity occurs will rob him. They frequent the dance halls and concert saloons, in fact, every place to which they can obtain admission, and leave no means untried to lure men into their company. As a rule, they are vicious in the extreme, they drink heavily, and are fearfully diseased.

Many of the street walkers are in the regular employ of the "panel houses," which abound in the city. These houses are kept by men, who are among the most desperate roughs in New York. The woman is either the mistress of one of these men, or in his pay. The method pursued is as follows:—The street walker secures her victim on the street, or at some concert hall or dance house. He is generally a stranger, and ignorant of the localities of the city. She takes him to her room, which is an apartment provided with a partition in which there is a sliding door or panel.

The confederate of the woman is concealed behind this partition, and, at a favorable moment, slides back the panel, enters the room, and rifles the clothing of the victim of the money and valuables contained in it. If discovered, the panel thief endeavors to disable the victim. The latter is no match for his assailant, and is from the first at a disadvantage. The thief is desperate, and is generally armed. He does not hesitate at anything, and, if necessary, will murder the victim, the woman assisting him in the fearful work. Then the body is left until near morning, when it is placed in a wagon engaged by the thief, carried to the river, and thrown into the water. Generally the robbery is accomplished without the necessity of resorting to violence. The victim either puts up with his loss in silence, or reports it to the police. The records at Police Headquarters contain reports of numerous robberies of this kind. Yet the evil goes on. Strangers in the city incur a terrible risk in accompanying street walkers and women whom they meet at concert and dance halls to their homes. In nine cases out of ten, robbery is certain. Murder is too often the result of such an adventure. Truly, Solomon was wise indeed, when he wrote:—"He hath taken a bag of money with him... With her much fair speech she caused him to yield, with the flattering of her lips she forced him... He goeth after her straightway, as an ox goeth to the slaughter, or as a fool to the correction of the stocks; till a dart strike through his liver; as a bird hasteth to the snare, and knoweth not it is for his life... Her house is the way to hell, going down to the chambers of death."

The concert saloons are among the worst features of the social evil. They flourish along certain parts of Broadway, Sixth avenue, and the Bowery, and are simply so many places where the devil's work is done. They provide a low order of music, and the service of the place is rendered by young women, many of whom are dressed in tights and all sorts of fantastic costumes, the chief object of which is to display the figure as much as possible. The liquors furnished are of the vilest description. The girls are hideous and unattractive, and are foul-mouthed and bloated. The visitors are principally young men, and even boys, though older men, and even gray heads, are sometimes seen among them. The women are prostitutes of the lowest order. They encourage the visitors to drink, shamelessly violate every rule of propriety, and are always in readiness to rob a visitor who is too far gone in liquor to protect himself. These places are frequented by ruffians, whose only object is robbery. They keep a watch over the visitors; and when one of the latter, overcome with liquor, staggers out of the place, follow him, lure him into a back street, rob him, and, if necessary to their own safety, murder him. Oftentimes they lure their helpless victims to the river front, and there rob and kill him, and throw his body into the water, where it is found by the harbor police.

The dance halls are often handsome places, but all are simply the rendezvous of street walkers, and men who come to seek their company. The principal establishments of this kind are the Buckingham Palace, the Cremorne Garden, and the Haymarket. At the Cremorne all are admitted free, but at the others an admission fee is charged for men. The "Buckingham" is the handsomest dance house in the city. We enter through a lobby into a bar-room, back of which lies the dance hall. This is a gaudily decorated apartment, two stories in height, with a gallery running around it on a level with the second story. Tables and chairs are scattered about the sides of the first floor, but the central space is kept clear for dancing. The galleries are also provided with tables and chairs. At the back is a dimly-lighted space, fitted up like a garden, where those who desire it may sit and drink, and at the side are a shooting-gallery and a restaurant. The place is always well filled. The women present are the inmates of the neighboring houses of ill-fame and street walkers. Each one is a prostitute, and each is intent upon luring some man into her clutches. The men are mostly very young, but on "gala nights," and during the "balls" which are given here in the winter, almost every class of society is represented by the male visitors. An orchestra in the gallery opposite the entrance provides the music, and dancing is constantly going on on the floor of this hall. Men and women are constantly passing in and out; drinking is going on in every part of the hall; and the air is heavy with tobacco smoke. In spite of its brilliancy and splendor, the place is but one of the numerous gateways to hell with which New York abounds. Men meet abandoned women here, and accompany them to their homes, risking disease, robbery, and even death, with a recklessness that is appalling. Young men of respectable families come here nightly, and spend hours in company with the abandoned women who

ALLEN'S DANCE HOUSE.

frequent the place. These same young gentlemen would shrink with a fastidious horror from even a few moments' conversation with the cooks and housemaids of their own homes. Yet here they find pleasure in association with women equally as ignorant and unrefined, and in every way unworthy to compare with "Biddy," who is honest and virtuous, whatever her other faults may be.

The lowest dance houses are situated on the river fronts and in the adjoining streets, and are largely frequented by sailors. The women at these places are generally residents of the house, whose sleeping rooms are above the dance hall. They are in the last stages of prostitution, and are fearful to behold.

A great deal of immorality is carried on in the city of which the police cannot take cognizance, and of which it is impossible to obtain statistics. This grade of vice is confined largely to persons of nominal respectability. The columns of certain city journals contain numerous personals by which appointments are made, and communications exchanged between persons engaged in intrigues. These people support the numerous assignation houses which abound in the city. About ninety of these houses, of all grades, are known to the police, but there are others which are conducted so privately that the police have no knowledge of them. It is said that some of the most fashionable are owned and furnished by men of nominal respectability. They put a woman in charge of the house, and share the large receipts with her.

Great efforts are made by benevolent people to lessen the amount of vice with which the Metropolis is cursed. The Midnight Mission, in Greene street, is the most successful of the various means that have been adopted to rescue fallen women from their wretched lives. It is open to every fallen woman who will seek refuge in it, and its invitations are scattered among this class by its agents. The women are treated with kindness, and encouraged to reform. They come voluntarily, and leave when they wish to do so. They are always welcomed; however often they may wander back into sin, the Mission never closes its doors upon them. "Until seventy times seven," is its rule. In a single year, as many as 282 women sought refuge in the Mission. Of this number, 73 were found good situations where they could earn an honest living, and 26 were restored to their relatives and friends. Year after year the Mission continues its good work, rescuing a few from sin and shame. The other reformatory institutions are, "The House of the Good Shepherd," the "House of Mercy," and the "New York Magdalen and Benevolent Society." They are all correctional establishments, and more or less force is employed in the treatment of those who are refractory. The majority of their inmates are sent to them by the police courts.

One of the greatest evils of the city is the existence of a class of men and women who make their living by practising abortion upon women who have been betrayed, and seek to remove the consequences of their sin. These abortionists are well known to the police, who spare no effort to break up the infamous business. They continue to flourish, however, in spite of the exertions of the authorities. They advertise

boldly in such city journals as will admit their advertisements, and reap large profits from the sale of drugs
and the performance of operations upon pregnant
women.   Their calling is illegal, and the statute book
denounces grave penalties against them.   To bring
on premature confinement, which shall result in the
death of a child, is made by the law of New York
manslaughter in the second degree.   In spite of this,
however, infanticide flourishes in New York, and every
year the city journals contain numerous accounts of
the death of women at the hands of professional abortionists.   They are arrested and punished whenever
a clear case can be made out against them ; but others
spring up to take their places, and the infamous business continues to thrive.   Some of the more cautious
practitioners will not undertake a premature delivery
of a woman, but content themselves with receiving
her, and carrying her safely through her confinement.
They require that she shall be "backed" by some
responsible man.   The child, when born, is sent to
some foundling asylum, or given to persons willing to
adopt it.   Often the practitioner places it in the hands
of some person to care for it, and, where the parents
are of good position in society, and possessed of wealth,
holds it as a means of extorting money from them.
Large sums are wrung from the parents in this way, in
order to avoid an exposure, and men and women have
been driven to despair and suicide by the wretches
in whose power they have placed themselves.

One of the most notorious women of this class was
the late Madame R——.   A large part of her income
was derived from the sale of drugs warranted to bring

on miscarriages.   She amassed a large fortune by her business, built a magnificent house on Fifth avenue, and lived in royal style.   She would never commit an abortion outright, but would safely deliver her patients, take care of the children born in her house, and use them as the means of extorting money from the parents. Her patients were invariably women of position in society, in the city and other parts of the country, and she would receive no one into her house unless "backed" by a man of known wealth.   At length her wicked ways threw her into the hands of the police. The evidence against her was overwhelming, and, to escape the just punishment of her crimes, the wretched woman committed suicide.

CHAPTER XXXI

JAY GOULD

EARLY LIFE OF THE GREAT FINANCIER—PERSONAL APPEARANCE—KNOWLEDGE OF LAW—
ENTERS THE ERIE ROAD—BLACK FRIDAY—HOW GOULD CAME OUT OF IT—A SHREWD
GAME IN "ERIE"—HIS WEALTH—ATTACKED IN WALL STREET—HIS METHOD OF OPER-
ATING.

There is not a village or town in the United States
in which the name of Jay Gould is not as familiar as a
household word.　He is a native of New York State,
and is in the neighborhood of fifty years of age.　He
is a small, puny man, scarcely larger than a boy of
sixteen, with black beard and hair, black eyes, and a
timid, shrinking manner.　He is secretive in everything, and has the rare gift of keeping his own counsel under all circumstances.　He is well educated, and
is the most daring and resolute financier in the United
States.　It is said that his knowledge of law is wonderful for an amateur, and that he can draw the most
difficult legal paper with the ease and skill of an old
practitioner.　He has few friends, and is suspicious of
all his associates, who return his distrust with equal
heartiness.

Mr. Gould began his business life in his native State,
after which he engaged in an unsuccessful venture in
Pennsylvania.　He then went to Vermont, where he
was made Superintendent of the Rutland Railroad,
which he soon placed upon a paying basis.　Its heaviest
stockholder was a Mr. Miller, whose daughter Mr.
Gould married in 1861.　Mr. Miller was also largely

interested in the Erie Railroad, and through his influence Mr. Gould, some years afterwards, was elected its President. His career in this capacity, and his connection with the late James Fisk, Jr., are too well known to make it necessary to relate them here.

He is credited, together with Fisk, with having brought about the famous "Black Friday" corner in the gold market, and it is asserted in Wall street that

JAY GOULD.

when the bubble bursted, he escaped loss by quietly selling out his millions of gold to his partner, Fisk, and consigning that individual to almost ruin. When he was driven out of the Erie Railroad, the public was astonished by the announcement that he had been compelled to make restitution to the Erie Company of $6,000,000 worth of property. With characteristic shrewdness he managed to make even this humiliation a matter of gain. The transaction was necessarily kept secret until it was concluded; but meanwhile Gould, knowing that the road's enrichment to so large an amount would send the stock up, bought all there was in the market. When the news of the restitution was made public, Erie stock rose rapidly, and Gould sold all he had at an enormous profit. He is said to have cleared $6,000,000 on the transaction.

Mr. Gould's wealth is very great, and is estimated anywhere from $10,000,000 to $50,000,000, but no one knows the true amount. His railroad interests are tremendous, and he is practically the owner of the telegraph system of the United States. He resides in a handsome mansion on Fifth avenue.

He is cordially hated by Wall street operators, many of whom have suffered severely from his remorseless combinations. In such matters he spares neither friend nor foe. A few years ago a party of Wall street men seized him near the Stock Exchange, and after handling him very roughly, threw him into a neighboring area. He saved himself from further harm by instant flight.

Mr. Gould rarely fails in his undertakings, and conducts them in a characteristic manner. They say in Wall street, that when he appears freely and frequently in the street, the brokers feel safe; but when he is missing for a day or two, Wall street begins to tremble and looks out for squalls. When he is about to put some great scheme in operation, he retires to his Fifth avenue house, and remains there until it is over, communicating all the while with his agents in the market by telegraph.

CHAPTER XXXII

THE NATIONAL GUARD

THE FIRST DIVISION—ITS ORGANIZATION—HOW ARMED—APPROPRIATIONS BY THE CITY—
PRIVATE EXPENSES—THE COMMANDER-IN-CHIEF—EFFICIENCY OF THE TROOPS—PAST
SERVICES OF THE FORCE—OVERAWING THE MOB—PUTTING DOWN RIOTS—A REINFORCE-
MENT TO THE POLICE—DISCIPLINE—THE ARMORIES—THE SEVENTH REGIMENT ARMORY—
PARADES.

The military organizations of the City of New York
constitute the First Division of the National Guard of
the State of New York, and are justly regarded with

SIXTY-NINTH REGIMENT ARMORY.

pride by the citizens of the Metropolis. The division
numbers about 6,500 men, and consists of four bri-
gades, which are divided into nine regiments of in-

fantry. In addition to these are one regiment and a troop of cavalry, and four batteries of artillery. The arms of the force, ammunition, and some other necessities, are provided by the United States. The regiments select their own uniform and equipments, and these are purchased by the members at their own expense. The city makes an appropriation of $500 a year for each regiment; but other expenses, such as the cost of parades, the hire of bands, and the fitting-up of armories are borne by the regiments.

The entire force is under the command of a Major-General, whose headquarters are at 155 Mercer street. The division is always at the orders of the Governor of the State, who is *ex-officio* Commander-in-chief of the National Guard of New York, and may be called into active service at his discretion.

The men are well-drilled, and constitute an efficient force, which can be relied upon in time of need. The majority of them are veteran soldiers, and saw service during the late Civil War. They have repeatedly proved their efficiency in the riots which they have been called upon to quell. They have promptly and bravely responded to every call upon them, preventing a terrible and disastrous riot when the banks suspended specie payments in 1837; putting down the Astor Place riot in 1849; preventing a serious riot at the time of the organization of the Metropolitan Police force; rescuing the city from the mob in the Draft riots in 1863; checking the Orange riots in 1871; and overawing the mob in the Railroad riots in 1877. The men are not holiday soldiers in any sense, but are trained troops; ready at any moment to play their part in the preservation of order in the Metropolis. They constitute a strong and effective reinforcement to the police, and the rougher element of the city know that they are no match for such a force as this, as they have learned from experience that the troops *will fire* when the word is given. The police, on their part, are encouraged by the knowledge that behind them stand the National Guard ready to support them when the task of preserving order is too great for them. The citizens appreciate this, and contribute liberally to the support of the military.

The discipline is very rigid. The men are not volunteers, but are regularly enlisted in the service of the State, and are liable to severe punishment for any infraction of discipline. Delinquent members, sentenced by court-martial to imprisonment, are confined in Ludlow street jail.

Each regiment has an armory, in which are kept its arms and valuable property. The armory is in charge of an armorer, who takes care of the arms, and keeps them in good order. A drill room constitutes the principal hall of the armory, and in some of these buildings reading rooms, a library, committee, and company rooms are provided. The regiments take a pride in decorating and furnishing their armories as handsomely as their means will permit. The Sixty-ninth Regiment armory and the armory of the Seventh Regiment are the handsomest in the city. The latter building is a notable structure, and occupies an entire block, bounded by Fourth and Lexington avenues and Sixty-sixth and Sixty-seventh streets. It is built of brick, with granite trimmings, and has the strength of a fortress and the elegance and comfort of a club-house. It cost over $300,000, and the interior was decorated and furnished at the expense of the regiment. The regimental drill room is 300 by 200 feet in size, and besides this there are ten company drill rooms, an officers' room, a veterans' room, a field and staff room, a gymnasium, and six squad drill rooms.

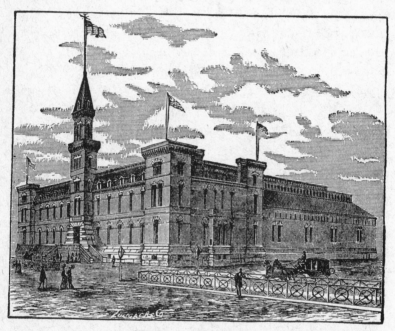

SEVENTH REGIMENT ARMORY.

The parades of the division are among the sights of the city, and draw great crowds to witness them. The martial bearing of the troops, their splendid uniforms and equipments, and the perfect discipline which marks every movement, elicit hearty applause from the citizens who line the entire route of the march.

CHAPTER XXXIII

WILLIAM H. VANDERBILT

THE RICHEST MAN IN NEW YORK—EARLY LIFE—BECOMES A FARMER—ENTERS THE RAILROAD WORLD—BECOMES VICE-PRESIDENT OF THE NEW YORK CENTRAL SYSTEM—SUCCEEDS THE OLD COMMODORE—THE VANDERBILT PALACES—LOVE OF FAST HORSES.

The richest man in New York is William H. Vanderbilt, Esq. He is the oldest son of the late Commodore Vanderbilt, and was born at New Brunswick,

New Jersey, on the 8th of May, 1821. He obtained his early education at the Columbia College Grammar School, and at the age of eighteen began his business career as a clerk in the banking house of Drew, Robinson & Co., of Wall street.   Here he remained two years, and gave such marked evidences of business capacity, that his employers began to contemplate taking him into partnership when he should have reached his majority.   His health gave way, however, before this plan could be carried out, and he left Wall street, and took a farm on Staten Island.   Devoting himself to his new pursuit with characteristic vigor, he brought the farm up in the course of a few years, and made it pay handsomely.   He then undertook the receivership of the badly crippled Staten Island Railroad, and soon brought that out of its difficulties, and became its president.   In 1864 he became vice-president of the Harlem Railroad, and soon after of the Hudson River Railroad.   Upon the consolidation of the Hudson River and New York Central Railroads in 1869, he was made vice-president and executive officer of the organization.   Since then his career has been a part of the railway history of the country. During the life of his father, "Billy," as the old Commodore affectionately called him, was his confidant and executive officer, and through him the far-reaching plans of the "railroad king" were carried into successful execution.   The united efforts of father and son more than trebled the value of the great railway lines in their hands, and little by little the ownership of the vast combination passed into their possession. "Billy" displayed the highest executive ability, and from the first took his place among the great railway managers of the country.   At the death of Commodore Vanderbilt, he succeeded his father in the presidency of the various roads under his control, and is now vice-president of a number of other roads in the West and South. He also became, by his father's will, the heir to the great bulk of the vast estate left by the Commodore. He is said to have more ready money than any man in America, and his railroads are a source of enormous income to him.

Mr. Vanderbilt was married in 1841 to Miss Kissam, of New York, and has a large family. He resides in an elegant mansion in Fifth avenue, and is now erecting two of the finest dwelling houses in the city, on Fifth avenue, between Fifty-first and Fifty-second streets. Mr. Vanderbilt will reside at the corner of Fifty-first street, and the adjoining house is for his married daughters. Two of his sons, Cornelius and William K. Vanderbilt, are also erecting splendid mansions higher up the avenue.

Mr. Vanderbilt is still devoted to his farm, and takes pride in regarding himself as a practical farmer. He has inherited his father's love for fast horses, and possesses some of the best trotters in the country. He is a good driver and is constantly on the road in fine weather.

CHAPTER XXXIV

CRIME IN NEW YORK

PROFESSIONAL CRIMINALS—THEIR NUMBERS—THE THIEVES—SUPERINTENDENT WALLING'S DE-
SCRIPTION OF THEM—THE THIEF LANGUAGE—GRADES OF THIEVES—BURGLARS—BANK ROB-
BERS—SNEAK THIEVES—CONFIDENCE MEN—HOW THEY OPERATE—THE PICKPOCKETS—
WHERE THEY COME FROM—THE ROGUES' GALLERY—THE RIVER THIEVES—DARING CRIMES
—THE FENCES—HOW STOLEN GOODS ARE DISPOSED OF—TRICKS OF THE FENCES—THE
ROUGHS—BLACKMAILERS—HOW THEY FLEECE THEIR VICTIMS.

Strange as it may seem, men and women of certain grades of intellect and temperament deliberately devote themselves to lives of crime. These constitute the "professional criminals," who make up such a terrible class in the population of every great city. In New York this class is undoubtedly large, but not so large as many people assert. That it is active and dangerous, the police records of the city afford ample testimony. It is very hard to obtain any reliable statistics respecting the professional votaries of crime, but it would seem, after careful investigation, that New York contains about 3000 of them. These consist of thieves, burglars, river thieves, fences, and pickpockets. In addition to these we may include under the head of professional criminals, the following:— Women of ill-fame, about 5000; keepers of gambling houses, and of policy and lottery offices, about 600, making in all nearly 9000 professional law-breakers, or about one professional criminal in every 136 inhabitants in a population of a million and a quarter. This is a startling statement; but unhappily it is true.

The population of New York is more cosmopolitan than that of any city in the Union, and the majority of the people are poor. The struggle for existence is a hard one, and offers every inducement to crime. The political system, which is based upon plunder, presents the spectacle of well known offenders going unpunished by justice; and is therefore so much encouragement to the ignorant and degraded to enter upon lives of dishonesty. The professionals are not all ignorant men or women, however. Among them may be found many whose abilities, if properly directed, would win for them positions of honor and usefulness. There seems to be a fascination in crime to these people, and they deliberately enter upon it.

The principal form which crime assumes in the Metropolis is robbery. The professionals do not deliberately engage in murder or the graver crimes; though they do not hesitate to commit them if necessary to their success or safety. They prefer to pursue their vocation without taking life; and murder, arson, rape, and capital crimes are, therefore, not more common, in proportion to the population, in the Metropolis than in other cities. Robbery, however, is a science here, and it is of it in its various forms that this chapter will treat.

The professional criminals of New York constitute a distinct community; they are known to each other, and seldom make any effort to associate with people of respectability. They infest certain sections of the city where they can easily and rapidly communicate with each other, and can hide in safety from the police.

Some time ago, Police Superintendent Walling thus described the thieves of New York:—

"New York thieves are of two sorts—those who steal only when they are tempted by want, or when an unusual opportunity for successful thieving is thrown in their way, and those who make a regular business of stealing. A professional thief ranks among his fellows according to his ability. Many professional thieves are burglars. They drink to excess, and commit so many blunders that they are easily detected by the police. They gamble a great deal. When successful they quarrel over their booty, and often betray each other. A smart thief seldom drinks, and never allows himself to get under the influence of liquor. He takes care to keep himself in the best physical trim; and is always ready for a long run when pursued, or a desperate struggle when cornered. He must always have his wits about him. A thief of this class makes a successful bank robber, forger, or confidence swindler. Professional thieves seldom have any home. Many of them find temporary shelter in a dull season in houses of ill-repute. They associate with, and are often married to, disreputable women, many of whom are also thieves. The smartest thieves do not have homes, for the reason that they dare not remain long in one place for fear of arrest. During the summer New York thieves are to be found at all the watering-places and seaside resorts. Later in the season they attend the country fairs and agricultural shows, and come back to the city at the beginning of the winter. They are fond of political meetings in

Jersey City and other places near New York, but do not appear at meetings in this city."

Being asked whether there were any places in the city where thieves were educated to their business, Mr. Walling replied:—"No; it would be impossible for such places to exist without being discovered Thieves educate themselves, or get their knowledge by associating with other thieves more experienced than themselves. Those people who believe in the existence of schools where boys are taught the art of picking pockets, have got their belief from works of fiction like Dickens's 'Oliver Twist.' The bucket shops and brothels of the city where thieves congregate, are the only places which can be called schools of crime."

For purposes of communicating with each other, the professional thieves have a language, or *argot*, which is also common to their brethren in England. It is generally known as "Patter," and is said to be of Gypsey origin. A few phrases, taken at random from it, will give the reader an idea of it: *Abraham*, to sham, to pretend sickness; *Autumn cove*, a married man; *Autumn cackler*, a married woman; *Bag of nails*, everything in confusion; *Ballum rancum*, a ball where all the damsels are thieves and prostitutes; *Barbary coast*, Water street; *Bill of sale*, a widow's weeds; *Booked*, arrested; *Bingo mort*, a drunken woman; *Brown stone*, beer; *Cain and Abel*, a table; *Cap-your-lucky*, to run away; *City College*, the Tombs; *Consolation*, assassination; *Doxie*, a girl; *Drawing*, pocket picking; *Duria*, file; *Family man*, a receiver of stolen goods; *Free*, to steal; *Gilt*, a crowbar; *Gilt-*

dubber, a hotel thief; *Madge*, private places; *Ned*, a ten dollar gold piece; *Olive*, the moon; *Plate of meat*, a street of a city; *Poncess*, a woman who supports a man by her prostitution; *Star the glaze*, break the glass.

Experienced thieves are thoroughly familiar with this language, and can speak to each other intelligibly, while a bystander is in total ignorance of their meaning.

The professional thieves are divided into various classes, the members of which confine themselves strictly to their particular line of work. They are classed by the police, and by themselves, as follows: Burglars, Bank Sneaks, Damper Sneaks, Safe Blowers, Safe Bursters, Sneak Thieves, Confidence Men, and Pickpockets. A burglar will rarely attempt the part of a sneak thief, and a pickpocket will seldom undertake a burglary.

The burglar stands at the head of the professional class, and is looked up to by its members with admiration and respect. He disdains the title of "thief," and boasts that his operations require brains, and nerve to an extraordinary degree. The safe blowers and safe bursters are also classed by the police as burglars, and are acknowledged by the craft as confederates. They number about 325 known professionals. The banks and the large business houses are their "game." They disdain smaller operations. When a plan to rob a bank has been formed, the burglar proper calls the safe burster, and sometimes the safe blower, to his aid. One man often prepares the way by opening a small account with the bank, and drawing out his deposits in small amounts.   He visits the place at different hours of the day, learns the habits of the bank officers and clerks, and makes careful observations of the building and the safes in which the money is kept.   Frequently a room in the basement of the bank building, or in an adjoining building, is hired and occupied by a confederate.   When all is ready, a hole is cut through the floor into the bank room, or, in rare cases, an opening is made through the walls from an adjoining building.   Once in the bank room, the services of the safe blower or burster are called into action.   The former takes charge of the operation when the safe is to be blown open by gunpowder. He drills holes in the door of the safe by the lock, and fills them with charges of gunpowder, which are ignited by a fuse.   The safe is carefully wrapped in blankets to smother the noise of the explosion, and the windows of the room are lowered about an inch from the top, to prevent the breaking of the glass by the concussion of the air.   The explosion destroys the lock, but makes little noise, and the door of the safe is easily opened.   Where it is desirable not to resort to an explosion, the safe burster makes the safe fast to the floor by strong iron clamps, in order that it may bear the desired amount of pressure.   He then drills holes in the door, into which he fits jack-screws, worked by levers.   These screws exert a tremendous force, and soon burst the safe open.   Sometimes, when small safes are to be forced open, they use only a jimmy and a hammer, wrapping the hammer with cloth to deaden the sound of the blows. The safe once opened, the contents are at the mercy of the burglars. These never attack a safe without having some idea of the booty to be secured, and the amount of risk to be run. Saturday night is gener· ally chosen for such operations. If the work cannot be finished in time to allow the burglars to escape before sunrise on Sunday, they continue it until successful, and boldly carry off their plunder in broad daylight. Where it can be done, the burglars prefer to enter the bank by means of false keys. One of them will frequent the bank and secure wax impressions of the necessary keys, and from these false keys are manufactured. Private houses are often robbed by means of such keys.

The bank sneak is simply a bond robber. He confines his operations to stealing United States and other bonds, preferring coupon to registered bonds, as they can be more easily disposed of. He frequents a bank for a long period, and patiently observes the places where the bonds and securities are kept. This he manages to do without suspicion, and when all is ripe for the robbery, he boldly enters the bank, makes his way unobserved to the safe, snatches a package of bonds, adding to it a bundle of notes, if possible, and escapes. If the plunder consists of coupon bonds, it is easily disposed of; but registered bonds require more careful handling. Generally, when the bank offers a reward for their recovery, the thief enters into communication with the detective appointed to work up the case, and compromises with the bank by restoring a part of the plunder on condition that he is allowed to keep the rest and escape punishment.

The damper sneak is also a bond robber, but confines his depredations to brokers' offices. Wall street is his field of operations, and has suffered heavily from him. He enters a broker's office, under pretext of waiting for a friend who has business with the house, or some similar plea, and watches his opportunity to get at the safe, which is generally left open during business hours. Seizing a favorable moment, he passes behind the counter unobserved, snatches whatever he can lay his hands on, and leaves the office. In the majority of instances he gets away with his plunder. He trusts everything to chance, and steals anything he can carry off.

The sneak thieves are the lowest in the list of professional robbers. They confine their operations principally to private dwellings and retail stores. They are in constant danger of detection and arrest, and are more often secured by the police than the other classes we have mentioned. The dinner hour, which in winter is after dark, is their favorite time for entering houses. They gain admittance by open doors or windows, or by false keys, and take anything within their reach. A favorite practice of sneak thieves is to call at houses advertised for rent, and ask to be shown the rooms. Another plan is to visit the offices of physicians and other professional men, and to steal articles of value in the waiting-rooms while they are left alone. The majority of those who steal from stores are women, who take articles from the counters while the clerks are busily engaged in laying out goods for their inspection. The practice of shoplifting has become so common, that many of the leading stores keep special detectives to watch the customers.

Confidence men make use of the credulity of country people and strangers in the city. A favorite plan is to watch the registers of the hotels, and get the names and addresses of the guests. The method is as follows:—Mr. Smith comes to New York, puts up at some prominent hotel, and after dinner saunters out for a stroll. A confidence man, who has been on the watch for his appearance, meets him some blocks away from the hotel, and, rushing up to him, seizes his hand, and exclaims delightedly, "Why, Mr. Smith, how glad I am to see you. When did you arrive? How did you leave them all in Smithville?" Mr. Smith is taken by surprise at being recognized in the great city, and if he is at all credulous, the confidence man has no trouble in making him believe that they have met before. The swindler joins him in his stroll, after a few moments of conversation confides to him that he has drawn a large prize in a lottery, and invites him to accompany him to the lottery office, and see him receive the money. On the way they visit a saloon and enjoy a friendly drink together. Another stranger now drops in, and is introduced to Mr. Smith by the swindler. The new comer draws the swindler aside and exchanges a few words with him, whereupon the latter tells Smith that he owes the stranger a small sum of money, and has unfortunately left his pocket-book at his office. He asks his unsuspecting victim to lend him the amount until they reach the lottery office, when he will return it. Smith produces the money, which is handed to the new comer, who then takes his departure, and the friends resume their stroll toward the lottery office. On the way the swindler manages to elude his victim, who seeks him in vain, and goes back to his hotel a sadder and a wiser man. Strange as it may seem, this is one of the most successful tricks played in the city. It is often varied, but is never attempted upon a resident of the Metropolis.

The pickpockets of New York are very numerous. The term pickpocket is regarded by the police as including not only those who confine their efforts to picking pockets and stealing satchels, travelling bags, and valises, but also gradations of crime which approach the higher degrees of larceny from the person, and highway robbery. The members of this class of the thieving fraternity are well known to the police, and the detectives are kept busy watching them. Their likenesses are contained in the "Rogues' Gallery" at police headquarters, and the authorities know the thieves well, as their careers embrace in every instance a long record of crime. Instances are not rare in which a whole family, from the oldest to the youngest, is equally deep in crime, the little ones having been thoroughly and systematically educated by their parents in the different branches of stealing, beginning with the simple picking of the pocket of some unwary person, and finally becoming able to commit the most daring burglaries. The pickpockets are largely recruited from the newsboy class. These boys grow up in such constant association with criminals, that their moral sense becomes so stunted that they step readily into lives of crime. They are utterly cut off from any saving or refining influence, and their lives throw them into the companionship of thieves and abandoned women, whose influence over them is all-powerful.

Pickpockets do not as frequently travel in gangs now as in former years. With the exception of the old and well-known professionals, most of this class of thieving is done by young men of 16 or 18 years, who rob men whom they find intoxicated of the money or valuables they may happen to have about them. It is difficult to keep the track of the residences of professional pickpockets, as they change them very often, and also give a different name every time they are arrested, so that they are best known by their aliases. The police endeavor to have all known professional thieves constantly under surveillance, but the task is a difficult one. In addition to constantly changing their places of abode, they are in and out of the city frequently. Several saloons and localities, however, have become notorious as resorts of pickpockets. A saloon and hotel near the Bowery and Canal street, a saloon near the junction of the Bowery and Fourth street, and one near the corner of Mercer and Houston streets, are well known to the police as resorts of thieves.

Most of the pickpockets now come, as we have said, from among the bootblacks and newsboys, who do a thriving business in the winter time, when overcoats are worn with outside pockets for small change. A newsboy, when offering to sell a paper, and while holding it before his customer's face, will skilfully extract from the change pocket in his customer's overcoat all that may be there. Great dexterity is sometimes acquired in this manner.

The ferry boats, the street cars, and the platforms and trains of the elevated railroads are favorite fields for the operations of pickpockets. The neighborhood of the Grand Central Depot is also busily worked by them. One or more thieves will work his way into a crowd of passengers, jostle them about, and rob them with the utmost ease. Some are so bold as to make scarcely any concealment of their work.

All professional pickpockets that are arrested, are photographed, and their pictures are placed in the "Rogues' Gallery" at police headquarters. It sometimes happens, though this is very rare, that one reforms and endeavors to gain an honest livelihood. In that case his picture is taken out of the gallery and privately kept by the Superintendent of Police or the Chief of the Detective Force, and if the reformation proves to be complete and thorough, the picture is either destroyed or given up to the original. The detectives claim that their efforts to arrest and convict pickpockets are not properly seconded by the police magistrates. In case a professional pickpocket who is well known to the police is arrested late at night on suspicion, he has to be taken to the police court by ten o'clock the next morning. It often happens that there are complaints in the detective office against this very man, and a full description given by some robbed person, which points out this one as the thief wanted. The police magistrates, however, insist that the evidence against the prisoner shall be immediately forthcoming; and, as it is frequently the case that the complainant may be out of town, or for some other reason cannot be immediately found, the prisoner is discharged.

One of the most dangerous and skilful classes of pickpockets consists of women and young girls. These operate with great success in dry-goods stores, churches, and other crowded places where ladies congregate.

Another dangerous class of criminals are the river thieves, or "River Pirates," as they are sometimes termed. There are about fifty of this class known to the police as professionals, and these are among the most daring and successful robbers in the city. The long line of the North River front of the island is well lighted, and as it is largely occupied by the piers of the great railroad and steamship lines, it is strongly guarded by private watchmen, as well as by the city police. The East River front is neither so well lighted nor so strongly guarded, and, therefore, constitutes the principal scene of the operations of the river thieves, though the North River front is by no means exempt from their depredations.

The river thieves work hard for their plunder. They operate in gangs of three or four, each of which has a large, swift rowboat, equipped with bags and tarpaulins. They row silently and with muffled oars along the wharves, darting under the piers occasionally to escape observation, until they reach the vessel, or vessels, they have marked during the day for robbery. Between midnight and morning is the time chosen for their work. Every one on board the vessel is asleep, even the man on the watch. Approaching the vessel silently, they clamber on board by means of her chains, or by a rope left hanging over the side.

RIVER THIEVES.

Moving cautiously about her decks, they secure whatever they can lay their hands on, fill their bags, and
lower them into the boat.   Though they will often
take original packages unbroken, they prefer to force
them open, and rifle them of their contents, which are
transferred to the bags.   Merchandise thus removed
from the original package cannot be identified if the
thieves are arrested with it in their possession, and
robbery cannot be proved against them.   They go
well armed, and, if discovered on board a ship, do not
hesitate to shed blood in their efforts to escape.   In
spite of the vigilance of the harbor police, the chances
are largely in favor of the thieves.   They choose their
own time and place of operation, and conduct their
movements so secretly, and with such system, that they
are generally apt to escape.   If pressed too hard by the
police boat, in their efforts to get away, they at once
open fire upon it, and sharp skirmishes often occur
between the officers of the law and the thieves.   Dark
and stormy, and especially foggy, nights are the favorite seasons for the operations of the river thieves.
They know every foot of the harbor on both sides of
the city, and are able to row for long distances under
the piers.   The North and East River fronts of the
city, and the wharves of Brooklyn and Jersey City, and
even vessels lying at anchor in the harbor, are busily
worked by them.   They rarely attempt to rob a
steamship, as the watch is stricter on those vessels
than on sailing ships, but several of the great European lines have suffered from their depredations.
Sometimes they find a schooner in charge of a single
man, or laid up for the winter.   The man in charge

is quickly overcome, and the vessel is literally stripped of everything that can be carried away from her, and is left a perfect wreck. Sometimes a desperate gang will boldly attack a vessel lying in the harbor, and endeavor to overpower her crew. They can be driven off only after a hard hand-to-hand fight.

One of the worst gangs that ever infested the waters of New York was led by Mike Shannahan. Under his guidance the pirates would sail up and down the East River in the schooner "Sunny Shower," in search of molasses. When unable to obtain it legitimately, they would steal it from the different piers. When a sufficient quantity was accumulated, they would sail to a retired nook in Long Island Sound, and there manufacture whiskey in large quantities. The vessel was supplied with everything necessary for the business, and, unmolested by the authorities, the gang soon made a large sum of money. One of their boldest exploits was the robbery of the bark Saone. The vessel lay at the upper quarantine station, and was loaded with coffee. Owing to the prevalence of yellow fever on board during the voyage, the cargo was ordered to be discharged in lighters. Pulling alongside in broad day, the pirates hailed the mate, and asked to be allowed to come on board, as they were thirsty. They found the mate was alone, and at once boarded the ship. Before he was aware of their intentions, the mate was seized, placed below the hatches, and tied to the ringbolts on the main deck. During all this time the Staten Island ferry boats, and other vessels, were passing and repassing continually. Taking off the hatches, the thieves transferred to their boat two hundred bags of coffee, and, bidding the mate good day, left the vessel. They conveyed their goods to the Floating Bethel for Seamen, moored, as now, in the East River, and concealed their plunder in an unused hatch until they were able to remove it safely.

The life of a river thief is full of hardship and danger. Apart from his encounters with the police and the crews of vessels, he has to battle with the elements and endure an extraordinary amount of exposure and fatigue. Constant night-work on the water, exposed to wind and storm, snow and ice, will break down the strongest constitution, and the river thief soon passes from the scene of his exploits to the hospital or alms-house, if, indeed, he is fortunate enough to escape the penitentiary.

Though the professional thieves are so successful in securing plunder, they would be at a loss to dispose of it to advantage were it not for the "Fences" with whom they deal. The "Fence" is simply a dealer in stolen goods, knowing them to be such. He is re-garded by the police as the most important person in the business of stealing, as without his assistance the thieves could not realize upon their plunder. The "Fence" is generally the keeper of a pawnshop or junk store in a part of the city inhabited by the poorer classes. His acquaintance among the professional thieves is extensive. When one thief wishes to com-municate with another whose place of abode is not known to him, he goes at once to the "Fence" to get the desired address, or to leave a message. All plun-der obtained by thieves, such as jewelry, watches, gold and silver ware, costly house ornaments, and articles

of clothing, for which the thieves have no use, and
which they cannot keep in their possession without
great danger, is brought to the "Fence" to be disposed of. The disposal of stolen property is often
attended with as much risk as the procuring of it, and
the "Fence" always demands his full share of the
profits for his part in the transaction. The crafty receiver knows very well that the thieves place themselves in his power when they come to him to dispose
of their plunder, and he does not hesitate to drive
hard bargains with the less desperate of his customers.
A thief frequently gets no more than enough to pay
his week's board for stealing a valuable watch. Whenever a burglary is planned by thieves a "Fence" is
always consulted, for without some means of hastily
removing and disposing of the goods no profit could
be gained by the undertaking. It is usual for the
"Fence" to provide a wagon, watch the building in
which the burglars are at work, and, at a prearranged
signal, to drive to the place and carry off the booty.
If a clothing house or fur store has been robbed, the
articles are at once stripped of their wrappings and
so altered in appearance that the owners would find
it difficult to identify their property. The "Fences"
keep melting pots in their houses, and articles of gold
or silver, including the cases of watches in many instances, are converted into bars of metal, which can
be easily disposed of without detection. Precious
stones are removed from their settings, and the gold
is either melted, or the marks by which it may be
identified are removed by burnishing. The marks on
dry-goods and clothing are removed by chemicals or

fine scissors, and even the trimmings and sometimes the shapes of garments are altered. Every fence store has numerous places in which stolen goods may be safely hidden, and every means is used to baffle the vigilance of the police. Every fence store in the city is known to the authorities, and is under surveillance, but in spite of this, so great is the skill of the "Fences" that it is a rare thing that one of them is ever brought to justice. The thieves are not their only customers; dishonest clerks, porters, and servant girls steal from their employers, and dispose of their plunder to the "Fences."

The roughs constitute another class of professional criminals. The rough is simply a brutal man, who seems lost to all the better feelings of humanity, and who engages in violence and crime simply for the pleasure it affords him. He is not necessarily a thief, though he often does steal for a living. As a general rule he lives upon the earnings of some woman of ill-fame, and though he beats and maltreats her himself, protects her from injury at the hands of others of his class. His favorite amusement is to attend picnics and celebrations in the suburbs or on board steamers, and to break up the enjoyment of the occasion by beating and robbing the pleasure seekers. At such times gangs of roughs work together, and women and children, as well as men, are the objects of their brutal violence. The rough is both a bully and a coward. He does not hesitate to commit murder or to outrage a woman, but he does this only when he can act without jeopardy to his own safety. He will not engage in a fair fight, and slinks away from real danger. He is often the proprietor of a panel-house, a policy-office, or a rat- or dog-pit, and his associates are his fellow roughs, thieves, and prostitutes. He is a politician by nature, and does the dirty work of the "statesmen" who rule in municipal politics. This gives him the only importance he enjoys, and also often saves him from punishment for his crimes. As soon as his misdeeds bring him into trouble, his political friends exert themselves to save him from punishment, and are generally successful.

Blackmailers are also classed by the police among the professional criminals. The object of these people is to live at the expense of others more fortunate than themselves, and to acquire the means of doing so by extorting money from them by threats. The blackmailer, though sometimes a man, is generally a woman. The well-known weakness of mankind inclines the community to listen with considerable readiness to charges brought by a woman, and men knowing this are often afraid to offer any resistance to the blackmailer. They fear that the charges will be believed, however they may deny them, and know that at all events they will produce a scandal; so they pay the sums demanded of them in the hope of hushing the matter up. Instead of accomplishing this, they simply place themselves in the power of the wretch, whose demands for money increase with every compliance of the victim. Innocent men have been driven to despair and suicide by these wretches. A firm stand at the first, with the assistance of the police, would end all the trouble at the start; but let a victim once yield, and he is certain to be bled as long as he will stand it.

Young men about to make rich marriages are the favorite "game" of the female blackmailer, who generally has a thief or a rough as her "backer." She knows, and indeed so does the young man, that any story about a man will find believers. She goes to the intended bridegroom, threatens to denounce him to his *fiancée* as her destroyer, and demands money as the price of her silence. Although the man knows he is innocent, he dreads the scandal, fears it will break off his marriage, and generally yields to the demand of the wretch. Should he refuse, the woman boldly goes to the young lady, and carries out her threat. This is her revenge, and she is too often successful.

A description of the arts resorted to by blackmailers to extort money from their victims would fill a volume. Their ingenuity and fertility of resource are wonderful. They rarely assail women, as they know the male relatives of a lady so attacked would bring the police upon them. Men are their victims, and they rely upon their fears for success.

CHAPTER XXXV

CREEDMOOR

THE NATIONAL RIFLE ASSOCIATION OF AMERICA—THE CREEDMOOR RANGE—THE GROUNDS —THE TARGETS—SHOOTING MATCHES—NATIONAL GUARD PRACTICE—AMATEUR MARKS- MEN.

The rifle range of the National Rifle Association of America is located at Creedmoor, a little village on Long Island, about thirteen miles from New York. The association owns a tract of eighty-five acres of land, enclosed with a substantial fence, and levelled and sodded with turf. Buildings for the use of the association and marksmen are erected within the grounds, and at the extreme end of the lawn thirty iron targets are placed, giving any desired range from 50 to 1200 yards. At various intervals are placed a "running deer" target, "a tramp" or "moving man" target, and a "ringing target," in the last of which a bell is rung when the centre is struck. A fine clock-faced wind dial is placed at a conspicuous point to show the marksmen the direction of the wind, and numerous flags and streamers are planted along the range for the same purpose.

Frequent shooting matches are held at Creedmoor during the year, and draw large crowds from New York, Brooklyn, and the surrounding country. The scene at such times is very brilliant, as the ladies attend the matches in large numbers, and take great interest in the sport. All the proceedings are regulated by a fixed code of rules, a violation of which subjects the offender to a forfeiture of the privileges

CREEDMOOR RIFLE RANGE.

of the range. Each regiment of the National Guard of New York and Brooklyn is required to practise at the Creedmoor range several times during the year, and prizes are awarded the best marksmen on such occasions.

The object of the Rifle Association is to improve the skill of its members in the use of fire-arms. Any person of respectability may enjoy the privileges of the range upon payment of a small sum and compliance with the rules. The range is very popular with amateurs, and some of the most skilful shooting in the country may be witnessed here.

CHAPTER XXXVI.

BAR-ROOMS

ARRESTS FOR DRUNKENNESS AND DISORDER—NUMBER OF LICENSED BAR-ROOMS—THE DRINK-
ING CAPACITY OF WALL STREET—AMOUNT OF BEER DRANK—THE LARGEST BAR IN THE
WORLD—AN ENORMOUS BUSINESS IN RUM—HIGH RENTS ASKED FOR BAR-ROOMS—THE ALL-
NIGHT HOUSES—THE BUCKET-SHOPS—GREAT AMOUNT OF DRUNKENNESS—WOMEN AS
DRINKERS—WHERE THEY GET THEIR LIQUOR.

About 35,000 persons are arrested and brought before the Police Courts of the Metropolis every year
for "drunkenness" and "drunkenness and disorder."
The Temperance Societies of the city, on the other
hand, do not number 20,000 members. The contrast
is startling, but becomes even more so when it is remembered that the persons arrested are only a small
part of the vast number who daily pay tribute to the
bar-rooms and rum-shops of New York. The Board
of Excise licenses 2430 places where liquors are sold
by the single glass or drink, or about one bar-room
to every six hundred inhabitants of the city. These
represent every grade of drinking establishment, from
the magnificent Broadway saloon to the "gin-mill" of
the Bowery and Sixth avenue, and the "bucket-shops"
of Baxter street. All these places enjoy a greater or
less degree of prosperity, and the proprietors grow
rich, unless they cut short their lives by becoming
their own best customers. For alcoholic and malt
liquors sold over the bar, hundreds of thousands of
dollars are spent daily. It is estimated that in the
vicinity of Wall street alone, 7500 drinks are taken

SPECIMEN OF WORK DONE INSIDE.

and 150 bottles of champagne are disposed of every day. The "bulls and bears" require heavy stimulants to keep them up to their exciting work, and their daily expenditure for such purposes is about $2500. Probably this may account for some of the queer scenes to be witnessed in the Stock Exchange.

The quantity of beer consumed in the city is about three times that of whiskey, which is the most common of the alcoholic drinks. The true-blooded German beer drinker will consume from one to two dozen glasses of his favorite beverage in twenty-four hours, and his American and other imitators follow closely in his footsteps.

The largest bar in the world is that at the Astor House, which transacts the bulk of its business between the hours of nine A. M., and five P. M. Its receipts average about $700 a day, or nearly $220,000 a year, Sundays excluded. A popular bar will take in from $200 to $400 a day, but the majority of the liquor dealers are content with from $30 to $50 a day. Some of these places remain open all night, and are filled with dram drinkers at all hours. At the first-class establishments the liquors sold are of good quality, but as the scale is descended the quality of the drinks falls off, until the low-class bar-rooms and bucket-shops are reached, in which the most poisonous compounds are sold, under the name of whiskey, brandy, gin, rum, etc. The prices charged are high and the profits are enormous.

The rents asked for bar-rooms in prominent localities are enormous. There is one man in New York who pays $10,000 a year for a small room. His principal trade is in whiskey, which he sells for twenty cents a drink ; for brandy he charges forty cents.

The bucket-shops are simply rooms located in the poorer sections of the city, where liquors of the vilest kind are sold by the pint, quart, or gallon. Their customers are the poor and wretched. Only the most deadly poisons are sold here.

It is impossible to estimate the amount of drunkenness in New York. The arrests represent but a very small part of it, as thousands of habitual drunkards manage to keep out of the hands of the police. Respectable men patronize the bar-rooms regularly, and are constantly seen reeling along the streets. So long as they are not helpless, or guilty of disorderly conduct, the police do not molest them. Systematic drinking, which does not amount to actual intoxication, but kills by slow degrees, is very common. Among the most liberal patrons of the bar-rooms and beer-saloons are young men and even boys, who thoughtlessly begin here careers that will one day end in sorrow.

Drunkenness is by no means confined to men. Women are largely addicted to it. Out of some 32,000 arrests in a single year for this cause, nearly 12,000 were females. In the more wretched quarters of the city women drink heavily, and are among the most constant customers of the bucket-shops. Even women of respectability and good social position are guilty of the vice of intemperance. They do not frequent bar-rooms, but obtain liquor at the restaurants patronized by them, and it is a common sight to see a well-dressed woman rise from a restaurant table under the influence of whiskey or brandy.

CHAPTER XXXVII

HENRY BERGH

THE FRIEND OF THE BRUTE CREATION—ESTABLISHMENT OF THE "SOCIETY, FOR THE PRE-
VENTION OF CRUELTY TO ANIMALS"—WORK OF MR. BERGH—HOW HE BECAME A TERROR
TO TWO-LEGGED BRUTES—A NOBLE RECORD.

One of the most familiar figures upon the streets
of New York is that of Henry Bergh, the President
of the "Society for the Prevention of Cruelty to Animals." Tall, erect, neatly dressed, and with a countenance remarkable for its expression of kindness and
benevolence, he never fails to attract attention as he
passes slowly along, seemingly preoccupied, but keeping a keen watch over the dumb creatures along his
route, to whose protection he has devoted his life.

Twenty years ago Mr. Bergh came to the conclusion that his mission in life was to protect dumb animals from the cruelties practised upon them. He
entered upon his self-appointed task with enthusiasm,
drew others into the good work, and in 1866 succeeded in organizing the Society of which he is the
president. The necessary legislation was carried
through the Legislature of New York through the efforts of the society, and its officers were empowered
to enforce the laws thus enacted.

Mr. Bergh is fifty-seven years old, and is possessed
of ample means. He is devoted to the cause he has
espoused, and serves the Society as its president without pay. Since he began his work he has created a

HENRY BERGH.

revolution in the treatment of dumb animals in New York. He spends much time on the streets, and his officers are scattered throughout the city, on the watch for cases of cruelty. A brutal driver, engaged in belaboring his horses, is suddenly collared, and looking up finds himself in the grasp of Henry Bergh, or one of his officers, and is made to desist from his cruel work. If a wagon is laden too heavily for the poor beast attached to it, the driver is made to lighten his load, or to take the horse out of the shafts. Sick and broken-down or crippled horses are taken from their drivers on the streets, and sent to the hospital of the Society, where they are properly cared for. Mr. Bergh has made himself a terror to the brutal drivers who once disgraced the city. Nor does he confine his good work to the streets. At the most unexpected times he will make a descent upon some wretched stable, where a suffering horse is being kept without proper care, and rescue the poor animal. The cruel owners of horseflesh have learned that it is useless to resist or to argue with him. He has the law at his back, and can summon the police to his assistance if need be. In aggravated cases he does not stop with relieving a tortured animal, but causes the arrest and punishment of the perpetrator of the cruelty. He is a sworn foe to dog and cock fights, and visits his heaviest wrath upon the persons engaged in such brutalism.

At first Mr. Bergh met with much opposition and considerable ridicule in his efforts to carry on his good work, but he has conquered both, and has gained the firm support of the best classes of the community.

CHAPTER XXXVIII

THE EAST RIVER BRIDGE

TRAVEL AND TRAFFIC BETWEEN NEW YORK AND BROOKLYN—THE FERRIES—PLANS FOR A BRIDGE—THE WORK BEGUN—THE GREAT BRIDGE—THE TOWERS—THE BRIDGE PROPER —THE CENTRAL SPAN—THE CABLES—THE ANCHORAGES—THE APPROACHES—PLANS FOR TRAVEL ACROSS THE BRIDGE.

To all intents and purposes New York and Brooklyn form one metropolis, and the day is not far distant when the two cities will be united under a single corporate government. The intercourse between them is constant and steadily increasing. About eighty millions of people annually cross the East River, and for many years the ferries have been utterly inadequate to the demand upon them. The boats are always crowded, and when the river is filled with ice or shrouded in fog, the passage between the two cities is more dangerous than a voyage across the Atlantic.

The necessity for providing a better, safer, and more regular communication between the two cities led a number of capitalists, some years ago, to conceive the plan of bridging the East River at a convenient point, and after much discussion a company was formed for that purpose. A charter was obtained from the Legislature of the State, and the necessary capital subscribed, the cities of New York and Brooklyn each assuming a certain proportion of the cost of the undertaking. It was determined that the structure should be a suspension bridge, and work was

BROOKLYN BRIDGE AND EAST RIVER.

begun upon it in 1871. The bridge is swung from two massive towers of granite, each of which rests upon a caisson sunk to the solid rock, which, on the New York side, is from 82 to 92, and on the Brooklyn side 45 feet below the surface of the water. The towers erected upon this foundation are 136 feet in length by 56 feet in width at the water-line, and rise to a height of 238 feet above the river at high water. They gradually diminish in size as they ascend, until at the cornice they are 120 feet in length by 40 feet in width. They are constructed of massive masonry, are pierced with two archways each, and rise high above the twin cities, forming the most conspicuous objects in any view of them from the East or North Rivers. The New York tower is located on the river shore near the foot of Roosevelt street, and the Brooklyn tower is just north of the Fulton Ferry house. The New York terminus of the bridge is in Chatham street, immediately below the City Hall Station of the Elevated Railway, and the Brooklyn terminus is in the square bounded by Fulton, Prospect, Washington, and Sands streets.

The bridge is divided into five parts: the central span over the river between the towers, 1,595 feet long; a span on each side from the tower to the anchorage, 940 feet in length; and the approaches— from the termini to the anchorages—the New York approach being 1,336 feet long, and the Brooklyn approach 836 feet long. The entire structure is 6,000 feet in length, and 85 feet in width, and includes a promenade of 13 feet, two railroad tracks, and four wagon or horse-car tracks. Four immense cables of steel wire, each 16 inches in diameter, pass from the anchorages over the towers, and from these cables are suspended the supporting wires which sustain the floor of the bridge. The deflection of the cables is 128 feet. Stays run from the cables and floor of the bridge to the towers to prevent the swinging of the structure, and enable it to resist the force of the heaviest gales. The centre of the floor of the bridge is 135 feet above high water.

At a distance of 940 feet back from the towers are placed the anchorages, which are constructed of massive masonry in the most substantial manner. After passing over the towers each of the four cables enters the anchor walls at an elevation of nearly 80 feet above high water, and, after passing through the masonry for a distance of 20 feet, is firmly secured by powerful anchor chains. The cables support the floor of the bridge from the towers to the anchorages in the same manner as in the central span, this portion of the bridge passing over the tops of the houses underneath.

The approaches extend from the terminus of the bridge on each side to the anchorages, and are supported by iron girders and trusses, which rest at short intervals on piers of masonry, or iron columns, built within the blocks crossed and occupied. The streets are crossed by stone arches, at an elevation sufficient to leave them unobstructed.

The bridge was thrown open to the public for the first time on May 24, 1883. Both cities were profusely decorated.

The procession which started from the City Hall,

Brooklyn, was led by Mayor Low and President Dimon, of the Common Council, followed by the city and State officials, the Brooklyn trustees of the bridge, Commodore Upshur and staff, and General Hancock and staff. There were also in line two detachments of United States troops. Mayor Low and the city officials stopped in the Brooklyn tower, while the United States troops moved across to await the President. In New York the Seventh regiment acted as military escort to the President and other distinguished guests.

William C. Kingsley, chief of the bridge trustees, awaited the party at the foot of the stairs. President Arthur and Mr. Kingsley walked together, followed by Mayor Edson and Secretary Folger, and the rest of the trustees and State officials. At the Brooklyn tower they were met by Mayor Low and the Brooklyn officials, and from there proceeded to Sands street station, where the opening ceremonies were held.

Lines of horse and steam cars traverse the bridge, taking up passengers at the City Hall in New York, and setting them down at the City Hall in Brooklyn, and *vice versa*. In this way the passage of the river is made safely and speedily, and the passengers enabled to enjoy a grand view of the two cities and the neighboring waters.

The bridge will undoubtedly prove a profitable enterprise, as it will enjoy an enormous patronage, which will increase from year to year.

CHAPTER XXXIX

GAMBLERS AND THEIR WAYS

LAWS AGAINST GAMBLING—NUMBER OF GAMBLERS IN THE CITY—THE FARO BANKS—FIRST-CLASS ESTABLISHMENTS—SPLENDID VICE—THE BROADWAY HELLS—THE SKIN GAME—DANGERS OF SUCH PLACES—THE DAY HOUSES—POOL-SELLING—TRICKS OF POOL-SELLERS—LOTTERIES—HOW THEY ARE CONDUCTED—POLICY DEALING—AN INSIDE VIEW OF THE GAME.

The statutes of the State of New York denounce severe penalties against gambling and gamblers, yet games of chance flourish in the Metropolis to a greater extent than in any other place in the United States east of the Rocky Mountains. There are said to be about 200 gambling houses in New York, and about 2,500 persons known to the police as professional gamblers, dealers in policy, and lottery agents. Of late years the laws against gambling have been enforced more rigidly than formerly, and the number of professional gamblers has somewhat diminished. Yet there are still enough of them to make their business a very marked feature of Metropolitan life.

At the head of the gambling fraternity are the faro dealers. This game is too well known to the average American to need a description here, and is very popular in this country because of its supposed fairness. There are between 90 and 100 faro banks in the city, some of which are palatial establishments. The finest of these are situated on Broadway and in the cross streets in the neighborhood of the up-town fashionable hotels. Outwardly they appear to be simply private dwellings, but they have a silent, deserted air during the day, giving no signs of family life. The blinds are kept down, and only men are seen to enter and leave the houses. They are furnished with great magnificence; the ceilings are elaborately frescoed, and costly paintings adorn the walls; the softest carpets cover the floors; the most costly furniture fills the apartments; and superb chandeliers hang from the ceilings and shed a brilliant glow through the rooms. The servants are colored, and the attendance is all that could be desired. Delicious suppers are spread nightly for the guests, and rare old wines and liquors are at the command of all who honor the place with their presence. In the various rooms of the house are all the conveniences for gaming. No one is asked to play, but it is understood that all who partake of the proprietor's hospitality are expected to make some return by risking something at the tables. In the best houses the games are generally fair, the proprietor trusting to the chances of the game, which are nearly all in favor of the bank and the skill of the dealer. Great care is exercised in the admission of visitors. The proprietors of these places discourage the visits of young men; they prefer the company of men of means who have something to lose. The guests are prominent men in the country, as a rule, lawyers, judges, professional men of all kinds, brokers, and the like. Members of Congress and State Legislatures, and public men generally, are among the most constant visitors to the first-class gambling houses. Poker is largely played in the private rooms of these establishments.

The second-class houses, or "hells," lie principally along Broadway and prominent streets leading from it. The visitors to these establishments are chiefly

SCENE IN A BROADWAY GAMBLING HELL.

strangers in the city, who are lured, or "roped," into them by agents of the proprietors. Faro is the principal game here, but fair games are unknown except among the professionals who frequent the place. The "skin game" is used with the majority of the visitors, for the proprietor is determined from the outset to fleece them without mercy. In these places everything pertaining to gaming is boldly displayed—chips, cards, faro boxes, roulette wheels, handsome gaming tables, and side-boards containing fine brands of liquors and cigars. The entrances to the houses are carefully guarded, the doors are secured by heavy bolts and bars, and numerous sliding panels afford every opportunity for inspecting the visitor before his final admission to the rooms. Though roulette is frequently played in these establishments, faro, as we have said, is the principal game. It is simpler than roulette, gives a heavy percentage in favor of the bank, and "skin faro," the only game played here, offers no chance whatever to the player. In "skin faro" the dealer can take two cards from the box instead of one, whenever he chooses to do so. The box is so arranged that the dealer can press on a lever within the box in the right-hand corner. When this is pressed upon, the mouth of the box is opened, so as to allow two cards to slip out at once. The cards being "sanded," stick close together, and the player cannot perceive that there are two. On the withdrawal of the pressure from the lever the mouth of the box is closed by a spring, so that only one card can slip out. There are some boxes made, called "sanded boxes," by the use of which the dealer can press on the end of the box and take out two cards, still keeping his fingers in the natural position, instead of being obliged to reach inside of the box in order to press the lever.

No tally is kept of these games, and the player is unable to tell how many cards have been dealt out. Should he discover the trick, it is highly dangerous to attempt to expose it, as nearly all the persons present are in league with the bank, and are united in the effort to get possession of the visitor's money. The safest plan is to bear the loss and get out of the place as soon as possible, as the men present will not hesitate to provoke a quarrel with or assault a stranger who disputes the fairness of the game. A quarrel once started, every advantage is taken of the player, and his life is not worth a farthing. The safest plan of all is to remain away from these hells. The man who enters any gaming-house in New York, especially a stranger in the city, is a fool, and deserves to lose his money. He who ventures into one of these second-class houses, risks not only his money, but his life. However wise a man may be in his own conceit, however he may rank as an oracle in his distant home, however brave, resolute, or skilful he may be, he is no match for a New York gambler. In nine houses out of ten his life is in danger unless he submits quietly to be robbed in the most barefaced manner.

The up-town houses conduct their operations principally by night. The "Day Houses" are down-town institutions. Ann street, in the rear of the *Herald* office, and several streets adjacent or convenient to Wall street, are the principal neighborhoods infested with them. Not long since a single block in Ann street contained five of these houses, and the majority, though several times raided by the police, still continue to flourish. The "Day Houses" occupy the

upper floors of buildings, the street floors of which
are devoted to legitimate business, and claim to be
"Club Houses." They are managed by the lowest
class of gamblers, skin games only are played in

LOW-CLASS GAMBLING DEN.

them, and the players have no possible chance of success. Yet they manage to do a profitable business.
Their visitors are Wall street brokers, clerks, salesmen, and men in regular business, who too often risk
here money that is not their own.

One of the worst and most demoralizing forms of gambling is "pool selling." The pool business is conducted more or less openly, notwithstanding that the laws of the State denounce severe punishments against it. The business is conducted by professional gamblers, and, though seemingly fair, is a swindle throughout. Pools are sold on horse-races, prize-fights, boat-races, swimming matches, political elections, and in short on every conceivable contest into which the element of chance or doubt enters. The pool is supposed to be made up of a fixed number of chances, each of which is sold at a certain price. The managers charge a percentage or commission on all tickets sold, and do not hesitate to sell as many as there are applicants for, even though the legitimate number is exceeded by such sales. It is said that on a recent presidential election as much as $2,000,000 was staked in pools. The commission on the sales charged by the proprietors of the pool rooms is from three to five per cent., and a certain well-known manager is said to have realized $60,000 from his commissions on the election mentioned above. A favorite trick is to receive the money invested in pools, and then spread reports which shall discourage the betters, and induce them to withdraw their bets. The managers return the amounts invested, minus their commission, which they retain, and in this way, while seeming to act with perfect fairness, fill their coffers at the expense of their victims.

The great evil of "pool" gambling is that it encourages young men and boys to enter into the combinations, and thus gives them a taste for gambling. The possibility of winning considerable money by small investments fascinates them. During a recent political campaign officers of two of the largest banks in the city called upon the Police Commissioners, and stated that they suspected that many of their clerks visited the pool rooms. They feared that the excitement and allurements of gambling might impair the integrity of these young men, and induce them to appropriate money belonging to the banks. Detectives were employed, and the suspicions of the bank officers were confirmed. Business men are constantly finding that their clerks and salesmen are regular visitors to the pool rooms. Messenger boys, bootblacks, and others who earn only a few dollars a week, invest all the money they can get hold of in buying pool tickets. Men of the highest respectability fall victims to the same vice, and the evil goes on increasing. The only persons who profit by it are the managers of the pools, who do not hesitate to resort to any trick to retain the money entrusted to them, and who coolly swindle their infatuated dupes out of their investments.

Another vicious form of gambling is the lottery business, closely connected with which is " policy dealing." Lotteries are of two kinds—the single number system, and the combination system. In the former, as many single numbers as there are tickets in the scheme, are placed in a wheel, and are drawn out in regular order. The first number drawn wins the capital prize, and so on until as many numbers are drawn as there are prizes. In the combination system, seventy-five numbers are generally placed in the wheel, and from these a certain set of numbers are drawn, according to the provision of the scheme. The chances are much greater *against* the ticket-holders in this system than in the single number schemes, as, in order for a player to win a prize, the various numbers must be drawn in the exact order represented on his ticket.

It is, of course, possible for a lottery to be fairly drawn, but it is a well-known fact that in the majority of the schemes advertised *no drawing of any kind ever takes place.* A bogus drawing is published, and, though prizes are assigned, not a single ticket holder ever receives one. Even if the drawing is fair, the business is to be denounced on the ground that it is not only illegal, but demoralizing. The purchasers of lottery tickets are, as a rule, persons unable to afford the expenditure—generally the very poor. This species of gambling has a fascination which holds its votaries with a grip of iron. They venture again and again, winning nothing, but hoping for better luck next time, and so continue until they have lost their all. There are hundreds of well-authenticated cases of men and women being reduced to beggary, despair, and suicide by lottery gambling.

The managers of the various lottery schemes are professional gamblers. They are without principle, and do not intend to pay any prizes to ticket-holders. They receive their money of their dupes, announce a bogus drawing, in which no prizes can be found by any ticket-holder, and then coolly ask their victims to try their luck again.

Policy dealing is one degree lower in infamy than the lottery business. There are about 400 policy shops in the city, whose principal customers are negroes, sailors, and foreigners. The mazes of policy are not well known to the general public. Few games are so well devised for a sure loss to the player, even when honestly played, and the more influential sellers make this assurance doubly sure by playing to suit themselves. The game consists in betting on certain numbers, within the range of the lottery schemes, being drawn at the noon or night drawing. Seventy-eight numbers usually make up the lottery scheme, and the policy player can take any three of these numbers and bet that they will be drawn, either singly, or in such combinations as he may select. The single numbers may come out anywhere in the drawing, but the combination must appear as he writes it in making his bet. He pays one dollar for the privilege of betting, and receives a written slip containing the number or numbers on which he bets. If a single number is chosen and drawn, he wins $5; two numbers constitute a "saddle," and if both are drawn the player wins from $24 to $32; three numbers make a "gig," and win from $150 to $225; four numbers make a "horse," and win $640. A "capital straddle" is a bet that two numbers will be among the first three drawn, and wins $500. The player may take any number of "saddles," "gigs," or "horses," paying $1 for each bet.

Now, all this seems very fair; but the policy managers are equal to the emergency. As soon as they receive the drawings, if they find that too many players are likely to win, they change the order of the numbers, or the numbers themselves, and thus condemn the players to a total loss. These altered numbers are printed on slips at a central office in Vesey street, and are distributed to the various policy shops. In some cases, after these copies have been sent out, it is discovered that the players have even then won too much to suit the managers. The copies are immediately recalled as misprints, and new copies altered to suit the managers are distributed.

All sorts of people engage in this wretched game, blacks and whites, rich and poor. The grossest superstitions are indulged in respecting "lucky numbers." Such numbers are revealed by dreams, which are interpreted by "dream-books." To dream of a man is "one;" of a woman "five;" of both "fifteen," and so on. A large publishing house in the lower part of the city sells thousands of copies of the "dream-book" every year, and among its purchasers are said to be many shrewd operators in Wall street. So great is the rage for policy playing that men and women become insane over it. The lunatic asylums contain many patients who have been brought there by this species of gambling.

CHAPTER XL

THE HUDSON RIVER TUNNEL

A DARING UNDERTAKING—THE WORK BEGUN—ACCIDENTS—DESCRIPTION OF THE TUNNELS—
THE PROPOSED DEPOT IN NEW YORK—PROSPECTS OF THE SCHEME.

One of the most daring undertakings ever attempted by modern engineers is now in progress. This is the construction of the great tunnel under the Hudson River, the object of which is to unite the city of New York with Jersey City, and to allow the railways now terminating in the latter place to enter the Metropolis.

This great work is to consist of two tunnels laid side by side, each 18 feet wide and 16 feet high. Work was begun on the Jersey City side, at the foot of Fifteenth street, on the 1st of November, 1879. The engineers began by sinking a well, 30 feet in diameter, about 100 feet inland from the river. This was securely walled with brickwork and shod with wedge-shaped steel at the bottom. When a depth of 60 feet had been gained, the solid bottom which was found was floored with Roman cement, and the work of boring the tunnel under the bed of the river was begun, and in spite of several accidents, in one of which, on the 21st of July, 1880, 20 men were killed, has been pushed forward steadily.

The tunnels will start from the foot of Fifteenth street, in Jersey City, and when finished will extend in a straight line from Pier No. 9, Jersey City, to Pier

No. 42, at the foot of Morton street, New York. The distance between the two points is a little over one mile, but with the approaches the entire length of the tunnels will be about two and a half miles. The tun-

THE TUNNEL

THE TUNNEL UNDER THE HUDSON RIVER.

nels will adjoin each other, but will be separate and distinct pieces of workmanship, uniting, however, under the grand arches at the working shaft on either side of the river. Each will consist of an immense tube of brick-work, two feet thick, laid in Roman cement, impervious to water, and capable of withstanding any pressure upon it. A single railroad track will be laid in each, and as one of them will be used for trains entering, and the other for trains leaving New York, collisions can never occur. At the lowest point the tracks will be about 60 feet below mean tide. At no point will there be less than twenty feet of earth between the crown of the tunnels and the bed of the river. It is expected that the different railways entering Jersey City will use the tunnels and land their passengers directly in New York City, the depot being probably located somewhere near Broadway and Bleecker street. Several years will be required for the completion of this great work, but its projectors regard its success as assured, and confidently expect that it will effect a complete revolution in the system of travel between New York and the New Jersey shore.

CHAPTER XLI

FASHIONABLE SHOPPING

FASHIONABLE STORES—HANDSOME GOODS—THE FIXED-PRICE SYSTEM—DETECTIVES ON THE WATCH—"STEWART'S"—ENORMOUS TRANSACTIONS THERE.

The fashionable stores of New York are to be found principally on Broadway, Fifth and Sixth avenues, and Fourteenth and Twenty-third streets. They embrace dry-goods, millinery, jewelry, fur, clothing, shoe, and other stores, and their customers consist almost entirely of ladies. They are fitted up elegantly, and contain the finest and most varied stocks of goods to be found anywhere in the world. In almost all these establishments the prices are written in plain figures on the articles, and the clerks are not allowed to deviate from them. Elevators connect the various floors, and convey purchasers from story to story, thus saving them the fatigue of climbing the stairs. Each floor is in charge of a manager, who directs customers to the counters where the goods they wish to purchase are sold. No one is urged to buy, but all the goods are readily shown to those who desire to examine them. Articles purchased are promptly forwarded to the residences of buyers, and every effort is made to render the task of shopping pleasant. All the while the customers are under the constant but unseen surveillance of detectives, and so perfect is this system that shoplifting is rare.

The principal retail firms possess large and magnif-

A. T. STEWART & CO.'S RETAIL STORE.

icent buildings, which are among the chief ornaments
of the city. The most imposing of these are the
buildings of A. T. Stewart & Co., the Domestic Sew-
ing-Machine Company, Arnold, Constable & Co.,
Lord & Taylor, and Tiffany & Co., the last being the
principal jewelry house of the country.

Stewart's is the best-known establishment in New
York. The building is a handsome iron structure five
stories in height, and occupies an entire block, as has
been described. The first floor is devoted to the sale
of miscellaneous goods, each class having its separate
department. It is generally thronged with buyers,
and presents a busy scene. It contains 100 counters,
the aggregate length of which is 5000 feet. The second floor is for the sale of ready-made clothing, suits
for ladies, furs, upholstery, &c.; the third floor is
devoted to carpets; and the other floors to the work
rooms of the establishment. The number of superin-
tendents, salesmen, and other persons employed in
selling and handling goods is about 1700. The business transacted is enormous, and averages about
$60,000, and has reached as high as $87,000, a day.
The greater part of the sales is made between noon
and five o'clock P. M., and between those hours the
vast store is thronged. Everything that can be
desired in the way of dry-goods, millinery, furnishing
goods, and the like, is to be found here. The sales
of silk amount to about $15,000 daily; dress goods to
$6000; laces to $2000; shawls to $2500; velvets to
$2000; gloves to $1000; hosiery to $600; embroid-
eries to $1000; carpets to $5500; and other goods
in proportion.

CHAPTER XLII

TENEMENT HOUSES

DENSITY OF POPULATION IN NEW YORK—NUMBER OF TENEMENT HOUSES AND INHABITANTS —CAUSES OF LIVING IN TENEMENT HOUSES—HIGH RENTS—HOMES OF THE WORKING CLASS—HOPES FOR THE FUTURE—VARIETIES OF TENEMENT HOUSES—A SPECIMEN—CLOSE PACKING—RENTS OF APARTMENTS—EVILS OF THE SYSTEM.

The immense population of New York, and the scarcity of house room in the thickly settled portions of the city, have given rise to a system of dwellings fortunately unknown in other cities of the country. These are known as tenement houses, and are simply vast barracks, inhabited by from two to twenty or more families. The average number of families to a house of this kind is eight. The city contains 20,000 tenement houses, inhabited by about 500,000 people, giving an average of 25 persons to each house. Some of these buildings are very small, however, and contain only two or three families, while the vast rookeries of the most densely populated wards contain from a dozen to twenty-five or thirty families. In one of the wards of the city the population is over 290,000 persons to the square mile, and in several it is nearly 200,000 to the square mile. About one-half of the people of the Metropolis live in these houses, and the crowding of such establishments is something that must be witnessed to be appreciated.

Nor is this crowding of the population the result of poverty. Land is so valuable that rents are enormously high. But few persons can afford the luxury

of a separate house, and workingmen, with families
dependent upon them, cannot think of having their
own establishments.   They must be content to share
a house with several families, and therefore confine
their establishments to a few rooms.   They are compelled to live within easy reach of their places of employment, and therefore are obliged to take up their
quarters in the most thickly settled portions of the
city.   Men earning handsome wages are compelled
to live in these vast barracks, because the rent of a
single house ranges from $1000 upwards. It is hoped
that the Elevated Railroads, which afford rapid transit
between the upper and lower sections of the city, will
enable the better class of working people to possess
homes of their own in the Harlem district and on the
mainland, where rents are not so high, and so thin out
the tenement-house population.

The city contains two classes of tenement houses.
Those of the first class are occupied by well-to-do
working people; those of the second by the very
poor.   The first are large, neat-looking structures,
and are kept as clean as the great number of people
occupying them will permit; the second are wretched
abodes of misery, and often of vice and crime.   The
better class tenement houses are constructed for the
purposes to which they are put; the second class are
simply buildings intended originally for a single family,
but now occupied by as many as they will contain.
These houses are very profitable to their owners, and
some of them pay as much as thirty per cent. on the
money invested in them.   Some of the central wards
of the city contain whole squares, and, indeed, many

TENEMENT HOUSE, BAXTER STREET.

consecutive squares, built up with houses of this kind. One of these, which is but a specimen of many, has a frontage of 50 feet and a depth of 250 feet. On each side of it is an alleyway running the whole length of the building, excavated to the level of the cellar, and arched over on a level with the street, with gratings in the flags with which it is paved to admit light and air to the vaults below. In these vaults are placed the water-closets of the house, which are drained into the street sewers. The water-closets are without doors, and the vapors and gases from them rise through the gratings into the alleyways above, and thence find their way into the house. The building is five stories in height, and has a flat roof. The windows on the sides open into the alleys and receive the poisonous gases which arise from them. Water is laid on each floor. The apartments for a family consist of a kitchen, which is also the living, or sitting-room, and one or more bed-rooms. The rooms are dark, badly ventilated, and into the most of them the sun never shines. The house contains 126 families, and has a population of 700 souls. As may be supposed, it is dirty, and full of bad smells. In the winter time it is close and unhealthy, and in the summer the heat of so many cooking-stoves renders it almost unbearable. What life is in one of these houses the reader can easily imagine. Yet each family pays for its apartment an annual rental which, in Baltimore, Philadelphia, and other cities of the country, would secure it a separate and comfortable house. From $10 to $30 a month is the average rental of a suite of rooms in a tenement house. The building we have described is not an exception to the general rule. The city contains whole blocks of such structures. There are many single blocks containing more people than some of our most thriving towns. The Fourth Ward, covering an area of 83 acres, contains 21,015 inhabitants; the Eleventh, with an area of 196 acres, has 68,779 inhabitants; the Seventh, with an area of 110 acres, contains 50,066 inhabitants; and the Seventeenth, with an area of 331 acres, contains 104,895 inhabitants. In 1880, the following cities contained populations as follows: Providence, R. I., 104,760; Richmond, Va., 63,243; Columbus, Ohio, 51,650; Hartford, Conn., 42,560; Taunton, Mass., 21,252; and Elmira, N. Y., 20,646. By contrasting the area of these cities with that of the wards named above, the reader will be able to form some idea of the terrible overcrowding of this portion of New York.

The tenement houses being so greatly overcrowded, it is impossible to keep them clean, and the majority of them are in bad repair. The mortality of these houses is fearful. In the summer season they are hot-beds of disease, and children die in them at a fearful rate. It is impossible for the authorities to enforce sanitary regulations in these buildings, and in spite of every effort on the part of the Board of Health to check the evil, the death-rate continues fearfully high.

The overcrowding of the tenement houses renders them nurseries of vice and crime. Children of all kinds are thrown together, and learn vicious ways, which develop as they grow older into worse traits. Privacy is impossible, and the various families may be said to live almost in common.

CHAPTER XLIII

JERRY McAULEY'S MISSION

WATER STREET—THE MISSION—ITS SUCCESS—JERRY M'AULEY—THE REFORMED THIEF—MRS.
M'AULEY—THE PRAYER-MEETINGS—THE AUDIENCE—JERRY M'AULEY'S METHODS—A
SCENE AT A PRAYER-MEETING—A WONDERFUL WORK.

In one of the vilest sections of Water street, right under the shadow of the anchorage of the great East River Bridge, is a substantial but modest-looking brick building, known as " 316 Water street." Over the door hangs a lantern bearing the inscription, " Jerry McAuley's Prayer-Meetings." When the shades of night come on, and the rays of the lantern shine out, revealing the legend inscribed upon it, they illuminate a region full of vice, crime, and suffering. The street is lined with long rows of rum-shops, rat-pits, low-down gambling dens, and thieves' dives of the worst description. Here and there are dance-houses, brilliantly lighted, and ornamented with gaudy transparencies. Strains of music float out into the night air, and about the doors and along the side-walks stand groups of hideous women, waiting to entice sailors into these hells, where they are made drunk with drugged liquors, robbed of their money and valuables, and turned helpless into the streets. Groups of drunken and foul-mouthed men and boys lounge about the street, bandying vile jests with the women, and often insulting respectable passers-by. High over all this sea of wretchedness and sin, Jerry

McAuley's lantern shines out like a beacon light, the
only sign of cheer and hope to be seen.   If you listen
you will hear sounds of music in this building also.
but the strains are of praise and thanksgiving—strange
sounds to be heard in such a neighborhood.

Some years ago a wretched frame building, that

JERRY M'AULEY.

had long been used for the vilest purposes, occupied
the site of the present edifice.   It had been for many
years notorious as a dance-house and rum-shop, and
was a terror to the neighborhood and a marked house
to the police. Great was the surprise of Water street,
therefore, when, one night in October, 1872, the place,

after having been closed for a short time, was opened as a Christian mission, and devoted to saving the drunken and sinful dwellers in this section of the city. Greater still was the surprise when it was announced that the Mission was to be conducted by Jerry McAuley and his wife. The work was slow at first, but it prospered, and at length assumed such proportions that the old building was found inadequate to the purposes of the Mission, and, in 1876, was torn down and the present edifice erected in its place.

The surprise of Water street at seeing Jerry McAuley and his wife in its midst in the guise of missionaries was not unnatural. Jerry was a tall, strapping Irishman, and had been for years one of the most notorious roughs in the city. He was a river thief by profession, and a habitual drunkard. He had committed every crime except that of murder, and for years had been the terror of Water street. At last he was arrested for one of his numerous offences, and was sentenced to a term in Sing Sing prison. While there he began to reflect upon his past life, experienced a change of heart, and embraced religion. Upon being released from prison, he returned to New York, and sought out the woman who had for a number of years lived with him, and been his partner in sin and crime. They were married, and began to devote themselves to the work of saving the souls of the wretched creatures among whom their lot had been formerly cast. The change in both was simply miraculous. They took the old dance-house in Water street, made it as neat as their means would admit, and then began their good work. Their meetings were well attended;

many came to see their old companions in their new characters, and others to make fun; but the earnestness of the devoted pair had its effect, and the curious and the scoffers became converts in their turn. Little by little assistance began to be held out to the Mission, and at length a strong body of Christian men and women came to its aid with money, a new building was erected, and the Mission placed upon a sound and safe basis.

Whatever the lives of Jerry McAuley and his wife may have been previous to their reformation, they have nobly atoned for them in the Christian work they have done in the past nine years. They have gone among the outcasts and the wretched, the sinful and the degraded, and have rescued them from their vile ways, brought them to a saving knowledge of God and his religion, and have started them in a new and better course of life. Their efforts often fail; many of their converts relapse into their old ways, but the number of those who are actually reformed is surprisingly large, and the lasting results achieved are great and glorious. No one, however wretched, however far gone in sin, is ever turned away; a helping hand is extended to all, and the vilest outcast is made to feel welcome and confident that there is still a chance for salvation left him.

There is no more interesting sight to be witnessed in the great city than one of Jerry McAuley's prayer-meetings. The audience is made up of men and women of various classes, including many who avoid other Christian agencies, who have never been in a place of prayer, or heard the Bible read except by the

prison chaplain; "poor, friendless men who have drifted
into New York from all parts of the world; drunkards,
thieves, roughs, and discharged convicts; sailors, boatmen, longshoremen, and many prodigal sons who have
wandered away from Christian mothers and have fallen
into crime and beggary."

MRS. M'AULEY.

The meetings are held in the chapel, which is a
pleasant, well-lighted and ventilated room, on the first
floor.   Near the entrance hangs a sign, inscribed as
follows:—"The use of tobacco in this room is strictly
forbidden;" and near the upper end of the room is
another, bearing this inscription:—"Speakers are

strictly limited to one minute." The room is neatly furnished, and is provided with a cabinet organ, at which Mrs. McAuley, a nice, lady-like woman, with a sweet, Madonna-like face, earnest, yet marked with the sadness of past trouble, presides.

The genius of the place is Jerry McAuley, the reformed criminal, and now the powerful messenger of the Gospel to the lost ones of the great city. He is a tall, well-built man, with sharp eyes, a long, sharp nose, and a quick, decisive manner. He is thoroughly in earnest in his work, and having been one of the class to whom he appeals, understanding their character and habits, being intense in his purposes, and animated by a desire to win sinners to the Saviour, he is able to speak with effectual power to these rough men, who listen respectfully to his words, and are attracted by those personal peculiarities that fit him for his work—a work which is unique, and has become one of the most important in the lower part of the great city. Before the meeting begins, and throughout its progress, he is all through the hall, attending to every arrangement, trying to make every one comfortable, and giving his warmest welcomes to the most degraded of all who seek admittance. His programme of the exercises of the evening, is thus stated in his own energetic way:—"We start the meetin' sharp at half-past seven; the man who reads the Bible takes till a quarter to eight—if he is a long-winded feller he stretches it out till eight—then I take hold of it, shut the speeches down to one minute, and on we go for three-quarters of an hour with testimonies." This programme is rigidly adhered to. Jerry knows the value of brevity, and, therefore, rigidly enforces the one-minute rule.

The audience drops in in little "gangs," as Jerry calls them, and by half-past seven the chapel is well-filled. As the clock points the half hour, Jerry opens his hymn-book, and calls out in a strong, cheery voice, "sixty-nine!" and thereupon the singing begins, led by the cabinet organ and the woman whose voice was once raised only in blasphemy. If the singing is a little faint, Jerry spurs up his audience by calling out, "Don't be afraid of your voices, boys; sing out with your whole soul;" and generally the volume of praise grows stronger and fuller. The singing over, a rough, but cleanly-looking young man, rises from his seat, and goes timidly to the platform, where he kneels for a moment in prayer. Then, rising, he opens the Bible, and reads the chapter for the evening, after which he gives in his rough way his own experience.

The testimonies roll in as the meeting progresses, strange and startling many of them, some so quaintly worded that they would provoke a smile in a more "respectable" prayer-meeting, but all given with an earnestness and pathos that is wonderful. Sometimes a drunken sailor will endeavor to interrupt the meeting. One night a man of this kind staggered to his feet, and hiccoughed, "Jesus saves *me*, too."

"That ain't so," replied Jerry, emphatically; "Jesus don't save any man that is full of gin."

And down sits the sailor, utterly abashed by the prompt retort.

Jerry acts as his own policeman, and meets all attempts at disturbance on the ground. The offenders are seized in his powerful grasp, led to the door, and put into the street.

As the testimonies are given, the audience is deeply moved. Yonder is a street-walker, kneeling on the floor, with her face hid in her hands, sobbing bitterly. Jerry smiles, beckons his wife, and the good woman goes down to the poor outcast, and whispers to her despairing soul the only words of hope she has ever heard. Others give evidence of their desire to be saved, and the meeting devotes itself to prayer for them. Jerry's keen eye sweeps the room, and at once detects the hesitating. In an instant he is at their side, devoting his rude but powerful eloquence to urging them to take the decisive step *then and there.* There is something wonderfully encouraging in his strong, hearty grasp of the hand, and in his earnest tones. "I was worse than you," he says; "but the good Lord saved *me.* I know there is a chance for you. Take hold of it, my boy, right now."

When nine o'clock strikes, there is a hymn, a short prayer, and then Jerry dismisses the meeting with a hearty invitation to come again the next night.

CHAPTER XLIV

METROPOLITAN AMUSEMENTS

THE PRINCIPAL THEATRES—METROPOLITAN AUDIENCES—EXPENSES OF A FIRST-CLASS THEATRE —SALARIES OF ACTORS—PRODUCTION OF NEW PLAYS—LONG RUNS—" BOOTH'S " THEATRE A MODEL ESTABLISHMENT—THE GRAND OPERA HOUSE—" WALLACK'S "—" THE UNION SQUARE "—" DALY'S "—THE ACADEMY OF MUSIC—VARIETY THEATRES—THE GRAND DUKE'S THEATRE—NEGRO MINSTRELS—CONCERTS—LECTURES.

In nothing does New York show its Metropolitan character more strikingly than in its amusements. At the head of these stand the theatres, which are more numerous and magnificent than in any American city. The Metropolis contains fifteen first-class theatres. They are as follows:—The Academy of Music, Wallack's, the Union Square, Daly's, the Madison Square, the Park, Booth's, the Grand Opera House, Haverley's Fourteenth Street, the Fifth Avenue, the Standard, the Germania, Harrigan & Hart's, the Thalia, and the Bijou Opera House. Besides these are a number of second-class and variety establishments, and the third-rate theatres of the Bowery and other sections of the city. They are open from the early fall until the late spring, with the exception of the Academy of Music, which is devoted chiefly to Italian Opera, of which only brief seasons are given. They are liberally supported by the residents of the city, and receive an immense patronage from the great throng of strangers constantly in New York. It is estimated that from $30,000 to $40,000 are nightly expended in the city in the purchase of theatre tickets, or from seven to eight million dollars in a single season.

The Metropolitan theatres are the handsomest and best appointed in the United States, and produce their plays with a splendor and completeness of detail unknown in any other American city. The companies are generally made up of actors and actresses who stand at the head of their profession. A Metropolitan audience is hard to please, and is keenly critical, as many would-be managers have learned to their cost. It will not tolerate sham, but is ever ready to encourage and reward true merit. To become a favorite on the New York stage is to win a proud position in the dramatic profession, and one that will command success in any part of the country. The leading theatres retain their players as long as they will stay, and many old actors still delight the audiences of the city who conferred the same pleasure upon the fathers and mothers of their present patrons.

The expenses of a first-class theatre in New York are enormous. The rent runs up into the tens of thousands per annum, and, besides the actors and actresses, anywhere from fifty to one hundred people are employed in each establishment in various capacities. The salaries of the company are liberal, and the leading-man and leading-lady receive very high pay. Wallack pays Miss Rose Coghlan, his leading-lady, $300 a week, for forty weeks in the year; Thorne, the leading-man at the Union Square, receives $200 a week; and John Gilbert, the best actor in Wallack's company, receives $125 a week. These are high figures. A salary of $100 a week is a large one, and many of the best artists in stock companies work like beavers for from $50 to $85 a week. It all depends upon the merit of an actor and his popularity with the public. An actor or actress who can draw full houses, and draw them steadily, whatever the attraction may consist in, is always certain of high pay. Out of their salaries they must provide, in some theatres, their costumes and other stage properties; in other establishments the manager pays half of the cost of the female costumes; and in one or two these are provided by the house. Now, as a large part of the attraction of a piece lies in the magnificent toilettes of the actresses, the reader can understand what a heavy expense the player or the management is under in providing them.

In the production of a new piece, new scenery and stage appointments must be provided, and a first-class house must expend many thousand dollars—often several tens of thousands—before the curtain rises upon the first performance. The risk is very great, and only the long runs which a successful play is sure to enjoy, would justify a manager in assuming it. The enormous number of theatre-goers in the city enables a manager to keep a popular piece on the boards for months. These long runs are extremely profitable to the management, and enable the players to perfect themselves in their rôles to a degree impossible in other cities. The two most profitable theatres in New York are Wallack's and the Union Square. They have the best companies, put their plays on the stage more carefully and elaborately than the other houses, and have a steady, assured patronage upon which they can depend with certainty.

The handsomest theatre in the city is "Booth's," at the south-east corner of Sixth avenue and Twenty-third street. It is a beautiful granite edifice, in the renaissance style, and is one of the largest of the city theatres. The interior is beautifully decorated, is provided with three galleries, and will seat over 2000 persons. The seats are so arranged that every one commands a perfect view of the stage. The frescos are far superior to any used in the decoration of an American theatre, and are genuine works of art. The stage is one of the most perfect in the world; the scenery is moved by machinery; and the changes of scene are executed with such quietness and ease, that they seem like a series of dissolving views.

The theatre was built by Edwin Booth, between 1867 and 1869, and was designed by him to be the most sumptuous temple of the drama in America. It was opened in January, 1869, and for several seasons was conducted by Mr. Booth. Here he produced his plays upon a scale of magnificence never witnessed before even in New York—his Shakespearian revivals being among the events of the dramatic history of the country. This entailed upon the establishment a degree of expense which proved Mr. Booth's financial ruin, and he was at length compelled to retire from the management. His successors have been but little more fortunate. The necessary expenses of the house are very great, and the theatre-goers of New York have not supported the efforts of the successive managers as they have deserved.

BOOTH'S THEATRE.

The Grand Opera House, at the north-west corner of Eighth avenue and Twenty-third street, ranks next to "Booth's" in magnificence. It is a massive structure of white marble, erected by the late Samuel N. Pike, of Cincinnati, as an opera house, about fourteen years ago. The location was unfortunate, however, and the opera house failed as a pecuniary venture

THE GRAND OPERA HOUSE.

from the start. In 1869 it was purchased by the late James Fiske, Jr. and Jay Gould. The front building was converted into offices for the Erie Railway, which was at that time controlled by these gentlemen. Under Fiske's management the Grand Opera House was the home of *Opera Bouffe*. The theatre is situated in a rear building, and is entered from Eighth avenue and

Twenty-third street by a magnificent lobby. The galleries are approached by the handsomest stairway in the city. The theatre is beautifully decorated, will seat over 2000 people, and is provided with one of the largest and best-appointed stages in the world. Of late years the establishment has been very successful — first-class attractions and popular prices being the policy of the management.

Wallack's Theatre is *par excellence the theatre* of New York. It is situated at the north-east corner of Broadway and Thirtieth street, and is one of the most elegant and beautiful houses in the city. It was opened in December, 1881, and is under the sole management of the distinguished actor, Mr. J. Lester Wallack. The old house, at the corner of Broadway and Thirteenth street, is now a German theatre. "Wallack's" is the favorite house with resident New Yorkers, and its audiences contain a larger proportion of city people than those of any of its rivals. Its company is the best in the city, is largely made up of old favorites, and is the model troupe of the country. The theatre is one of the most prosperous in New York, and naturally so, as the performances here are given with a degree of perfection unequalled anywhere in the world.

The Union Square Theatre is situated on Fourteenth street, three doors east of Broadway, and faces Union Square. It was originally leased and fitted up by Sheridan Shook, as a variety theatre. In 1872 it was opened by its present manager, Mr. A. M. Palmer, as a first-class theatre, and devoted chiefly to the sensational school. Under Mr. Palmer's management it has been a magnificent success, ranking as the most profitable house in the Metropolis. Its receipts for the first five years of Mr. Palmer's management amounted to over a million dollars. The auditorium is very beautiful, and the plays produced here are brought out upon a scale of unusual magnificence.

"Daly's Theatre" is situated on Broadway, opposite Wallack's. It is very handsome, and is under the management of Mr. Augustin Daly, the well-known dramatist. It is devoted to the sensational school, and ranks among the most successful establishments in the city.

The Academy of Music is the Opera House of New York. It is a plain building of red brick, situated at the corner of Fourteenth street and Irving Place. It is the largest theatre in the city, and will seat 2400 people. It is magnificently decorated in crimson and gold, and its auditorium equals in beauty and splendor that of any European opera house. The scene during opera nights is very brilliant, the audience being in full dress, and comprising a thorough representation of the *élite* and fashion of the Metropolis.

There are several German theatres in New York, in which plays and opera are rendered in the language of the Fatherland. The principal of these are " The Germania," formerly "Wallack's," at the corner of Broadway and Thirteenth street, and " The Thalia," formerly " The Old Bowery," situated on that classic thoroughfare below Canal street.

Variety theatres are numerous. Of these the principal are Harrigan & Hart's, on Broadway, opposite the New York Hotel, and "Tony Pastor's," on Fourteenth street, between Third and Fourth avenues. These establishments draw large audiences, and are very profitable.

The third-class theatres are situated principally on the Bowery. The price of admission is low, and the performance suited to the tastes of the audience. The majority of these remain open during the summer months.

Perhaps the most remarkable dramatic establishment in the city is the Grand Duke's Theatre, or, as it is better known to its patrons, "The Grand Dook Theatre," in Water street. It was formerly located in Baxter street, and began its career in a very humble way; but with increasing prosperity removed to more suitable quarters in Water street. The prices of admission are as follows:—Boxes, 25 cents; orchestra, 15 cents; balcony, 10 cents; gallery 5 cents. The establishment is managed and controlled by boys, and its audiences consist chiefly of bootblacks, newsboys, and the juvenile denizens of the east side of the city, ranging in age from three to 20 years. The company is composed of youths yet in their teens, and the performances are of the blood-and-thunder order, interspersed with "variety acts" of a startling description. The house and its appointments are primitive, and the stage and scenery equally so. The orchestra is made up of amateur musicians, and is placed out of sight at the back of the stage. The footlights consist of six kerosene lamps with glass shades. Two redplush lounges, stuffed with saw-dust, and in a sad state of dilapidation, serve as boxes; while the orchestra stalls are represented by half a dozen two-legged benches, and the balcony and gallery are composed of a bewildering arrangement of step-ladders and dry-goods boxes. The manager acts as his own policeman, and enforces order by punching the heads of disorderly spectators, or by summarily ejecting them. The performances are crude, but they satisfy the audience, and never fail to draw forth a storm of applause, mingled with shrill whistles, cat-calls, and other vocal sounds. The boys are satisfied. What more could be desired?

Negro minstrelsy is very popular in New York. The Metropolis has a warm corner in its heart for the " burnt-cork opera." Several handsome minstrel halls provide nightly entertainments during the season, which are largely attended by respectable audiences.

Concerts and lectures are also well patronized. Chickering's, Steinway's, and Association Halls, and the great hall of the Cooper Union, are the principal centres of these attractions.

CHAPTER XLV

LIFE UNDER THE SHADOW

POVERTY IN NEW YORK—THE DESERVING POOR—SAD SCENES—"RAGPICKERS' ROW"—HOW THE RAGPICKERS LIVE—AN ITALIAN COLONY—SOUR BEER—DRUNKENNESS IN "RAGPICKERS' ROW"—BOTTLE ALLEY—A RELIC OF THE FIVE POINTS—A WRETCHED QUARTER—THE DWELLINGS OF POVERTY—THE CELLARS—LIFE BELOW GROUND—BAXTER STREET—THE CHINÉSE QUARTER—A HOSPITAL FOR CATS.

It is a terrible thing to be poor in any part of the world. In New York poverty is simply a living death. The city is full of suffering and misery. Some of it the wretched people who endure it have, no doubt, brought upon themselves by drink, by idleness, or by other faults, but a large majority are simply unfortunate. Their poverty has come upon them through no fault of their own ; they struggle bravely against it, and would better their condition if they could only find work. They are held down by an iron hand, however, and vainly endeavor to rise out of their misery. They dwell in wretched tenement houses, in the cellars of the buildings in the more thickly populated parts of the city, and in the shanties in the unsettled regions lying west of the Central Park. A few families, even in the midst of their sufferings, manage to keep their poor quarters clean and neat, but the majority live in squalor and filth. But little furniture is to be seen in the rooms of the poor. Everything that can bring money finds its way to the pawnshops for the means to buy food. Many of these wretched homes have been stripped of all their contents for this purpose.

HOMES OF THE POOR.

A cooking-stove sometimes constitutes the only article of furniture in a room, and the inmates sleep upon pallets on the floor. Not a chair or table is to be seen. Often there is no stove, and the only food that passes the lips of the occupants of these rooms is what is given to them in charity.

The inmates of these wretched homes are often families who have seen better days. Once the husband and father could give those dependent upon him a comfortable home, and provide at least the necessaries of life. But sickness came upon him, or death took him, and the little family was deprived of his support. In vain the mother sought to procure work to keep her children in comfort. What work she could procure was at intervals, and the little she earned barely sufficed to keep a roof over their heads. Little by little they sank lower, until poverty in its worst form settled upon them. The city is full of such cases, and the Missionaries whose labors among the poor bring them in constant contact with such scenes of suffering, confess that they do not know how these poor people manage to live. Whole blocks are filled with families on the verge of starvation, suffering every kind of privation. They would gladly work if they could get employment; but the city is so full of sufferers like themselves that they cannot escape from their wretched condition. "Bottle Alley," "Ragpickers' Row," sections of the Five Points, and other localities, present scenes of misery which almost surpass belief. Many of the dwellers here pick up a bare subsistence as street scavengers. They gather up whatever they can find, and sell it to the junk and rag stores for whatever it will bring. They carry the mass of refuse they collect during the day to their homes, sort it out there, spread out the rags, or hang them up to dry, pile up the other materials in the yards and courts of their dwellings until they can dispose of them, and thus add to the wretched appearance and filth of their quarters.

To those who visit these sections of the city, each one seems worse than the other. "Bottle Alley" appears as bad as can be, yet "Gotham Court" seems in some respects even worse, and "Ragpickers' Row" appears more wretched still. "Ragpickers' Row" is the most wretched haunt occupied by human beings in the New World. It is easily found. You leave the Bowery at Bayard street, go down two blocks to Mulberry street, and it is just around the corner. Anybody can tell you where the ragpickers live. There is no mistaking the place. "A junkman's cellar in the front house opens widely to the street, and, peering down, one may see a score of men and women half buried in dirty rags and paper, which they are gathering up and putting into bales for the paper mills. This is the general depot to which the rag-picker brings his odds and ends for sale after he has assorted them. Just as we emerge from this cellar a ragpicker, heavily laden, passes up the stoop and enters the hall above. Following him, we come to a small, badly-paved courtyard, which separates the front from the rear houses. Standing here and looking up, one beholds a sight that cannot be imagined. Rags to the right of him, rags to the left of him, on all sides nothing but rags. Lines in the yard draped

CHINESE QUARTER.

with them, balconies festooned with them, fire-escapes decorated with them, windows hung with them; in short, every available object dressed in rags—and such rags! of every possible size, shape, and color. Some of them have been drawn through the wash-tub to get off the worst dirt, but for the most part they are hung up just as they were taken from the bags, and left to the rain and sun to cleanse them. The exterior of the buildings is wretched enough; the interior equally so. Some of the rooms, on a cloudy day, are as dark as dungeons, with but little light coming in through the dirty window on the front and the smaller one on the back. Every inch of the ceiling and walls is as black as ink. Against this dark background are hung unused hats of odd colors and still odder shapes, musical instruments of various kinds, pots, kettles, and pans, pokers, joints of raw meat partly consumed, strings of Bologna sausages, the gowns of the women, and great pipes. The beds are almost invariably covered with old carpets, that still retain some bits of their original colors. None of the chairs have backs, and hardly any of them have four legs. Seated on these uncertain supports, or oftener on an empty soap-box or upturned boiler, are the ragpickers. Every man in the house has his hat on, including one in the bed napping after the hard work of the early morning. Not one bareheaded man is seen anywhere. Some of them are sitting dreamily by the stove, but most of them are sorting old rags or cutting up old coats and pantaloons that are too rotten to wear, and stuffing the bits into bags for the junk dealer. In one room is a woman plucking a well-seasoned goose with her dirty hands. In another place four men are seated on a big chest, with a bit of Bologna sausage in one hand and a chunk of bread in the other, making their noon-day meal. These same hands have just been turning over the filthy scraps from the garbage-boxes and the gutters. On the ground floor a man, who looks for all the world like a brigand, is stirring broth over the fire, and the horrible odor of rottenness that comes from the pot is enough to knock one down.

"None of the members of this Italian colony speak English, except here and there one who has mastered a few common phrases; but there is one word that all of them understand, and that is, 'Beer.' Here, as in 'Bottle Alley,' kegs are found in several of the rooms, where the contents are dealt out at a cent a glass. It is nearly all sour stuff, given to the men for helping on the brewers' wagons, or sold to them at the end of the day for a mere trifle. 'Is there much drunkenness there?' asked the writer of a police-officer. 'Oh, yes, sir,' he replied; 'we can go in there, or in any of these alleys, any night, and get a cart-load of drunken and disorderlies. We don't take them one by one, but gather them up in a hand-cart, and wheel them off to the station-house. They are not usually people who live there, but bummers who go there to drink.'" For these wretched quarters the people who live in them pay from five to six dollars a month rent out of their earnings, which rarely exceed fifty cents a day.

"Bottle Alley" is another terrible neighborhood. It is a portion of the old Five Points, and is the abode

SHANTIES, EIGHTH AVENUE.

of misery and wretchedness. How it came by its name no one knows, but it was probably so called because of the trade in old bottles carried on by a junkman who lives in its rear. The alleyway, about four and a half feet wide, is cut through the front house, and, running back about thirty-five feet, it opens into a little courtyard that faces the rear building. It is irregularly paved with cobble-stones, is covered with filth, and looks as though it might be a passage-way leading from a stable. Standing at the entrance, and looking in from the street, no one would ever dream that the tumble-down building in the rear was the abode of human beings.

The cellar is a queer hole. Passing down a flight of stone steps (every one of which is out of joint with its neighbor) and through a dilapidated doorway, you stand in an apartment ten by fourteen feet, with a ceiling so low that you can scarcely stand up with your hat on. One of these walls is of bare logs, the others of undressed stone. There are no chairs to sit on, only a few rough boxes. An Italian family of five persons occupies the room, paying five dollars a month rent, and taking lodgers—sometimes eight to twelve—at five cents a night. To add to their income they sell sour beer at two cents a pint or three cents a quart. The place is filthy beyond belief. The two upper floors are not quite so bad; but they contain sights that baffle description. The inmates are hud-dled together in disregard of cleanliness and decency. The rooms are dirty and the air is foul. The food is gathered principally from the garbage-boxes of the streets or from the offal of the markets. The cooking is done from time to time, and fills the rooms with horrible odors. There are no bedsteads. Filthy-looking mattresses are spread on the floor, or on boards placed upon supports. The inmates never undress, but go to bed with their clothes on, including their boots and shoes. The children are wan and pinched in appearance, and are frightfully dirty. What wonder that sickness and disease hold high revel here?

Bad as is the lot of these people, they at least exist upon the face of the earth. Those who dwell in the cellars of these wretched quarters are infinitely worse off. The cellars are all located below the level of the pavements. They have but one entrance, and a single window gives light and ventilation. There is no outlet to the rear, and the filth of the streets drains steadily into them. They are occupied by the poorest of the poor, and the amount of misery and wretchedness, of dirt and squalor to be witnessed in them surpasses description. In the winter time a stove heats the place, and renders the air so foul and stifling that one unaccustomed to it cannot breathe in the room. Many of these cellars are lodging-houses, into which the wretched outcasts who walk the streets during the day crowd for shelter at night. They pay from two to five cents for a night's lodging, and sometimes as many as from twenty-five to fifty persons are packed in these terrible holes.

Baxter street is another scene of misery, and, alas, of crime. It is the centre of the Italian and Chinese colonies. Its dwellings are equal in wretchedness to those described. It is a terrible neighborhood, and at night even the police venture into it with caution.

Drunken rows, fights, and stabbing affrays are of nightly occurrence.

John Chinaman finds his home in this and the neighboring streets. He is a stranger and a waif in the great city, but he has managed to establish a distinct quarter here. In other portions of the city are Chinese laundries, where the almond-eyed Celestials conduct the business of washing and ironing at rates which could not possibly afford a decent living to white men; but here are the headquarters of the Mongolians, their gaming houses and opium dens. Though peaceable as a rule, they are sometimes very troublesome, and the police find them hard customers to handle. They are inveterate gamblers, and one of their chief dissipations consists in stupefying themselves by smoking opium. The opium dens are simply dirty rooms provided with wooden bunks, in which the smokers may lie and sleep off the effects of the terrible drug. Many of these places are patronized by white people, and some number women of the lower class among their customers.

One of the greatest curiosities in New York is the " Hospital for Cats." It is located at No. 170 Division street, in the midst of the tenement-house section of the city, and is conducted by Mrs. Rosalia Goodman, a philanthropic German lady. She devotes the greater part of her time to the comfort and relief of neglected and persecuted felines, and is quite an enthusiast in her singular avocation. The house she occupies is a three-story wooden structure, dating back to the Dutch period of the city. She has lived there for a number of years, and makes a comfortable living

HOSPITAL FOR CATS.

by renting rooms, retaining two for herself and her cats. Besides many pets who for years have been kindly cared for, the family is being constantly increased by the addition of unfortunate tabbies whose wants are brought to the notice of the worthy lady. Lean and hungry cats, prowling around in search of food; cats who bear scars received by having bootjacks, bricks, and crockery-ware hurled at them by unappreciative hearers while they were performing a midnight concert; cats who come out with broken limbs and disordered fur from an interview with naughty little boys; cats who are hungry and in distress, or who have strayed away from their homes, are brought here, and are kindly received and cared for. So well is the idiosyncrasy of Mrs. Goodman known in the neighborhood, that whenever one of her neighbors finds a cat in distress, it is taken to her, and is always welcomed. Her room presents a most singular appearance. It is literally filled with cats of all sizes and descriptions, who crowd around the good lady, perch upon her shoulders, and nestle in her arms. She prepares their food with her own hands, and carefully ministers to all their wants.

CHAPTER XLVI

THE METROPOLITAN PRESS.

THE DAILY NEWSPAPERS—HOW THE LEADING JOURNALS ARE CONDUCTED—THE VARIOUS DE-
PARTMENTS—PRINTING-HOUSE SQUARE—EDITORS' SALARIES—THE " NEW YORK HERALD "
—THE HERALD OFFICE—JAMES GORDON BENNETT—CIRCULATION OF " THE HERALD "—
THE TRIBUNE " THE TALL TOWER "—WHITELAW REID—PROFITS OF " THE TRIBUNE "—
" THE TIMES," THE LEADING REPUBLICAN JOURNAL—" THE SUN," A LIVELY PAPER—
CHARLES A. DANA—PROFITS OF " THE SUN "—THE EVENING PAPERS—WEEKLIES—MAGA-
ZINES.

The daily newspapers of New York stand at the
head of the American press. There are 12 leading
daily morning papers; 7 leading daily evening papers;
10 semi-weekly; nearly 200 weekly papers; and about
25 magazines and reviews published in the city. These
have an annual circulation of over one thousand million copies. They are devoted to general news, politics, literature, science, and art—in short, to every
subject that can interest or attract the people of the
Metropolis and the country at large. They employ
millions of dollars and thousands of men in their publication, and their profits vary from handsome fortunes to smaller sums than their proprietors desire
to see.

The morning papers are those which give tone to
the Metropolitan press, and are the models after
which the journals of other American cities are pat-
terned. The principal are, the *Herald*, *Tribune*,
Times, *World*, and *Sun* in English, the *Staats Zeitung*
in German, and the *Courier des Etats Unis* in French.
Some of these papers are the private property of

their publishers, while others are owned by joint-stock companies.

The management of the daily newspapers is admirably systematized, and its various departments are conducted with the regularity and precision of clockwork. Each paper is in charge of an editor-in-chief, who controls its general policy, and assigns his various assistants their respective tasks. He is responsible to the proprietor and to the public for the course of the journal, and sees that the work in the various departments is promptly and faithfully performed. The night editor occupies one of the most responsible positions in the office. He takes charge of the paper about seven or eight o'clock in the evening, and controls it until it goes to press, about three or four o'clock in the morning. He receives and edits the telegraphic news, and the reports of the various reporters, decides what shall or shall not appear in the paper, a task which often requires the nicest tact and good judgment, and sees that the journal is properly put to press. Where important news is expected he often holds the paper back until daylight. The foreign editor has charge of the correspondence from Europe and other countries, and generally writes the editorials relating to matters abroad. The financial editor prepares the financial reports showing the daily state of the money market, and writes the articles which appear in the paper relating to such matters. His position is one of great responsibility and importance, as he must be thoroughly informed of the progress of events, not only in New York, but in the various monetary centres of this country and Europe. He plays no small part in shaping the financial policy of the country, and largely influences the opinions of his readers.   His duties bring him in constant contact with the leading bankers and brokers of the country, and afford him many opportunities of making money apart from his salary.   The city editor has charge of all the local news of the paper, and of the reporters and their work.   The leading dailies employ from twelve to thirty or forty reporters, and expend large sums in the collection of news.   The reporters present written accounts of their observations to the city editor, who revises them and puts them in proper shape for the paper.   He assigns each reporter his special duties every morning, noting them down in a book kept for that purpose.   Special reporters are assigned to duty in Brooklyn, Jersey City, Newark, and the surrounding towns, to the law and police courts, public meetings, conventions, parades, churches, lectures, and, in short, to every source from which news can be drawn.   Sometimes very little work is to be done; at others the whole force of the office is busy, and extra help has to be engaged.   There are also musical and dramatic critics, who write the reports of the prominent performances at the various places of amusements, and a literary editor, who reviews the publications sent to the paper for notice, and gets up the literary news.

Each daily is in charge of a publisher, who attends to the printing-office, the press-room, the counting-room, and the various matters connected with the practical work of getting out a newspaper.   He manages all its financial matters, and upon his energy depends the pecuniary success of the journal.

Almost all the leading morning and evening dailies are located in large buildings in and near Printing-House Square, as the triangular place on the east side of the City Hall Park at the north end of Park row is called. In the centre of the open space is a bronze statue of Benjamin Franklin, erected by the printers of New York; and around the so-called square are a number of restaurants and drinking saloons, which are kept open all night, and are patronized principally by newspaper men, printers, and kindred spirits.

The salaries paid by the city journals are not high. The leading editors, and the more prominent men on the various dailies, are paid from $3,000 to $12,000 a year; but, considering the amount and the character of the work done, the pay is not large. As the most of these are married men, and the cost of living in the Metropolis is high, newspaper men, even with large salaries, rarely have an opportunity to put by much for a rainy day. The large salaries are very few in number, however—scarcely half a dozen in the whole city—and the majority of newspaper men work hard on very small wages. As a rule they die poor, though the proprietors of the journals which they have helped to make successful usually win large fortunes.

At the head of the city dailies, as well as of the American press, stands the *New York Herald*. It is the wealthiest and most prosperous journal in the country, and is the private property of Mr. James Gordon Bennett, who was carefully trained by his father, the founder of the paper, as his successor. The story of *The Herald* is familiar to every reader, and we need not repeat it here. It is a noble monument to the energy, enterprise, and ability of its founder. *The Herald* office is a magnificent structure of white marble at the corner of Broadway and Ann street, one of the most conspicuous locations in the city. The cellars are occupied by the press-rooms, which are connected with the composing-rooms by elevators, by means of which the "forms" are carried between the two extremes of the building. Three costly Hoe presses, of the latest patent, are kept running from midnight until seven o'clock in· the morning, working off the daily edition. Every mechanical appliance that ingenious experts can suggest, and abundant means procure, is furnished by the liberal proprietor, so that the means to spread *The Herald* far and wide shall be the best in the world. The business offices occupy the street floor, which is raised about two feet above the sidewalk, and these are fitted up in elegant style, and are connected with the editorial and composing rooms by winding stairways of iron, speaking tubes, and slides, through which small boxes travel up and down. The editorial rooms are on the second and third floors, and are the most uncomfortable in the building. They are dark and badly ventilated. The best lighted front on Broadway, and are occupied by Mr. Bennett, the managing editor, the editor in charge, and *The Herald's* secretary. On the same side of the building is the "Council room," a long, narrow apartment, in which are a desk for the chief editorial writer, a type writer, and a long table, at which the council of editors assemble at a stated hour each day to discuss the subjects to be treated of in the next day's paper. The composing rooms are under the Mansard roof, and contain every appliance for the prompt dispatch of the work of the establishment, and a small army of compositors.

Mr. Bennett is in every sense the manager of *The Herald*. He is not a writer, but he is an excellent business man, a good listener, a quick decider, and a firm supporter of those who serve him well. To him is due the credit of nearly all the great successes of the paper. He conceived and put in execution the Stanley expedition, and almost all the great undertakings which have made *The Herald* the representative of American journalism. He orders the lengthy telegrams from abroad—the interviews with leading statesmen, journalists, and prominent actors in European affairs. He spends much of his time in Europe, but never loses his grip upon the management of *The Herald*, with which he is in constant communication by telegraph. When at home his eye is upon every department of the paper, and there is a general shaking up throughout the office.

During Mr. Bennett's absence he is represented by the managing editor, Mr. Thomas Connery, one of the most competent newspaper men in the Metropolis.

The circulation of *The Herald* is about 60,000 during the week, and 50,000 on Sunday. Its advertising business is immense, and its Sunday issue is a quintuple sheet, with from fifty-five to sixty columns of *bona fide* advertisements. It is worth a fortune to its owner every year, and can count upon the most magnificent future of any journal in America.

The Tribune is located in one of the loftiest buildings in the city, at the corner of Nassau and Spruce streets, and fronts upon Printing-House Square. The building is of brick, was erected at a cost of $600,000, and is surmounted by a lofty tower with an illuminated clock, which makes it one of the landmarks of the great city. The history of *The Tribune* has been an eventful one. Founded by Horace Greeley, it was, until his misfortunes came upon him, the most powerful Republican journal in the land. After Mr. Greeley's death, he was succeeded in the chief editorship by Whitelaw Reid, and great changes were made in the paper, the new building was erected, the stock of the association passed into new hands, and finally Mr. Reid became the nominal owner of a majority of the shares. It is well known, however, that the real owner is Jay Gould, and this knowledge has greatly weakened the popular confidence in the financial articles of the paper, which were once one of its chief sources of strength.

The Tribune is owned by an association, and represents property worth over $1,000,000. Between 1865 and 1878 it cleared a profit of $1,637,000, which was paid out in dividends, or invested in property. Its profits average about $100,000 a year and have done so for some years past. The offices of the journal are the most elegant in New York, the rooms being large, airy, and well lighted, and fitted up with every comfort and convenience. The managing editor, Mr. Whitelaw Reid, is also the publisher of the paper.

He is one of the most accomplished newspaper men in the country, a thorough business man, and a rigid disciplinarian. The daily circulation of the paper is about 35,000, the semi-weekly edition circulates 20,000, and the weekly about 75,000 copies. During Horace Greeley's life the circulation of the weekly was more than double the above number.

The Times occupies a handsome building at the intersection of Park Row and Nassau street, and stands opposite *The Tribune*. It is the leading Republican journal of New York, and was founded by the late Henry J. Raymond, under whom it pursued a brilliant career. After Mr. Raymond's death it encountered severe trials at the hands of incompetent men, but finally the majority of the stock passed into the hands of Mr. George Jones, and he assumed the business management of the paper. Under him it has been a great success. Its present circulation is about 35,000 copies on week days, and 40,000 on Sunday. Its annual profits are about $200,000.

The World is the leading Democratic daily, and has comfortable quarters in Park Row, just out of Printing-House Square. It is said to be controlled by Jay Gould, and its course in financial matters gives strong grounds for believing this assertion. Its circulation is estimated at from 15,000 to 30,000.

The Sun claims to be the organ of the working people, and is independent in tone. It is a four-page paper, closely printed, and a model of condensation of news and general information. It is ably edited, and is one of the brightest and most sparkling journals in the country. The editor-in-chief, and its principal

owner, is Charles A. Dana, one of the veteran journalists of the Metropolis.   The paper was founded by the
late Moses Y. Beach, about thirty years ago, but never
achieved any reputation, and finally became so offensive that it was regarded as a nuisance.   It was read
only by sewing and servant girls and small advertisers,
and was rapidly going down hill.   In 1868 an association, headed by Mr. Dana, bought the paper and
placed it under the charge of that gentleman.   Mr.
Dana at once elevated the tone of the journal, infused
new life into it, employed an able corps of assistants,
and soon made the new *Sun* one of the most popular
and best paying journals in the city.   It now occupies

THE EVENING MAIL BUILDING.

a handsome building in
Printing-House Square,
at the corner of Frank-
fort street, and has the
largest circulation of
any city daily, an aver-
age of 130,000 copies
being sold every day.
Its profits since 1869
have run from $99,000
to $164,000 (in 1876)
yearly.   The *Weekly
Sun* has also a tre-
mendous circulation.

The evening papers
have large circulations,
and are very profitable.

The principal are *The Post, The Express, The Mail,
The Telegram,* and *The Graphic.   The Post* is re-

garded as the "solidest" evening paper in the Metropolis. It is read largely by cultivated persons, and its book notices and reviews are considered the best of those of any city journal. *The Express* is the organ of John Kelly, who is its principal owner. *The Mail* is owned by Cyrus W. Feld, the originator of the Atlantic Telegraph, is a bright, pleasant paper, and is much liked. *The Telegram* is owned by James Gordon Bennett, and may be regarded as an evening edition of *The Herald*. It is published in the same building. It has the largest circulation of any of the evening journals, is ably edited, and is a thoroughly good newspaper. Its local reports are a specialty. *The Graphic* is the only illustrated daily in the world, and is the property of a stock company. It is doing well, and enjoys a large popularity, because of its illustrations of current events.

The weekly press embraces the prominent religious, literary, scientific, art, and mechanical journals of the country. These are fairly prosperous as a rule, and are scattered broadcast throughout the land.

The magazines are numerous, and are devoted to all subjects. *Harper's* and *The Century*, formerly *Scribner's*, stand at the head of the list of literary journals.

CHAPTER XLVII

THE FIRE DEPARTMENT

THE METROPOLITAN FIRE DEPARTMENT—FIREMAN'S HALL—THE BOARD OF FIRE COMMIS-
SIONERS—DIVISIONS OF THE DEPARTMENT—THE FORCE—UNIFORM — THE ENGINE-HOUSES
—INTERNAL ARRANGEMENTS—THE ENGINES—THE HORSES—HOW THEY ARE TRAINED—
THE SIGNAL TOWERS—THE ALARM BOXES—FIRE DISTRICTS—THE FORCE ON DUTY—SCENES
AT A FIRE—THE INSURANCE PATROL AND ITS DUTIES—THE "FIRE DEPARTMENT RELIEF
FUND"—LIFE OF A NEW YORK FIREMAN—HEROIC DEEDS.

The Metropolitan Fire Department has its headquarters at No. 155 Mercer street, in the old building
known as "Fireman's Hall." It is under the control
of three Commissioners, appointed by the Mayor and
the Board of Aldermen, for a period of six years. The
President of the Board of Commissioners receives an
annual salary of $7500, and the others $5000 each.
The Commissioners appoint the officers and members
of the force, make and enforce the rules for their
government, and are responsible for the good behavior
and efficiency of the department.

The Fire Department is divided into three bureaux,
as follows:—1st. The Bureau for Preventing and Extinguishing Fires, under the charge of the Chief of the
Fire Department, who receives an annual salary of
$4700; 2d. The Bureau for the Enforcement of
the Laws Relating to the Storage and Sale of Com-
bustibles, the head of which is the Inspector of Com-
bustibles, whose salary is $2500 per annum; 3d. The
Bureau for the Investigation of the Origin and Cause

of Fires, at the head of which is the Fire Marshal, with a salary of $2500 a year.

The force consists of a chief engineer, an assistant engineer, 10 district engineers, and 850 officers and men, of whom over 700 are constantly on active duty. There are employed in the service of the department 42 steam fire-engines, 4 chemical engines, and 18 hook and ladder trucks. These are quartered in handsome and conveniently arranged engine-houses distributed throughout the city. Each company consists of a foreman, assistant foreman, an engineer of the steamer, a stoker, a driver, and 7 firemen. The men are carefully picked for the service, and are subjected to rigid examinations, for the purpose of ascertaining their physical and moral conditions. They are required to be free from vicious habits, which would impair their usefulness to the force, and must come well recommended by citizens of known respectability. As a rule, they are fine-looking, hardy fellows, and take pride in maintaining the high reputation and efficiency of the department. They are uniformed in dark-blue cloth, with flannel shirts of the same color. The buttons and metal trimmings of the dress are silver. When off duty they wear a cloth cap of peculiar shape, but on duty the head-gear consists of the usual stout leather fireman's hat.

The officers of the force receive liberal salaries, and the men are paid $1200 a year, and furnished with quarters. All are required to give their entire time to the service, and no member is permitted to engage in any outside employment. A certain number are always kept on duty at each engine-house. Leaves

of absence are granted at stated periods, but an alarm
of fire at once terminates the leave, and summons the
fireman back to duty. In such a case he must proceed at once to the fire, if it is one to which his company is summoned, or to the engine-house if the fire
is out of his district. A watch is kept at the engine-
house, day and night, and detachments of the force
are required to patrol their districts regularly to look
out for fires. The most rigid discipline is maintained,
and the force is ever on the alert and ready to move
to the scene of danger at a moment's warning.

Each fire company is provided with a handsome
and conveniently-arranged engine-house, so located
as to be central to the district to which the company
is assigned. These buildings are generally of brick,
but some are of brownstone. The engine-house is provided with an engine-room and a stable on the first
floor; a basement, in which is placed the furnace by
means of which the building is heated, and the water
in the engine kept hot during cold weather. The upper
floors contain the quarters of the officers and men,
rooms for reading and study, a drill-room, library, etc.
Every portion of the building is kept scrupulously
clean and neat; the floors and wood-work are fresh
and free from dirt, and the glass- and metal-work are
brightly polished. In the lower room is the telegraph
instrument and the alarm-bell, over which a watch is
kept at all times. All the members of the force must be
present at ten o'clock at night, when, with the excep-
tance of the watch, they are allowed to go to bed.
They must make their preparations to be roused at

any moment, and are allowed but a few seconds to dress when called up by an alarm.

The steam-engines used by the department are made by the Amoskeag Manufacturing Company, of Manchester, New Hampshire, and cost the city about $4000 a piece. They are of the second-class in size, are beautiful specimens of machinery, and are very powerful. One of the largest of these is propelled by steam, and was purchased by the city in 1873. It weighs about four tons, and is capable of propelling itself at the speed of a rapid trot. When standing in the house, the boilers of the engines are kept supplied with water and steam from a heater in the basement, at a pressure of about seventy pounds per square inch. The fireplace is kept charged with kindling-wood and other combustibles, and it requires but one minute after the fire is lighted, which is done the instant the alarm is sounded, to raise steam enough for action, and to propel the large engine at a quick pace.

The Chemical engines consist each of a pair of large cylinders, constructed on the plan of the Babcock Fire Extinguisher, mounted upon a handsome carriage, drawn by horses. These cylinders contain about 75 gallons of water each, and are capable of sustaining an internal pressure of 400 pounds per square inch. Each carriage is provided with a reel and several sections of hose, mounted in front of the cylinders and behind the driver's seat. When an alarm is sounded, a chemical engine is despatched to the scene in advance of the steamer, and often succeeds in extinguishing the flames before the arrival of the larger engine. In many instances, these self-acting engines have been used to great advantage in connection with the steamers. The department also employs a large and powerful floating-engine, placed on board of a steamboat. This is used for extinguishing fires on vessels or on the wharves. When not on duty the steamboat lies near the Battery, in order to be able to move promptly to any point in either river. Several engines are kept in reserve by the department to replace any that may break down in service. These can be called out only by the chief engineer of the force. The Hook and Ladder Companies are provided with long trucks, steered by a wheel and gear at one end, for the conveyance of their ladders and

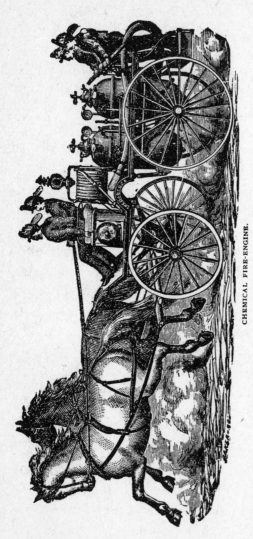

CHEMICAL FIRE-ENGINE.

other apparatus. They are quartered in houses similar to those of the steamer companies, and are subject to the same discipline.

There are about 200 horses attached to the department. These are large, powerful, and spirited animals, and are kept with the most scrupulous care. They are stabled in the engine-houses, and are groomed every day, and fed punctually at six o'clock, morning and evening. If not called out during the day, they are exercised in the streets near the engine-house. They are thoroughly trained to the work before them, and exhibit a high degree of intelligence. They are kept harnessed all the time, and an automatic attachment, connected with the fire-alarm gong, releases them from the stalls the moment the signal is struck. The instant they are free they back out from their stalls, trot to their places at the engine, truck, or wagon, and stand ready to be hitched. This requires but three seconds, and the noble animals exhibit the greatest impatience to be off the moment the harnessing is completed.

As soon as an alarm is given all is excitement in the engine-houses. The men are roused from their sleep at night by the sharp strokes of the heavy gong, hastily don their clothes, and come rushing down the stairs to their places at the engine. The horses back out to their stations, are attached to the engine, the fires are lighted, the doors of the building are thrown open, and in fifteen seconds during the day, or in one minute at night, from the time the alarm is sounded, the steamer and the hose-carriage are in the street, and on a sharp gallop towards the fire.

Seven lofty bell-towers are distributed throughout the city, and on the summit of each of these is placed a telegraph alarm connected with the central office, and in charge of a lookout. A sharp watch is kept over the city below by the lookouts. Being thoroughly familiar with the various sections of the city, they can locate a fire with perfect accuracy, and, as soon as one is discovered, they telegraph the location to the central office, from which the alarm is repeated to the engine-houses, each of which is connected with the central office and the police headquarters by a special telegraph line.

For the purpose of communicating the alarms of fire promptly, 600 fire-alarm boxes are scattered throughout the city. Each box is attached to a telegraph pole, or to the side of some building. The boxes are made of iron, are about 25 inches high, by 12 inches wide and 4 inches deep, and are provided with an outer and an inner door of iron, securely locked. As the locks are of the same size and construction on all the boxes, one key will open any box throughout the city. Each member of the police force, the fire department, and the insurance patrol is provided with a key, and a key is also deposited at a place adjacent to the alarm-box, and designated upon the box itself. All persons having keys are warned not to give an alarm unless absolutely certain there is a fire, and are forbidden to open the boxes except for the purpose of giving an alarm. They must securely lock the box after the signal is given, and must not give up their keys to any person save the proper authorities. Each box contains a telegraphic battery and an alarm-bell. These are placed behind the inner door, which is never opened except when it becomes necessary to repeat the alarm. Between the outer and inner doors is an iron catch or handle, connected with the battery. In giving an alarm, the outer door of the box is opened, and the catch is pulled down firmly once. This works a spring, by means of which a wheel attached to the battery is set in motion, and sounds the number of the box upon the gong at the central office, from which it is telegraphed to the engine-houses. Should it be necessary to repeat the alarm, the inner door is opened, and the Morse key of the battery is struck ten times. A lock attachment to the box prevents the key from being withdrawn after the alarm is given except by the officer of the department.

The city is laid off in districts for fire purposes. Certain companies are assigned to each district, and are not permitted to move beyond their proper districts without orders from the chief engineer or the central office. When an alarm is sounded, about one-sixth of the force is sent to the fire; a second alarm calls out another sixth, and so on until the force required is obtained. When on the way to a fire, only the driver, the engineer, assistant engineer, and stoker are permitted to ride on the engine. The rest of the men go on foot. The foreman runs ahead of his engine to clear the way for it, and the driver must follow, but not pass him. The engines have the right of way in the streets, and a free passage is made for them, even in the most crowded streets, with a rapidity that is sometimes astonishing. Fast driving, racing, and improper conduct on the part of the men, in going to or coming from a fire, are sharply punished.

Upon reaching the scene of the fire, the company at once proceed to connect their engine with a fire-plug, and get a stream of water on the flames as soon as possible. As soon as the chief engineer—who is required to be present at all fires—arrives, he takes command of the force present, and issues all orders. Thus discipline is maintained and all confusion avoided. The men are trained to their work, and go at it with coolness and deliberation, and without any unnecessary shouting or noise. Orders are given briefly, and are promptly obeyed. The reserve force of the nearest police-station is always sent to a fire, and this force at once takes possession of the streets, keeps back the crowd, prevents disturbance, and allows the firemen room to perform their duties. This arrangement also ensures the safety of the property removed from the burning buildings to the streets.

The life of a New York fireman is a hard one, and is full of danger. It not only requires the constant exercise of the greatest courage, coolness, and daring, but also imposes upon the fireman the greatest hardships. He is liable to be called up at any hour of the night, and after returning from a severe fire, worn out with fatigue, may be instantly summoned to another in a different section of the city. It sometimes happens that for days the men are without either sleep or rest, and have scarcely time to partake of food. However great their fatigue and exhaustion may be, they must respond promptly to every call upon them. In the torrid heats of summer they drop at their posts from sunstroke, and in the bitter winter weather suffer fearfully from the cold. Their hands and feet are sometimes frozen as they perform their duties, drenched through to the skin with the mercury below zero. They bear themselves gallantly, however, and shrink from no exposure, no hardship, or danger in the discharge of their duty. Scarcely a fire occurs but is made memorable by some heroic action by a member of the force. Now it is a child, a woman, or an aged person who is rescued from some burning building at the imminent peril of the rescuer's life; again,

NEW YORK FIREMAN RESCUING A CHILD FROM THE FLAMES.

a gallant fellow will dash into a smoke-enshrouded edifice in the hope of saving the lives imperilled within, only to lay down his own life as the price of his heroism.

CHAPTER XLVIII

HARRY HILL'S

THE BEST KNOWN DANCE-HOUSE IN NEW YORK—THE HALL—THE AUDIENCE—THE FEMALE VISITORS—THE PERFORMANCES—DANCING—HARRY HILL—THE MIDNIGHT HOUR—HARRY HILL ON DUTY.

At the corner of Houston and Mulberry streets is a singular-looking structure with a flashy entrance, in front of which hangs a huge colored lantern, on which is the name of the proprietor of the place. This is one of the most noted establishments in New York, the well known " Harry Hill's," a favorite resort of the " fancy," and the best kept dance-house in the city. The main entrance is for men, who are charged an admission fee of twenty-five cents, but close by is a private door for women, who are admitted free. Passing in by the public entrance, you find yourself in a bar-room, at the further end of which is a stairway leading to the principal hall.

The hall has grown with Harry Hill's prosperity, and consists really of a series of rooms which have been added from time to time, and are of different heights. At one end is the bar, from which liquors and refreshments are served, and at the other, is a stage, upon which low variety performances and sparring matches are given. The room is ablaze with light and heavy with tobacco smoke. Tables and chairs are scattered through it; there is a gallery at one side, and a wine-room opening from it. From eight o'clock until long

HARRY HILL'S.

after midnight the place is filled with a motley crowd. The women present are street-walkers ; the men represent all classes of society. Some are strangers who have merely come to see the place; others are out for a lark; and others still have come in company with, or to meet, some abandoned woman. The women are generally in the flush of their prosperity, and are well dressed: the proprietor will not admit those who have sunk so low as to cease to be attractive. Some are handsome, but all bear the inevitable marks of their degraded calling. They drink heavily, for that is expected of them, their male friends paying the score. Among the men you will see prominent judges, city officials, detectives in plain clothes, men of prominence in other parts of the country, army and navy officers, merchants, roughs, and thieves. They join the women, drink with them, and too often accompany them to worse places.

The performance on the stage is interspersed with dances in an open space in the hall, and a Punch and Judy show forms a popular feature of the evening's entertainment. Visitors are forbidden to smoke while dancing, and good order is enforced by the proprietor.

Harry Hill keeps a watchful eye over the proceedings. He claims that his is a respectable establishment. He knows the character of his female guests, and the purposes for which the men come. Whatever may happen after a man leaves the place in company with a woman, he is careful that no crime shall be committed in his house. If he sees a man whom he likes, or who he thinks may be of service to him, drinking heavily, he takes care of him, prevents him from falling into the hands of a street-walker, and sends him to his home or his hotel. He is a powerful, determined man, and acts as his own policeman, repressing disorder, and ejecting all who pass the bounds of outward propriety. He has been in the business for over twenty years, and is said to be very wealthy. Those who profess to know, estimate the profits of his "respectable establishment" at over $50,000 a year.

The place is most crowded, and business is briskest, from eleven o'clock until an hour or two after midnight. Men who do not dance, are expected to spend considerable money in liquors and refreshments for themselves and the women present. The performances on the stage are broad and coarse, and the songs suggestive, if not openly indecent. The liquors are wretched, and the drinkers soon fall under their influence. Then Harry Hill is most watchful. He is all over the hall, checking a quarrel between women, reminding men that swearing and noisy behavior are not permitted, and enforcing order with a heavy hand. After one o'clock the women begin to drop off, accompanied by their male companions, who follow them to the panel-houses they frequent, and where the foolish victim is sure to be robbed of his money and valuables by the woman's confederate, and perhaps is beaten or murdered. Harry Hill well knows the danger these men will encounter, but he utters no warning word. It is not his business to save men from the consequences of their folly, and so long as his "respectable establishment" is not the scene of disorder, violence, or crime, he is indifferent.

CHAPTER XLIX

JOHN KELLY

"BOSS KELLY"—BIRTH AND EARLY LIFE—EDUCATION—BEGINS LIFE AS A STONE-CUTTER—
ENTERS POLITICAL LIFE—BECOMES AN ALDERMAN—ELECTED TO CONGRESS—HIS CAREER
IN THE HOUSE OF REPRESENTATIVES—IS ELECTED SHERIFF—LOSS OF HIS FAMILY—
ASSISTS IN OVERTHROWING THE TWEED RING—LEADER OF TAMMANY HALL—APPOINTED
COMPTROLLER—REMOVAL FROM OFFICE—PERSONAL CHARACTERISTICS.

One of the most noted men in New York is John Kelly—or, as he is commonly called, "Boss Kelly"— the leader of the Tammany Hall Democracy of the Metropolis. He is credited by his friends with being one of the most skilful political leaders in the country, and denounced by his enemies as the very embodiment of political trickery and corruption. His friends are warmly devoted to him, and his enemies hate him with an intense bitterness. His sway over his particular branch of the Democracy is absolute, and he can control its vote, and make or unmake political fortunes with a power unsurpassed by that of any old-world despot. Mr. Kelly is of Irish parentage, and is a native of the Fourth Ward, the classic region which produced his famous predecessor, "Boss Tweed." He received his preliminary education in the parochial school of St. Patrick's Cathedral, which he left at the age of twelve years. He subsequently attended the night schools established by the Board of Education, and displayed an ardent desire to obtain a liberal education. Upon leaving the Cathedral school, he was apprenticed to learn the trade of a grate-setter and soapstone-cutter, in which he became a proficient workman. He was a steady, resolute young man, without vicious habits, and exhibited a strong devotion to his widowed mother. In after years he edu-

JOHN KELLY.

cated his younger brother and established him in business, and extended similar assistance to his sisters, all of whom have become women of remarkable character.

At an early day Mr. Kelly turned his attention to municipal politics, and, attaching himself to the Democratic party, soon became one of its leaders. In 1853 he was elected a member of the Board of Aldermen, and in 1854 was elected to Congress, defeating the Hon. Mike Walsh, one of the most notorious politicians of his day. In 1854 he was reëlected by an overwhelming majority, and received his famous title of "Honest John Kelly," an honor which his friends claim he richly deserves. He took an active part in Congress, winning a good reputation as a debater and a hard-working member, and was regarded by his associates as a cool, clear-headed adviser in public affairs. Near the close of his second Congressional term, he resigned his seat in the House of Representatives, and was elected Sheriff of New York by a large majority of the voters of the city. In 1865 he was reëlected to the same position. He served both terms with credit to himself and fidelity to the city, making many friends among the Bench and Bar, and adding greatly to his popularity. During this period he was very prosperous in his business affairs, and won a handsome fortune; but his life was saddened by the death of his wife in 1866, his only son in 1868, and his two daughters in 1870 and 1872. Thus left alone, his health gave way under the pressure of sorrow and care, and in 1869 he made a visit to Europe, remaining abroad nearly three years. Returning in 1871, improved in health and spirits, he entered heartily into the reform campaign which resulted in the complete overthrow of the Tweed Ring. His services were rewarded by his selection by the Democracy as the person most competent to reorganize the party in the city on an honest and healthful basis. He accomplished his task to the satisfaction of his political associates, and has ever since maintained his position as the leader of the Tammany Hall Democracy. He was subsequently appointed to the lucrative office of Comptroller of the city, from which he was recently removed for political reasons by the Mayor.

Mr. Kelly resides in an elegant mansion at the corner of Thirty-eighth street and Lexington avenue. He is in the prime of life, being in his fifty-ninth year. He is below the average height, with a stout, hardy frame, and a pleasant, intellectual, but unmistakably Irish face. He wears a full, but close-cut beard and mustache, of a reddish hue, with hair of the same color. Both beard and hair are now largely sprinkled with gray. He is earnest and impressive in manner, firm and decisive in character. Being a close student of books and men, he has accumulated a large fund of knowledge and experience. He is familiar with the French and German languages, has an extensive acquaintance with the standard literature of the age, and is a devoted student of political economy and practical politics. He is rarely deceived in men, and is thoroughly independent in character. His enemies acquit him of having gained any portion of his large wealth by corrupt means. He has figured prominently of late years in municipal, State, and national politics, and is generally believed to have caused the election of the late President Garfield by bringing about the defeat of General Hancock in New York, in the last presidential campaign.

CHAPTER L

RELIGION IN NEW YORK

NUMBER OF CHURCHES IN NEW YORK—VALUE OF CHURCH PROPERTY—THE DUTCH REFORMED CHURCH—THE EPISCOPALIANS—GRACE CHURCH—ST. THOMAS'S—"THE LITTLE CHURCH AROUND THE CORNER"—THE LUTHERANS—THE PRESBYTERIANS—THE FIFTH AVENUE CHURCH—THE BAPTISTS—THE METHODISTS—ST. PAUL'S CHURCH—THE CONGREGATIONAL-ISTS—THE QUAKERS—THE UNITARIANS—THE ROMAN CATHOLIC CHURCH—ST. STEPHEN'S—ST. PATRICK'S CATHEDRAL—THE JEWS—THE TEMPLE EMANU-EL—LOWER NEW YORK DES-TITUTE OF CHURCHES—FASHIONABLE RELIGION—STRANGERS IN CHURCH—THE MUSIC—PROFESSIONAL SINGERS—A TENOR'S SENSATION—THE FIFTH AVENUE PROMENADE—PEW RENTS—CHURCH DEBTS—RECKLESS EXTRAVAGANCE.

There are more than five hundred churches, chapels, and places used for religious worship in New York, with seating accommodations for about 600,000 people. These are divided among the Orthodox Protestant de-nominations, the Roman Catholics, Quakers, the Greek Church, and the Jews. Of these, the Protestant churches number nearly 450, the Catholics over 40, the Quakers 5, the Greek Church 1, and the Jews 27. The total value of church property in the city is about as follows: Protestant, $30,000,000, exclusive of en-dowments; Catholic, $8,000,000; Jews, $2,000,000; the Greek Church, $10,000. Apart from their church property, the various denominations own numerous schools, hospitals, and charitable and benevolent insti-tutions, which swell the value of their real estate to an enormous figure. It is of the churches, however, that we propose to treat here.

The oldest denomination in the city is the Dutch Reformed. It was planted here by the first settlers of New Amsterdam, and the church records extend back, unbroken, to 1639. The denomination is now very strong, and possesses twenty-five churches and chapels. Several of these are located on Fifth avenue, and are among the handsomest in the city. The "Holland Church," at the corner of Fifth avenue and 29th street, is a fine edifice of Vermont marble, in the Romanesque style, and is surmounted by a tall spire, crowned with a gilt weather vane. The "Collegiate Church," at the corner of Fifth avenue and 48th street, is an imposing structure of brownstone, in the modernized Gothic style, and one of the most beautiful churches in the city.

Next in order of age is the Protestant Episcopal Church, the successor of the Church of England, introduced into the city by the English when they obtained possession of the colony. It now possesses ninety-four churches and chapels, a general Theological Seminary, and a number of charitable and benevolent institutions, schools, etc. The principal church edifice is Trinity, which is described in another chapter. Grace Church, on Broadway, at the corner of 10th street, is, next to Trinity, the wealthiest Episcopal Church in New York. It is a handsome Gothic structure, built of white granite, and occupies one of the best positions in the city. The interior is richly decorated, and the stained glass windows are very beautiful. There are two organs in the church, connected by electricity, an arrangement which enables the organist to use either or both from a single key board. The music is very fine, the choir being made up of celebrated professional vocalists. The Rector, Dr. Potter, is one of the most eloquent and effective pulpit orators in the Metropolis,

and large congregations assemble to hear him. At
the morning service a greater display of wealth and

REV. HENRY C. POTTER, D.D.

fashion is presented
here than at any other
city church. Grace
Church has been the
scene of more fashion-
able weddings and
funerals than any
other place of wor-
ship. Until about a
year ago these cere-
monies were presided
over by the famous
Sexton Brown, per-
haps the most noted
man connected with
the parish. He was a

shrewd, long-headed fellow, this same Brown, and knew
more of New York society than any man of his day.
The congregation have sadly missed him. Peace to
his ashes.

St. Thomas's Church, at the corner of Fifth avenue
and 53d street, ranks next to Grace, as a fashionable
place of worship. It is very massive, and is built of
brownstone, in a mixed style of architecture, in which
the early English predominates. Its tower contains a
fine chime of bells. The interior is extremely beautiful, though somewhat dark, and is decorated with
superb frescoes by John La Farge and sculptures by
A. St. Gauden. There are two organs, connected by
electricity, and the music, which is among the best in

the city, is under the direction of the famous organist, George William Warren. St. Thomas's is rapidly surpassing Grace Church in the number of its fashionable weddings and funerals, and is noted for the wealth and magnificent display of its congregation.

St. Bartholomew's and the Holy Trinity, which almost face each other on Madison avenue, the former being at the corner of 44th street, and the latter at the corner of 42d street, are beautiful edifices, and are sumptuously fitted up and decorated internally. The Church of the Heavenly Rest, on Fifth avenue, near the Windsor Hotel, is handsomely decorated with frescoes. Over the street entrance stand four immense angels sounding trumpets.

One of the most noted Episcopal places of worship is the Church of the Transfiguration, on 29th street, east of Fifth avenue. It is popularly known as "The Little Church Around the Corner." It is a pretty, rambling sort of structure, built of brownstone, beautifully ornamented and decorated within, and of a size that by no means merits the popular title given it. A pretty churchyard, shaded by fine trees and laid off with green sward lies between the church and the street, and luxuriant vines clamber over the edifice, giving to the place a charming rural aspect. The congregation is a very fashionable one, and the services are conducted upon an elaborate scale. The popular name of the church originated in this way: Some years ago, Mr. George Holland, an old and popular actor, died in New York, and his friends made application to the Rector of the Church of the Atonement, in Madison avenue, to conduct the funeral services in that church.

They were met with a point-blank refusal, but at the same time the Rector intimated that there was "a little church around the corner, where they sometimes held funeral services for actors." Joseph Jefferson, who was one of the parties making this request, exclaimed, impulsively, "Then God bless the little church around the corner, say I." Application was made to the Rector of "the little church," and the funeral services were held there. Since then, several actors have been buried from it. The church-going members of the dramatic profession attend it, and contribute liberally to its support.

St. Augustine's Chapel, in Houston street, east of the Bowery, is a part of Trinity Parish. It is built of brownstone, in the Gothic style, and its steeple is surmounted by a crystal cross, which on Sunday and special nights is illumined by gas jets placed within it, and can be seen shining out high over the dark city, a blessed symbol of hope and cheer.

The other prominent Episcopal churches are St. George's, Ascension, Calvary, St. Paul's, St. John's, Trinity Chapel, and St. Peter's.

The Lutheran Church ranks third in the order of age. The city contained many members of this faith at the time of its capture by the English, and by 1702 they had grown strong enough to build their first church. They are now numerous, and constitute a very wealthy body, possessing twenty-one churches.

The Presbyterians organized their first society in 1716, and for three years were allowed by the authorities to worship in the Town Hall. Previous to this they were subjected to a petty persecution by the

Established Church, one of their ministers being fined, in 1707, for exercising the functions of his office, and were obliged to meet in private houses. In 1719 the first Presbyterian church was built, in Wall street near Broadway. At present they constitute one of the strongest and wealthiest denominations in the city, and besides a number of noble benevolent and charitable institutions, own ninety-four churches, divided among the various branches of the denomination, as follows: Presbyterian proper, seventy; United Presbyterian, eight; Reformed Presbyterian, seven; Congregationalist, nine.

REV. JOHN HALL, D.D.

The Fifth avenue Presbyterian Church, at the corner of Fifth avenue and 55th street, is the largest and finest Presbyterian Church in the city. It is built of brownstone, in the French Gothic style, and its tower is the highest in New York. The interior is very beautiful, and is elaborately and magnificently decorated. The floor slopes from the entrance to the pulpit, giving to every seat a commanding view of the preacher. The church cost over a million of dollars, and is paid for. The congregation is large and enormously wealthy, numbering more bank presidents and insurance men than any similar body in the Union. The pastor is the Rev. Dr. John Hall, one of the most gifted pulpit orators of the day. He is a man of gigantic frame, great scholarship, and wonderful capacity for work. He hates sensationalism, and gives the people plain and practical sermons. The church is always crowded when he preaches.

REV. THOMAS ARMITAGE, D.D.

Like the Presbyterians the Baptists had to contend with persecution in their efforts to establish themselves in New York. They were treated with great harshness by the civil authorities and the Established Church, and were often obliged to immerse their converts by night, to avoid arrest. It was not until 1725 that they erected their first church, in what is now Gold street. Since then they have grown and prospered, and are now very numerous and wealthy, having fifty churches in the city. The First Church, in East 39th street, is a wealthy organization, with a handsome edifice. The Fifth avenue Baptist Church, in West 46th street, is the leading church of this denomination, and possesses the best arranged church edifice and the wealthiest congregation. The pastor is the Rev. Dr. Thomas Armitage, one of the most learned and eloquent divines of the Baptist faith.

The Methodists rank among the oldest denominations in the city, having been organized in 1766, by Philip Embury, a local preacher from Ireland, who held religious services in his own house, in what is now Park Place. Only half a dozen persons attended his first ministrations, but the society grew rapidly, and in 1768 the Methodists erected their first church, in John street, which venerable edifice is still standing. Since then their growth has been rapid, and they now have sixty churches and chapels, with a membership of about 20,000, and church property valued at several millions. The principal church is St. Paul's, at the corner of Fourth avenue and 22d street. It is a fine structure of white marble, in the Romanesque style, with a Rectory adjoining it, of the same material. Both buildings were the gift of the late Daniel Drew to the church.

REV. W. M. TAYLOR, D.D.

The Congregationalists have been included among the Presbyterians, in speaking of that body. They

have nine churches, the principal of which is the Tabernacle, at the corner of Sixth avenue and 34th street.
It is a handsome brownstone building, and is under the
pastoral care of the Rev. Dr. W. M. Taylor, an eloquent divine.

The Friends or Quakers, came into the city at a
very early day. They built their first meeting house
in 1703, and at present own five places of worship,
besides other valuable property.

The Unitarians built their first church in 1819. They
now have five churches. The principal are "All Souls,"
on Fourth avenue, just above Union Square, and the
Church of the Messiah, at the corner of Park avenue
and 34th street. The latter is under the charge of the

REV. ROBERT COLLYER.

Rev. Robert Coll-
yer, formerly of
Chicago, one of the
most brilliant pul-
pit orators of this
or any other coun-
try.

The Roman
Catholic Church is
the strongest in the
city, in point of
numbers, its
strength lying in
the vast Irish and
other foreign popu-
lations of New
York. The first church of this denomination stood on
the site of the present St. Peter's, at the corner of Bar-

clay and Church street, and was built in 1786. In 1815 St. Patrick's Cathedral, at the corner of Mott and Prince streets, was built, and was the Cathedral of the diocese until the completion of the new Cathedral, on Fifth avenue. At present the wealth of the Church in New York is very great. There are fifty-five Catholic Churches and chapels in the city, besides a number of benevolent and charitable institutions, schools, etc. The Church authorities have been unusually fortunate in their purchases of real estate, which have largely increased in value, and besides this have received constant and liberal assistance in the shape of grants of money from the city.

Though the great body of Roman Catholics in New York consists of their poorer and more wretched classes, the church includes among its membership a large class of wealthy and cultivated citizens and their families. Almost the only churches in the poorer and more crowded sections of the city are Catholic, and this immense field is being cultivated by them with an energy and zeal well worthy of imitation. A number of the churches are located in the most desirable portions of the city, and are attended by wealthy and fashionable congregations. They are very handsome, and the music is exquisite. The most fashionable church, as well as one of the most beautiful, is St. Stephen's, on 28th street, between Third and Lexington avenues, and extending through the block to 29th street. The interior is beautifully decorated with frescoes, and the altar, of pure white marble, is one of the most magnificent in the Union. The altar-piece, representing the Crucifixion, is a noble work of art, and the music the best in the city. The church will seat 4000 people, and is always crowded. Father McGlynn, the rector, is one of the most gifted pulpit orators in the city.

The new St. Patrick's Cathedral is the grandest church edifice in America. It occupies the entire square bounded by Fifth and Madison avenues, and 50th and 51st streets, and stands on the highest and most commanding site on the avenue. It was begun by Archbishop Hughes, in 1858, and was dedicated by the Cardinal Archbishop McCloskey, on the 25th of May, 1879.

The foundations of the Cathedral rest upon a bed of solid rock, in which excavations therefor had to be made. The first course is of Maine granite, dressed with the chisel, and from this springs a pure Gothic superstructure, similar in architecture to the style adopted in Europe during the thirteenth and fourteenth centuries. The building is three hundred and thirty-two feet in length, one hundred and thirty-two feet broad in the nave and choir, and one hundred and seventy-four feet broad at the transepts. It is constructed of white marble, from the Pleasantville quarries, in Westchester County. Like the Cathedrals at Amiens, Rouen, and Cologne, St. Patrick's is free from heaviness and over-ornamentation. The Fifth avenue front consists of a central gable, one hundred and fifty-six feet in height, with towers and spires. The design of the grand portal contemplates the statues of the twelve apostles to be placed within it. The interior of the Cathedral is as fine as its exterior. The massive columns which support the roof are of white stone, thirty-five feet in height, and clustered, having a combined diameter of five feet. The ceiling is groined, with richly moulded ribs and foliated bosses. The springing line of the ceiling is seventy-seven feet from the floor. The organ gallery is in the nave, between the towers. The high altar is forty feet high, and the table was constructed in Italy, of the purest marble, and inlaid with semi-precious stones. The bas-reliefs on the panels have for their subjects the Divine Passion. The tabernacle over the altar is of white marble, decorated with Roman mosaics and precious stones, and with a door of gilt bronze. The altar of the Blessed Virgin is at the eastern end of the north side aisle of the Sanctuary, and is of carved French walnut. The Sacristry is placed in the east of the south aisle of the Sanctuary, and St. Joseph's altar, of bronze and mosaic, is in front of it. The altar of the Sacred Heart is of bronze. The Cardinal's throne is on the gospel (right) side of the altar, and is of Gothic design. The altar of the Holy Family is of white Tennessee marble, and the reredos of Caen stone; over the altar hangs a painting of the Holy Family, by Costazzini. The Cathedral is lighted by seventy windows, thirty-seven of which are memorial windows. They were mainly made at Chartres, France, cost about $100,000, and were presented by parishes and individuals in various parts of the country. The total cost of the Cathedral, up to the present time, has been a little over $2,000,000. It is estimated that $500,000 more will be needed to complete it.

The exterior of the building is to be richly ornamented with statues. Two towers are yet to be built at the northern and southern angles of the Fifth ave-

ST. PATRICK'S CATHEDRAL.

nue front. They will be three hundred and twenty-eight feet in height, from the ground to the summit of the cross on each. For a distance of one hundred and thirty-six feet from the ground they will be square in shape, after which they will assume the form of octagonal lanterns for fifty-four feet more, and above these will soar beautiful spires for a further distance of one hundred and thirty-eight feet. The towers and spires will be adorned with buttresses, niches containing statues, and pinnacles, which will conceal the change from the square to the octagon.

The Jews have been in New York since the earliest days of the colony, and among the Dutch settlers found tolerance and protection. They have multiplied rapidly, and now constitute one of the largest and wealthiest classes in the city. They have twenty-seven synagogues, and own several large and well-supported institutions for the relief of the unfortunate of their own faith. They have two splendid synagogues on Lexington avenue, but their principal place of worship is the Temple Emanu-el, at the corner of Fifth avenue and 43d street. This is one of the most magnificent structures in New York, and the noblest specimen of Saracenic architecture on the Western Continent. It is built of brown and yellow sandstone, with the roof of alternate lines of red and black tiles. The centre of the façade on Fifth avenue, containing the main entrance, is flanked by two minarets, beautifully carved in open work. Five large doors lead into the vestibule, from which one passes into the interior, which is a rich mass of Oriental coloring.

Very few churches are to be found in the lower part

of the city, almost all being located above Canal street. Trinity, St. Paul's, and one or two others, are all that supply the religious wants of the dwellers in this section. One ward in this region, containing 30,000 people, has not a single place of worship in it, with the exception of a Chinese Joss house, which is kept, by its votaries, in the background.

The morning services at the various churches, especially at the more fashionable temples, bring out a goodly crowd of worshipers, and it is difficult to obtain a seat. At the fashionable churches the lady members of the congregations have a bad habit of waiting until the services have begun before putting in an appearance. Then they sail up the aisles, to their softly cushioned pews, arrayed in all the finery to which they have devoted so much attention during the past week. These late entrances disturb the worshipers, but they enable the ladies to show off their toilets, and that, after all, is what the churches are for, so far as they are concerned. Strangers are expected to stand in the aisles near the door, and wait until the sexton can show them to seats. A certain fashionable sexton is said to have derived quite a snug income from the "tips" bestowed upon him by visitors wishing to obtain eligible seats. A good story is told of a certain high-toned church. A gentleman had been standing in the main aisle during the greater part of the service, vainly waiting for the sexton to show him to a seat. At last, finding the process tiresome, he leaned over, and, in a whisper, asked the occupant of a pew in which there were several vacant seats, "What church is this?" "Christ's," was the whispered reply. "Is He at home, to-day?" asked the stranger. The pew owner took the hint, and rising, asked the inquirer into his pew.

The music at the fashionable churches is superb. The organist is a professor of high reputation, and the choir is made up of professional singers, who devote themselves to concerts and public amusements on secular days. In some of the highest toned temples you will find among the male singers persons whom you may have seen at some of the variety or concert halls during the week. The "Music Committee" ask only for good voices, and do not trouble themselves about the daily lives of the choristers. When the sermon begins the choir curtains are drawn, and the singers, who are not employed to listen to the sermon, seek rest from their fatigues in flirting or reading, or compose themselves for a peaceful nap. Not many years ago, the tenor of one of the best choirs in the city was also the popular singer in a Bowery "Free and Easy." He had a magnificent voice, and his secular engagements were constant and profitable, often keeping him in the concert halls all through Saturday night, and until the small hours of Sunday morning. The tenor, unfortunately, had a weakness for his glass, and it was a constant wonder to his friends that he contrived to get his head clear enough by church time on Sunday morning to take his place in the choir of St. ——'s Church. For a long while, however, he managed to fill both engagements creditably, but at length misfortune overtook him. He had sung, with great *eclat*, at the "Free and Easy" on Saturday night, and had gotten through the morning service at church, as far as the sermon, with equal credit. The eloquence of the preacher lulled him into a profound slumber, and all through the sermon he was dreaming of the Bowery and the jolly crowd assembled to hear him render his great song of "Muldoon." The sermon over, he was roused from his dreams by a fellow member of the choir, who whispered that they were waiting for his solo. Still half asleep, and with his head yet full of the saloon and the applause awaiting him, he staggered to the choir rail, and looking about him, broke out, lustily:—

> "Come and see me, I'll trate ye dacent,
> I'll make ye drunk, I'll fill yer can;
> Sure, when I walk the strate,
> Says each one I mate,
> There goes Muldoon; he's a solid man."

The reader may picture to himself the sensation the tenor's solo produced in the church.

It is the custom for church goers on Sunday morning to promenade Fifth avenue after service. At such times the street is uncomfortably crowded, but the display of fashionable costumes is worth seeing. On Easter Sunday, if the weather be fine, the ladies are out in all the glory of new toilets, one of the most inexorable laws of fashion requiring such displays. Then the Fifth avenue temples pour out vast throngs of these magnificently dressed creatures, and the crowd is heavily reinforced by the congregations of churches not on the avenue, all bent on seeing and being seen.

The churches are supported mainly by the money received from the rents of the pews. Few persons not connected with some fashionable place of worship can form any idea of the amount of money spent in this way. The annual rental of some pews is equal to the house rent of a family of moderate means. The income derived from the pews is obtained in various ways in the different churches. In some, nearly all the pews are sold, and the owners pay a certain percentage of the valuation annually; in others, pews are sold at auction, to the highest bidder; but most of the churches have an annual rental of the pews. In the fashionable churches the rents run from $500 to $700, and in some even higher rents are demanded.

Many of the leading churches of the city are heavily encumbered with debt. Some time since the New York *Tribune* published a list of some fifty odd churches, giving the amount of the mortgage resting upon each. These mortgages ran from $9000 to $471,000, and none were registered prior to 1869. They footed up a grand total of nearly two million and a half dollars.

The recklessness with which the city churches rush into debt is appalling. No other class of real estate in New York is so heavily incumbered as that of its religious associations; and this in spite of the fact that no sort of property has a more uncertain tenure of its income, the whole depending in a large measure on the popularity of the ministers in charge, and on the good will and prosperity of the members. Nearly the whole of the debts thus created is for the purpose of enlarging the churches or constructing new ones. Scarcely any of the congregations go in debt for the purpose of increasing the minister's salary, or to enlarge the contributions to missionary funds or charitable enterprises. All is for show. Old fashioned, comfortable churches, free from debt, are torn down, or sold, and new edifices, rich and costly in every detail, are erected. A little money is advanced, the church is plastered over with mortgages, and the next generation is left to pay for the vanity of the present. Sometimes the mortgage is paid, but too often the reverse is the case. The mortgage is foreclosed, the beautiful temple is sold, and perhaps is converted into a theatre, concert hall, livery stable or factory.

So handsome are the churches, as a rule, so conspicuously do wealth and fashion thrust themselves forward on all sides, that the poor rarely seek them. They are too fine, and the pride of the honest poor man will not permit him to take his place in a house of worship where he is certain to be looked coldly upon and made to feel his lack of worldly goods. Fashion and wealth rule with iron hands, even in the house of God, and in these gorgeous temples the class who were nearest and dearest to the Master's heart have no place.

CHAPTER LI

ALONG THE BOWERY

ORIGIN OF THE NAME OF THE STREET—NOTABLE BUILDINGS—CHEAP RETAIL SHOPS—BEER
SALOONS—CONCERT HALLS—THE JEWS—THE BOWERY BECOMING GERMANIZED—THE BOW-
ERY IN BY-GONE DAYS—THE "BOWERY BOY"—THE "BOWERY GIRL"—A GORGEOUS CREA-
TURE—SUNDAY IN THE BOWERY—NIGHT SCENES IN THE BOWERY—THE STREET-WALKERS—
THE GERMAN BEER GARDENS—THE SHOOTING-GALLERIES—THE THEATRES.

Next to Broadway, the Bowery is the most characteristic street in New York. It derives its name from
the fact that, during the days of the Dutch, it was lined
with the "boweries" or farms of the early settlers,
being at that time merely a country road. It commences at Chatham Square, and extends in a straight
line to Eighth street, where the Third and Fourth avenues begin. But few buildings of note are to be found
along its extent. These are the Thalia Theatre, formerly known as "The Old Bowery," the Windsor
Theatre, the Bowery and Dry-Dock Savings Banks.
The last building is an elegant structure of yellow
sandstone, in the Gothic style of architecture. As a
rule the houses on the Bowery are from two to three
stories in height, and are plain and unattractive. They
are devoted mainly to retail stores of the cheap order,
one peculiarity of which is that about half the stock
is displayed on the sidewalks. Soda fountains, peanut and fruit-stands impede the progress of the passers-by at every step, and street-venders of all kinds
hawk their wares along the entire course of the street.
The Bowery is crowded day and night with a motley

throng; several lines of street-cars traverse it; and the trains of the Elevated Railroad speed rapidly by overhead. The street is the paradise of beer saloons,

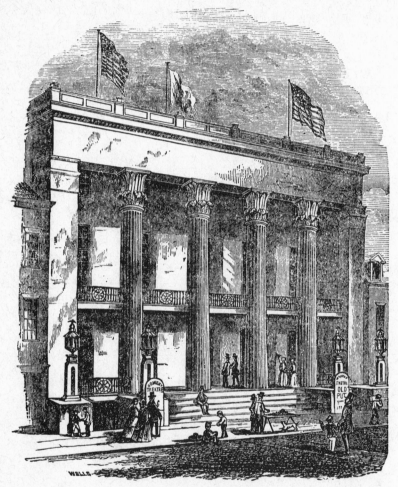

THE OLD BOWERY THEATRE.

bar-rooms, concert and dance halls, cheap theatres, and low-class shows. The Jews are well represented in the retail stores, and seem to do well. The population of the street is largely German, and at night and on holiday occasions the Bowery constitutes the favorite resort of the pleasure-seekers of this nationality. German restaurants, beer saloons and gardens, theatres and music halls, abound here; the signs are German, and the dishes in the eating-houses the same. You may go for squares sometimes without hearing an English word spoken.

Half a century ago the Bowery was the chosen haunt of the ruffian element of New York. It was shunned by respectable people, and given over to the "Bowery Boys," rowdy firemen, thieves, and women of doubtful or disreputable character. The "Bowery Boy" was an institution of Old New York, and lives yet in the memory of many of the veteran citizens. Chanfrau, the actor, has preserved a faithful picture of him in his "Mose." With his red shirt, stunning necktie, black pants carefully tucked into his boots, his coat on his arm, his tall hat, ornamented with a broad band of crape, set one-sided on his carefully soaped locks, and his face smooth shaven, he paraded the Bowery with the pride of a lord of the universe. His attire was simplicity itself, but of a striking kind. Jewelry he avoided as low and vulgar, his only ornament being a gold or brass figure representing the number of the fire "mersheen" with which he ran. This he wore in his shirt-front, and he regarded it with the fondest pride. He stood on his dignity, and it fared ill with the person who dared to insult him. A fight was his glory, and it must be confessed he bore himself gallantly, and fought squarely. He was a rough, but not a bully; he never made war upon women and children, or took delight in breaking up a peaceful picnic or dance, but was ever ready to defend the helpless, especially the fair sex. As a rule, he worked steadily at butchering or some other trade during the week, and paid his way as he went. His diversions were an evening at the Old Bowery Theatre, a run to a fire, or a fight, all of which were highly enjoyed. A dog-fight on the end of the wharves on Sunday morning was, perhaps, his greatest pleasure. He was devoted to his girl, and kept a jealous watch over her, and under his protection she was safe from insult or harm.

The original "Bowery Girl" must have been made of a rib of the original "Bowery Boy," so exactly was she his counterpart. There was this difference, however, between them. While he affected a severely simple style of dress, she loved to deck herself out in all the glories of dry-goods and millinery. A more gorgeous creature could not be found. Her janty bonnet, set rakishly on one side of her head, bloomed in all the colors of the rainbow; her short skirts showed the neatest-turned ankle and the trimmest little foot, with a perfectly marvellous stocking. And then her air—as, with parasol poised in one hand, the other arm swinging to the motion of her body, her dainty nose pointing upward, she passed at a quick gait peculiar to herself along the Bowery, or through Chatham square—it was the perfection of East Side poetry. No wonder that the "Bowery Boy" bowed down before her, and worshipped. She was irresistible. Both are beings of the past. The bar-room loafer, the sneak-thief, the red-faced bully, and the half-drunken street-walker have taken their places.

The Sunday law is a dead letter in the Bowery. Beer saloons, rum-shops, concert and dance halls, are in full blast. The German element is out in force. The Atlantic Garden is thronged, and the clink of beer-glasses mingles sharply with the strains of the orchestra. The cheap clothing stores and the pawn-shops drive a thriving trade, and the vile dens of vice which line the lower part of the street are crowded with their wretched habitués. All along the street you hear the sharp crack of the rifles in the shooting-galleries. The sidewalks are full, the street cars are overcrowded, and the elevated trains are jammed.

To see the Bowery in its glory, one must visit it at night. It is a blaze of light from one end to the other. The saloons, theatres, concert halls, and "free-and-easys," are gayly ornamented with lamps of all colors, and the lights of the street-venders give to the side-walks. the appearance of a general illumination. The concert halls are filled, and sounds of music and shouts of laughter float out from them into the street. Wretched transparencies mark the entrances to the low dives, in and out of which a steady throng pours. The pavements are full of abandoned women, boldly plying their trade, regardless of the police, who are out in force along the thoroughfare. Turn into any of the concert or dance halls, and you will find the majority of the company present young men and boys, and girls not out of their teens. The larger German music halls have the only respectable audiences to be found in the Bowery. To these the children of the

Fatherland resort in great numbers to enjoy their beer and listen to the music. The husband and father takes his wife and family along with him, and the pleasure here is innocent and orderly. The shooting-galleries are a feature of the streets, and are brightly lighted and open to the sidewalk. They are ornamented with targets consisting of gaudily-painted figures, and offer innumerable inducements to passersby to try their skill. The theatres are brilliant with transparencies and illuminated glass signs, and are well filled with pleasure-seekers. The admission is cheap, and the performances adapted to the tastes of their patrons. Men and women in all stages of intoxication stagger along the pavements, and here and there is a sturdy policeman with some offender in his grasp, hastening on to the station-house. Vice offers every inducement to its votaries, and the devil's work is done nightly upon a grand scale in the Bowery. The horse-cars, with their colored lights and jingling bells, and the rapidly rushing elevated trains overhead, give an air of briskness to the street. The scene is gay and animated, but must be witnessed to be properly appreciated.

CHAPTER LII

NEW YORK HOTELS

GREAT NUMBER OF HOTELS IN NEW YORK—FIRST-CLASS HOTELS—THE AMERICAN AND EURO-
PEAN PLANS—THE ASTOR HOUSE—THE ST. NICHOLAS—THE METROPOLITAN—THE GRAND
CENTRAL—THE NEW YORK—THE FIFTH AVENUE—THE WINDSOR—OTHER HOTELS—INTE-
RIOR ARRANGEMENTS—NIGHT SCENES—COST OF FURNISHING A HOTEL—DEAD BEATS—
HOW THE DETECTIVES WATCH SUSPICIOUS CHARACTERS.

No city in the world surpasses New York in the
number and excellence of its hotels. There are said
to be about 700 hotels of all grades in the Metropolis,
the majority of which do a profitable business, and some
of which return large fortunes to their proprietors.

The first-class hotels are magnificent structures of
marble, brownstone, iron, or brick, and are ornaments
to the streets in which they are situated. They are
furnished in magnificent style, and provide every
comfort and luxury for their guests at moderate
charges. The assertion that the New York hotels
are extortionate in their prices is untrue; where the
charges are high the accommodations furnished are
in keeping with the price. A stranger in the great
city can consult his tastes and means in the choice of
a "stopping-place," for there are hotels suited to
every need. Almost every house has a number of
permanent guests, and the proprietor is thus assured
of a certain income; while the vast throngs of strangers who daily enter and leave the city provide a tran-
sient custom unequalled in its proportions in any city
of the New World.

The hotels are divided into two classes — those which are conducted on the American plan, in which the guest is provided with a room, lights, attendance, and a certain number of meals per day; and those conducted on the European plan, where the charge is only for rooms, attendance, and lights, the guest taking his meals *a la carte* in the hotel restaurant, or wherever he sees fit. Each class has its advocates, and each its advantages.

ST. NICHOLAS HOTEL.

The Astor House is one of the oldest hotels in New York, and the only first-class house in the lower part of the city. It is conducted on the European plan, and is admirable in all its appointments. Its restaurant is famous, and its lunch-counter furnishes meals to several thousand people every day. It does a prosperous business, and is very popular with visitors from New England. It is a massive structure of granite, on Broadway opposite the Post-Office, and its name has long been among the household words of the Metropolis.

The St. Nicholas is an elegant marble building, on Broadway, between Broome and Spring streets, is conducted on the American plan, and is one of the most thoroughly comfortable houses in the city. Its public rooms on the street floor look out upon Broad-

METROPOLITAN HOTEL

way, and constitute one of the pleasantest lounging-places in New York. It is a favorite with Western people, and is a fortune to its proprietor, Mr. Uriah Welch, whose sterling qualities and unfailing kindness to his guests have won him hosts of friends. Its patrons are attached to it, and rarely leave it for newer houses.

The Metropolitan Hotel is at the corner of Broadway and Prince street, and occupies nearly half of the entire block, extending back to Crosby street in the rear. It is built of brownstone, with an imposing front on Broadway, and is one of the largest of the

GRAND CENTRAL HOTEL.

Metropolitan hotels, containing about 400 rooms. It is popular with New Englanders and Western people, and does a profitable business.

The Grand Central Hotel is a monster establishment, and is said to be the largest hotel in the United

States. It is situated on Broadway, between Bleecker and Amity streets, and extends back to Mercer street. The Broadway front is of marble, and the building rises to a height of eight stories, with two additional stories in the central dome. It is surmounted by a handsome mansard roof, and is one of the most imposing edifices on Broadway. It is magnificently furnished, and will accommodate over 1000 guests. The dining-room will seat over 600 at one time.

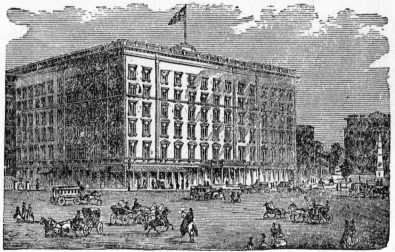

FIFTH AVENUE HOTEL.

The New York Hotel is a plain red brick building, occupying the square bounded by Broadway, Mercer street, East Washington Place, and Waverly Place. It is one of the most elegant and exclusive houses in the city, and is the favorite with wealthy visitors from the South.

The Fifth Avenue Hotel is located at the junction of Broadway, Fifth avenue, and Twenty-third and

Twenty-fourth streets. It occupies the most conspicuous site in the city, and is a magnificent edifice of
white marble, six stories in height. It cost over
$1,000,000, and is superbly furnished and kept in the
most expensive style. Its patrons are principally persons of wealth, and it is a favorite with politicians of
the Republican faith.

The Windsor Hotel is situated on Fifth avenue,
and extends from Forty-sixth to Forty-seventh
streets. It is built of red brick, with brownstone
trimmings, is eight stories in height, and is palatial in
all its appointments. It is the highest up town of all
the great hotels, and shares with the "Fifth Avenue"
the wealthiest and most fashionable custom of the
city and country.

The other prominent hotels are the Albemarle, the
Brevoort, the Buckingham, the Clarendon, the Coleman, the Everett, the Gilsey, the Glenham, the Grand,
the Hoffman, the Brunswick, the Irving, the Park
Avenue, the Rossmore, the St. Cloud, the St. Denis,
the St. James, the Sturtevant, and the Westminster.

The accommodations provided by the first-class
houses are unequalled in any part of the world. The
parlors are sumptuously furnished, the halls softly car-
peted, the public rooms elegantly decorated, and the
chambers the perfection of comfort. Elevators connect the various floors, and every convenience is at
hand for the use of the guests. The table groans with
all the luxuries of the season, and the service is perfection.

At night the scene in a first-class hotel is very interesting. The public rooms are thronged with guests

and residents of the city, and are brilliantly lighted; the parlors are filled with guests enjoying the pleasures of social intercourse, the dining-rooms are crowded with ladies and gentlemen, many in evening dress, and groups of promenaders stroll up and down the halls of the parlor floor.

The cost of furnishing a first-class hotel is enormous. As much as half a million dollars is often expended for this purpose. The expenses of the house are very great, but the profits are in proportion. The Fifth Avenue Hotel is said to clear $250,000 annually, and the other leading houses are proportionately profitable. The city is always full of strangers, and a handsome and well-kept hotel is sure of a large transient custom. Thousands of city people make their homes at the hotels, and thus constitute a class (enormously profitable to the proprietors of the houses) unknown in other cities. It is this class of hotel livers that support the smaller establishments. These people are away at the watering-places during the summer, but return to their old quarters with the fall of the leaves.

All the New York hotels suffer more or less from impostors or dead-beats. The best houses seek in every way to exclude improper characters, but, in spite of the vigilance of the proprietors, such persons will find their way into them. Each house employs one or more private detectives to watch over the safety of its guests, but hotel robberies are of frequent occurrence, and often assume considerable proportions.

CHAPTER LIII

THE TRAMPS.

NEW YORK THE PARADISE OF TRAMPS—WHO THEY ARE—THEIR MODE OF LIFE—WORTHLESS CHARACTERS—SLEEPING IN THE PARK—THE TRAMPS' ABLUTIONS—THE TRAMPS' LODGING HOUSE—UNFORTUNATE WANDERERS.

New York is the paradise of tramps. This term is generally applied to able-bodied men and women who are too lazy to work, but prefer to pick up a precarious living by begging food and clothes from house to house. In the mild weather they sleep in the parks and public squares, and in the winter take refuge in the police-stations, as has been described. During the warm season they leave the city in large numbers, and wander through the country, going sometimes as far west as Ohio, following regular routes; but in the winter they flock back to New York, where they are sure of food and shelter. Some remain in the city throughout the year. They are dissipated, as a rule, and the majority have been brought to their present condition by love of drink. They will steal, and even commit highway robbery, rape, or murder, if they have a chance, and are a terror to the householders of the upper portions of the city. They haunt the beer saloons and low class bar-rooms, beg for drinks, and will even drain the few drops left in the empty beer kegs on the sidewalks. They will solicit passers-by for money, and in this way often manage to collect enough to buy whiskey or beer. Their food they beg at the doors of residences, keeping a sharp lookout all the while for an opportunity to steal something of value when the servant's back is turned.

The Central Park is a favorite lodging-place with

THE TRAMPS' BATH.

them in warm weather. Under the cover of darkness they creep into the shrubbery, and make their beds on the grass. Sometimes they sleep on the benches scattered through the grounds, but as they are apt to be disturbed by the police, they prefer the shrubbery. Madison Square is also one of their favorite sleeping-places, but, as they are sharply watched by the police, they are obliged to sleep in a sitting posture on the benches. In the morning they perform their ablutions in the pretty fountains.

BEER TRAMPS.

The more fortunate tramps patronize the cheap lodging-houses of the Bowery, where a bed can be had for ten cents a night. An old church for colored people, at Prince and Marion streets, has been turned into a tramps' lodging-house. Each occupant is provided with food, lodging, and a bath, in return for which he must assist in sawing, splitting, and bundling kind-

ling-wood, the sale of which provides a part of the
revenue of the house. The place is not popular, however, as the tramp disdains to work. Nightly scores
of men and boys apply for lodging, but refuse to ac-
cept it when told they must work for it.

Many deserving persons are classed among the
tramps. They are friendless, homeless, and without
money or work, and must adopt the tramp's life in
order to maintain existence. Such persons gladly ac-
cept any work offered them, and escape from their
wretched companionship as soon as able to do so. It
is easy to distinguish them from the genuine tramp,
however, for they are eager to work; while the
tramp, pure and simple, regards an offer of labor as
an insult.

CHAPTER LIV

THE POST-OFFICE

THE MODEL POST-OFFICE OF THE UNION—THE BUILDING—THE POST-OFFICE PROPER—THE
BOX AND STAMP DEPARTMENT—INTERNAL ARRANGEMENTS OF THE POST-OFFICE—BUSI-
NESS OF THE OFFICE — HOW THE WORK IS CONDUCTED.

The New York Post-Office is the largest and best
conducted establishment of its kind in the United
States. It is a massive edifice of Dix Island granite,
triangular in shape, and occupies what was once the
southern end of the City Hall Park, at the junction
of Broadway and Park Row. It is five stories in height
above the street, and is surmounted by a Mansard
roof with several domes, the roof constituting an extra
story. Below the sidewalk there are also a basement
and a sub-basement. The architecture is a combination of the Doric and Renaissance styles, and the
domes, which rise above the roof, are modelled after
those of the Louvre at Paris. The girders, beams,
and joists used in the building are of iron, and the
vast structure is as solid as skill can make it. The
interior is handsomely fitted up, with elevators connecting the various floors, and is divided between the
Post-Office and the United States Courts.

The Post-Office occupies the sub-basement, the
basement, the first and second floors, a gallery about
25 feet wide running around the entire building between the first and second floors, and a portion of the

fifth floor. Entrances to the building are placed on all the sides except the north front facing the City Hall. The main entrance is in the centre of the southern front by a noble portico, and from this broad iron stairways lead to the top floor. The third and fourth floors are occupied by the United States Courts and their offices. The fifth floor is devoted to the janitors, and to the storage of material belonging to the Post-Office.

The engines and other steam machinery used in heating the building and running the elevators, are placed in the sub-basement, the basement proper being used for the reception and sorting of the mails.

Entering from the street the visitor finds himself in a broad corridor running around three sides of the building. Here are the windows for the sale of stamps, envelopes, etc., the drops for letters and papers, and 5795 boxes, each of which is provided with a metallic door with a lock and key. The boxes are arranged in alcoves, thus giving double room. Here is the general delivery and the ladies' window, and at the end of the corridor on the Park Row side is the Foreign Department, with a separate drop for letters for each country, and a window for the sale of stamps for such letters. The drops for the United States are arranged by States, and there are also drops for the principal cities of the Union, and a separate one for New York. This arrangement saves much trouble in assorting the letters deposited in the office.

The space enclosed by the boxes is of a triangular shape. Light is admitted through the windows of the balcony, but chiefly through a large skylight, 100 feet square, and 30 feet above the first floor. Above the skylight is a court open to the weather, and giving light and ventilation to the inner rooms of the floors above. At the south-western end of the room, at a conspicuous point, is an electric annunciator, the largest ever constructed, which gives notice of the time of the arrival and departure of all mails. Scattered through the room are tables and cases of boxes for mailing and distributing purposes. At the north end of the room is a semi-circular case, containing 682 large, deep boxes, into which the packages of letters ready for the mails are thrown. At the back of each box are hooks for the attachment of bags, into which the matter slides at the opening of the door.

The mails are received on the City Hall side of the building, along the whole length of which are elevators —ten in number—running to the basement, where everything except letters is distributed and mailed. All the employés of the Post-Office enter the building by the portico from this side. The large basement room contains a number of wardrobes, with locks and keys—one for each employé of the office. In the south-west corner, under the portico and pavement, is a space, enclosed by massive iron screens, extending almost to the ceiling. Here are stored all the mail-bags belonging to the United States not in use.

Upon the second floor of the building are located the Money Order Office, the Registered Letter and Special Agency Departments, the Wholesale Stamp Department, and the private offices of the Postmaster and his assistants.

The total cost of the building was between six and seven million dollars.

The business of the New York Post-Office is immense. Besides its transactions with foreign countries, it is in communication with nearly 40,000 post-offices in the United States. 84 mails are despatched, and 86 received, every day. About 300,000,000 letters, papers, etc., are received and forwarded annually, and over 1200 men are employed in the work of the establishment. The average annual receipts of the office are about $3,000,000, and the annual expenditures about $1,000,000; so that the office yields a net annual profit of about $2,000,000.

The work of the office is conducted with the most perfect system, much of which is due to the efforts of the Hon. T. L. James, formerly Postmaster here, and afterwards Postmaster-General of the United States. The immense business of the establishment is so simplified that it goes on like clockwork, without a perceptible hitch.

CHAPTER LV

CASTLE GARDEN

THE BUILDING—THE OLD FORT—EARLY HISTORY OF CASTLE GARDEN—BECOMES AN EMIGRANT DEPOT—ARRIVALS OF FOREIGN STEAMERS—LANDING THE EMIGRANTS—AVERAGE WEALTH OF THE NEW-COMERS—PASSING THE SURGEON—REGISTERING EMIGRANTS—INTERNAL AR-RANGEMENTS OF CASTLE GARDEN.

At the north-western angle of the Battery Park is a singular-looking circular structure of stone, to which have been added several out-buildings of wood, all enclosed on the land side by a high wooden fence. This is Castle Garden, the famous emigrant-landing depot of New York. The stone building was erected between 1807 and 1820, and was intended for a fort, but in the latter year was found to be too weak to bear the weight of the guns intended for it. It was sold by the General Government, and was converted into a summer-garden, where refreshments were sold and indifferent concerts given. In 1832 a grand ball was given here by the citizens to Lafayette, on his last visit to this country, and in 1843 a reception to President Tyler was held here. Subsequently it was converted into a concert hall, and here Jenny Lind and several other celebrated singers made their first appearance in America. In 1847 it was leased to the Commissioners of Emigration, and has ever since been the principal emigrant depot of the country. It was partially destroyed in 1876, but has since been rebuilt.

When a steamer with emigrants on board drops her

EMIGRANTS LANDING AT CASTLE GARDEN.

anchor in the river, several large barges are towed alongside, and to these are transferred the emigrants and their baggage. As soon as the barges are loaded, they are cast off, and are towed to Castle Garden, while the steamer proceeds to her pier in the North River. When the barge is made fast to the landing at Castle Garden, the baggage is taken into a hall of the building, where it is claimed by its owners, and examined by the Custom-House inspectors. Some of the new-comers have scarcely any baggage at all, while others are possessed of large quantities of it. Formerly each emigrant was questioned as to the amount of money brought with him, but this practice has been abandoned. It is estimated that the average amount is about $100 for each person, and $50 more for personal property. Taking this average, and estimating the total number of arrivals at 250,000 in a favorable year, it will be seen that these new-comers increase the wealth of the country in a single year by $37,500,000.

The Custom-House inspectors having passed the baggage, it is sent to a room provided for its proper storage. The surgeon of the establishment then examines the emigrants to see that no paupers, or criminals, or persons affected with contagious or infectious diseases are among them. After the inspection is over, the emigrants are passed into the rotunda, or principal hall of the building, filing, one by one, by the registration desk, where their names, age, nationality, destination, the vessel's name, and date of arrival, are carefully registered, as a means of identifying the person should it be necessary to do so at any time in the future. The floor of the rotunda is divided into enclosures, containing a telegraph-office, post-office, money exchange office, railroad ticket offices, and a restaurant. Those of the new-comers who have friends awaiting them are allowed to depart with them, after the latter have satisfied the authorities as to their real characters; others who wish to remain in the rotunda are allowed to do so for a stated time; those who wish to go to a boarding-house, are recommended to houses licensed by, and under the supervision of, the Commissioners; and others still, who wish to proceed at once to their destinations in other parts of the country, can purchase their railway tickets and have their baggage checked at the offices in the building. The sick are cared for in a temporary hospital until they can be transferred to Ward's Island, and the helpless are kindly looked after, and sent to the institution provided for them on the same island. A labor exchange is established in the building, where those who wish to procure work can secure situations. Interpreters, speaking all the various European languages, are provided, and every care is taken to protect the emigrant's interests, and to guard him from the dangers which threaten him during his first few days of strangeness and inexperience in the great city.

CHAPTER LVI

THE MARKETS OF NEW YORK

THE MARKET-HOUSES—UNSIGHTLY STRUCTURES—THE MANHATTAN MARKET—SCENES IN THE MARKETS—NEW YORK'S SOURCE OF SUPPLY—THE MORNING HOURS—SATURDAY-NIGHT MARKETS—THE OYSTER-SALOONS—FULTON MARKET—THE "CORNER GROCERIES."

The markets of New York, with the exception of the Manhattan and Tompkins markets, are about as unattractive and wretched structures as could well be imagined. They are dirty, in various stages of dilapidation, and are regarded by the citizens as first-class nuisances. The amount of business conducted within them is enormous, however, but even this is surpassed by the aggregate transactions of the street stands and retail stores in their immediate vicinity, which to a stranger appear to form a continuation of the market itself.

The principal establishments are the Fulton, Washington, Jefferson, Catharine, Union, Clinton, Franklin, Centre, Tompkins, Essex, and Manhattan. The Manhattan market is the property of a private stock company, and is a magnificent structure of brick and stone, lying at the foot of Thirty-fourth street, on the Hudson River, and covering about three acres. It is used mainly for the sale of butchers' meats, and a large part of it is devoted to the purposes of an *abattoir*. Its location is unfortunate, being difficult of access.

The best-known markets are the Fulton and Washington. The former is now undergoing reconstruc-

tion, and the new market will be a handsome and
clean edifice. The old one was an eyesore to the
neighborhood.

Bad as the outward appearance of the markets is,
the interior presents one of the most interesting sights
of the city. The stalls are filled with the products of
every portion of the Union, and with fruits and delicacies from foreign climes. The display of meats is
extensive and enticing, and at Thanksgiving and
Christmas times the number of turkeys that find their
way here is perfectly astounding. The country for
miles around New York abounds in market gardens
and truck farms, and these send their rich stores of
fruits and vegetables in profusion, while similar products from every State in the Union are also displayed
for sale. Steam has made even the most distant States
of the West and South producers for the New York
markets. Large as the supply is, the markets are
never overstocked. Over a million of people purchase their food here, and the demand is unceasing.
Everything finds a sale at good prices. The Metropolis is the first American city to be supplied with the
various products of the country. As the spring opens
the South sends its fruits and vegetables to these
markets, beginning with Florida. As the season advances the source of supply moves northward and
westward, so that the Metropolis enjoys the benefit
of all the changes of season to a greater extent than
would be possible in a provincial city.

The business of the markets begins about four
o'clock in the morning. The first comers are the
caterers for the hotels, the restaurants, the fashionable

FULTON MARKET IN WATERMELON SEASON.

boarding-houses, and the mansions of the very rich, and the proprietors of the "corner groceries" and meat stores of the city. These purchase largely, and the best of the stock of the dealers is soon disposed of. Prices are high at this season, but as the morning advances they decline. Towards six or seven o'clock a perfect army of boarding-house keepers makes its appearance, and now begins the season for "bargains." By ten o'clock the market is wellnigh exhausted, and the remainder of the stock is disposed of to the poor, who cannot afford to purchase better food at the prices which rule the earlier hours.

On Saturday night, the night before Thanksgiving, and on Christmas Eve, the markets are in their glory. Brightly lighted, filled with the most tempting articles, and thronged with eager purchasers, they do a lively business, and are perfect Babels of noise and confusion.

In many of the markets, rooms are built in the enclosure, some of which are handsomely furnished. These are used for restaurants and oyster-houses. The Fulton Market has long been famous for its oysters, and at almost every hour of the day during the season its most noted saloons are thronged with lovers of the delicious bivalves. Ladies in rich dresses, and gentlemen swells, pick their way through the dirt and grime, and crowd the saloons in quest of their favorite delicacy.

The Fulton Market is a vast bazaar. Almost anything can be purchased there. Side by side are book and periodical stands, with full stocks of the latest literature, eating-stands, oyster-saloons, bar-rooms, cheap jewelery stores, hardware, crockery, and dry-goods stands, all of which seem to do well.

Comparatively few of the people of the city purchase their supplies at the markets. They buy of the provision dealers who procure their supplies from these establishments, and sell to their customers at a considerable advance upon the market rates. The location of the markets and the immense distances of the city render this system a necessity.

CHAPTER LVII

THE CROTON WATER-WORKS

THE SOURCE OF NEW YORK'S WATER SUPPLY—CROTON LAKE—THE CROTON AQUEDUCT—A WON-
DERFUL WORK—THE HIGH BRIDGE—THE " HIGH SERVICE" SYSTEM—THE CENTRAL PARK
RESERVOIRS—HOW THE WATER IS SUPPLIED TO THE CITY—ENORMOUS WASTE.

Seventy miles from New York is a group of 23
small lakes, occupying portions of Westchester, Put-
nam, and Dutchess counties, and a small corner of
Connecticut.   They lie in a lovely region, and are
noted for the purity and abundance of their waters.
They are drained by the Croton River, which along the
lower portion of its course flows through Croton Lake,
40 miles from New York, and finally falls into the
Hudson above Sing Sing.

During the early part of the century New York began to realize the necessity of providing an abundant
supply of pure water for drinking and other purposes.
A number of plans were offered, some looking to the
Bronx River as the source of supply, and some to
other localities; but no definite action was taken until
the great fire of 1835 taught the citizens the danger
of leaving the Metropolis longer without an adequate
supply of fresh water.   Then it was determined to
bring water into the city from Croton Lake, and in
May, 1837, the construction of an aqueduct from the
lake to the city, a distance of 40 miles, was begun.
Five years were employed in the work, and on the 4th
of July, 1842, the Croton water was distributed through
New York.

The work was begun by throwing a massive dam across Croton River at its outlet from the lake, which raised the water to a depth of 40 feet, and gave to the lake a retaining capacity of about 500,000,000 gallons. The dam is constructed of massive masonry, and is 230 feet wide and 45 feet high, and over it the waste water flows in a fine cataract. The aqueduct begins at the dam, and consists of a tunnel of brick, stone, and cement, arched above and below, with a width of seven and a half feet, and a height of eight and a half feet. Along its entire course it falls 13 inches to the mile. After leaving the gateway of the dam it follows the left bank of the Croton River for five miles, when it turns southward, penetrating two lofty hills of solid rock by means of tunnels, and takes a generally southerly course to the High Bridge, opposite New York. For a part of the way it rests upon the ground, and at other points is supported by a series of stone arches. During its course it crosses 25 considerable streams, besides many brooks. It is conveyed over the Harlem River by the High Bridge, a splendid stone structure of 15 arches, eight of which, 80 feet wide and 100 feet above the tide, rise out of the river. The bridge is 1450 feet in length and 21 feet in width, and is provided with a parapet on each side. The great height of the arches prevents the bridge from obstructing the navigation of the river, and vessels pass and repass under it with perfect ease. On the bridge is laid an immense iron pipe, seven and a half feet in diameter, through which the water is conveyed from the tunnel to the opposite shore. Two other pipes, three feet in diameter, are also laid on each side of the great pipe, through which an additional supply of water may be conveyed to the New York side. Above the pipes is the floor of the bridge, which is laid off as a promenade. The bridge is an imposing structure, is visible from a long distance, and forms a prominent feature of one of the loveliest landscapes in the world.

HIGH BRIDGE.

At the northern, or Westchester, end of the bridge is a gate-house, which is used for the purpose of regulating the flow of the Croton water from the tunnel into the pipes over the bridge; and on the New York side is another gate-house, by which the water is admitted to the aqueduct, which resumes its course from this point to the reservoirs in the Central Park. At this end of the bridge two large reservoirs are located, known as the "Storage" and "High Service" reservoirs. The latter of these is designed for the supply of the elevated regions of Carmansville. Powerful engines pump the water from the aqueduct into this reservoir, supplying 100,000 gallons daily. A handsome tower of granite rises at the side of the reservoir, and the water is pumped to the top of this, from which it falls into the pipes that supply the district of Washington Heights.

Two and a quarter miles below the High Bridge the aqueduct reaches a gate-house at the corner of Tenth avenue and One Hundred and Tenth street, from which the water is conveyed in pipes to Ninety-third street between Ninth and Tenth avenues. Here is another gate-house, and from this point the water flows into a new section of the aqueduct, which conveys it to, and discharges it in, the two large receiving reservoirs in Central Park. The cost of the Croton Aqueduct and the original reservoirs was about $9,000,000.

The reservoirs are two in number, and have already been mentioned in connection with the Central Park. The older or southern reservoir was built at the time of the construction of the aqueduct, and covers an area of 35 acres, with a water surface of 31 acres and a capacity of 150,000,000 gallons. The new reservoir covers an area of 106 acres, with a water surface of 96 acres and a capacity of 1,029,888,000 gallons. When full it has a depth of 38 feet. It is divided by a wall, so that in case of accident only one-half of the reservoir need be emptied. It is provided with an elaborate system of gates, by means of which any desired quantity of water may be taken from it. The affluent gate at the northern end distributes the water equally into each section of the vast basin, or into one section only if desired. At the southern end is a handsome gate-house of granite, by means of which the water in both reservoirs is distributed into the pipes running southward into the city. Here the great forty-eight inch mains which supply the city begin, and here is a vast but systematic arrangement of blow-off valves, stop-cocks, ventilators, and other contrivances, all contained in a large vault below the level of the gate-house. The blow-off valves are used for letting the water out into the sewers of the city when repairs are to be made to the reservoirs. On the floor of the gate-house is a series of iron wheels which work large screws, which, in their turn, raise or lower the gates, admitting the water to the great mains or shutting it off from them. One of these mains extends towards First avenue, another to Third avenue, a third to Madison avenue, and the others to the principal longitudinal streets of the city. There is a third reservoir on Fifth avenue, between Fortieth and Forty-second streets. It is a massive, fortress-like structure of stone, rising high above the street, covering four acres of ground, and possessing a capacity of 20,000,000 gallons. It is the principal distributing reservoir for the lower part of the city.

The aqueduct brings to the city a supply of 104,-000,000 gallons of water daily, and the reservoirs contain, when full, about ten days' supply. In ordinary seasons the quantity of water is abundant; but in times of unusual dryness the greatest care is required to keep the city supplied. The Central Park reservoirs are connected with the police and fire headquarters by telegraph, and in seasons of drought, when the water is carefully dealt out, news of the location of a fire is telegraphed to the gate-house of the new reservoir, and a full force of water is turned on to the mains of the district in which the conflagration occurs.

In spite of the warnings of the Croton Board, the people of the city use the water as lavishly in seasons of drought as in times of plenty. They are charged for the privilege they enjoy, a water-tax being levied upon each building in which the Croton is used. This tax amounts to about $6000 a day, or $2,000,000 a year.

The total cost of the water-works of New York, including the laying of the mains and other expenses, has been about $30,000,000. The total consumption of water daily is about 95,000,000 gallons. Over 400 miles of mains are laid under the streets of the city, and about 100,000 buildings of all kinds are supplied with pure water.